RUSSIAN POLITICS

COMPARATIVE POLITICS AND INTERNATIONAL STUDIES SERIES

Series editor, Christophe Jaffrelot

This series consists of translations of noteworthy manuscripts and publications in the social sciences emanating from the foremost French researchers, from Sciences Po, Paris.

The focus of the series is the transformation of politics and society by transnational and domestic factors—globalisation, migration, and the post bipolar balance of power on the one hand, and ethnicity and religion on the other. States are more permeable to external influence than ever before and this phenomenon is accelerating processes of social and political change the world over. In seeking to understand and interpret these transformations, this series gives priority to social trends from below as much as to the interventions of state and non-state actors.

MARIE MENDRAS

RUSSIAN POLITICS

The Paradox of a Weak State

HURST & COMPANY, LONDON

Liberté • Égalité • Fraternité
RÉPUBLIQUE FRANÇAISE

This book is supported by the French Ministry of Foreign Affairs, as part of the Burgess programme run by the Cultural Department of the French Embassy in London. (www.frenchbooknews.com)

First published in French as *Russie: L'envers du Pouvoir*,
© Odile Jacob, 2008
First published in English in the United Kingdom in 2012 by
C. Hurst & Co. (Publishers) Ltd.,
41 Great Russell Street, London, WC1B 3PL
© Marie Mendras, 2012
This English translation © Ros Schwartz, 2012
All rights reserved.
Printed in India

The right of Marie Mendras to be identified as the author of this publication is asserted by her in accordance with the Copyright, Designs and Patents Act, 1988.

A Cataloguing-in-Publication data record for this book is available from the British Library.

ISBN: 978-1849041133

This book is printed on paper from registered sustainable and managed sources.

www.hurstpub.co.uk

To Lars

CONTENTS

CONTENTS

CONTENTS

ACKNOWLEDGEMENTS

A book is an intellectual and human adventure. My gratitude goes to friends and colleagues who have accompanied me in building scholarship in Russian studies, from my student days at Sciences Po, the Institute for Oriental Languages and Civilisations, and Harvard University, to my research and teaching years in Paris and London, enriched with many trips to Russia.

My home institutions in Paris have provided me with excellent working conditions and intellectual stimulation: the Centre National de la Recherche Scientifique (CNRS), the Centre d'Etudes et de Recherches Internationales and Sciences Po University where I teach Russian politics and foreign policy. Colleagues, research assistants and students have always been my best support and source of inspiration. A two-year professorship at the London School of Economics in 2008–10 gave me a wonderful opportunity to carry out the project of publishing *Russie: L'envers du Pouvoir* (Odile Jacob, 2008) in English. At the LSE and at Chatham House, I found a rich and stimulating environment. This manuscript, finalized in October 2011, is a slightly revised and updated version of the French book.

To me, Russian politics means people, not only institutions. The most rewarding part of fieldwork is the encounter with men and women who tell their stories, explain their social and political institutions, express their beliefs and doubts. I remember conversations with teachers and pupils at a school in a small town in the Urals in 1995 as vividly as I remember the Valdai Club meetings with Russian leaders in the 2000s. At every level of authority, and in every town and city I visited, my interlocutors generously shared their experiences with me: governors, mayors and deputies, regional and local functionaries, judges and lawyers, human-rights activists and environmentalists, economists and businessmen, journalists and think-tank experts. My task has been to decipher, assess and analyze their words and deeds. I offer all of them my thanks.

I am very grateful to my colleagues in Moscow, Saint Petersburg, Tver, Novgorod, Nizhnyi Novgorod, Irkutsk, and other cities, who invited me to share research projects and speak at conferences and helped me build my toolbox and *esprit critique*. In the confines of this page, I can only name a few institutions and individuals.

Scholars with such institutes as the Academy of Sciences, the Moscow State Institute for International Relations (MGIMO), INION, and RGGU, have always been excellent interlocutors in the fields of history, geography, anthropology, and international relations.

At the Levada Center for the study of public opinion, leading sociologists Yuri Levada, Boris Dubin, Lev Gudkov, and Aleksei Levinson have taught me how to study their own society and interpret Russians' opinions and attitudes. Their journal and website, often quoted in this book, are remarkable publications.

With the Institute for Law and Public Policy, I worked closely in the 1990s and 2000s. Olga Sidorovich organized numerous conferences in provincial cities, always in cooperation with a local university or law institute, and published monographs and a unique journal, *Konstitutsionnoe Obozrenie* (Constitutional Monitoring), which for twenty years has been analyzing constitutional and institutional developments in post-Communist states.

The Carnegie Center in Moscow has been a friendly and stimulating base during my stays in Moscow. I am indebted to Dmitry Trenin, Lilia Shevtsova, Nikolay Petrov, Masha Lipman, Andrey Ryabov, and the whole team. Thanks to Nikolay Petrov, who introduced me to other political geographers like Dmitry Oreshkin, Natalya Zubarevich, and Aleksey Novikov, I have learned from them how to analyze federal-regional issues as well as electoral geography.

The Higher School of Economics is the place where long-time friends now teach and conduct research: demographer Anatoli Vishnevsky, historian Igor Klyamkin, economist Evgeny Yasin, political scientists Andrei Melville, Mark Urnov, and Vladimir Ryzhkov, who is also a former deputy and opposition politician.

Vladimir Gelman and his fellow political scientists at the European University in Saint Petersburg have been a source of inspiration; away

ACKNOWLEDGEMENTS

from the nexus of power, they propose original analyses of post-Communist social and political change. Elena Nemirovskaya's Political School is an oasis of free discussion among young elites from all regions of Russia. The School's seminars offer precious insight into contemporary developments.

It would be impossible to study political and social evolution in Russia without the courageous work of reporters and journalists posted on the Internet and printed in a few independent outlets. I am thankful to them, and my thoughts go to Anna Politkovskaya, who was assassinated in October 2006.

Most of my Russian colleagues have kindly contributed to the work of the Observatoire de la Russie at CERI/Sciences Po by presenting papers and speaking at conferences. Their cooperation with us, European scholars, is invaluable.

This book is coming out in English thanks to the unwavering support of CERI Director Christian Lequesne, and CERI English publications editor Irina Vauday, and a generous grant from the Bureau du Livre of the French Cultural Services in London, headed at the time by Paul Fournel.

My deep gratitude goes to Stephen Holmes of New York University, Stephen White of Glasgow University, Lilia Shevtsova of The Carnegie Moscow Center and James Nixey of Chatham House, who carefully read the English-language manuscript, and whose comments, corrections and suggestions made it so much better. All remaining imperfections are mine.

The Federation of Russia

1. KALUGA
2. OREL
3. TULA
4. MOSCOW
5. LIPETSK
6. RIAZAN
7. MORDOVA

8. CHUVASHIA
9. MARI-EL
10. NIZHNI NOVGOROD
11. VLADIMIR
12. IVANOVO
13. KOSTROMA
14. YAROSLAVL

⊙ Cities with federal status
(Moscow and Saint Petersburg)

Republics
(respublika)

Regions *(oblast)*
and territories *(krai)*

ARCTIC OCEAN

BERING
SEA

CHUKOTKA

SEA OF
OKHOTSK

MAGADAN

KAMCHATKA

YAKUTIA

KRASNOYARSK

SEA OF
OKHOTSK

KHABAROVSK

SAKHALIN

IRKUTSK

BURIATIA

AMUR

ZABAIKALSKI
(CHITA)

UST-ORDYNSKI

AGINSKI-
BOURIATIA

China

JEWISH
AUTONOMOUS
REGION

Japan

PRIMORIE

Mongolia

Vladivostok

600 km

Atelier de cartographie de Sciences Po, 2011

-------- Districts *(okrug)*
and autonomous region

———— Districts *(okrug)*,
merged in *oblast* or *krai*,
no longer subjects of the Federation

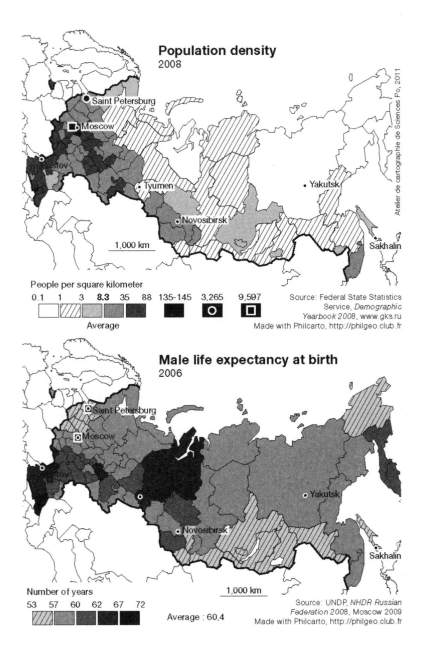

Population density
2008

Saint Petersburg

Moscow

Rostov

Tyumen

Yakutsk

Novosibirsk

Sakhalin

1,000 km

Atelier de cartographie de Sciences Po, 2011

People per square kilometer

0.1   1   3   **8.3**   35   88   135-145   3,265   9,597

Average

Source: Federal State Statistics
Service, *Demographic
Yearbook 2008*, www.gks.ru
Made with Philcarto, http://philgeo.club.fr

Male life expectancy at birth
2006

Saint Petersburg

Moscow

Rostov

Tyumen

Yakutsk

Novosibirsk

Sakhalin

1,000 km

Number of years

53   57   60   62   67   72

Average : 60,4

Source: UNDP, *NHDR Russian
Federation 2008*, Moscow 2009
Made with Philcarto, http://philgeo.club.fr

PROLOGUE

In his seminal study of France, *The Old Regime and the Revolution*, Alexis de Tocqueville concluded that 'the most dangerous moment for a bad government usually is when it starts to reform'. This maxim was generously applied to Mikhail Gorbachev's reforms and the fall of the Soviet Union. The reverse proposition may be more appropriate for Russia after twelve years of rule by Vladimir Putin. The lack of reforms and the stifling of political and social life are the root causes of the contest that destabilised the regime in late 2011.

Two decades after the end of the Soviet Union, the Russian political system is in turmoil. Among society as a whole as well as among the elites, a growing clamour of voices is questioning the viability, efficacy and legitimacy of the power system consolidated by Vladimir Putin since 2000. Widespread corruption and electoral fraud have triggered criticism and protest from a small but vociferous segment of civil society. The political crisis is particularly significant as it stems from the poor judgement and dysfunctional behaviour of the leadership's inner circle. By its very nature, such a closed decision-making group is ill-equipped to tackle political problems beyond the restricted horizon of the chosen few.

The final updating of this book was completed in October 2011, just after Putin publicly announced that he would stand for president for a third time, on 4 March 2012 . This prologue was written in the early days of 2012 just as the volume was about to go to press. I wish here to shed some light on the post-electoral protest and the reversal of fortune suffered by Vladimir Putin and the 'dominant' party, United Russia. The core findings and theses of this book help analyse the destabilisation precipitated by the electoral cycle of 2011–2012.

In the realm of institutional studies, the research I conducted on elections, federalism, and the defeat of constitutionalism in the 1990s and 2000s substantiate the main argument that a democracy cannot be built solely on elections, but needs both a free and fair vote and the rule of law if it is to prosper. 'Electoral democracy' is a misnomer, all the more so when electoral campaigns are unfair, ballot boxes stuffed, and results made up behind closed doors. The Orange Revolution in Ukraine in December 2004 was a case in point: hundreds of thousands of Ukrainians occupied Maidan Square in Kiev for nearly three weeks to protest the rigged presidential election and call for new elections. Russian leaders probably believed they were immune to political accidents.

From a sociological point of view, Russians' support for Putin throughout the 2000s was undoubtedly an essential ingredient in the building of a personalised, clientelistic and authoritarian regime. As explained in chapters 4 and 5, support for the elected president was not to be equated with genuine popularity in a country where people were offered no credible alternative to Putin. In this *bezalternativnaya sistema* (one-choice-only system), most opposition figures had no access to the public spotlight or television. Many Russians agreed with Putin but distrusted his government, administrations, and 'business oligarch' friends.

Consequently, as soon as the leader's authority and charm fail to impress, which is almost inevitable after twelve years at the helm, support for the system as a whole dwindles. And if the leadership cannot or do not want to resort to large-scale repression, they are faced with a genuine political challenge.

The paradigm of 'elite loyalty' proves absolutely crucial. As Putin's power system is being contested by a more assertive civil society, its survival depends on the attitudes of the economic, administrative and intellectual elites that generate Russia's wealth. And the behaviour of the elites in turn depends on the wider mood in society. The crux of the matter is the triangular schema presented in chapter 8—society, elites at large, and the ruling groups—and the way in which the three bodies interact. In their response to urban discontent in December 2011, the central authorities tried to sow the seeds of distrust and discord between the active and affluent middle class and society as a whole. The ability of new figures and movements to propose an alternative government depends on enough citizens withdrawing support from the current system. Without street demonstrations in many Russian cities, opposition leaders would not have been able to gather political momentum and form a united front.

The regime began to feel vulnerable in early autumn 2011 and was openly challenged after the rigged elections of 4 December. The moment of truth occurred on 24 September 2011 when Vladimir Putin and Dmitry Medvedev, in a grimly humourless double act, announced that they would swap seats a few months later, with Putin regaining the presidential chair, and Medvedev casually taking over the post of Prime minister occupied by his mentor since 2008. In open contempt for their citizens, the two men insisted that the arrangement had been sealed a long time ago. This public announcement reinforces one of my main arguments, namely that the 2008 'non-succession'—the invention of an executive tandem—was a major distortion of the spirit and letter of the 1993 constitution. The arrangement was devised to provide Putin with a loophole to circumvent article 81 of the Fundamental Law, which limits a president to two consecutive terms. It also generated the *de facto* transfer of considerable prerogatives from the president to the head of government, without any revision of the constitution.

The effect of the advance notification of yet another staged succession in September 2011 was devastating. Russians felt humiliated, at best indifferent. The reaction came quickly, and was unexpectedly strong. Several close allies of Putin disapproved of the pre-arranged game of musical chairs, the most high-profile being Finance Minister Kudrin who was forced to resign. On several occasions, Vladimir Putin was booed in public. More important still, the Internet buzzed with vitriolic criticism of Putin, shrewd jokes and mocking caricatures. Millions of people surfed the web, viewing the renowned blog of the lawyer and staunch Putin opponent Aleksei Navalny, to the *Grazhdanin Poet* (Citizen Poet) postings of the writer Dmitry Bykov and thousands of other lively sites. Protesters organised themselves via Facebook, getting prepared for election monitoring on 4 December. The Internet, in particular YouTube, transformed the traditionally predictable elections into an astounding, mutifaceted expose of the ballot-rigging and gross violations of voting procedure in every corner of the Federation of Russia. It is also thanks to Facebook that the demonstrations of 10 and 24 December 2011 were adeptly organised in several dozen Russian cities.

What added backbone to the anti-Putin protest was the unlikely chorus formed by a few establishment figures like Aleksei Kudrin and Patriarch Kirill, popular writers like Boris Akunin, non-parliamentarian opposition leaders like Vladimir Ryzhkov and Sergey Udaltsov, high profile bloggers and journalists like Alexei Navalny and Mikhail Fishman, and longtime dissidents like Sergey Kovalev and Liudmila Alexeeva. Protesters were mostly urban-dwellers, younger rather than old, and representing diverse political strands, from democratic, neo-Communist, to nationalist. While no overall leader galvanized the emerging waves of protest, several individuals and movements have given some structure to the angry citizens' stand.

Universal suffrage is not a benign institution. Even in an authoritarian regime, where the police and intelligence services are very powerful, ballots cannot be tampered with endlessly. And in December 2011, the authorities came unstuck. Having acted in an unconstrained and unsanctioned manner for many years, electoral commission staff, bureaucrats and top government officials alike overstepped the mark. The fraud was palpable, there for everyone to see with their own eyes, on a computer screen or a mobile phone: ballot boxes already stuffed with votes, empty polling stations which reported a 90% voter turnout, bawls between independent Russian observers and electoral *apparatchiki*. The most extraordinary declaration occurred in Rostov province, entertaining millions surfing the web: on television on 4 December a young female presenter, in all seriousness, announced the preliminary results, declaring that the total of all parties' percentage of the vote was 146%—to accommodate the instruction from on high to allot 59% of the vote for Putin's party, her colleagues having forgotten commensurately to reduce the other parties' percentages. As usual, Chechens who mostly stayed home, were responsible for a 93.3% turnout and a 99.4% vote for United Russia. According to seasoned election experts from Russia and abroad, fraud was estimated at around 10–15% on average.

The authorities believed that they had held the popular will in check and that Russians would not risk rocking the boat. They nevertheless had to use administrative manipulation and fraud to produce the desired outcome: a majority of seats for the dominant party, United Russia, in a legislative ballot which was meant to be a rehearsal for Putin's reelection as president in March 2012. They thereby further degraded the key institution of free universal suffrage, the expression of popular sovereignly, at a time when they most needed that institution on which to build legitimacy. They played with voters and with legal as well as 'illegal' oppositions. They tried but failed to fake a 'managed pluralism'. What happened reveals how little attention the leadership devoted to social realities in their own country and to developments outside Russia, and how little they knew about the political histories of neighbouring European countries. It has often proved to be an unsuccessful gamble to introduce pluralism in elections yet seek to retain absolute power over all public institutions and control over economic resources.

The Arab revolts of 2011 and the fall of well-entrenched dictatorships in Tunisia, Egypt, Libya and Yemen have raised alarm in Moscow and taught Putin at least one lesson: to stay in power, repression is not the solution, and some kind of compromise has to be found.

Election-rigging is not a new phenomenon in Russia, yet earlier elections had not generated similar protests. Four major factors may explain what occurred in 2011.

The first is, very simply, the passing of time, the perils of repetition and fatigue. Putin won his first race in 1999–2000. The electoral cycle of 2011–12 is the fourth such 'managed' contest, with roughly the same parties and presidential candidates taking part, Medvedev having played the role of stand-in for Putin in 2008. Always the same primitive discourse and stage-managed campaign. And invariably similar results whatever the context: about a two-thirds turnout and over two-thirds of votes going to the incumbent. Putin's rule has been hit by the well-known phenomenon of erosion; he can no longer reinvent himself.

The second reason is disappointment, bordering on deception, at Medvedev's stepping aside to let his patron back in the presidential seat. Dmitry Medvedev was not meant to be the real boss, and most Russians understood the ruse and voted for him in 2008 in order to keep Putin. Nevertheless, political life became so stifled, and Putin so confident that he could stay on for ever, that many wished for Medvedev to fight for reelection. Even in his master's shadow, a younger and more amiable man offered some prospect for more modern and open ways. To more critically minded people, as well as to middle-class conservatives, Putin's one-man rule no longer held out the promise of a better future.

A third reason is corruption. The protestors of 2011 for the first time accused Putin, his friends and party cronies of being 'thieves and crooks'. They meant that the system is corrupt both economically and politically. Hence, the two can no longer be separated. Putin is the national leader and the patron of the oligarchic and unaccountable system that is analysed in the second half of this book. Until the war in Georgia and the international financial crisis of 2008, most Russians believed Putin to be a tough but fair and efficient leader. As the oil windfall dwindled and the rulers felt less confident, people started to look at them more critically. Their wealth appeared to be huge and disproportionate in contrast with Russia's stagnant economy and glaring social disparities.

A fourth and momentous cause of post-electoral unrest is the growth of the Internet. In 2011, the number of regular Internet users reached 50% of the populace, among whom a growing number are active users of Facebook, Twitter, YouTube and the like. They are fluent in hightech communication and compulsive networkers. They are opening new modes of social or group interaction where they outwit official webmasters, FSB experts, and spindoctors.

The irony in Vladimir Putin's misfortunes in 2011 is that he fell into a trap of his own making. He believed that the formulae that had worked so well over ten years would continue to perform. For example, he decided to crack down on media freedoms and relied on biased confidential sources of information. He freed administrative bosses of democratic accountability and judiciary sanction, but needed them to rule the country, which they were bound to do less and less effectively. He has deprived himself of the best Russian minds, the dedicated men and women who could have conducted long overdue reforms, in Moscow and in other Russian cities, towns and rural areas.

Vladimir Putin did not think in terms of 'already twelve years in power', but rather 'another twelve years ahead' since he was aiming at getting relected president twice for a six-year term. Society, however, is never perfectly still and orderly. The social realities fluctuate, even without reform from above or demands for change from below. Putin was concerned not to repeat Gorbachev's 'mistakes' that, in his view, led to 'the greatest geopolitical catastrophe in the twentieth century', i.e. the fall of the USSR. He ought to have paid more attention to Boris Yeltsin's mistakes and Brezhnev's stagnation, the famous *zastoi* which he started to reproduce.

All politicians, in Moscow and in the provinces, Putinites and opponents alike, feel the necessity to address society's mood and needs, to be attentive to the 'moral temper', to use Nathan Leites's phrase. Before 2011, neither side was particularly keen to talk to the 'masses'. The times have changed. The regime may still rely on the conservative mood of many in Russian society who look on, anxious not to live through troubled times again and prepared to go along with the current power, or a similar type of rule, with or without Vladimir Putin.

Since the late 1990s, rulers have hollowed out public institutions and disregarded the democratic principles of good governance. That has helped them consolidate their unchallenged grip on power, but it has backfired. When it needed them, the Putin regime lacked the efficiently run federal, regional and local institutions required to reform government and create new social momentum. The paradox of Russian politics is that of a strong power based on a weak state.

INTRODUCTION

It is often said, both inside and outside Russia, that Vladimir Putin restored order and power and revived Russia as a strong state. Wonder at Great Russia's rebound implies that the Putin model is good, since it suits the country's particular circumstances. The economy has seen steady growth from 2000 to 2008, the population's standard of living has improved and, with the exception of the poorest section, Russia is becoming a consumer society. Oil and gas revenues have given Russia the means to regain its place in world affairs. The country was severely hit by the world financial crisis of 2008, but the economy started to grow again in 2010 at a more modest pace.

Until the blatantly rigged elections of December 2011 that unleashed public protest, order seemed to reign: the Parliament always appeared to be in agreement with the Executive, as did the courts, and disruptive elements seemingly occupied only a very marginal position in society. Ordinary Russians supported the existing government and were happy to have elected Putin's young protégé Dmitri Medvedev as President, so as to be sure to retain the architect of this stability, Putin himself, as leader of the nation.

One big shadow looming over Russia since 1999 is terrorism that strikes Moscow at regular intervals, and extreme violence in the North Caucasus on a daily basis. The commanding authorities and media under their control present terrorism as a world evil. Russians are getting used to living with the Sword of Damocles and do not expect terrorism to recede.

The scenario painted by the admirers—and by the servants—of the regime was that of collective satisfaction among citizens and satisfied consumers. Everything was good compared to the chaos that followed the break-up of the USSR in 1991 and the collapse of the Communist regime.

And so the Putin system, aided by the high price of hydrocarbons, was seen as the key to Russia's remarkable recovery, achieved without the direct support of the West, thanks to Russia's distancing itself from the democratic prescriptions of Europe and the United States, considered unsuited to the situation in post-Soviet Russia. The economic upturn until the crisis of 2008 is indisputable. With revenues doubling in five years, the state coffers were comfortably full, and between 2002 and 2008 real salaries doubled on average, as did GDP per capita during the same period. Russia bounced back from a long way down, only returning to its 1991 economic level in 2006. The economic recovery was therefore a healthy development that has saved the country from stagnation, but not yet set it on the road to rapid, solid economic prosperity and social cohesion.

The setback caused by the credit crunch and the fall in commodity prices in 2008–2009 has shown that post-communist modernization falls short of systemic reform and long-awaited diversification of a rent economy. Russian and foreign economists stress that Russia is still in a catch-up phase, and are concerned about inflation and the concentration of resources in the hands of a few large state-owned conglomerates. The still considerable social disparities recall the bumpy history of the last two decades.

The elites are aware of their country's deep-seated problems and are frustrated with the decline in population, the dereliction of the health system, the bureaucracies' ineptitude and the irrepressible corruption that reaches out to the very top of the political pyramid. They are evidently keen to underline the dangers threatening Russia and jeopardizing its global ascension. Russia is facing a tough challenge, repeat the politicians, for if things are going well, then the threat of losing what has been accomplished is all the greater: central government control is therefore all the more vital. Economic progress requires a curb on pluralism and competition, in other words on freedoms, while those who oppose government policy are condemned for taking an anti-nationalist stance. The laws on non-governmental organizations (NGOs) and on extremism, for example, were introduced in 2006 to thwart individuals and organizations (NGOs, associations, parties) voicing opinions or acting against 'state interests'. Furthermore, media criticism is seen as jeopardizing the rebuilding of a strong state, and must therefore be silenced.

This then is the challenge: how to explain, by means of in-depth analysis of political and social Russia, the contradictions of the current situation, which is a mix of political repression and Internet contest, of weakened public institutions and a reinforced central government, of anti-Westernism and active cooperation with Western partners. The Russian state prides itself on being 'strong', but what kind of *state*, and what form of *strength* are we talking about?

This book attempts to answer the question that arises from this extraordinary paradox: Russia is generally praised or criticized for its intense statism and centralism, for the government institutions' grip on society and the Kremlin's ability to unite lands and peoples. However, analysis of the modern-day Russian state arrives at opposite conclusions. The state as an institutional construction and embodiment of public life is weak and dysfunctional. The nature of the Russian polity has been transformed during the drift towards authoritarianism, personalized power and patron-client networks. Energy wealth and the economic growth of the 2000s are undoubtedly shoring up a system where power and resources are concentrated in the hands of individuals and networks that are not accountable to society. How then do we explain the persistence of a mythical vision of Russia, both inside Russia and abroad?

More than twenty years have passed since the fall of the Berlin Wall and the collapse of the communist system. This book goes to print shortly after the twentieth anniversary of the August 1991 putsch against Gorbachev—the last and failed attempt at stopping reforms and saving the Soviet state. In December 1991, the USSR died, as did the centuries-old Russia empire.

The present work aims to shed new light on the recent history of post-Communist Russia and offer an interpretation of the political and social changes taking place. It also seeks to develop a critical analysis of the political regime under Putin since 2000, the most recent stage in Russia's transformation. The executive duo formed in May 2008, the Putin-Medvedev 'tandem', was led by Prime Minister Putin, with President Medvedev in the position of loyal associate. After a four-year interval, Vladimir Putin is striving to get his presidential post back in 2012. If he succeeds, he will be a weak president confronted to mounting criticism and protest.

Looking back at the Gorbachev reforms and their immense consequences with the hindsight of two and a half decades gives us the necessary distance to at least attempt a formalized and well-argued critique of a political system that is still today in the process of change. This analysis does not claim to be putting forward a definitive model of Russian society and government, and it will certainly need expanding and refining over the coming years. However, the social scientist cannot always wait for the end of a process, as the completion of a historical cycle is more symbolic than real and does not spell the end of developments or changes in a society. Current trends should not erase from the scholar's memory and critical apparatus the lessons learned from the many episodes that had a profound effect on the different stages of the transformation in the 1980s, 1990s and 2000s. It is up to us, political scientists, sociologists and contemporary historians, to weigh up and fit together the pieces of a fast-moving historical puzzle without claiming to see the whole picture at any given moment.

This is all the more important since for the last few years the Russian authorities have been doing their utmost to act in precisely the opposite way from the scientific approach. For Vladimir Putin and his advisers, an event that has not been 'a victory' never happened. According to their narrative, the Orange Revolution that rocked Ukraine at the end of 2004 did not happen; it was an American attempt at subversion, as proved by subsequent events, since the Orange coalition did poorly and lost the presidential election of January 2011. Another example of rewriting history: Chechnya is 'back to normal', and the war waged by the Russian Army for years is summed up as a battle won in the 'fight against terrorism'. Any other analysis is considered ill-intentioned, antipatriotic and biased.

The silencing of criticism from within Russia gives added importance to analysis and interpretation by outside observers who do not risk constant interference in their private and professional lives when they touch on sensitive issues. The subject of this book is in principle the most sensitive issue of all, since it tackles the question of the Russian state and government, in other words the issue of political power, an area that is dangerous by definition in a context where the rulers jealously guard their preserve. The gist of the official response can be summarized as follows: 'The state is harsh and intransigent; it can be so because it has become strong again. That comes as a disappointment to some, but the majority of Russians are delighted'.

The ruling elite is irritated by, but does not completely censor, the 'rants' of independent journalists, experts and political opponents who criticize the regime's abuses of authority and violations of freedoms and basic rights. But at the same time, the real world of the exercise of power by officials in the Kremlin and their henchmen is a taboo subject. There is no way of penetrating the secretive inner workings and cronyist practices of those in power. As soon as an issue touches on financial interests, judicial affairs or reciprocal gifts between influential figures, the authorities use all the means at their disposal to silence the troublemakers. The other dangerous subject is the excessive use of force by the state and the groups it protects, like the ruling clan in the republic of Chechnya, supposedly pacified because it is controlled by fear. The two wars in Chechnya have left at least 150,000 dead since 1994; on the Russian side some tens of thousands have been killed, mainly soldiers, including young conscripts.

As long as one plays by the rules, there are no obstacles to studying the decline of public institutions, media control, petty corruption and poor governance, even for Russian academics. At regular intervals President Medvedev, and sometimes even Prime Minister Putin, paint a dark picture of their country and underline flaws in government.[1] Their official think tanks publish blunt reports that make the reader wonder why the power-wielders have met with such little success in solving some of the haunting problems since 2000. Why does an authoritarian regime convey a negative image of its political and social organizations, continually condemn corruption within the state and regularly deliver up provincial governors, mayors, company directors to public opprobrium?

One answer is that the servants of the regime are easy scapegoats, responsible for Russia's ills in place of the boss. Another answer lies with the leadership's contempt for both social organizations and representative institutions. Vladimir Putin chose to concentrate power in a few selected places: the presidential administration, the government, the special branch of the Federal Security Service (FSB), the Interior Ministry and the police, the energy and industrial giants, and international diplomacy. Ultimately, one can write about public institutions since those institutions, in essence and in formal organization, are of no primary interest to those who claim to govern them.

This book suggests an interpretation of contemporary Russian politics which takes as its starting point the study of the state, a question that has been relatively neglected by Russian and foreign analysts. The familiar narrative framework chosen by many observers since the collapse of the USSR has been the transition towards democracy and a market economy: is Russia following the expected exit route from Communism and heading naturally towards Western-style democratization?

My analysis of the political regime through a study of the state, and relations between state and society, does not call into question the relevance of studies of transition towards democracy (see Bibliography). It offers a counterpoint and a slightly different approach, perhaps more 'French' than Anglo-Saxon.

This line of attack is well understood by Russian scholars, but with a few exceptions, they do not trust it for their own research. The state has too long been an impossible and unappealing subject. It fairly soon emerged that Russian experts, like the journalists and spin doctors (*polittekhnologi*), seized on Anglo-Saxon methods of analysis, adopting the terms 'delegative democracy', 'managed democracy' and 'electoral authoritarianism', precisely because this thinking was foreign to them; it was less painful for them and more neutral to write and speak of their own country using these foreign tools, detached from the profound realities which they had such difficulty formulating.

By choosing the construction and deconstruction of the state as a narrative framework, I am seeking to dispel the illusion of Russia's successful consolidation through authoritarianism and the pushing back of democracy, an illusion upheld by the ruling powers. On the contrary, as this book endeavours to show, the methods and the authoritarian mindset advocated by Russian rulers are undermining the state, public institutions and the law, and hampering Russians' social and cultural development.

The Putin regime has overwhelmingly sought to re-establish the paradigm of the interventionist and controlling state. In so doing, it has rejected that of the unifying, negotiating state, representing diversities and specificities without crushing them in a political straitjacket. Federalism has become a hateful notion, even though formally the state is a federation. In the economic sphere, those in power have monopolized a considerable share of the country's resources and curbed the independence of industrial and financial players, thus prejudicing free competition in the new market economy.

This book examines the relationship between state and society— between those who wield executive power and hold a monopoly on 'legitimate violence' and those who are governed. On what basis is the interaction between those who govern and those who are governed organized? Is there a form of consensus between them?

The problem of causality is particularly pertinent since the same unanswerable question always arises: are the people to blame for the shortcomings of their government? Or are the authoritarian rulers and their mindset, allegedly inspired by 'oriental despotism', responsible for an apathetic, subjugated society incapable of embracing democracy?

A significant part of this study focuses on the mindsets and attitudes of the ruling elites and ordinary Russians, on the quality of the leaders, their advisers, the values they claim to defend. Inward-looking suspicion of 'the Other' (foreigners, strangers, and dissidents) is the hallmark of Russian society, as well as a wariness towards the institutions of government. Threats and enemies are often imaginary, and these perceptions are more persuasive than is reality in a Russia that appears to be quite the opposite of a country that is besieged and under threat. Never, in all its history, has Russia objectively been in a situation of greater security. The Cold War is over, Russia is better integrated into international institutions, and most of its neighbours have an interest in trade cooperation. Vladimir Putin has chosen to promote a siege mentality and suspicion of the outside world among his citizens. He convinced Russians, through media propaganda, that the Georgians were enemies and that a military conflict was inevitable in 2008. He has also pushed Russians to be inward-looking, to guard against competition, and to be content with a very mediocre public life in which they do not participate. The regime's authoritarian line represents a setback compared with the remarkable transparency and openness instigated by Mikhail Gorbachev when Russians felt for the first time that they were fully entering the world in every way.

After the 1990s, which were marked by the dismantling and very imperfect rebuilding of government organizations, Vladimir Putin sought to undermine all the institutions that did not come within the compass of the central state from his point of view. Whereas Boris Yeltsin had let institutions decline, his successor pursued a systematic strategy of hollowing out public institutions. Putin's system of rule is focused on the executive power and its economic networks, and on the administrative and corporatist control of actors and resources. It succeeded in establishing the economic and political sovereignty of the central federal state, which was achieved at the expense of the autonomy of the provinces, and of independent stakeholders, like the Yukos oil company and its CEO, Mikhail Khodorkovsky.

The paradox of this new authoritarian model is that it pushes ordinary Russians outside the political arena and gives them a form of autonomy and freedom that they did not have during the Communist era. They may distance themselves fully from public affairs and stay away from any form of social mobilization. The private individual is now free while the public citizen is very weak. A *civil society* struggles to exist in Russia, but finds it difficult to become a *political society*, because of the lack of democratic and effective public institutions to carry forward protest and claims. Russians are willingly escaping the reach of institutions in which they have no faith and which the Kremlin is seeking to undermine, like the Parliament and elected assemblies. They are also suspicious of alternative institutions— NGOs, foreign businesses and government opponents. They do not want to see the re-establishment of a police state, but rather a form of economic, social and moral order. They tolerate the existing regime, but are increasingly able to impose their individual choices, in particular the choice not to take part in the political charade spearheaded by the Kremlin. They no longer think that elections are free and fair, and know that they do not choose the successors to the Head of State or the government, or the leaders of provincial administrations. Dmitri Medvedev was designated by Vladimir Putin to occupy the position of President; the population endorsed this choice on 2 March 2008, via a controlled, rigged ballot. And the new President, according to the agreed scenario, appointed his mentor as Prime Minister. Putin's famous 'stability' was guaranteed. Officially, the Constitution lived, and the 'free vote' too. The negative consequences of the 2008 political trick are unfolding before our eyes at the end of 2011.

Society has not been completely stifled, since individuals find ways of adapting and circumventing. Most Russians do not participate in public life, because it has been emptied of content. They have no hold on state institutions and they deal with this by turning away from them, to the extent that those in power no longer know how to manage the populace or control them effectively. The following pages open a few doors into this strange political and social world that is neither democratic nor neo-Communist.

The opening chapter analyzes the construction of the state and the empire during the Tsarist period. As in every country, the mindsets of the elites and of ordinary citizens are forged by the past and major historical events. In Russia especially, this heritage has been doctored and rewritten to suit the needs of those in power. The relationships of Russians to the government, the state, and to Russian soil have been shaped by these successive reconstructions of the national imagination.

Chapter 2 offers an analysis of political and social change under and after Gorbachev and puts forward two paradigms: opening up to the outside world as the key to transformation; national-imperial identity as a major impediment to post-Communist liberalization.

Chapters 3, 4 and 5 focus on political developments since the collapse of the USSR, and the problems of building institutions and holding free elections. They are not a straightforward chronology of two turbulent decades. The aim, rather, is to gain an understanding of relations between the ruling elites and society, between the actors at the top and the grass-roots, between economic interests and political ambitions, by looking primarily at the political scene. From the end of the 1990s, the decay of democratic institutions was accompanied by a curtailing of rights and freedoms.

Society's attitudes are the subject of Chapter 6. Opinion polls and Russian sociological studies bring to life and interpret the views and behaviour of Russia's 140 million inhabitants.

Finally, the last three chapters offer an interpretation of the system of rule under Putin.

1

THE MYTH OF A STRONG STATE

LEGACY OF THE EMPIRE AND AUTOCRACY

'Without a Constitution, without political rights, Russia is not yet a modern state'.

Anatole Leroy-Beaulieu, 1888[1]

'Russia is not a state; Russia is a world'. This phrase, attributed to Catherine the Great, is still repeated by Russian historians and philosophers. It perfectly encapsulates the attitude of many Russians towards their country, from the bottom to the top of the social ladder. More than twenty years after the fall of the Berlin Wall, the notion of sovereign states strictly demarcated by borders has not taken root in Russian minds. In a 2007 opinion poll, the vast majority of Russians stated that Belarus and Ukraine 'are not foreign countries' and that 'Europe belongs to another world'.[2] This reveals that Russians have difficulty both in seeing the countries that were for a long time part of Russia's imperial sphere as 'other', and in conceiving of European countries as close neighbours.

This fractured representation of the regional and global environment is symptomatic of a country that has experienced and written its national history as an imperial history in a world that is shut off from outside influences. The state is seen first and foremost as an imperial power confronting the outside world, whereas the state as a form of government, from the Tsarist period to that of the omnipotent Communist leaders, remains the affair of the small group of decision-makers at the top. Russian historians have focused mainly on the history of the building of the empire and that of the Tsars. The social and human history of the empire's peoples has been explored in ethnographers' monographs (to use the Russian term), travel journals and literary works.

Imperial State, not Nation State

From the fifteenth century onwards, Russia sought to build a territorially integrated empire, not a nation state. Expansion was continuous, the Moscow princes pushing back the territory's borders towards secure natural frontiers—seas, rivers and mountains. For too long, the eastern Slavs of the central plain that stretched for thousands of miles with no natural protection had suffered from foreign invasions, especially by the Mongols. The recomposition of a Russian political entity around Moscow had barely begun when the territory expanded. The Grand Principality of Moscow (called Muscovy by European observers) did not have time to build institutions; it had already become the centre of an imperial enterprise. The history of the Russian state and that of the empire were one and the same, from Ivan the Terrible's sixteenth-century conquests of the khanates of Kazan and Astrakhan on the Volga, peopled by Finnish and Turkic tribes. From that point on, the empire was multi-ethnic and multi-faith.[3] The *Rus*, also called *Zemlya Russkaya* ('Russian land'), became *Rossiya* and *Vserossiiskoe gosudarstvo* ('State of all Russia').[4] We translate the word *Rossiya* as 'Russia', likewise *Rus'*, which leads to confusion. *Rossiya* became the generic term for the multinational ensemble created by the Tsar. Until the break-up of the USSR in 1991, the empire stretched from the Baltic countries to Vladivostok, from Kiev and Tbilisi to the lands of the far Siberian north.

By the seventeenth century, expansion had transformed Russia into a continental empire reaching as far as the Pacific. In the eighteenth century, the tsar ruled over Siberia, Ukraine, Belarus, the Baltic and the Kazakh steppes. By the nineteenth century, the empire also encompassed the Caucasus, Central Asia and the Far East. The expansion westwards and to the south-west, from the Baltic to the Caucasus, involved the incorporation of European nations, generally organized as states, such as Georgia and Lithuania. It was a tough challenge, particularly in the Caucasus where strong resistance dragged Russia into long and bloody battles. Russia's push towards Europe primarily reflected a desire for openness and to be part of the Western world's modernization process. The chief reason was not a concern for military security; only the Napoleonic campaigns threatened the Russian empire with occupation.

Conquest eastwards and south-eastwards, as far as the Pacific and the mountains of Central Asia, Mongolia and China, was however motivated principally by the wish for natural boundaries, and secondly by the search for habitable land and the lure of Siberia's resources (sable, gold and, later, raw materials). One of the driving forces for the colonization of the Kazakh and Siberian territories was the *mujik*, the Russian peasant escaping or freed from serfdom, who headed eastwards and built his *isba* in an attempt to survive in the steppe. Adventurers and merchants were also pioneers of the conquest of the East. Russia's populating of these inhospitable terrains in Asia was often tantamount to an unofficial colonization, with no established rules and no frontier. The Tsarist administration came down later to impose the Tsar's laws.[5]

After the end of the Tatar occupation and Ivan the Terrible's conquests, Russia continued to build its empire. The continuous drive to expand and gain greater power went hand in hand with a vitality and a capacity to absorb crises, wars and population explosions. Russia was certainly not static. However, weaknesses and imbalances began to emerge. The country was spreading into inhospitable terrain, marshland (on which the new capital by Peter I was built), or areas that were very cold or unprotected. People were living with the impression that the ground underfoot was not stable and that they might be forced to pack up their belongings and leave at any moment.

The immense space was used by the rulers and their subjects as a reservoir and a source of vitality as well as an opportunity for escape and liberation, or of forced isolation and exile. If a conflict could not be resolved through negotiation, the use of force or banishment was the answer. The Tsarist regime, with its administrations and its army, was not reassuring; it did not give the people a solid foundation, but was a weight that could descend and crush individual lives, divine will being invoked at such times.

Perhaps this complex history, where opposing realities are inextricably intertwined—confinement and the vastness of the territory, the omnipotence of the emperor appointed by God and the diversity of the peoples and resources, the attraction of Europe and the specificity of

Greater Russia—explains the very particular relationship the Russians have with time, authority and property: a sense of eternity mixed with an awareness of life's precariousness, a mixture of dependence and suspicion towards the state and the government.

The nineteenth-century European vision of Russia was often a simplified one, that of a vast, static country that was backward and impervious to outside changes. This perception was based on the autocratic system, serfdom and poverty, taking little account of the more profound changes happening beneath the carapace of a closed, autocratic regime. The failures of the Crimean War in 1856 and of Alexander II's reforms in the 1860s added to this image of an inert Russian Empire. However, the second half of the nineteenth century was a period of intense change, the effects of which cannot be overstated, in particular demographic changes and the growing part of non-Slavs in the overall population.

One of the major consequences of Russia's policy of colonizing territories by populating the land with Slavs was that Russians did not remain concentrated in metropolitan areas. At no time in its history has Russia been conceived as a metropolis surrounded by colonies. In contrast with the French and British empires, it has no territory overseas. Everything is empire, and everything is colony. The Slav was subjected to the autocracy and arbitrariness of state representatives just as much as the Tatar or the Yakut, and probably more than the Pole or the Armenian. At certain points in the Tsars' empire, the Russian peasants and nobles had a lower status than other nationalities.

The Eastern Slavs did not become clearly divided into Russians, Ukrainians and Belorussians until the fifteenth and sixteenth centuries. Russian ethnicity was not consolidated into a nation state, since those who spoke Russian already belonged to a multinational complex, the growing empire. It was easier for the Ukrainians to develop their own national culture since Ukrainian developed into a national language, unlike Russian, which became the language of the empire and so was not, strictly speaking, a national language.

Russians feel that Russia in its vastness was built at the cost of great hardship and costly conquests, but that they have never benefited from it directly. Their view of their own history became clear when the USSR collapsed. Many were shocked at the 'ungratefulness' of the non-Russian nationalities who resented Russia's political, economic and military domination over the centuries. They did not see themselves as a colonizing people but as the builders of a Eurasian power that protected the Christians of the Orient and was inspired by a civilizing mission.

Nineteenth-century historians described the building of the empire in positive terms. The extension of the Tsar's sovereignty to vast regions of Asia and to Christian countries to the West was natural. Vasily Klyuchevsky wrote the history of Holy Russia, of the empire, not the history of the nations of which it was composed.[6] Nicolas Karamzin starts his history of Russia with this remarkable sentence: 'From the Caspian Sea to the Baltic, from the Black Sea to the Arctic, amid deserts known to the Greeks and Romans, more from fairy tales than from the correct descriptions of eyewitnesses, there lived a thousand years ago peoples given to nomadism, hunting and agriculture. From these diverse tribes it pleased Providence to create the most spacious state in the world'. A staunch advocate of autocracy, Karamzin defends a strong regime and a prudent reform policy as the guarantors of the continuity of the empire in its entirety.[7] The American historian Marc Raeff stresses the 'elites' and the people's

lack of awareness of the imperial[ist] nature of their country. […] the conquest of an empire to the east and south-east happened so slowly, one could almost say 'organically', that the Russians barely realized it. It is true on the other hand that Russians at the time were aware of the conquests of the Caucasus and Central Asia. But, just like most of the colonial conquests in Africa and South-East Asia in the nineteenth century, these often took the form of local military initiatives and served to fuel the exotic and warlike romanticism of a small social and artistic elite. This lack of awareness explains the extraordinary ignorance of the creation, not to mention the nature, of this empire, even in educated circles, as well as the conviction that the assimilation of the indigenous peoples into Russian civilization was natural, inevitable and desirable.[8]

Ironically, this view of the colonization process as natural and civilizing was reinforced by the Bolshevik reconquest and the Sovietization of the entire imperial complex inherited from the Tsars. The paradox lies in the Bolshevik critique of the pre-1917 'prison-house of nations', a prison which they would take over, consolidate and perfect in the 1920s, '30s and '40s. Once Sovietized, these peoples officially became part of the modern, positive history of the march of socialism. The Stalinist interpretation of Russian history was nationalist and imperialist: since Russia was more economically advanced than the periphery, and closer to socialism, Soviet expansion had a progressive impact on the backward nations. Later in this book we will discuss the profound impact of the Bolshevik domination of the historical memory of today's Russians, and in particular their difficulty in understanding and accepting the break-up of the USSR.

At no time in Tsarist or Soviet history did Russia see itself as a metropolis surrounded by colonies. The 'national' community was the imperial complex, embracing all ethnic groups and provinces. Expansion stimulated the building of an 'imperial nation', to the detriment of a purely Russian identity. Russians felt Russian because they spoke Russian, were attached to the land and belonged to the Russian empire, were subjects of the Tsar and belonged to the Orthodox Church. Ethnic affiliation was not a determining factor for the Eastern Slavs. The concept of nation was first and foremost imperial. And there has never been an equivalence between the Russian people and the Russian state. After 1917, the Communist government extended this notion of an imperial-national community through the ideology of the 'Soviet people', while at the same time profoundly transforming it. Russia therefore has never been a nation state and this option seems just as impossible in the twenty-first century, even if the ideology developed by the Putin regime in recent years has pushed Russians towards the notion of a 'Russia for Russians', which ties in with the ideology of a 'specifically Russian route' to modernization.[9]

The question of nationalism in Russia, both in the past and today, is inextricably bound up with the state's imperial history.[10] Russia and empire, Soviet Russia and the USSR all merge. Russians in the 'national-ethnic' sense of the word are a people without a specific *habitus*, and whose language, which has become the *lingua franca*, does not distinguish them from other peoples of the empire. The authoritarian nature of the Tsarist and Soviet regimes, the lack of reform and public freedoms, and the absorption of society by the state have made national consciousness the exclusive preserve of the elites. The peasant obeyed the Tsar and God; the Orthodox Church and religious belief formed the basis of the absolutist regime.

The Communist regime upheld a strong Soviet patriotism so that it could undermine the Greater Russian identity more effectively (and also, of course, Ukrainian, Armenian, Georgian, Lithuanian, etc. identities). However, when the USSR was invaded by Hitler's Germany, Stalin realized that he had to play the identity card and encourage Russian nationalism. During World War II, the Orthodox Church regained a central position in defending the fatherland.

The major upheavals of 1989–1991 highlighted the weaknesses and the contradictions of Russian nationalism, which was caught between nostalgia for past glory and the utopia of Russian or Slavic purity. Yeltsin's and Putin's governments, in different ways, have encouraged the search for a romantic ideal of the nation, when the real challenge facing post-communist Russia with its legacy of empire was to build a state, a public institution capable of representing and governing all the populations of the federation as a whole, at local, regional and national level. After more than a decade of Putin's leadership, the building of a modern, federal and secular state is abandoned in favour of the ideological construction of a Russian Orthodox nation, thus breaking with the long multinational past of Tsarist and Communist Russia. The creation of a national identity 'in reverse' is one of the pillars of the Putin system.

A People, not a Nation

A major effect of Russia's expansion through settlement was the dispersal of Russians across the empire's far-flung provinces. The Russian people were not concentrated in a specific, clearly defined territory. There was no Russian state in the ethnic sense of the word. From the beginnings of expansion in the sixteenth century, Muscovy was multi-ethnic and multi-faith. The term *Rossiya* designates the imperial state and has no ethnic connotation, whereas the word *Rus*, which appeared in the ninth century to designate the territories of the Slavic tribes of the East, is the root of the adjective *russkii*, which has an ethnic and linguistic meaning. The Russian language makes a clear distinction between this term, specific to the Russian people, and the adjective *rossiiskii* which refers to the state, and to all the inhabitants of imperial Russia (*Rossiya*). The difficulty in explaining these fundamental distinctions is that the two words are usually both translated as 'Russian'. Nowadays, as during the Tsarist period, the adjective *rossiiskii* is synonymous with 'national' or 'state' (*gosudarstvennii*).

The Eastern Slavs' close intermingling with other tribes and peoples for ten centuries makes it difficult to identify a Russian *ethnos* in the sense of a race and a language. On the other hand, a Russian feels Russian and has no doubt about his Russianness, based on the fact that he belongs to a solid body which is the Russian people. For him, it is first and foremost a way of being, a way of life. When Nobel Prize laureate Ivan Bunin wrote about the Russian landscape from exile in Paris, he expressed an immense nostalgia for a reality which he placed above all else. The poor, peasant way of life is idealized as embodying a specifically Russian purity and truth. When the Russian soldiers defended Holy Russia in 1812 and the USSR in 1941–1945, they were defending their land. Emigration has never reached significant proportions since Russians do not wish to leave their country, even if life is hard there. The huge wave of exiles after the Bolshevik Revolution can be explained by the certainty of perishing under the new regime. Remaining was not an option.

Dostoevsky describes the pride of the Russians who travelled in Europe where everything was so much more civilized. Back home, they say that in Russia everything is better. The aristocrat speaks French, but he likes his country. Only an understanding of this feeling, of this pride in being Russian, can enable us to comprehend the ease with which Putin's controlled media stage the resurgence of national pride at the cost of jeopardizing good relations with Georgians, Tatars, Ukrainians and other communities living in the Russian federation.

Once elected through direct universal suffrage in June 1991, the President of the new federal post-Communist Russia, Boris Yeltsin, found himself facing a conundrum. How should he address his fellow citizens now that the term 'Comrades' (*Tovarishchi*) was banned and the word 'Citizens' (*Grazhdane*) considered outmoded? Yeltsin had to find an expression that would embrace all the populations of the vast Federation and he chose the little-used noun *Rossiyane* ('inhabitants of Russia'). He could not use the word *Russkie* ('Russians') if he wanted to include the non-Russian nationalities of the present-day Russian Federation. Later Vladimir Putin opted to use the word 'compatriots', or 'dear friends' in public. In his less formal conversations and exchanges, he simply says 'Russians'.[11]

The national sphere was traditionally the 'imperial' sphere. And the political sphere, the *gosudarstvo*, was built on this territorial and autocratic foundation. The word *gosudarstvo* translates as 'state', but its etymology is very different. The *gosudar* is the 'sovereign', the *gosudarstvo* is the 'domain of the sovereign', in the way that the kingdom is the domain of the king.[12] Imagine if the word 'state' in English today meant the same thing as 'kingdom'. The Tsar was master over everyone and everything, he was the state. The modern notion of sovereignty did not develop from this word, since Russian history did not give way to the sovereign people until the beginning of the twentieth century. The modern principle of sovereignty and the Russianized word *suverenitet* were therefore imported from the West: in 1990–1991 the Soviet republics declared their *suverenitet*, in other words, the political independence of their nation and the end of Russian domination. The Russian Socialist Federal Soviet Republic (RSFSR), headed by Boris Yeltsin, also claimed its sovereignty in July 1990, eighteen months before the USSR ceased to exist, which created an unprecedented legal and political situation. Moscow was the capital of two 'sovereign' states, one embedded in the other.

Enlargement through incorporating adjoining lands created a massive territory, with no physical barriers. No sea, no high mountains, separated one province from another. Russians felt at home wherever they went. They did not see themselves as a colonizing people but as the founding and dominant people of a great European and Asian power. The Russian people were the biggest community of the greater whole that was the nation or the imperial people. The Tsar's power was based on three pillars: autocracy, Orthodoxy and *narodnost'*.[13] It is hard to translate this third term, which means 'community of the people' and, for the Russians, belonging to their Russian community. It thus embodies the ambiguity of the national identity.

The difference between the notion of 'peoples' (*narody*) who live within the empire and the 'national imperial community' became a major political issue in the nineteenth century. In the eighteenth and nineteenth centuries, the empire, which had remained predominantly Russian and Slav until the end of the seventeenth century, incorporated new non-Slav and non-Orthodox peoples and nations. The conquest of the countries of the Caucasus and of Central Asia, and thrusts westward involving confrontations with other imperial powers, gradually changed the make-up and the nature of the empire. From Muscovite *Rus'*, then Great Russia, *Rossiya* was transformed in the late nineteenth century into a sprawling patchwork, almost the entire periphery of which, from the west to the Siberian south, was a mosaic of different territories, most of them with their own strong national, ethnic and religious identities. According to the first census of 1897, 55.7 per cent of the empire's population, excluding the Grand Duchy of Finland, was non-Russian.[14]

Often it is only the conquest of Siberia that is remembered as the pioneering colonization drive to push back Russia's borders. Thomas Barrett points out that conquering the frontier, both southwards and eastwards, was a lengthy affair:

The lower Volga was as non-Russian as Siberia until the late eighteenth century... [15] The Russian advance through the north Caucasus was much more than a military conquest: it was also a frontier process involving the in- and out-migration of large numbers of people, the settlement and creation of new communities and the abandonment of old ones. And, as on all frontiers, borders were crossed and allegiances shifted continually by Russians and Ukrainians, by mountain peoples, by Armenians and Georgians. To understand the Russian annexation of the north Caucasus, we must look behind the military lines to the movements of peoples, the settlements and communities, the transformation of the landscape and the interactions of neighbors, not just in war but also in everyday life. [16]

Thomas Barrett also alludes to the role and the diversity of the Cossacks and the specificity of the Chechens.

Other scholars have analyzed the construction of imperial Russia, emphasizing the importance of migrations, displacements and mixing of populations. [17] However, it is striking that many Russian history textbooks still being published in Russia and in the West devote very little attention to the human, sociological, cultural and economic aspects of the expansion of the empire. [18] Furthermore, the effects of the increase in the proportion of 'foreign' peoples and the reduction of the percentage of Russians in the overall total should not be underestimated. First of all, the push towards new frontiers, at the expense of other states, consolidated Russia's status as a major power and promoted the image of a 'developed' Russian people capable of dominating non-Slavic nations. This aspect definitely played a part in the development of Russian nationalism, fuelled by imperial pride. But in the latter half of the nineteenth century, the conquest of territories with strong ethnic and religious identities stirred up the resentments and demands of the Empire's non-Russian nations. The 'national question', or the 'question of nationalities', was one of the major factors that weakened the imperial power prior to the break-up of the empire during World War I and in the wake of the 1917 revolution.

Another facet of Russia's eighteenth- and nineteenth-century expansion was the even greater dispersal of Russians to all corners of the newly captured markets. Russians were present throughout the imperial territory, their language was the *lingua franca* imposed on everyone, and their Tsar was the sovereign of all the empire's inhabitants. How was it possible to define a separate political identity that had no territory, no language, and no government, that would distinguish the Russian community from the imperial community? The merging of Russian identity and national-imperial identity explains why Russian nationalism took on specific forms which the Bolshevik powers sought to eradicate after 1917, in the attempt to eliminate Russianness from Sovietism.

The Ruler Ruled but did not Govern

From the late fourteenth century onwards, with the creation of the Grand Duchy of Moscow, and after the Mongol occupation, territorial expansion was the driver for the imperial state's political and economic development. To govern the empire's many provinces, the autocratic ruling powers gradually put in place an administrative system based on the rural commune, that made no claims to be modelled on Europe's modern states. As historian Richard Pipes sums up, 'Russia's geographic location, on the edge of an enormous [Asia], with a fluid frontier and restless neighbours, had induced her rulers since the fifteenth century to expand more rapidly than the country's resources warranted, with the result that the growth of the territory had usually outstripped the means available for its administration and defense'.[19]

In *The Empire of the Tsars and the Russians*, Anatole Leroy-Beaulieu describes 'the Muscovite administration' as 'primitive and rudimentary'. 'In the seventeenth century, Russia was as yet but a rudimentary embryonic organism; outside of the Church, she possessed only two institutions, one at the base, the other at the summit, of the state, and both not particularly favourable to the development of individuality: the commune with mutual solidarity of the members, and autocracy; the bond between them—serfdom'.[20] He emphasizes the political necessity of centralization in order to consolidate the autocracy and unify the lands and the people, but he also stresses the ineffectiveness of this system of governance: 'Russian centralization, although naturally a result of the physical and historical conditions of the empire, encountered a double principle of weakness and ineffectiveness, both on the ground and in Russia's history. This enterprise encountered two major obstacles, the material vastness of the territory to be governed, and the ignorance of the people from among whom agents had to be recruited. This explains the impotence of an administration that was legally omnipotent'.[21]

The notion of centralization, then, is not so pertinent. An autocratic regime is not automatically centralized and governed with an iron fist from 'on high'. Historical interpretations are diverse and often contradictory, as evidenced by the controversies over the nature of power and modes of government in Tsarist Russia, and they cannot simply be reduced to a centralized state model. The current debate as to whether the Russian Federation should be re-centralized so as to improve government efficiency shows that the Moscow elites lack a culture of governance that involves delegating power, allowing the regional authorities budgetary autonomy and trusting local government (see Chapter 4).

The constant shortage of financial, material, military and administrative resources to manage such a vast and diverse territory resulted in different modes of administration in different provinces. The administrations were neither excessive nor fully supervised from above. The Russian administration always lagged behind in consolidating positions gained by the army, the Cossacks or adventurers.

For the historian and sociologist Igor Klyamkin, the central problem in Russia from the outset has been the lack of a political relationship between those governing and the governed, and therefore the absence of a modern state in the European sense. The existence of the *state* requires a capacity for abstraction, whereas *power* is a very concrete reality embodied by the Tsar, his army and his officials.

The population of the Russian empire was illiterate; the nobles and the merchants depended on the ruler's will both for their social position and the use of their property. Religion and the army were tangible manifestations of power, while the law and the market remained abstract entities. Klyamkin contends that Tsarist Russia was a traditional, pre-modern society. The local and peasant institutions, the *veche* and the *zemskiy sobor*, were not representative bodies; Klyamkin is critical of historian Boris Mironov for writing of 'local democracy'.[22]

Richard Pipes' interpretation of Tsarist history revolves around the notion of patrimonialism. The Tsar owned the land and the resources, and had the power of life and death over his subjects. Russia's economic and social organization was characterized by the absence of private property, and therefore of public property distinct from the sovereign's property. At the close of Peter I's reign, the state even confiscated the lands belonging to the Church and the monasteries. It was only in the second half of the eighteenth century that a small privileged minority gained private ownership of the land and some capital goods.[23] As property ownership developed, a tentative notion of civic rights also burgeoned.

The seventeenth and eighteenth centuries saw the beginnings of institutionalization with the publication of the *ukases* (the Tsar's edicts) and laws, but the Tsar's autocracy was still absolute. Peter I legitimized the status of Emperor, giving him temporal as well as divine authority. With militarization and the establishment of the 'Table of Ranks', the Tsar was no longer exclusively *bozhestvennyi* (divine), he was also a man. Additionally, Peter liked to disguise himself as a simple soldier, a mere mortal. During the same period, the Tsar's power was consolidated around an administrative system controlled from the capital and a reinforced, modernized army. Maintaining control over vast territories in Europe and Asia required a strong, absolute power. Autocracy remained virtually unchallenged until the beginning of the nineteenth century, for it was seen as the guarantor of the empire's integrity.[24]

The highly influential historian and conservative thinker Nicolas Karamzin wrote in 1811 that 'the severity judiciously applied' by the autocrat ensured that he ruled over an 'integrated Russia'. 'Autocracy was the foundation of Russia; it is what brought Russia back to life; any modification to its structure is damaging and will necessarily lead to its destruction. Composed of such multiple and diverse elements, each with their own interests, can it be governed otherwise than by a sole and absolute power who alone is capable of giving a uniform impetus to this immense expanse?'[25] In other words, the Tsar reigned over the empire and over a community of subjects. The notions of society and of state were of little relevance.

It is also pertinent to mention the necessary recourse to repression and emergency procedures that were an integral part of the autocratic regime up to the end of the Romanov dynasty, in 1917. The Tsars passed emergency legislation to quell unrest and opposition, which underscores the fragility of the state and the ineffectiveness of the Tsarist administration's policies.[26] The ideology of omnipotence required the staging of regular shows of strength; it was important not to show any weakness and not to tolerate any criticism.

The revolutionaries who took power in 1917 very quickly constructed a new ideology of omnipotence and compulsory unanimity, immediately resorting to emergency measures and the arbitrary. The most striking similarity between the *ancien régime* and the new is the conception and practice of a supreme ruler with no counterbalance, no limit to his authority, engaged in a permanent battle against the enemy within and the enemy without.

The Dilution of the State within the Soviet System

The Bolshevik method for reconquering the nations and territories that made up the former empire profoundly marked both the mindset of non-Russian Soviet citizens and influenced the course that the break-up of the USSR would take in 1989–1991.[27] The years of civil war, 1918–1921, were particularly violent in those provinces seeking to break away from the empire. Fighting in the Caucasus went on into the 1920s and in Central Asia until the 1930s.

With the founding of the USSR in 1922 and the domination of the Soviet Republic of Russia within the formal federal grouping, the empire became a countryless state. All references to a geographical or human reality disappeared even from the name of the state: the Union of Soviet Socialist Republics. The state was temporal and temporary since the coming world revolution—the Bolsheviks' supreme aim—would wipe out capitalism and unite all countries in a global Communist entity. The USSR's official internationalist doctrine in the 1920s, even if it was soon diluted in favour of 'socialism in one country', eliminated slogans promoting Greater Russia or the Russian nation from the official ideology. But these slogans made a comeback during World War II: Stalin had to revive Russian patriotism and Orthodoxy in order to mobilize men and resources.[28] He also took advantage of the German occupation in the western part of the USSR to deport nationalities accused of 'collaboration' with the Nazis. The Chechens, the Ingushes, the Tatars of Crimea and numerous other peoples were decimated. In the USSR, as in today's Russia, World War II was seen as the 'Great Patriotic War'.

Post-1917 Russian history blurred all classifications. The revolutionary mood reinforced the idea that the masses, so long subjugated by Tsarism, supported the new regime; the privileged classes of the *ancien régime* had opposed the expression of the people's will and lost all legitimacy: they were enemies of the Revolution. The Bolshevik regime built its legitimacy on this doctrine of popular assent, in the absence of any elections or democratic process. And yet, the reality of popular support was far from being established. Historians' research on the archives opened up in the 1990s widely confirms Merle Fainsod's theories. Back in the 1950s, this American historian analyzed the Smolensk archives, which contained poignant testimonies from peasants, workers and clerks who had fallen victim to the arbitrary nature of the Soviet regime.[29]

However, the people were not in a situation to challenge the new government, which controlled the army. It was impossible for resistance movements to develop in Russia or Ukraine, as terror was inculcated to prevent any dissidence and the formation of organized groups against the Soviet regime. The Bolshevik government managed to impose itself and survive as a result of mass repression. The only public criticism of the regime and its abuses was voiced abroad, among émigrés living in Europe.

This is not the place to retrace the first phase of decolonization of the Tsarist empire between 1914 and 1922, the reconquest by the Soviet powers in the 1920s and 1930s, and the territorial annexations and boundary changes during World War II and the following decade. However, it is worth pointing out that the boundaries of the Soviet Republics were determined by the dismembering of the Tsarist empire after 1914 and the nations that proclaimed their independence between 1918 and 1920, like Armenia and Georgia, and the Baltic states which were reconquered during World War II. After having promised freedom to the oppressed nations of the empire, Lenin did his utmost to impose the new Bolshevik law on their territory. The national elites were forced to recognize Soviet rule; otherwise the territories would be reconquered *manu militari*.[30]

The federal structure of the Soviet state was a tactical weapon. In June 1923, Stalin convinced the Central Committee to create a territorial system dividing all nationalities large and small into federal republics, autonomous republics and regions, which fitted inside each other according to often arbitrary borders. The advantage of this *matrioshka* (Russian doll) system was that it could only be managed by an oppressive, centralized government that allowed the governments and parliaments of the republics no autonomy. A bureaucratic and police culture prevailed, making the USSR a pseudo-federalist body crushed by a central government that was much more totalitarian than during the Tsarist period.

The Russian Socialist Federal Soviet Republic (RSFSR) was soon deprived of key republican institutions. It effectively constituted the gigantic trunk of the USSR. Its capital was confused with that of the USSR, Moscow; the titular nationality, Russian, was that of the dominant nationality. Keen to avert possible Russian nationalist sentiment, Stalin abolished in the RSFSR the national institutions that had been established in other republics. From 1925, the Russian Republic had neither its own Communist Party nor its own Academy of Sciences. Deprived of its first secretary, Russia had no channel of communication, or representative of its interests within the ruling party. The Republic maintained a parliament and a government, but these remained hollow edifices until the Gorbachev years. The real institutions, those of the Communist Party, merged into the institutions of the USSR. Russia as an entity was also weakened by its own federative structure, composed of 'autonomous republics'.[31]

Despite the Leninist theory of the decline of the state, the Bolshevik model soon became a hierarchical and repressive monopolistic one-party state resulting in the subjugation of society. According to the expression coined by the historian and sociologist Basile Kerblay, 'the masses were the antisociety'.[32] The modernization of the state, in the sense of developing political rights and checks and balances to the executive power, was dead and buried. Russia turned its back on Europe. Soviet modernization proved to be industrial and urban, not political. The USSR was an immense country where all the resources—natural, human and economic—came under the control of the ruling class, in other words the Communist leaders and Party *nomenklatura*.

Stalin's terror, from the forced collectivization of the farms to the purges and war, put an end to any pretence of public institutions. The Soviet population did not live in a state, but in a gigantic camp ruled by arbitrary power, and fear. The Gulag—the labour camps where millions of prisoners were enslaved—was the highest level of imprisonment, the equivalent of solitary confinement inside a prison.[33] The administration system, secret police and Party officials were not institutions but 'organs' of execution.[34]

The State as an Instrument of Power

The Russian conception of the state was therefore inextricably connected both to the construction of the empire and autocracy, and to Soviet and Stalinist history. The idea that there is a natural and inevitable correlation between the authoritarian regime and the vastness of the territory still has currency today both in Russia and Europe, a century after the end of Tsarism and more than half a century after the death of Stalin. Even today, in Paris, Berlin or Moscow, observers—often people with serious political and economic responsibilities—conclude the discussion with the familiar pirouette: 'The Russians have centuries of autocracy behind them, that is all they know, and that is how they consolidated their immense territory. Whenever reforms were introduced they jeopardized the country's integrity, and the Russians prefer to defend their state rather than to modernize politically'. This facile explanation is often heard in Russia, even in Ukraine, Georgia and other countries that formerly constituted the USSR. No wonder it is so often echoed in Europe.

By giving credence to this statement, commentators consider the matter closed. In so doing they are missing the opportunity of probing deeper and anticipating where Russia is heading. Is there really a Russian paradigm where the state is inevitably autocratic and society submissive, even in the twenty-first century? No foreign conception of the state penetrated political thinking in Russia until the eighteenth century, when the influence of European philosophers and thinkers, mainly German and French, began to stir up intellectual circles in Saint Petersburg and Moscow. German influence was indisputably the strongest when it came to the almost metaphysical conception of the state, which encompasses the law and government but also the whole of society. In this formulation, social structures receive their legitimacy from the state rather than from the institutions produced by the expression of the people's will or from market mechanisms. French influence exerted itself on Russian thinking through the model of a centralized, egalitarian Jacobin state, born of revolution. The people had won their sovereignty and entrusted it to state institutions. Russian socialists and anarchists drew on a very broad range of sources, including the European thinkers who were the precursors of socialism and Marxism.[35] In comparison, relatively little was known about the American model as the Russian elites did not travel there, whereas they did journey the length and breadth of Europe in the nineteenth century. America remained *terra incognita*; the reading of de Tocqueville gave them their first glimpse. As Nathan Leites and Alain Besançon point out, the influence of ideas is found above all in Russian literature. Dostoevsky depicts better than anyone the spirit of the Slavophiles and the search for a Russian truth.[36] Boris Souvarine sums up this particular situation:

Driven from politics, free thought sought a refuge in literature and philosophy. The great writers of Russia, from Pushkin to Tolstoy, gave lustre to this epoch [...] enlightened youth passionately embraced the doctrines of Fichte and Schelling, Hegel, Feuerbach, and later John Stuart Mill and Spencer, Büchner and Darwin. Petrashevsky's circle studied Saint-Simon and Fourier, Cabet and Proudhon, Louis Blanc and Lamennais, which earned for its members prison and exile ...[37]

Russian thought concerning the state, power, the relationship between those governing and the governed drew little inspiration from the rich reservoir of the Greeks and Romans, nor even from the debates of the sixteenth and seventeenth centuries on the writings of Hobbes, Locke and Montesquieu. Russian philosophy followed a rather separate path, with religion continuing to occupy a dominant position. In Russia, divine right only began to be questioned in the nineteenth century. The merciless repression of the Decembrists in 1825 nipped any questioning of the Tsar's power in the bud.[38]

The discussion pitted Slavophiles against Westernizers. Most experts on this period, however, concur in playing down the antagonism between these two stances, highlighting rather their convergences. The tone varies, the ideal vision of Russia too, but no Westernizer was completely anti-Slavophile.[39] The core issue was the fundamental nature of Russia, its civilization or non-civilization, its religious culture, its very individual path isolated from the major avenues of European civilization. Could Russia's 'nature' adapt to European-style modernization or must Russia find its own means of progress? According to historian James Billington, Russian intellectuals were more interested in 'social questions' than in constitutional and institutional issues. 'A distinctive feature of Russian culture from the 1840s to the early 1880s was its extraordinary preoccupation with what the Russians call 'social thought'. [...] Its concerns were not primarily political, and may be best understood in terms of psychology or religion'.[40] Mikhail Petrashevsky and his group were sceptical of 'both the institution of private property and the value of constitutions'.[41] The conception of the state and the need for uniform laws and effective government did not catch much attention until the end of the nineteenth century. Constitutional liberalism came late in Russia. 'The Russian bourgeoisie had not developed the same interest in political and civil liberties as the bourgeoisie of western Europe'.[42]

It is against this background that the Marxists developed the notion of the decline of the state, the source of all forms of alienation. Lenin published *The State and the Revolution* in 1917. The key idea was directly inspired by the writings of Karl Marx who asked future revolutionaries 'not to transfer the bureaucratic and military machine from one pair of hands to another, as has been done until now, but to smash it'.[43] The Soviet period, from the end of the 1920s until the beginning of the 1980s, was hardly conducive to reflection on political or social issues. But this intellectual vacuum was masked by an ideological doctrine that occupied minds and entrenched negative perceptions of the state, political rights and economic freedoms. At the level of ideas, the Bolshevik revolution and the Soviet doctrine had 'resolved' the question of the state and that of the sovereignty of the people and freedoms. All the constraints and suffering inflicted on individuals were justified by the Revolution and the fight for Communism, in particular the loss of individual freedom. In the doctrine of the Brezhnev era, the USSR was defined as 'the state of the entire people'. That was the high point of Soviet political thinking on the state!

From Bolshevik history, Russia learned of the twofold danger of a group backed by an armed force taking power and the threat of an ignorant, credulous people, easily subjected to the will of their political masters. Mistrust of the 'masses', those millions of anonymous individuals, remains astonishingly alive in people's minds and behaviour. Russians themselves do not trust each other, do not see themselves as vested with a responsibility for their country, and prefer not to be involved in making important choices. And so the idea of the general will, so central to the French Revolution, and to Communist doctrine in a different way, is completely absent from the political debate. Chapter 6, 'A Distrustful Society', shows the extent to which Russian mentalities have been marked by this legacy, which has resulted in a distrust of public institutions and explains Russians' reluctance to accept the law as the basis of public life in an open, pluralist regime. The question is, who determines the law, who applies it and how?

The state is power, reiterate Russian intellectuals today as they did in the past. Yuri Pivovarov and Andrey Fursov have constructed a paradigm, the 'Russian System', which shows how Russia is made up of three elements: the Power, the Population, and the Superfluous Man (individual or collective). The relationship between the three is virtually non-existent.[44] On the other hand, the ideologists of the Putin regime prefer to base their analysis on historical roots, on the eternal Russian political culture which unfailingly guides the nature of the political system. The useful idea of 'Russian specificity' (*osobost*) has thus been cobbled together to distinguish the Russian system from democracy and from 'Western-style' sovereignty of the people. In 2007, Vladimir Putin's chief ideologist, Vladislav Surkov, cited the early-twentieth-century Russian philosopher Nicolas Berdyaev, contending that the Russians' traditional 'communitarianism' leads to institutions being seen as secondary: Russia does not depend on its institutions but on its people and on its wealth. Power-wielders claim to explain through tradition and beliefs a Russian state of affairs that deserves a philosophical debate and scholarly analysis. They prefer to talk about a deep-rooted culture rather than listen to a sociological and political critical explanation, of which they are very much afraid.[45]

Soviet society and the ruling elites agreed on one positive and indisputable quality of the state: the state as great power, the 'external sovereignty' as Hegel defined it. And it is precisely this reality of power (*derzhava*) that was the first victim of the transformations set in motion by Gorbachev. The socialist bloc collapsed in 1989, then the USSR in 1991. Mikhail Gorbachev had rooted his entire policy of renewing the state and society in a strategy of openness between the USSR and the Western world. He believed that Soviet power could be exercised in a climate of openness and negotiation, as opposed to one of hostile competition. The equation proved false.

The next chapter analyzes the very special relationship, veering from attraction to rejection, between the USSR and the Western world. The opening up of the USSR precipitated change by introducing the legitimacy of the external gaze, the 'deregulation' of information and the participation of multiple stakeholders. After 2003 Vladimir Putin went back on this strategy of virtuous openness, prompting Russia's return to a state of inward-looking withdrawal.

The driving force for Gorbachev's reforms was the state, the modern, competitive, powerful state, capable of carrying the active population along with it. He was interested in Soviet society, in its citizens, because he was interested in the future of the USSR as a state and major power. And, because he was concerned with bolstering society, the 'human factor', he was therefore interested in people, in the individual. This was at the heart of the will to reform, focused simultaneously on the state, society and the individual, making it both ambitious and risky.

It was the introduction of free suffrage and of private property, in addition to openness to the outside world, that disrupted the strategy for reforming the socialist system and the Soviet state. These two major institutions of Western democracies overturned Gorbachev's scenario and dragged the Soviet world into an unprecedented transformation, eventually resulting in its dislocation. The Soviet state was unable to withstand the change.

2

DOMESTIC REFORM AND OPENING
TO THE WORLD

'The USSR is absolutely unique: over twenty or thirty years, not a single Communist was born there'.[1]

Alexander Ginzburg, 1988

The Soviet state died in the historic tempest of 1991, without putting up any resistance. Nobody lamented it enough to organize a counter-revolution. Not even the Communist Party of Russia, dissolved after the putsch of August 1991 and then refounded in February 1993, placed the restoration of the USSR and the Soviet regime at the heart of its agenda. Did no one care about salvaging the Soviet state then? How can this strange phenomenon be explained, considering that the Soviet elites had remained in place up to this point?

The political, economic and social change that began with *perestroika* (restructuring) in 1986 soon evolved into a process that turned against the state and against the ruling party that was at the heart of the government machine. The drive for change was unequivocally expressed in the new doctrine and the concrete actions undertaken. Conceived by Mikhail Gorbachev with a view to modernizing and consolidating the Soviet system, the reforms led to the collapse of the Communist regime and of the USSR. Twenty years on, the Russians still cannot comprehend how such rapid destruction was possible, and they blame it on Gorbachev and the Communist reformers. Mikhail Gorbachev's political destiny was heroic and tragic.

Throughout this book we will see how the Russians' unpreparedness for these upheavals and their inability to understand the reasons for the USSR's demise have been a barrier to Russia's democratization and modernization. The same questions arise time and again: Could the fatigue of a system of government and society's weariness be enough to jeopardize an already declining regime? Did the USSR die of exhaustion or from Mikhail Gorbachev's reforms? Was the West pulling the strings and encouraging the reformers to destroy their country in spite of themselves, thus ending the Cold War and establishing American supremacy?

The controversy still rages, in Russia more than in the West, concerning Russia's capacity to implement fundamental reforms and break with the Soviet-era way of life and system of government. Was Russia ready for such an upheaval, and did the Russians push for change, or deep down have they always resisted a radical breakaway from the world of the past? The answer to this question also determines the interpretation of Putin's policy of reneging on the democratic promises of the early years of the reforms. The theories on which analyses of the 1980s and 1990s are based are therefore crucial for discussion of the 2000s.

In today's Russia, memories of *perestroika* and then the Yeltsin years are hazy and very broadly negative. They have deliberately been besmirched by Vladimir Putin who, since 2004, has officially presented the end of the USSR in 1991 as 'the greatest disaster' in twentieth-century geopolitics.[2]

I propose here to explain both how the political, economic and social changes introduced since Gorbachev's 1986–1989 reforms were inextricably linked to the opening up of the 'besieged fortress' to the Western world, and why Russian society, the elites and the new economic players did not buy into democratization, liberalization and the building of a modern and democratic federal Soviet state. The two pillars of change—free, universal, plural suffrage, and private property—destroyed the USSR, but did not lead to the building of a constitutional state.

Opening Up: the End of the Besieged Fortress

When Gorbachev was appointed Head of the Party in March 1985, the inefficiency of the Soviet system was no longer the subject of any serious debate, either in the absolute or in connection with the economic development of capitalist countries. The USSR embarked on reform because it could no longer remain shielded against the outside world behind the high walls of the socialist fortress. External pressure was growing, bringing the Soviet leadership face to face with an alarming realization: the country no longer had the ability to confront outside challenges, its competitiveness and power were waning, and it was starting to lose the battle waged since the 1920s against the capitalist foe. Pressure from the surrounding world was more decisive than pressure from within, which came from a minority section of the elites and of society.

The irony of history is that the Bolshevik system, born of rejection of the Tsarist regime, died decades later from the same sickness as Tsarism: backwardness and economic and social imbalances in a nation having trouble with its empire, a government undermined by the arbitrary nature of the exercise of authoritarian governance, and its untenable international position. How was it that in the 1980s the Communist leaders found themselves facing a situation comparable to the one that had led to the fall of the Tsarist government three-quarters of a century earlier? They too had evaded the crucial question of the nation and state modernization.

The Bolsheviks chose to ignore essential problems that pre-dated the Revolution and related to the hybrid nature, both Russian and imperial, of the nation and the state, and to the search for a 'special path' that was neither Western nor Asian. One major disruption followed another: the Stalinist dictatorship and insularity (socialism in one country and Terror), World War II in 1941, the break-up of the external and internal empire in 1989–1991 (sovereignty of the central European satellites and the Soviet republics), and currently the disintegration of the Caucasus societies following the war in Chechnya and the conflict with Georgia, accompanied by the return to an authoritarian and nationalist government.

At each of these historic milestones, Russia's relationship with the outside world determined whether its internal policy was one of openness towards the West or of isolation. Gorbachev's reform went hand in hand with the requisite Europeanization of the USSR. All of Gorbachev's speeches were punctuated with his famous expression 'common European Home'. Yeltsin oscillated between close cooperation with the West and Westernization of the law on the one hand, and the dereliction of democratic principles, culminating in the war in Chechnya, on the other. This contradiction revealed the profound ambivalence of Russia's relationship to 'civilization' which, in the language of the 1990s, meant Western civilization. During the following decade there was a pendulum swing. The Putin regime's shift towards authoritarianism and nationalism was accompanied by a growing hostility towards Western countries.

As a rule, change generally comes about in response to challenges from outside, from the surrounding society. Sociologists and ethnologists have described how traditional societies can remain virtually unchanged over the centuries, then, at a particular point, be propelled into a cycle of change that disrupts ancestral balances. In a peasant society, innovations can only come from the outside. Interaction often comes from an external economic factor that challenges the community's internal equilibrium. The well-known example of Tikopia shows how a small community on one of the Solomon Islands in the Pacific Ocean lived cut off from the outside world until the disruption caused by the arrival of boats seeking labour for plantations on other Solomon islands. The chiefs were called on to arbitrate and exercise power of a political nature, whereas until then the chief's authority had been purely ritual. Land-related conflicts increased as a result of population growth and the emigration of the men for work.[3] This new paradigm, brought about by the influence of outsiders on a society that had hitherto been isolated, transformed relations within the community and resulted in a challenge to the leaders' authority.

It is interesting, although somewhat iconoclastic, to consider Soviet society for a moment as a traditional, closed, hierarchical society and shake off the idea that it was first and foremost an urban, industrial, hence modern society. In his remarkable book on the conservative modernization of Russia, Anatoly Vishnevsky explains the very specific nature of the urbanization and industrialization of the USSR.[4] Entire cities were built in just a few years to support the industrial leap forward and uproot the peasant population. But these immense population transfers and these gigantic construction sites did not create the basis for a modern urban society. Vishnevsky described this pattern as '*bourgs* without bourgeois' or *urbanisatsiya po derevyanski*, which can be roughly translated as urbanization where the new city-dwellers retain their rural habits, norms and outlooks on life. Neither the production of steel and lead piping nor great leaps forward in space technology are sufficient for genuine modernization. Modernity is not solely technological and industrial but, above all, cultural and sociological.

The central state was not the most influential factor in the lives of Soviet citizens: the most concrete influences were the factory or the administration, the town or the village, the support networks. Even in the vast capital, relationships between people and day-to-day 'accommodations' were considered more important than institutional relations.[5] Relations of proximity are particularly important in traditional, closed societies.

It was the appearance of an external, international society, and chiefly the Western world, that permitted the transformation of traditional society. In opening up the USSR, Mikhail Gorbachev destroyed the basis of the system: the besieged fortress. He upset the equilibrium, or rather the stable disequilibrium of the Soviet community. And yet he had not set out to destroy that balance, but to improve the efficiency of the economic and political system. He knew instinctively that, in order for his reforms to be accepted, they must not profoundly disrupt the existing system. But, once introduced, the reforms built up their own momentum and shook the political edifice. The history of the years 1987–1991 is the history of a traditional society overturned by innovation and openness to the outside world.

When a leading group embarks on major reforms, it does so as part of a process of change already underway, and the reforms reflect the changes in society, be they slow or fast. But society is not necessarily sensitive to these slow developments and may not feel ready for, or even concerned by, the reforms. And the impetus to modernize does not always come from the expected quarter. In the case of *perestroika*, a top Party official propelled to the summit carried the torch of innovation and openness since he saw it as being of economic, social and political benefit to his country. For five years, Gorbachev met resistance from the conservatives who sought to curb the reforms and ended up organizing the putsch of 19 August 1991.

Another Party boss, Boris Yeltsin, who had fallen out with Gorbachev in 1987, was elected President of the Russian Federation in June 1991. He then demanded the position of leader, taking on the role of revolutionary against Gorbachev who had become a conservative in spite of himself, isolated in his position as President of the USSR. Gorbachev had not been elected through direct universal suffrage, but indirectly by the deputies of the Supreme Soviet, whereas his rival Yeltsin had obtained the endorsement of the ballot box in the Russian Republic thanks to the constitutional reform instigated by Gorbachev. Now the latter found himself the *unelected* leader of an immense Soviet federation made up of republics with presidents elected through direct suffrage.[6] For a few months, until 25 December 1991, the Soviet population lived in a strange state of limbo. The USSR collapsed, and democracy and free elections were established in the republics where the national elites were demanding independence; Yeltsin's Russia was one of those fifteen republics. Gorbachev's tragedy was that he saw his destiny as bound up with that of the state and the Party which became defunct in 1991. The reformer had to step down on 25 December 1991, superseded by other reformers who had profited from the liberalization of the institutions which he had instigated in 1986–1987. A few years later, a KGB officer who had worked in East Germany in his youth arrived at the helm brandishing the slogans of 'modernization' through order, centralization and 'vertical power'. Vladimir Putin was to spearhead an illusory modernization of Russian society, based on wealth creation, inequalities and inward-looking hostility to Europe and the United States and their democratic values.

The Central Relationship with the West

In the Soviet Union of the 1980s, the question of reform was inextricably linked to the question of openness, and above all to the ambivalent but central relationship with the enemy, the West. There was an ambiguity towards the capitalist world, which was held in contempt but at the same time exerted an allure. Gorbachev followed the Bolshevik culture of anti-capitalism, but sought to bring the USSR closer to Western modernity.

For seven decades, the Soviet authorities had a Hegelian relationship with the West, with attraction and rejection combining in a negation of the Other, although they constantly compared themselves to the West. The paradox of revolutionary Russian history is that its ideological credo came from the West. The Bolsheviks appropriated Marxism, which was born in Germany, conceived for Western capitalist societies, and then adapted by Russian socialists, Plekhanov in particular. They then jealously defended the authenticity of their Marxism; no other form would be recognized as authentic without direct allegiance to Moscow. And so, to break away from the West, the revolutionaries sought to stop 'imitating' it, but they ended up by taking the capitalist world as a standard and entering into a long race against it. 'We will catch up with and overtake the West!' declared Nikita Khrushchev in 1957.

This rejection of the Soviet Union's 'Other' was simultaneously a dismantling of the country's relation to itself. In no other major state did those in power work so hard to obliterate their own history. They not only denied the history of Tsarist Russia, but at each turn they denied the Soviet history of their predecessors. Stalin buried the New Economic Policy (NEP) of the 1920s, Khrushchev de-Stalinized, Brezhnev relegated Khrushchev to oblivion, Gorbachev erased the Brezhnev period from positive history, labelling it the time of stagnation, Yeltsin crushed Gorbachev and accelerated the dismantling of the state over which he presided, and Putin made the younger generation of Russians learn that the Yeltsin years were nothing but chaos and poverty.

Soviet and Russian historiography is a succession of lulls punctuated by 'feats of arms': the Revolution, the civil war, Stalinist industrialization, the Great Patriotic War, the conquest of the socialist bloc, nuclear arms, oil and gas energy, the fight against terrorism. The Communist leaders failed to create a true history for themselves. As a result the ideology was inflated, becoming a substitute for a national history and collective consciousness. Devoid of historical and spiritual references, the cultural matrix of the Soviet people—citizens and leaders alike—was replaced by an ideological and temporal explanation of the universe, theirs and that of others. The regime operated with two ideological registers, which combined together in what was termed Marxism-Leninism: the negation of the Western model and a utopian project (the advent of Communism). It had to push the allegory of the future to extremes since it had erased the historical roots of national identity and rejected European identity on ideological grounds. From the end of the 1920s, the Soviet regime's abandonment of 'world revolution' as the ultimate goal illustrates its turning inwards towards a national utopia whose identity depended first of all on its antonym, capitalism.

Communist doctrine thus created this imaginary universe, this 'radiant future' so well portrayed by Alexander Zinoviev,[7] which is a mirage scenario, a distorting mirror that makes it possible to cohabit with the Western world without the Soviet citizen being reflected in it, for then he would see the aberration of the system governing and imprisoning him.

It was essential for the Communist regime, as it is again today for Putin, to sustain the population's perception of a hostile outside world and to erect a barrier of ignorance. The image of the Enemy was integral to the Soviet edifice, as it is in today's authoritarian Russia. Zinoviev, an excellent logician, emphasized the active rather than passive negation of the Other by the Soviet authorities. The negation of Western values reaffirms the existence of those values. Jon Elster considers that 'he whose independence requires the destruction of another being, depends deep in his soul upon that other being and cannot, without self-contradiction, wish for its destruction'.[8] The Cold War and the 'balance of terror', which meant that the two military blocs could not enter into a military confrontation without the risk of mutual annihilation, marked the pinnacle of this paradigm. By remaining faithful to the Hegelian process, the convergence initiative spearheaded by Gorbachev led to the destruction of socialism. Socialism could not be reconciled with the Western system since it existed by basing its identity and its reality in unwavering opposition to the other world.

Gorbachev was neither a philosopher nor a dissident. At the end of the 1980s, unaware of the danger in which he was placing the Soviet regime, he instigated the exit from 'active negation'. He proposed modernization through a rapprochement with European civilization, seeking a convergence between the positive aspects of the Western model and the positive aspects of socialism. He had no regard for the 'angry exclamation' by Khrushchev—'we will bury you!'—and, breaking publicly with the doctrine of defeating capitalism, he wrote that 'no one could ever subordinate the other'.[9] His starting point was the acknowledgement that the Soviet economy was less efficient than that of the capitalist economies and that it was necessary to cooperate with Europe and the USA in order to modernize the USSR. Effectively it was necessary to reduce military spending and to revive other sectors of the economy. Consequently, the Soviet people would see their standard of living improve, which would incite them to be more actively involved in *perestroika*.

Gorbachev's Perestroika *and the Quest for Modernity*

The USSR opened itself up to Europe and to a Western modernity, which it had eschewed and yet desired for such a long time. This opening up beyond the Soviet universe had an extraordinary knock-on effect for Gorbachev's initially moderate reforms. Unlike 1965–1968, when the post-

Khrushchev leadership attempted a timid reform of the planned economy, the lid did not come down in time.

Change in the USSR did not take place just within the two or three years of Gorbachev's reforms, but had its roots further back in Soviet history. During the last decade of Brezhnev's leadership, dubbed 'developed socialism' but stigmatized later as the era of 'stagnation', there was growing doubt and anxiety among the ruling elites. All the economic and social indicators pointed to a profound crisis of the system, a malaise within society and among the elites, and a loss of competitiveness in the rivalry with the West.[10] For our purpose, it is important to highlight the main characteristics of the problem facing the Soviet Communists at the beginning of the 1980s. The economy was in decline, despite the abundance of raw materials; the demographics were disastrous, to the point where infant mortality was so high that the figures were no longer published; the army was bogged down in Afghanistan; the technological gap with the West was widening (Reagan's 'Star Wars' programme had the Soviet leadership in a panic);[11] the satellite countries of central and eastern Europe were in the throes of major crises which exposed the vulnerability of the Communist regimes. The crises and shortcomings of the system were criticized with increasing openness in the years that preceded the appointment of Mikhail Gorbachev to the head of the Central Committee of the Communist Party of the Soviet Union in March 1985. And yet, the elites did not prepare for reform sufficiently. The subject was on everybody's mind, but the institutions were stymied both intellectually and politically, which prevented strategic proposals from being put into practice. After Brezhnev's death in November 1982, some Communist Party leaders considered economic reforms to be vital. Yuri Andropov, chief of the KGB who then took over as head of the Party, demanded an 'acceleration' and improved 'discipline'. The realization that the USSR lagged far behind the West both economically and technologically caused alarm, and the KGB was the institution best placed to be pessimistic with regard to the future.

Andropov and the KGB instigated reforms within the institutions they considered still to be robust and least prone to excesses. But the envisaged reforms consisted of relatively modest tinkering. With their thinking distorted by seventy years of abuses and setbacks, none of these people had the ability to conceive of a mode of governance other than socialism. There was a grave lack of political nerve in a power system stuck in a false collegial administration characterized by an opacity that led to disinformation and lies.[12] Yuri Andropov's replacement by Konstantin Chernenko in 1984 illustrates the decline of the Politburo made up chiefly of ailing old men: the new Party leader also died in office, like Andropov and Brezhnev. Gorbachev was chosen for his youth (he was 54 in 1985). Discussions on the nature and implementation of the reforms were hampered by the closed system of the Central Committee of the Communist Party and the hostility of the old guard. The secrecy of the inner circle and the veneer of propaganda prevented any real examination of the problems and any truly innovative proposals. Those who advocated reform were cautious, as ideas could not be discussed freely, even within the ruling bodies. There was still heavy censorship, and the general public remained unaware of the infighting within the Central Committee of the Party and the Politburo. The policy of *glasnost* ('transparency', i.e. the liberalization of information) did not begin until later, in 1986–1987, as a corollary to economic *perestroika*.

It is important to emphasize this lack of open, productive debate prior to Gorbachev's reforms, for this was still the hallmark of the Russian way of doing things. Top-down reform, led by the Party's new General Secretary, was not the fruit of mature reflection, even less of a well thought out, structured programme. It was spurred by economic urgency, the political will at the very top of the Party, the KGB, and by the intellectual input of a generation of scientists and experts who saw reform as the last chance to haul Russia out of the slump and economic stagnation. *Perestroika* involved a doctrinal overhaul, an opening up to the West, and economic and political decisions taken on an ad hoc basis. It quickly developed from a simple reform into a radical transformation of the system's very foundations.

The debate became extremely heated and animated during these exceptional years of freedom of speech and spirit of criticism. There was great excitement in intellectual, scientific and artistic circles. Economists grappled with whether or not to open the economy up to private ownership, to competition and market forces; historians were divided into anti-Communist liberals versus conservatives who defended the socialist fatherland; the legislators considered the overhaul of the Soviet Constitution as part of the democratization process. The renowned economist Leonid Abalkin, of the Novosibirsk school with Tatiana Zaslavskaya, wrote in 1989: 'Above all we must re-think the nature of socialism in a completely different way, the diversity of its models, its humanist nature and its driving forces'.[13] The Communist elites in Moscow were overwhelmed by the speed and scale of the phenomenon that was shaking up the entire system, and which ended up dismantling the vast territorial and human entity that was the USSR.

By 1989, the Communist Party and the Soviet administrations had lost the people's trust. So who could lead the reforms? In the fifteen republics that made up the USSR, including the Federative Republic of Russia, the Communists had lost their authority and legitimacy. There were alternative elites, especially in the republics most eager to break away from the empire—the Baltic countries, Armenia, Georgia and Ukraine. The Moscow-driven 'top-down' reform of socialism prompted protests from the national elites in the republics, following on the heels of the independence movements in Poland, Hungary and Czechoslovakia.

By the time Gorbachev and his team realized that the cadres of the Communist Party were no longer the architects of change, it was too late to shift the burden onto the so-called 'state institutions' (*gosudarstvennye organy*). Most republics of the USSR seized their autonomy the moment the Communist Party hierarchy lost its authority and capacity for repression.

The Soviet edifice did not survive the battle waged by the elites and the societies of the most western parts of the USSR, chiefly the Baltic countries. From the political point of view, once the Communist Party with its unwieldy system of republican, regional and local organization was discredited, the Soviet state strictly speaking did not stand for much. From the day Gorbachev made it clear that he would not use mass repression, the USSR no longer existed in the minds of the Estonians, Lithuanians, Latvians and Western Ukrainians, and the possibility of regaining their national identity seemed realistic and imminent. These countries had harboured a deep resentment against the Soviet state since the accords between Hitler's Germany and the Stalinist USSR in 1939–1940, which made them particularly resistant to the idea of the Soviet state.

The Government Misinforms Itself

Faced with resistance from the Party organizations, Gorbachev attempted to revitalize the state organs, the administrations, the municipal and regional councils and the republican assemblies. One of the slogans of the liberalization drive in 1988 was 'All power to the Soviets', and the principle of pluralist elections (several Communist Party or independent candidates competing) was put forward. Events deviated from the planned path and the Soviet citizens in the non-Russian republics took advantage of the opening up of the electoral competition to declare their autonomy, followed by the declaration of sovereignty. The transformation of the ballot into open elections for the sake of appearances was the decisive factor in the break-up of the USSR in 1991, a scenario which Mikhail Gorbachev had never envisaged.[14] He and his peers were trapped in a warped vision of Soviet federalism. According to them, the national republics formed political and economic entities, but retained their own cultural 'specificities'. The borders of each republic were merely 'administrative' and not political, explained Gorbachev at the beginning of December 1991,[15] still refusing to come to terms with the reality staring him in the face: on 1 December, Ukraine's population of 46 million had held a referendum and voted for independence, thus breaking away from the USSR, the imperial Russian entity. Furthermore, pluralist elections for the republican assemblies had already been held a year earlier, the results being a clear indication of the strength of the independence movement.

Gorbachev's government was suffering from the legacy of decades of disinformation. It had only a fragmentary and often erroneous knowledge of what was happening in the country, as Gorbachev admitted frankly in his memoirs. It was hard for ideas to circulate in the closed, authoritarian regime, and the media were unable to fulfil their role as providers of critical information or to act as a communications channel. The government was disinformed, both by its subordinates and by the gagged media, and it disinformed its own population which, in turn, was powerless to express its condition and mood through political and social channels. It was even impossible to have an objective view of the situation in the USSR, above all for the Party leaders who were prisoners of their own closed, propagandist system. And yet, the Soviet elites continued to express a certain faith in socialism, since they found comfort and security in this method of social organization.

Aleksander Lukin illustrates this attitude in his book examining the values of the Russian democrats during *perestroika*.[16] He provides numerous testimonies to a fairly naïve trust in the system, even though it was unanimously agreed that this system did not function well. In the 1960s and 70s, the *Komsomol* (Communist Youth) and the young party members, the future top echelons of the political elite, from whose ranks the Gorbachevian and Yeltsinian reformers would emerge, maintained their confidence in the Communist organizational system, probably because they would be treated well within it and because they did not have strong views on possible alternatives. They were as wary of Soviet propaganda as they were of Western discourse, the tone of which was anti-Communist, urging these young people to fight against the world of which they could easily become a part. Capitalism and Western democracy remained alien and unfamiliar.

The fear of losing more and more ground in comparison with the West and of widening the economic divide between the USSR and the capitalist countries was one of the major motivations driving one section of the Soviet elites. The Communist leaders in Moscow also feared being overpowered by local leaders, the Uzbeks, Azerbaijanis and Georgians who could no longer be forced into submission as in the past. One of Gorbachev's flagship measures in 1986 was the battle with Uzbekistan's 'cotton industry', in other words against the corrupt bosses of the Central Asian republic. Another was the so-called 'dry law' to combat alcoholism, especially by pulling up vineyards in Georgia. In both cases, the General Secretary of the Party antagonized the leaders and the elites of these two republics and exacerbated the distrust of the 'periphery' towards the 'centre'. Relations between Moscow and the republics were in fact organized along centre-periphery lines, in a division of labour and a political subordination of the non-Russian elites and peoples to a Russian central power. Thus excluded from policy-making and hence from *perestroika*, the elites in the republics took advantage of the instability created by change to push for autonomy and free themselves from the diktats of Moscow. The process gathered momentum after the fall of the Berlin Wall, and the Soviet republics demanded independence, a goal they had set only three years earlier, with the exception of the Baltic countries which had never accepted their enforced incorporation into the USSR during World War II.

A Better Life

The change was not merely a reaction to decline and backwardness; it was also the result of a desire to live a better life, to travel and to be on equal terms with the rest of the world. The reformers' prime motivation was a vision of a more efficient, more prosperous and therefore more powerful USSR. But for them, this desire went hand in hand with a certain belief in the ability of the socialist system to perform better. The spirit of *perestroika* and of *glasnost* is only understandable in the context of this contradiction between the ambition to modernize and a head-in-the-sand attitude to the enormous crisis affecting the Communist system.

Many observers have written that Mikhail Gorbachev embarked on *perestroika* and continued along this already dangerous road in 1988–1990 simply to win and then consolidate his own power in the face of the 'conservatives'. In isolation from the general situation, the contention that Gorbachev was forced to carry out reforms to gain the edge over his rivals is not convincing. It does not chime with his character: he was a convinced socialist but was attracted to the unknown world, the West.

It is certain that after each succession, which was always problematic as there were no clear rules governing the inner circle of the CPSU, 'ideas' and 'slogans' took on a particular significance as they became the stamp of one personality versus another. Andropov's mottoes were 'acceleration' and 'discipline', which sent a clear signal that he intended to attack the networks of Central Asia, and 'corruption'.

Gorbachev too needed to find a specific discourse within the overall doctrine from which he could not yet deviate in 1984–1985. This hallmark was an instrument, admittedly, but it heralded real change, as history has doubtless shown. It is reductive to claim that he was trapped in a discourse and a system of reforms originally conceived solely to counter his adversaries in the Politburo, and that subsequently the scenario got out of hand and he was forced to carry out reforms which he allegedly never seriously envisaged.[17]

In 1986–1987, the very concrete question facing Gorbachev was how to develop the political, economic and social institutions so as to modernize the country and make it more 'efficient' and more competitive. There was a need both to boost the efficiency of the regime, in every area and not just the economy in the strict sense of the word, as well as to improve performance in comparison with the other industrialized countries. Gorbachev's innovative contribution was in making a connection between internal performance and performance vis-à-vis the outside world.

A discrepancy between the Western interpretation of reform and Gorbachev's conceptualization soon became apparent. Effectively, seen from the point of view of the Western democracies, the transformation courageously initiated by the Secretary General of the Communist Party bore an ideological stamp. The regime was moving towards a socialism with a human face, opening up to freedoms and espousing European values, which meant that it was breaking away from the Communist ideology and Soviet values. From the point of view of the Gorbachevian reformers, there was no doubt that there was a break with doctrine, but abandoning the prevailing ideology and system of government was not on the agenda. The conception of *perestroika* was clearly embodied in the word itself: *perestroika* means 'reconstruction' or 'restructuring', first and foremost it implied *institutional* changes. Mikhail Gorbachev reasoned in terms of adapting the Soviet institutions, for example by liberalizing foreign trade or initiating plural and competitive elections. He never advocated abolition of the Party institutions or of the state. On the contrary, he saw the state as an actor in the modernization process—that was his 'legalistic' mind; he had studied law and thought that bills and institutional frameworks were key to reform. From Gorbachev's point of view, the Party was too ideological, too clientelistic. His approach may seem naïve, but it reflected the elites' ingrained respect for the legal architecture of Sovietism. In the absolute, with no opportunity to make comparisons with the legal systems of democratic regimes, Soviet law represented for them a solid, rational edifice that formed the backbone of socialism and enabled them to see it in a positive light. In my view, this penchant for the law reveals a steady loss of faith in doctrinal ideology among the ruling elites from the 1950s. Mikhail Gorbachev did not feel he was leading a country of passionate Bolsheviks, but good Soviet citizens who were still lagging behind on the road to modernization.

Analysis of the Soviet regime's transition must take into account this emphasis on gradual institutional reform, initially adhering to so-called Soviet or Communist values. The movement quickly gathered momentum and went beyond its master's control. From 1988 to 1989 *perestroika* turned into a critique of the foundations of the Soviet regime. The instigators of *perestroika* were caught off-guard by this challenge, which necessarily implied the end of the *ancien régime*. The latter had an institutionalist, 'legalistic' approach, remaining firmly within the entire Soviet framework. And Gorbachev and his advisers' misreading of the geographical and national-identity realities in the USSR can be explained by this erroneous premise of leaving the basic architecture of the USSR unchanged. They did not conceive the general structure as multiple and multi-layered. As a result, they believed that overhauling the *modus operandi* of the Communist Party and some state institutions was sufficient, and would not have any effect on the national, republican edifice of the Soviet Federation. History has shown that the architectural façade led the leaders in Moscow to make a monumental conceptual error: they believed it was possible to reform the state-Party pyramid without provoking reactions from the capitals of the republics, Tbilisi, Kiev, Tallinn and Vilnius.

Gorbachev was not a Machiavellian character, nor did he have the soul of a tyrant. He had no desire to resort to mass repression against Eastern Europe in 1989, against the Georgians in 1989, the Azerbaijanis in 1990, or the Balts in 1991, even though on each occasion there was a very strong temptation, and he allowed matters to get out of hand for a few days or hours in various capitals of the USSR before ordering a halt to armed reprisals. In Vilnius and Riga, in January 1991, an attack was launched on the Parliament and the television headquarters, then the order was withdrawn and the incident left few victims. Gorbachev knew that a major crackdown would empower his enemies in the Kremlin and put an end to *perestroika*.

The salient innovations of the era that began in 1985–1986 were the refusals to resort to force and the seeking of support from Western partners, but these innovations could not be taken for granted at the time. The fast-paced events of 1989–1991 clearly confirmed Gorbachev's commitment to peaceful means. It was undoubtedly the combination of his refusal to use violence, and openness towards the West, that led to the failure of the August 1991 putsch against Gorbachev.

During the *perestroika* years and at the beginning of Yeltsin's presidency, reflections on the nature of the embryonic political regime lacked depth and rigour. Events were moving too fast. The situation was analyzed at a given moment in comparison with the past—managing the exit from Communism—and in anticipation of the general direction of the historic movement, ensuring the transition towards democracy and a market economy. Vigilant and uncompromising analysis of the system of government and of economic and social policy remained all too rare and went unheeded. The extraordinary speed of territorial, institutional, legislative and strategic change was not conducive to a precise and systematic analysis of the regime at a given time, since it seemed that any analysis would rapidly be overtaken by events. This lack of ongoing reflection at the different stages of the transformation could only be remedied after the event and still hinders analysis today. Self-criticism on a day-to-day basis would have been invaluable both to observers and the Russian protagonists. The latter were often caught off-guard by trends they had failed to anticipate. And they rarely took the time to try and understand the causes of unexpected developments that challenged their conviction and their strategy.

Out of the Barrel

The collapse of the USSR can be explained in large part by divisions and differences between ethnic Russian society and societies inhabited by Soviet citizens of non-Russian ethnicity. The fact that the overwhelming majority of inhabitants of the Russian Republic were not actively involved in the reform had immense consequences for the history of the Gorbachev, Yeltsin and Putin periods, and will continue to have an impact in the years to come. Average Russians did not openly demand profound changes to the system in the 1980s. Each individual reacted with differing degrees of enthusiasm to the new freedoms of speech, pluralist elections and economic initiatives, which remained restricted to small cooperatives. Russians experienced the reforms as 'top-down', and withdrew their support from the Kremlin once they saw that the proposed changes offered them no material benefits or guarantees for the future. They were caught unawares by the collapse of the state, and this caused them, with the benefit of hindsight, to develop a negative view of the entire 'top-down' effort at reform.

They lost the bearings of their day-to-day world, from which they had derived a certain comfort, even if life had not been much fun and not very comfortable. The satirical writer Vladimir Voinovich gives an apt illustration of the Soviet people's resistance to change in his metaphor of the barrel:

We are born, we live and we die in a barrel. We do not know what happens outside the limits of the barrel and cannot remember how we ended up in it. [...] Those who live in the barrel have their own idea of good and evil. [...] the most freedom-loving ones try to escape, they climb up the barrel's rusty sides, fall down, then climb up again. The most persistent either lose their lives or make it to the rim. And suddenly a new, never-seen world opens up before them: grass, flowers, animals [...], water, solid ground and air [...] A boundless world! But everyone must obtain his own food and everyone has to take care not to be trampled, bitten or swallowed. Good God, what's going on here? Quick, back in the barrel.[18]

The Russians' failure to embrace the ongoing reform of 1989–1991 is closely related to the difficulty they had in conceptualizing an alternative that they simply could not envisage. For how could they represent access to freedoms and democracy in words or images with no clear referent to help them? The only referent was the Western world, but that was largely in their imaginations since 99 per cent of the Soviet people never pierced the Iron Curtain of the Cold War. And for the few tens of thousands of leaders and members of the *nomenklatura* who had travelled abroad, admittedly the West had a face, but it was always associated with a form of exoticism, of radical otherness.

The Soviet Union's people lived in a propaganda system, and Western discourse was presented to them as such. And so they were wary and thought that all rhetoric from on high was artificial. They felt trapped by the wretchedness of day-to-day life, far removed from doctrinal discourse. They did not imagine that the reforms were made to help them and did not demand to play a part as a social community. The impetus for reform could not have come from a strong social demand.[19] It was imposed in a world that was still closed, where the *nomenklatura* and the bureaucratic and industrial apparatus had reached their limits and were unable to move forward in an atrophied political society and a non-competitive economy.

The one moment when a part of society began to stir was in 1989–1990 when everything seemed up for grabs and the actors no longer played the roles implicitly assigned to them. During this period, it makes sense to speak of social movements, of a growth in collective awareness, of upheaval and emergence from apathy. People were transfixed by the promise of reforms. This lasted for two years at most because economic and social change made life much more difficult. The polls show that very quickly Russians stopped feeling directly involved in the general change. As the years went by, they increasingly came to believe that the change had been imposed on them by a handful of reformers, or by the West. They felt betrayed by their own elites. And when Vladimir Putin told them that 1991 was 'the greatest geopolitical disaster of the twentieth century', they were in agreement with him. They have erased from their memory the years of liberalization, *glasnost* and openness, to remember only the collapse of 1991, the loss of power and the ensuing economic problems.

Understanding the Unexpected

A society's cultural features can survive long after the factors that created them have ceased to operate.[20] In Russia's case, in 1988–89, the Soviet people found themselves brutally and unexpectedly confronted with new ideas, beliefs and assertions, the origins of which eluded them. Even if criticism of the one-party system and of the command economy had been percolating throughout the USSR in a low-key way for at least two decades, no one foresaw the major cultural upheaval represented by the eradication of the system and its all-embracing ideology. The Soviet people were not just witnessing a weakening of the doctrinal framework. They realized, to their astonishment, that the very ground rules were being challenged; the old rules no longer had authority, and the new ones were unknown. They did not have the benefit of years of reading, listening to foreign media and public debate led by alternative elites to help them think about and prepare for a different form of society and government. The situation was radically different from that in Poland, where for most Poles the trade union *Solidarnosc* and the struggle against Russia and Communism were part of everyday life.

To extend Ronald Inglehart's contention that cultural change takes a long time to come about compared with the shorter time it takes for economic innovation, the question we need to ask is that of the levels of *understanding* of the individuals who make up the community: understanding in the sense of a grasp of the facts and ideas. We also need to ask about the level of participation, albeit modest and from a distance, in the major developments in national policy. To gain such an understanding would have required a longer period of openness, of *glasnost*, before the final collapse of 1991. But events succeeded each other at a dizzying speed. The word *perestroika* appeared in 1986, *glasnost* in 1987, liberalization in 1988, and a few months later the incredulous Soviet people witnessed the first fall, that of the Berlin Wall, and with it the system of the hermetic socialist entity. The twenty months that followed October 1989 are impressive, for they drastically altered the map of the continent, and of the world. This was the beginning of a brick-by-brick dismantling of the entire national and territorial organization of the Soviet empire. The Soviet people discovered the new concepts of 'sovereignty' and 'independence', 'representation' and 'democracy'. Liberalization and democratization had already been superseded, the developments and transitions swept away by the radical nature of events. The definitive terms—democracy, freedom, market—clearly indicated that a page of history had been turned. This was the history not of a development of the Soviet system, but very much of its root-and-branch transformation.

Apart from a few thousand intellectuals and officials, very few Russians in the Soviet Republic of Russia were prepared for such a radical upheaval. They simply did not have the time either to imagine it or to formulate it. They were incapable of projecting themselves into an unforeseeable future.

The question then is not so much whether the Russians were for or against the change, but how well they were able to grasp and come to terms with the new situation, and especially the crumbling of the former social, cultural and state edifice. There was nothing ideological about the exercise; it was absolutely pragmatic, and was carried out in extreme haste, more akin to an earthquake than a palace coup.

After a natural disaster, the victims wonder what they have lost forever, what they have managed to salvage, and what aid and compensation they can hope for. The Russians asked themselves the same agonizing questions and received very little help from the officials or their employers. Their reflex was to concern themselves first of all with what they could salvage. Who, in such a major upheaval on such a vast scale, would welcome the crumbling of the old edifice and rejoice at the inevitable arrival of a new world? Only societies driven by the desire for national independence, like those of the Baltic republics or those Russians who had long been fighting the arbitrariness of the Communist regime could be happy and optimistic, for they had envisaged and were prepared for, at least mentally, the end of the Soviet system.

In this complicated situation, the change in people's mentality did not keep pace with the revolutionary transformation of their society. Quite the opposite in fact. The sociologist Yuri Levada emphasizes the negative and hostile reactions of the Russians once they were able to stop and take stock of the scene after the battle. Surveys carried out in 1993 show extreme anxiety, reactionary attitudes, and anger with the elites that had thrown them into the unknown. Feelings of loss and insecurity largely prevailed over the sense of liberation and renewal.

It has often been said and written that the Soviet people missed the Communist state, that they harboured a nostalgia for the 'strong state' that ruled their lives. The testimonies and studies gathered soon after 1991 suggest a more nuanced attitude. Russians were not attached to Communism as an ideology and strong rule. What they missed was the system that provided daily subsistence and security. Their attachment was to the former way of life, to a certain carefreeness 'in the barrel', a life of few constraints and few responsibilities. In addition, the humiliation of the USSR's collapse also created a yearning for superpower status and the attendant external recognition.[21] The Russians could not imagine Russia as an 'ordinary country' without being a great power. 'Russia will only join the ranks of "ordinary countries" if it is able to define and articulate its national security interests according to its own criteria, and not simply in imitating Western policies and points of view'.[22]

The Misunderstanding over Ideology

According to Lev Gudkov and Boris Dubin, the doctrine of transition to democracy was tacked onto Russia as an anti-totalitarian doctrine, creating the illusion of 'liberation' from Communist ideology. But both the Marxist-Leninist credo and the 'national consciousness' that constituted the sense of belonging to a Soviet entity had already been heavily corroded.[23] Erosion of the ideology had weakened the Soviet regime, both in Russia and in the other Republics.[24] Russian sociologists underline the limits of critical thinking in the early years of the Yeltsin regime. Still in 1996, when the war in Chechnya was raging and Boris Yeltsin was highly unpopular but wanted to be re-elected President, the slogan 'Stop the Communists!' was waved as a red rag; the threat of a return to the *ancien régime* was the argument brandished by the ruling elites. This dichotomic vision of Russia, torn between communist authoritarianism and chaotic democracy, prevented a more nuanced study of mentalities and attitudes, and blinded observers to the fact that even after the formal collapse of the previous regime, the fallout from it remained a heavy burden.[25]

All Putin's government had to do was revive the essential elements of this legacy to create an authoritarian system. Going back to familiar attitudes was the key to Putin's regime, and this explains how he succeeded in winning Russians' loyalty. This allegiance was without emotion or enthusiasm. What outside observers saw as a worrying deviation from the path to democratization and Europeanization, the Russians saw as continuity and security. The fundamental difference in perception was repeated, as in 1989–1991 when outsiders applauded the victory of freedom, whereas a majority of Soviet citizens were distraught at the loss of their system of government and their day-to-day mode of survival.

Drawing on an interesting study carried out in 1990 in Russia and in Ukraine, Donna Bahry showed that the post-Soviet people were much more concerned about the very concrete question of the institutions that governed or no longer governed them than by cultural and ideological considerations of freedom and democracy. They were not against freedom, but feared the destabilization of the institutional framework. The study shows that the democratic spirit existed. However, an important factor reveals its limitations: intolerance. The interviewees showed little tolerance towards others, people who were different, foreign regions, the unknown.[26]

Westerners ideologised the scenario of a reform that broke radically with the despicable Soviet past. They read it as a complete rejection of the Communist system and felt there was nothing more to be said. In the USSR, however, this was not the case. Even in intellectual circles, the critique still remained poorly formulated, badly coordinated, sometimes pro-Western, sometimes anti-Western, in any case uncertain and divided as to the goals to be achieved. This maturation period for developing ideas and plans was too short to permit a frank *a posteriori* critique of *perestroika* and its impact on Russia's history. Twenty years later, many Russians still wonder whether the collapse could have been avoided. And the answer is anti-Gorbachevian, since society did not have a sense of participating in the shaping of its own history.

Western analyses of the transition have posited the critique of the authoritarian or totalitarian system as the prime vehicle, and breaking the ties with the *ancien régime* as the main driving force. Rationality took precedence, based on the observation that the former Soviets could only be delighted to be rid of a bad system and see it replaced by a better one. We observed that it was not the case in Russia. While very innovative in their analysis of Latin America in the 1970s, the work of Juan Linz and Alfred Stepan had its limitations when it came to the societies of the former USSR,[27] as has been demonstrated by several American and European experts.[28] Some variables were under-estimated, for example Soviet Russians' lack of support for the accelerated transformations of the last years of Gorbachev's leadership, and the post-Soviet administrations' exceptional resistance (see chapter 4). This note of caution aside, Juan Linz's theoretical and methodological contribution is invaluable. He emphasizes a number of crucial points: the propensity of new democratically elected leaders to 'refuse to be accountable at a later date'; the dangers of imperfect pluralism; the clever promotion of 'generic values' like patriotism, social justice and order, rather than the building of a new utopian ideology that would exert a 'utopian strain in politics' and reduce the scope of cooptation of the elites by the new regime.[29]

Adepts of the transition paradigm saw the rejection of Marxism-Leninism and the advent of a new regime as evidence of the overthrow of Communism. Conversely, some historians of Communism in the West emphasized the resistance of a deep-rooted system of beliefs and the permanence of the credo of the elites, who stayed in power after the interment of the Communist Party. According to them, *Homo Sovieticus* was still alive.[30]

Analysis of the ideology's function draws on a lengthy controversy that went on during the entire Soviet era. For some historians, like Martin Malia and Annie Kriegel, ideology was the foundation of the entire Soviet system. Its function was not solely to indoctrinate the masses, but also to provide a common language, a 'parlance' as Martin Malia calls it, and guidelines for action. Others saw ideology as an instrument, a system whose chief purpose was propagandist and repressive. According to sociologist and psychoanalyst Nathan Leites,[31] the ideology—or what he called the '*system of beliefs*'—was an 'operational code' and unveiled the ruling elites' neurotic mentality.

In my view, the various interpretations of the role of ideology all make an important contribution to the understanding of the Soviet reality at different points of its seventy-year existence. But the question that remains unanswered is: did the Soviet population buy into this credo?

Malia is right when he presents the Marxist-Leninist doctrine as providing the backbone for the entire workings of the Communist Party, the economy and Soviet society. However, he is unconvincing about the explanatory and programmatic functions of ideology. Of course, the doctrine legitimized a revolutionary history and erased anything that was inconvenient. But it did not offer an explanation for the developments experienced by the Soviet people, it remained distant from day-to-day events, and had a mythical character which each person in their own way was conscious of, even the least educated of the 300 million inhabitants of the USSR. From the outset, belief in the radiant future was built on a utopia that was unattainable during a human lifetime. The political system was therein cut off from the social body. The mentality of the ordinary Soviet, to use Yuri Levada's term, was composed of many layers that did not make up a simple easy-to-read mind. Even if the official ideology remained 'Marxist-Leninist' to the end, it changed profoundly in the decades that followed Stalin's death, both in its doctrinal aspects and in its political and social function. In the 1960s and 70s it was no longer a 'system of beliefs' in the sense described by Nathan Leites with regard to the revolutionary years and then the Stalinist era. Nor did it shape an entire 'Soviet mentality' any longer, but it was the framework within which the Soviet citizens thought, spoke and understood what the leaders communicated to them.[32] It was the grammar and lexicon of a social system. A society and an elite can be dazed by an ideology, and function emotionally and mentally in relation to it; that does not automatically mean that they believe in it. In Brezhnev's USSR the touchstone was utopia, and not illusion. Utopia, in other words the unattainable goal, provided the doctrinal justification for the decisions made by the Party, despite what the population might have wished, and thus guaranteed the authority of the ruling class.

In *The Passing of an Illusion*, François Furet sought to explain why, in Europe too, people believed in Communism, why the Communist illusion was so seductive throughout the world and across all cultures.[33] But it was utopia that captured minds and political movements, and not the illusion of the fulfilment of a project that, in essence, had to remain utopian and therefore unattainable. The Russians did not lose their beliefs; they did not have, or no longer had, any. They lost some very concrete bearings, referents, representations. I choose not to use the word 'values' (*tsennosti*), as they could not choose their values, which is why I prefer the notions of principles, habits and dependency.

The ideology of implacable opposition to the capitalist world was crucial to ensuring the unquestioning acceptance of the Party's authoritarian policies. Devoid of its ideological foundation, repression was difficult to implement, and yet it remained essential to the survival of the Soviet regime. Hannah Arendt, Claude Lefort and all the intellectuals who reflected on the totalitarian phenomenon have pointed out that the weakness of the totalitarian regime was that it relied on mass repression. In an authoritarian regime, repression is more moderate, more diffuse, but it remains just as essential to the survival of those in power. Assessing the degree of acceptable tolerance to give the population breathing space without jeopardizing those in power is a complex exercise, as Gorbachev's failure to liberalize the USSR illustrates. Vladimir Putin's determination to repress the opposition with increasing brutality, even though it is very much a minority and already weakened, shows that he is afraid of unrest and fears for himself.

Violence is essential to totalitarian regimes, and it remains central to post-totalitarian regimes that are still authoritarian and arbitrary (the USSR after Stalin). It almost disappeared in the post-authoritarian Russia of 1991–1992, but only for a very brief interlude. Conflicts occurred in some regions of the former USSR, such as the battle between Ingushetia and Ossetia in 1992, but the conflict was not provoked by the Kremlin. The brief period of rejecting the use of armed force as a means of resolving political differences came to an end in 1993 with President Yeltsin's attack on the unruly parliament, and the war in Chechnya from December 1994 (see chapter 3).

What were the objectives envisaged by the reformers? Did they share a well thought out vision of the future USSR that was freer, more modern and more dynamic? Or should the emphasis be placed on the economic rationale, namely the reforms that were necessary to resolve the economic crisis and improve performance?

Once again, Alexander Lukin's study offers valuable insights. He recounts the transformation of the Russian democratic elites' value system between 1986 and 1991. He pinpoints the trigger moments, when all of a sudden a good *Komsomol* member began to see the past he had been taught through new eyes, discovering to his confusion that he had swallowed a sizeable chunk of the official version of history. He then embarked on the liberal path and a completely different way of thinking about Russia's development, in opposition to Communism, based on combating totalitarianism. The democrat espoused democratic values, which had triumphed elsewhere, without thinking of the direct consequences for Russia, the state and the ruling system. Those years were exceptional as regards the general state of mind and enthusiasm for renewal, sentiments which since 1992–1993 have receded amongst ordinary Russians, hamstrung by the struggle for survival and antagonized by the financial and political elites' behaviour.

Lukin emphasizes the fact that, even at the height of *perestroika*, the reformers did not turn their backs entirely on Soviet values and behaviour, but relegated them to a secondary level. Some of these attitudes resurfaced very quickly, like the evasion of responsibility, disdain for the public good, suspicion and circumvention of rules, which explains both the reversal of attitudes during the Yeltsin years and the easy acceptance of Putin's methods. The cultural change had not reshaped Russian society as profoundly as the institutional reforms had led people to believe.

The intellectuals and politicians were not particularly innovative when it came to political organization, owing both to a lack of interest in the state and a lack of knowledge of their own political history, and probably too because they referred, consciously or unconsciously, to Western models, often poorly understood within Russia. Their immersion in the images and realities of the state through the Western prism left them in thrall to a dichotomic vision of politics: liberal or authoritarian, social or individualist, pro-Western or 'specifically Russian', competitive or neo-Soviet. Twenty years after Gorbachev's *perestroika*, Russia had not produced a Condorcet, Sieyès or Benjamin Constant. No great minds or politicians of substance applied themselves to the question of the means of transformation of the state or of post-Communist society. It even proved difficult for private property, the prime institution of transition, which failed to enter into the value system or the institutional and legal frameworks.

Property and Free Vote: The Public-Private Separation at Stake

Currency and property on the one hand, free votes and representation on the other, are the two fundamental vectors that enabled Russia to move out of the Soviet era and into a modernity envisaged initially as Western. They always advanced in tandem, and pointed in the same direction, sometimes with a slight time lag.

The development of these two major phenomena has shaped Russia's overall political, economic and social history after 1989. It has been a bumpy process with several breakdowns: for example President Yeltsin's armed attack on the parliament of 3 and 4 October 1993, Yeltsin's controversial re-election of 1996, the transfer of power to Vladimir Putin at the end of 1999, and the Medvedev pseudo-succession in 2008 represented major blows against free elections; the financial scandals of

1997–1999, the arrest of entrepreneur Mikhail Khodorkovsky in October 2003 on charges of tax evasion and the subsequent dismantling of Yukos oil company were direct attacks against property rights.

Property and free elections offer an exceptionally rich narrative framework for studying the vagaries of Russian history between 1989 and 1991. They help define the question of sovereignty: popular sovereignty, independence of the states, autonomy of the provinces, monetary policy and defence of property. The narrative framework I have chosen for the purposes of this book covers the elections and relations between the new citizens, the reconstituted elites and political power. The following chapters describe the turbulent development of the new democratic institutions, particularly free elections, in an attempt to explain the derailing of the democratization process and offer an interpretation of the current regime's oligopolistic authoritarianism. In support of the political narrative, it is important to summarize the key issues relating to property and economic sovereignty, and their close link with the political regime.

The major transformation of the economic regime was the introduction of private property and hence the defining of public property. The Communist experience emphatically and brutally showed the major distortion created by state property alone, i.e. property under the control of a non-accountable elite, not subject to citizens' scrutiny or sanction. In the USSR everything belonged to everybody, nothing belonged to anybody.[34] There was widespread chaos, a permanent violation of property rights. The prime example is the disastrous exploitation during the Communist decades of mineral resources, the land, the air, the rivers and the seas—all the country's resources and physical heritage. As the official principle was that state property was by definition protected against the abuses of private interests, there was no mechanism in place to ensure the best use of natural resources in a manner that safeguarded the environment and protected people and future generations. The environmental toll is terrifying, and the 1986 Chernobyl nuclear disaster typifies the lack of concern for the safety and security of the local population.

The reasons for this behaviour go back much further in Russian history and cannot be explained solely by the Soviet economic system, which was indifferent to environmental and human costs. The empire had not developed a property system that was enshrined in law or in people's minds. Until the mid-nineteenth century, serfdom and the ruler's absolutism had hindered the establishment of a unified property law that was independent of the ruler's will.

Whereas the nations of Europe underwent major upheavals in the Middle Ages and then during the Renaissance, Russia lived in isolation from the rest of the world. Russia knew neither Antiquity nor the Middle Ages, nor the Renaissance, wrote the Russian philosopher Ivan Kireevsky.[35] Russia had no Roman law, nor did it develop the concept of private property, associated with the transition to a mercantile and industrial society.

When England, France and Germany experienced the revolution of their political systems one after the other, Russia did not budge at institutional level. It expanded and modernized in some areas, but individual property was not seen as a positive value that fostered the development of a merchant and industrial bourgeoisie. Historian Richard Pipes explains how the rejection of land ownership deprived Russians of all the levers by which the English had managed to curb the power of their monarchs. The Tsars received levies or payments from all land, and so a regular taxation system would have been pointless and there was no need to convene a parliament to discuss taxes, as in England. In Russia, the legal institutions, which in Europe were the corollary of property, remained very basic and essentially acted as instruments for administering the territory. It was not until 1762 that the monarchy released the upper aristocracy from mandatory service; in 1785 the aristocracy was given jurisdiction over its estates, and only in 1861 was serfdom abolished.[36]

Property is both a concept and an institution. Since Classical times, philosophers and politicians have questioned the nature of property, its necessity or its superfluous and artificial nature, and the power of God and the sovereign over worldly goods. In *The Republic*, Plato attacks property as fomenting greed, conflicts and inequalities. In his day, Athens had a highly developed private property system, and observers could therefore construct a critique of the city's fall. In *Laws*, he does not reject all property, but insists on the state's role in curbing excessive wealth and excessive poverty. Aristotle challenges Plato. He sees property as an indestructible and positive institution that must not be placed in the hands of a state. He refutes the idea that common property would be better protected by the community, claiming that it becomes the subject of machinations and that no one can defend it better than a single owner. The chaos of the Communist economies vindicates his argument.

Private property and law are inseparable, since the safeguarding of property demands a public authority capable of protecting it. The Russian empire went for centuries without creating solid property legislation that was binding, or establishing the fundamental institutions of a modern state. No real public sphere was created that would have made it possible to define the private sphere, i.e. the separation of state and sovereign. Russia's history has thus been marked by the absence of law, private property and public affairs, and by the obstinate battle of the rulers, imperial and then Bolshevik, against these cornerstones of the modern economy and bourgeois society. As Pipes writes, 'the history of Russia offers an excellent example of the role that property plays in the development of civil and political rights, demonstrating how it makes possible the maintenance of arbitrary and despotic government'.[37]

In European countries and in the United States, the building of state institutions has been closely linked to the development of property status and ownership rights. The right to land was a concrete security which guaranteed survival and which powers that be would defend. Political government exists to protect property. Individuals organize themselves into a political community when it is in their interest to do so. People create rules of cohabitation that establish organized powers, whether absolute monarchy or parliamentary democracy. John Locke points out that 'forfeiture gives the third despotical power to lords for their own benefit, over those who are stripped of all property'. The protection of private property goes hand in hand with the battle against absolutism.[38]

It is interesting to compare the construction of the modern state of France with that of England since the eighteenth century. The government's supremacy is less strong in England since the greater pluralism and keener competition give entrepreneurs and wealthy financiers a direct influence on politics, particularly through the institution of parliament. In France, according to Hilton Root, 'failing to distinguish between private interests and public welfare, the government found it hard to mobilize confidence in its conduct of public business'. Root concludes that 'drawing the distinction between obligation to the state and obligation to family members [was] an important component of successful modernization'.[39]

The positive meaning of 'private' emerged precisely in reference to the concept of free power of control over property that functioned in capitalist fashion, states Habermas. The modern history of private law shows how far this process had already advanced during the mercantilist phase. [...] these codifications guaranteed the institution of private property and, in connection with it, the basic freedoms of contract, of trade and of inheritance.[40]

Max Weber, writing on the rule of law, stresses the necessity of account-ability, which is the greatest obstacle to the application of law in Russia today, and which compromises the full guarantee of property rights.[41]

Economic Sovereignty

In his work *Money Unmade*, David Woodruff presents his account of the transformation in Russia based on the themes of monetary sovereignty and the development of private and public property.[42] He contends that post-Communist state-building should have been driven by monetary sovereignty, property and free competition. But the legacy of Commu-nism, the issues of federalism and provincial autonomy held back the modernization of the open, capitalist state.

The weakness of Russia's central government can be explained by sit-uational factors: the speed of events, the government's lack of prepara-tion, financial negligence by the federal state which ran the regional administrations, and businesses' failure to restructure and find their own means of survival.

A crucial factor that was generally ignored by the reformers of the early 1990s dragged the Russian state into an acute crisis: the weakness of the rouble across the entire territory and the growth of bartering and currency substitution. Russia's financial crisis ended tragically with the crash of the rouble in August 1998.

In the command economy of the Brezhnev years, there was no official currency. The rouble was the formal instrument of trade with the outside world, made out in dollars. It was entirely unconnected with the coun-try's economic reality. The Soviet people themselves juggled several 'cur-rencies': the rouble—monopoly money used for buying daily bread and cabbages; the diplomatic rouble for buying in the *beriozkas* (the shops reserved for the elites); and barter, i.e. exchange in kind. They therefore had no training in economics to prepare them for capitalism and mon-etary trade. Barter took place on an extraordinary scale in Russia after 1994. Not only were wages and pensions almost no longer paid, but when they were, it was often in kind. I collected poignant accounts from inhab-itants of the Sverdlovsk, Ulyanovsk and Yaroslav regions between 1994 and 1997: up to two years of unpaid wages for the nurses in a country hospital; family allowances paid in sweets and biscuits; workers in a sauce-pan factory paid in saucepans—which it was then up to them to sell.

Woodruff deconstructs the perverse mechanism of barterization, or the demonetization of Russia. Reforms, and in particular the end of government orders for industries and therefore the need for profitability, pushed most ex-Soviet factories into bankruptcy. But the local and regional authorities could not allow their territory's economy to grind to a halt and see their citizens unemployed, with few prospects of a rapid restructuring. Consequently, the mayors and governors had to work with industrialists to maintain at least some manufacturing activity, even operating at a loss. Devoid of financial resources, people developed barter systems, and also unofficial currencies, local 'roubles'. Currency plays an essential role in the building of a sovereign state, as does having a tax system. The sovereignty of the Russian Federation and government authority could not be built solely on the basis of a new Constitution and the legitimacy of a president elected by universal suffrage who was committed to liberal reforms.

Vladimir Putin had learnt the lesson. As soon as he became President, in 2000, he spearheaded fiscal reform and stabilization of the rouble. Filling the state coffers was the priority at that point.

Comparing Russia with Poland, Woodruff highlights the legal, political and economic weaknesses of the Russian transformation—failings that Poland avoided.[43] His view is that the difference can be explained by the nature of privatization in Russia, which was pushed through without prior negotiations and resulted in lengthy legal battles over the guarantee of ownership rights. In principle, in Russia, the freedom to acquire is open to all, but in practice the law consolidates property distribution and the negotiating power that owners derive from it. The fair distribution of property comes under the jurisdiction neither of the legislators nor of the courts.

The actual notion of Russia's national sovereignty eluded the grasp of the elites in Moscow, who until 1991 were ruling not only the Russian Republic, but the fifteen republics of the Soviet Union. National defence is a good example. Boris Yeltsin did not establish the Russian Federation's national army until May 1992. The new Russian authorities did not realize the urgency of the matter until the newly independent Ukraine passed a decree forming its own army and disputed the Soviet military bases and academies on its territory. From the moment the USSR ceased to exist, the Red Army was defunct. The fact that Russia was not the Soviet state, but one portion of it, impeded the process of building a national state.

When such a sudden historic disruption occurs, the elites bear a particularly heavy responsibility. The political and economic leaders' and the intellectuals' lack of preparation and often inability to support the change in society and the reforms of public institutions should be examined before we jump to hasty conclusions about the ordinary Russians' preference for an authoritarian government.

The Paradox of Mistrust

Trust beyond a person's immediate circle demands a sufficient standard of living and institutions that operate democratically. When survival is a daily battle, people cannot take the risk of trusting and being betrayed: 'While traditional societies can survive even if one trusts only those whom one knows personally, modern societies can function only if people do not assume that strangers are enemies'.[44]

How did the Communist leaders create allegiance to the regime? The feelings shared by the majority of Soviet citizens were not trust, even less respect, but *detachment*, in comparison to the compulsory and permanent mobilization of the first Bolshevik decades; *individualism* (relying on oneself and family first and, beyond that, playing on patronage politics); and, ultimately, a pronounced and enduring *rejection of responsibility*.

In this de-ideologized and demobilized environment, propaganda however continued to play an essential part. Even if the Soviet people were suspicious of the regime and of the Truth from on high, they remained hostages to the Party line, to the general ambiance, to the prejudices which were still deeply rooted in a society that was not free.

The Sovietism of the 1970s was confined to the achievable, stifling all ambition: increased wealth was not an aim because it was unattainable. The phenomenon of long queues was emblematic: an expectation had to be created within the individual and then fulfilled or, conversely, not fulfilled. Those in power thus kept the individual in suspense, his fate depending on the whims of the administrations and the vagaries of the harvests or the transport system. Everyone was competing against everyone else: 'My neighbour hasn't got what I've got; I haven't got what my neighbour's got'. There was tremendous hostility towards others. As people could not express their aggression towards the regime freely and publicly, they gave vent to it by attacking other ordinary people like themselves, or drowned it in alcohol, suffered depression or engaged in black humour at home. There is a wealth of incredible anecdotes from the Brezhnev era bearing witness to this expression.[45]

In other respects, the entire production machine was officially focused on a defence objective: building socialism as protection against the threat from the enemy, so as not to allow the capitalists to assert their power, and consolidating the defence of the USSR. It was not until a new acute crisis occurred that the needs of ordinary people were included on the Party's agenda, for example the supply of bread, cereals and dairy products when the food disaster was looming. The paradigm of the 'nation in danger' faded in the 1990s, but re-surfaced with Putin.

The image of the enemy, of the nation in danger, is at the core of the relationship between rulers and ruled, cementing its legitimacy. The threat that comes from the Other, from the Chechen and the American alike, from the Jewish industrialist to the NGO Médecins sans Frontières, makes it possible to create a closed Russian society and to protect the leaders' strategies and interests from any interference from outside their world. The existence of the enemy also forges a bond between Russians and their leaders in the face of the Other; and the police, the state's armed force, are seen as protecting a population under threat. And this is all the more true in that the rejection of democracy by those in charge deprived them of those bonds which, in a democratic society, unite the various social bodies and institutions in a more solid and lasting way than fear and isolation. For these reasons, the paradigm of trust does not work in the case of Russia.

Do other nations trust their leaders? Or do they have a sense of belonging, of sharing rules and abiding by contracts, that is more essential than trust in people? Prevention and the battle against threats and potential enemies do not create relations of trust between a people and its rulers, even less with respect to the abstract entity of the state, or towards the police, the intelligence services and public services. The people's relationship to these institutions which, since the arrival of Vladimir Putin at the helm, have asserted their muscle is therefore a relationship of subordination and not one of loyalty or trust. When this subordination needs to be consolidated by forms of repression, control and isolation of society—of some protagonists in particular—then the Hannah Arendt paradigm[46] comes to mind, since the government veers towards an authoritarian model: totalitarian power is only strong as long as the structures of oppression exist. Once these are weakened, power crumbles.

In the case of Russia, Inglehart's general hypothesis that cultural changes lag behind situational changes does not hold.[47] On the one hand, the change in mindset can be one step ahead of the institutional and economic environment, while on the other, the pioneers of change, organized in political and social movements, can spur the institutions to reform. In the Russia of Gorbachev's last years and the early Yeltsin years, there were no objective or convincing factors suggesting that people's mentalities would be averse to democratization and openness. Those who claim so today are rewriting the facts after the event, in the *post factum* rationalization of developments that were not predetermined. As Russians' outlooks did not become democratized, it is convenient to think that they would never have been able to develop in this way, under any circumstances.

The Russians' cultural atavism, said to explain a taste for despotism and wariness of modernity, is an unacceptable premise since it is rooted in prejudices. Naturally, these prejudices are held by the Russians themselves, by those in the higher echelons of power, among some intellectuals and by a section of the population that did not learn a critical knowledge of their own history when young. But can we rely on the 'politically correct' as the basis for our analysis of the Russians' political culture, and of their propensity or lack of propensity to be open to other ideas and other ways of life?

Our entire objective is to go beyond generally accepted ideas, so neatly wrapped up in official discourse, and trace the origins and the complicated and contradictory paths of change in Russia. To do this, we must guard against the convenient models of 'convergence' of Eastern societies towards Western societies. The rapid implosion of the USSR and the Communist Party naturally led most observers, Russian and foreign alike, to expect the former Soviet societies to embrace Westernization with enthusiasm.

And indeed Russians began to buy into Western values from the start of the 1980s, without clashing with traditional Soviet patriotism. The elites were on a course towards a modernity that was appealing both ideologically and materially, without worrying about the effects on the Soviet state. They did not seriously envisage the end of the USSR until 1990. So Soviet patriotism did not hinder reform or dampen the democratic spirit. On the contrary, the universality of the newly adopted values relegated any consideration of power and Soviet specificity to a secondary position. The reversal occurred abruptly, after the collapse of the USSR in 1991. With the loss of 14 republics and 150 million inhabitants, the question of national identity suddenly arose. Yeltsin's Russia had half the population of Gorbachev's USSR, and comprised only three-quarters of the land, most of which was in Siberia and the Far East. Russian identity became a crucial and highly sensitive issue since it was posed in terms of loss and weakening. It was the considerable price to be paid for shedding Communism and Russia's imperial history. By 1991, 'European-style' modernization was thus associated with the ruin of the state and with the shrinking of both the territory and the population. Soviet patriotic values gradually resurfaced, upheld initially by opposition political forces, in particular Vladimir Zhirinovsky's nationalist far right, and then by the Kremlin and its cronies. When Vladimir Putin came to power in 1999–2000, conditions were conducive for a new attempt at ideologizing the nation and power.

National Identity in the Turmoil of Change

Boris Yeltsin was the first president of a Russian Federation whose identity was no longer either Communist or imperial.[48] He had played on the awakening of nationalities in order to take power; he invoked Russian identity to defeat Mikhail Gorbachev and take over from the Communist regime. However, for all the above reasons, the Republic of Russia was not a Russian nation-state but a Russian Federation (*rossiiskaya federatsiya*). Moreover, Yeltsin planned to instrumentalize his leadership of the biggest Republic of the USSR to take the helm of almost the entire Soviet complex, with the likely exception of the Baltic states. His ambitions were thwarted after the failed putsch of August 1991, as the collapse of the USSR did not leave room for the counter-project of a union of the republics. The Commonwealth of Independent States (CIS), established in December 1991 to put a formal end to the USSR, remains to this day a very loose association that brings together the leaders of eleven of the fifteen ex-republics (the three Baltic countries and Georgia are not members) around ad hoc issues. The myth of the Soviet people is well and truly buried.

At the end of 1991, the Russian Federation stood alone facing its destiny. The elites did not seriously believe in the independence of the other Slavic countries, Ukraine and Belarus. The shock was so profound that it took time for its consequences to sink in. Nor was the population yet able to mourn what we call the empire, but what for them was simply Russia, Great Russia, their motherland and native land (*rodina*). The hardline nationalists vowed fierce hatred for Mikhail Gorbachev and the 'modernizers'. In their view Gorbachev had destroyed the empire, in other words Russia, and caved in to the West. He had buried the hopes of the national state and of power. The words *derzhava* and *derzhavnost'* (power) are part of the nationalist lexicon, along with *otechestvo* (fatherland). The most extreme tendencies, spearheaded by the association *Pamiat'* (memory) and the newspapers *Den'* (the day) and *Zavtra* (tomorrow), were racist, anti-Semitic, and advocates of a strong government that should not encumber itself with democratic processes. They were critical of the breakup of the Soviet Union.[49] The journalist and writer Alexander Prokhanov presented himself as an 'imperialist' and 'statist' (*gosudartvennik*); he made no secret of his hostility towards the West.[50] The well-known writers Valentin Rasputin and Yuri Bondarev lent their support to this imperial and reactionary vision of Russia. This movement remained a minority tendency in the 1990s, but gained new momentum in the next decade, spurred on by Vladimir Putin and his ideology of 'sovereign democracy'.

Another national vision was that of Alexander Solzhenitsyn, who also had a limited audience in Russia. The famous dissident, author of *The Gulag Archipelago*, who defended traditional Russian and Orthodox values, did not win over his compatriots. His return to the motherland in 1994 left the vast majority of Russians indifferent and they were unaffected by his death in August 2008. His message was both patriotic and, for Russians, archaic. He advocated a Slavic union (Russians, Ukrainians and Belarusians), but rejected any close ties with non-Slavic peoples of the former empire. For Solzhenitsyn, Slavonic identity, Orthodoxy and a simple life were the glue that held the nation together. Local democracy and spiritual values, as well as protection against some aspects of Western democracy, were the condition for the renewal of Russia.[51]

Boris Yeltsin sought Solzhenitsyn's support, but the former exile remained cautious. He was a harsh critic of the Yeltsin's regime's economic developments, 'dictated by the West', social inequalities, corruption among the elites and the first war in Chechnya. A few years later, the great writer was unable to resist the rise of Russian nationalism and the attendant xenophobia. He gave his support to Vladimir Putin. The Orthodox clergy joined in this movement of national revival. Boris Yeltsin had worked to build better relations with the Church. Vladimir Putin involved the Patriarch Alexis II, and now his successor Kirill, very closely in all major state events. The patriarchate generally aligns itself with the state's decisions on matters of domestic and foreign policy. It even acts as a vanguard for Putin's doctrine of merging the Russian nation and the Orthodox Church in one identity. Since 2006, the Church has been waging a battle to introduce religious education into schools.[52]

The pro-Yeltsin 'legitimist' elite had already attempted to occupy the 'national idea' ground by promoting a mix of economic progress and state interventionism, combined with a hardening of the foreign policy line, especially with regard to NATO's enlargement. For the most part, this elite was the product of the pro-Gorbachev modernizing elite of the 1980s. However, it had not emerged unscathed from the upheavals of 1989–1992. In the main it had been disconcerted by the fall of the Soviet state and the shrinking of the country. Falling back on the Russian Federal Republic had not been greeted as a positive step towards the building of a modern, more homogeneous state (since present-day Russia is made up of more than 85 per cent Russians, as against less than 50 per cent in the former USSR). Many 1980s 'modernizers' and democrats had not foreseen the threat to the territorial integrity of the Soviet complex represented by restructuring and openness. Like Gorbachev, they believed that the Soviet empire could be modernized and liberalized without breaking up into its respective national state communities. They thus demonstrated the importance of the 'national-imperial' heritage in their vision of Russia and of the world. Confronted with the loss of the republics, a large section of the intelligentsia and the ruling elites (administrative, economic and political) were opposed to the 'lottery' of free elections and the tyranny of the majority.

Communist voters remained sensitive to the question of a return to Soviet values, not because they wanted to reinstate the USSR, but to defend their material security and have a government that looked after them. 'The idea of restoring the USSR is not only not imminent, but is even unthinkable to the majority of Russia's population', concluded the sociologists Klyamkin and Lapkin in a remarkable study carried out in 1996.[53]

It is true that Gorbachev's introduction in 1989 of universal suffrage with a free and secret vote accelerated the process of independence for the republics and undermined the authority of the central state. Believing they were fostering the emergence of a community of Soviet citizens, Gorbachev and the reformers gave the republican elites the means to build new communities of citizens, at the national-republican level, and to exit the USSR.

Polls illustrating the reasons for voting in the elections throughout the 1990s show that the majority of Russians dreamed neither of a revival of the USSR, nor of great power schemes.[54] Ordinary people, those who had not grown rich or reached the upper echelons of government, were concerned first and foremost with their living conditions and short-term material security: holding on to their jobs, earning wages, keeping their homes. They had no interest in rousing ideologies or imperial ventures. They were sorry that their country was no longer a major power and felt humiliated by Russia's diminished power. They were suspicious of their leaders, whom they considered mediocre and corrupt. However, questioned more specifically on what they would be prepared to do to help regain Russia's prestige, they replied that they did not want to be involved, that they did not want to be betrayed once again.

While preserving a certain nostalgia for Russia's past glory, Russians initially saw the creation of a more limited, more compact, more Russian Russia, as the chance to finally take on a fitting national identity in keeping with the territory. In the 1990s, in the main they were more accepting than their elites of the republics' independence. In the opinion polls, they did not express the wish for a 'reintegration' of the neighbouring countries since they saw them first and foremost as representing a risk of impoverishment and conflict. Asked about the values they held dear, throughout the reform years, Russians stressed their attachment to 'traditional Russian values'. These values relate to a way of life and human interaction, and not to an authoritarian government.[55]

Russian society in the 1990s was in an inward-looking phase. There was a renewed impetus towards localism and regionalism. No one was prepared to sacrifice themselves for 'their neighbours', in the city or the neighbouring region, and even less for the former Soviet territories. The Russians of Russia had no concern for the fate of Russians who were now minority populations in the former republics (chiefly Ukraine, Estonia, Latvia and Kazakhstan). They felt no solidarity or kinship, which is perhaps the best indicator of a lack of nationalism, in the sense of a gathering of all Russians in one single nation-state. Furthermore, the Russians of Estonia and Latvia preferred to remain in their countries of residence.[56]

In people's minds, the national community was closer to the state-federal territory and the populations that inhabited it. This new vision, calmer and more realistic than that of a Russian 'ethnic' nation, offered an environment that was conducive to the advance of democratic ideas during the Yeltsin period. Russian society was not asking its leaders for huge voluntarist projects, but for economic and social stability, and institutions that worked. And yet, the government was unable or unwilling to consolidate the rule of law. The economic hardship created by the collapse of the Soviet system and the mistakes made during the reforms partially explain the failure of Russia's first post-communist government. Moreover, the elites expressed more disarray than ordinary Russians at the loss of Russia's great power status from the very beginning, and, thanks to skilful information campaigns, carried society along a more revanchist path in the 2000s.

3

THE DEFEAT OF CONSTITUTIONALISM

'A society in which the observance of the law is not assured, nor the separation of powers defined, has no Constitution at all'.

Article 16 of the *Declaration of the Rights of Man and of the Citizen*, 1789

At the beginning of the 1990s, all efforts were invested in the economy: free pricing and trade, and new legislation relating to property, companies and finance. Privatization enabled a section of the former elite and young entrepreneurs to grow rich; some even built colossal fortunes. Meanwhile the question of the state was only being addressed by a few legal experts and a handful of intellectuals. The Kremlin simply maintained a road map of the democratic institutions and the legislation necessary for the transformation to capitalism, particularly privatization. Ultimately, even the drafting of the new Constitution escaped public debate. After the constitutional crisis that saw a stand-off between Yeltsin and a large group of deputies in October 1993, with the army's intervention resulting in large numbers of dead and injured, the draft Constitution was revised on the quiet and was not subject to any criticism until the referendum of December 1993.

Paradoxically, the adoption of a new Constitution in December 1993 marked the beginning of the end of constitutionalism. By constitutionalism, I mean the process of building a state subject to the rule of law based on respect for the pre-eminence of the Constitution under the control of an independent constitutional court, a state in which the separation of powers is guaranteed by free, fair elections and true competition between political parties, and where there are independent tribunals with the power to sanction servants of the state, both elected and appointed. 'Politically, constitutionalism means that the basic law is the translation of the social pact concluded between all the elements of the country'.[1]

The lack of in-depth reflection on the significance of the transformations and on their long-term political consequences can be explained to a large extent by the accelerated pace of historical events between 1988 and 1993. By the time the new architects of the republican and federal state finally took the time to consider the new organization and draft a constitution, concrete problems had already built up in all the Federation's provinces. The foundations of the state and the mechanisms of government had not yet been laid, and Russia was in a sense suspended over a legal and institutional void. But the many pressing problems made it imperative for those on the ground to find immediate solutions. Central government in Moscow and provincial and local politicians put in place makeshift solutions that quickly became institutionalized, and were enshrined in regional and municipal legislation and regulations. These multiple processes occurred independently of each other, generally with no concern for harmonization or even communication at national-federal level.

The crux of Gorbachev's tragedy and then of Yeltsin's lay in their inability to create a coherent whole based on the new realities that differed from one province to another (Soviet republics, then Russian republics and regions). Local ruling groups' inventiveness and dynamism were not acknowledged in the strategies of the Moscow policy-makers who planned to reform the state, the legal system, the economy and society without taking into account the territorial and human diversity or the people's mood. The differences in electoral behaviour from one constituency to another, between different social classes and generations, caught the reformers off guard. From the first ballot of 1989, the Soviet citizens acted like voters capable of exercising free will. Universal free, direct and plural suffrage resulted in the peaceful implosion of the USSR, then highlighted the fragility of the federal edifice of Yeltsin's Russia. The reformers had not foreseen the impact that the expression of the people's sovereignty would have on their political plans.

And so, from 1988 liberalization took shape on the basis of a misunderstanding. Gorbachev was seeking a new legitimization of the regime through the ballot box, but did not understand the ingratitude of the citizens who used the new democratic instrument he gave them to 'jeopardize *perestroika*'. In June 1991, Boris Yeltsin made opportunistic use of universal suffrage to challenge Gorbachev and seize power. In September-October 1993, he did not waver for long before dissolving all the elected assemblies and calling in the army to crack down on parliamentary opposition. He abandoned negotiation and consensus-seeking in favour of resorting to force. In Soviet-style thinking, Yeltsin and his advisers were struggling to secure their hold on power by building a new monopoly over central state institutions. Strangely, they let republican and regional public institutions go their own way and left the fundamental issue of federalism unattended.

The liberalization process begun by Gorbachev's reforms was brought to an end by two crises: the army's storming of parliament in October 1993 and the war against Chechnya in December 1994.

The First Elections: Sovereignty and Representation Put to the Test

There was regular contact between the elites and ordinary citizens through the ballots that punctuated the history of the democratization process from its beginnings in 1989 to its subsequent dismantling. We will be focusing on voting as the key theme of the 1990s, and analyzing the development of the political regime after the adoption of the new Constitution of December 1993. We start with a brief summary of the elections that took place between 1989 and 1993.

1989 was the year of parliamentarianism. By having a new parliament elected in the spring—the Congress of People's Deputies—through a multi-candidate election in some constituencies, the leaders were seeking legitimacy through the ballot box. Gorbachev thus hoped to oust the conservative and incompetent politicians and promote a generation of young and efficient Communists. The extension of suffrage to non-Communist candidates had a much more radical effect than foreseen. It led to the Communist Party itself being challenged in some republics and big cities, especially Leningrad where the Communist old guard was swept away.

The year 1990 saw the first institutional break-up of the USSR. In the republics, the parliamentary elections hastened their bid for autonomy. Very soon the newly elected assemblies passed laws that would lead them to demand their 'sovereignty' and, in 1991, their independence. Again, the Party reformers had not anticipated such a backlash against the regime. After having revised the Soviet Constitution once again, Gorbachev was elected by the deputies on 15 March 1990 to the newly created post of 'President of the USSR', with far-reaching powers. However, it was at the point when he enjoyed almost total power as head of both state and the Party that these two institutions collapsed. A year and a half later, the Communist Party of the Soviet Union (CPSU) and the USSR would be defunct. Gorbachev tried to propose a project for a new, more flexible Soviet federalism, but it was already too late. To counter the undermining of central government and try to salvage a centralized USSR, the conservative opposition organized the putsch of August 1991. The irony of history is that Mikhail Gorbachev was freed from house arrest by the man who wanted to be the leader: Boris Yeltsin.[2]

The President of the Russian Republic, elected through universal suffrage, pushed Gorbachev to resign, putting an end to the Soviet state on 8 December 1991. That day, in Belovezhskaya Pushcha, Belarus, the presidents of the new independent states of Russia and Ukraine, and the chairman of the parliament of Belarus decided to establish the Commonwealth of Independent States, joined subsequently by Kazakhstan, then by the Republics of Central Asia and Armenia. The USSR was no longer. On 25 December 1991, Gorbachev formalized the demise of the state over which he presided and resigned from his post.

In the following years, Georgia, Ukraine and Moldova formerly became members of this poorly organized 'community'. The CIS never became a confederation, or even an alliance of states or an economic community. It remained a talking shop for the governments of twelve ex-Soviet republics, dominated by Moscow, to which Ukraine signed up with reservations. The Baltic countries had ruled out any agreement with the new post-Communist Russia since regaining their sovereignty. In August 2008, when the Russian army occupied significant parts of Georgia, the latter withdrew from the CIS. In 2011, eleven states are members of the CIS.

Yeltsin, like Gorbachev before him, inherited the territorial and administrative organization of the Russian Soviet Federative Socialist Republic (RSFSR) and had to reorganize the modes of government within this federal structure. The USSR was formally a multi-tiered federation, a *matrioshka* in which Russia was a Soviet Republic, organized in a federation of autonomous republics. Among the string of independence claims of 1991, some autonomous republics also insisted on sovereignty. Chechnya declared its independence unilaterally and withdrew from the Russian Federation; Abkhazia refused to submit to the Georgian government. Sovereignty conflicts began to destabilize the Caucasus. In March 1992, Yeltsin persuaded the deputies to vote for a highly controversial 'Federation Treaty', which was not even mentioned in the proposed Federal Constitution of December 1993.

The question of restructuring the state was overshadowed by the breakup into sovereign republics, to the detriment of other fundamental issues relating to the renewal of the state: constitutional architecture and parliamentarianism, the separation of powers and the role of the courts. The Russians were at a loss, faced with choosing a political regime. They had never had to think in terms of institutional balance, of the legislature acting as a counterweight to the executive. President Yeltsin soon found himself facing opposition within the new parliament elected in 1990, with deputies' visions for the new political system varying widely. To decide the issue, he proposed putting four questions to the vote, in particular support for economic reforms (without specifying which ones) and support for the President and Parliament. The outcome was no surprise. The Russians replied that they supported the President, much more than they did Parliament; Yeltsin was a very real figure, whereas the hundreds of deputies could not appear as an efficient 'power centre'. There is evidence of a similar attitude fifteen years later, when Russian society put its trust in Vladimir Putin but did not rally to defend the role of parliament. This reveals the failure to instil a profound democratization. The *vlast'*—real, tangible power—lay with the Kremlin. From the start of the post-Soviet regime, the separation of powers was considered a weakness. Similarly, federalism was perceived as a structural failing, since it reinforced the possibility of provinces breaking away.

1993 was a crucial year, made up of successes for democracy and dramatic retreats. The referendum of 25 April, despite the flawed design of the questions, was the ballot that gave the most nuanced insight into the new Russian electorate. The maps drawn up at the time (see maps at the end of the chapter) show the formation of a geography and a sociology of the electorate, for the very first time in Russia's history. Three Russias emerged: legitimist Russia, which supported Yeltsin and the spirit of reform, despite the difficulties; protest Russia, opposed to change and faithful to the Communist or nationalist vote; and spectator Russia, which abstained, thus expressing its freedom not to participate, either due to indifference or distrust of the political leaders.[3]

Calling in the Army and the End of Enchantment

By summer 1993, the state and its institutions were hamstrung. No progress had been made either on the federal question or the problem of separating and dividing up power; on the contrary, things had gone backwards. The debate over the new Constitution had led to serious dissension among the political elites in Moscow and in the capitals of the republics and the regions. It seems that most of the protagonists clung to the old Soviet Constitution of the Russian Republic, many times overhauled and now incomprehensible, for they feared that close scrutiny of the entire state edifice would lead to the suspension of their positions as deputies, judges or ministers. The new Constitutional Court, which met for the first time in November 1991, was called on to give a ruling on the most diverse questions, for lack of arbitration and consensus on the authority of the president, the government and the elected bodies.

The deputies elected in 1990 were the first to resist the renewal of the Constitution, and many of them rejected the principle of holding a people's referendum on the adoption of the Basic Law. The President of the Parliament, Ruslan Khasbulatov, spoke out publicly against the referendum. He and Vice President Alexander Rutskoi[4] led a parliamentary revolt against President Yeltsin. They were opposed both to the federal project and the restructuring of institutions proposed by the Kremlin advisers and the constitutional commission.[5] At the same time, tensions were growing in the north Caucasus. Chechnya declared its independence in October 1991 and broke all ties with the federal institutions; it refused to take any part in the process of setting up a Constitution. In 1992, the Ingushes and the Ossetians entered into a bloody conflict; and the Abkhazians fought the Georgians to gain their independence.[6]

On 21 September 1993, President Yeltsin promulgated a decree suspending the Constitution and dissolving the federal parliament and all the elected provincial and local councils. A large group of deputies, led by Khasbulatov and Rutskoi, occupied the parliament in the White House (renamed the House of the Government of the Russian Federation in 1994). The discussions with the Kremlin ended in stalemate. Yeltsin resolved to win the trial of strength by storming parliament. On 3 and 4 October 1993, the White House and the television tower came under army fire. Around two hundred people died in this clash, mainly employees who happened to be in the buildings, and passers-by. The exact toll will never be known, and no investigation will be carried out. The 'conspirators' were arrested, imprisoned, tried and then released within a few months. Alexander Rutskoi succeeded in being elected governor of the Pskov region in 1995.

In the days following the events of 3 and 4 October 1993, the media attempted to legitimize the tragedy. The rebel deputies were allegedly jeopardizing the post-Communist revolution; the use of armed force was justified by the danger of a counter-revolution. The threat of 'civil war' was invoked, whereas the conflict was actually between two institutions, the presidency and its administration on the one hand versus the elected Assembly on the other, and not between organized social movements. Most of Boris Yeltsin's advisers abided by this interpretation, which exonerated them of a radical departure from the democratization process. They stuck to their contention that all the avenues of negotiation with the rebels had been exhausted. In actual fact, both sides wanted to monopolize power in their own camps, dismissing pluralism and the separation between executive and legislative powers. As with the decision to bomb and invade Chechnya one year later, the new rulers used the argument of 'the threat of extremism' to justify the disproportionate use of violence and ultimately to shirk taking responsibility for their actions.

In November 1993, President Yeltsin had the Constitution rewritten in a vein that was more presidentialist and deliberately vague as to the functioning of the Federation. The powers of the federal and provincial authorities were not clearly set out, and the process for forming parliament's upper house remained undefined. The draft new Basic Law provided no clear solution to the most sensitive problems of radically reforming the state.

Even more importantly, the Constitution was adopted in highly controversial conditions. Almost half of the 89 subjects of the Federation had not approved the bill. The Chechen and Tatarstan republics did not hold a ballot. Some twenty regions and republics had a turnout of under 50 per cent, the required threshold for the poll to count; another twenty or so voted against it. After an indescribable shambles, the Kremlin finally decided to count the votes solely on a federal basis, as if the entire Federation were a single constituency. The results by province had no impact on the adoption of the Basic Law (note that the rules had not been set prior to the referendum and that a large proportion of voters thought that by voting no, their republic would be standing up to Moscow). Publication of the definitive but still incomplete results was delayed for weeks. It is not certain that at national level the 50 per cent turnout threshold was reached. The uncertainty cast a shadow over the entire constitutional process and on the legislative elections held at the same time, already creating mistrust of the 'democratic vote'.

There was a significant loss of confidence between the referendum on Yeltsin and the reforms of 25 April 1993[7] and the referendum on the constitution of 12 December 1993. In April, 58 per cent of Russians indicated renewed trust in the president, elected by universal suffrage on 12 June 1991 with an abstention rate of 34 per cent, whereas abstention in December rose to 45.2 per cent. The election of the deputies to the two chambers reveals a majority protest vote in many constituencies. The disrepute of the assemblies surpassed that of Boris Yeltsin and his government.

The parliamentary institution never recovered from the storming of the White House in October 1993. Russians have not forgotten the vision of a quarrel at the top, between the President and the Vice president, between the Kremlin and the deputies. The President had the army at his disposal, and was therefore strong, whereas the deputies were weak and could only take refuge and resist. In his *Memoirs*, Mikhail Gorbachev describes his very bitter reaction and condemns Yeltsin for calling in the army. 'Nevertheless, late on 3 October the government was in control of the situation and could have continued to seek a mutually acceptable solution to the impasse, but it was at this moment that the inclination of the president to "act decisively", which he understood as using force irrespective of the consequences and the number of victims, manifested itself'.[8] He has never forgiven Yeltsin for sidelining him after the putsch of August 1991, and has constantly accused him of having derailed the reforms begun in 1987 and disrupting the democratization process.

The Constitution drafted in November 1993 is a reflection of the contradictions and conflicts besetting Russia at the time. The bill was amended on the quiet, since the constitutional conference of the previous summer had been dismantled and all the parliamentary authorities dissolved by the presidential decree of 21 September. So it was a group of experts close to the Kremlin who revised the draft and produced a

Basic Law that reflected the climate of crisis in the autumn of 1993. The bill was even more presidentialist than the previous draft, and, above all, it remained nebulous and uncertain regarding the institutions of federalism. The powers of the executive authorities in the republics and the regions that made up the Federation and the exercise of these powers in relation to central government were not specified. Furthermore, the status of the republics was different from that of the regions (*oblast'*) and territories (*krai*), even if the Constitution affirmed the equality of all the Federation's subjects (*sub'ekty*).[9] Crucial issues such as the basis of the building of the state, the division of responsibilities and the rules of subsidiarity remained shrouded in ambiguity and vagueness.

Conversely, the key principles forming the basis of state and society were the subject of a perfectly clear preamble. Russia declared itself to be democratic and respectful of rights and freedoms in terms similar to those of the French Constitution. It joined the major democratic countries in setting out the guiding values and principles for the restructuring of the state. It is hard to say, retrospectively, almost twenty years on, whether the authors of the bill truly believed in the essence of these principles, or whether they saw them as rather formal, cosmetic declarations of intention that it was appropriate to include in order for their country to be seen as part of 'Western civilization'. Becoming a 'civilized' country was one of the mantras of these early post-Communist years. The desire was genuine and the possibility seemed real.[10]

The arbitrariness of the decision to invade Chechnya on 11 December 1994 can be explained to a large extent by the disdain for the elected assemblies and the very tense atmosphere in which the new Constitution was rewritten and then submitted to a referendum. There was no debate in parliament, no thought given to a republic's right to embark on a process for leaving the Federation. The Kremlin decided on a massive use of force without declaring a state of emergency or asking the deputies for their endorsement. At the same moment, experts were putting the finishing touches to a new military doctrine. Published in October 1993, the document affirmed the abandonment of the no-first-use policy and adopted the concept of a deterrent. Western governments then accorded more importance to this doctrinal rapprochement than to the lack of public oversight of the army or to the post-colonial conflicts in the Caucasus. The appeal of democratic political life based on negotiation and compromise died on 3 October 1993.

The War in Chechnya

The war in Chechnya contributed to Boris Yeltsin's unpopularity in 1995. Why wage war on this Caucasus republic? A few weeks after the hostilities began, opinion polls indicated that a majority of Russians were in favour of withdrawal, even at the price of Chechen independence. Only 13 per cent supported the military intervention; 65 per cent had a negative assessment of Yeltsin's role in the Chechnyan crisis.[11]

Why force a Muslim people to remain when they no longer wanted to be part of the Russian Federation? The population of Russia was not convinced that the principle of territorial integrity of the Federation and the domino theory invoked by the Kremlin justified a war in which many young conscripts were to die. Many opinion polls and testimonies showed that an imagined community was emerging in Russian society in the early 1990s that was different from the Russia envisaged by its leaders. The reality of a smaller, but more coherent, less multiethnic Russia was more welcomed amongst ordinary people than in elites circles.[12]

In December 1994, a small group of leaders decided to end General Dudayev's separatist regime in Chechnya through the use of armed force. The military intervention was intended to last two weeks; it lasted sixteen months, until the ceasefire of August 1996 which paved the way for the withdrawal of Russian troops and saw the start of a very turbulent inter-war period in Chechnya. The same scenario was repeated in 1999–2000, when Vladimir Putin resumed hostilities to take political and military revenge. The independence declared by the Chechen parliament in 1991 was never recognized by Moscow or by the international community.

The first war in Chechnya left tens of thousands dead and hundreds of thousands of wounded and displaced persons. The tiny Caucasus republic bordering on Georgia had a total population of 900,000 prior to the conflict, including around 200,000 Russians, who were the first victims of the bombings, as they lived in the cities, mainly the capital, Grozny. They were forced to flee and become refugees in the Russian Federation. The conflict led to the very rapid 'ethnic cleansing' of Chechnya. Within a few months, there were no more than a few thousand Russians and non-Caucasians left. As for the Chechens living in the towns, they invaded neighbouring Ingushetia. They lived there for years in makeshift conditions. To win back Chechnya, Moscow brandished the argument of belonging to Russia, and at the same time emptied that republic of its entire Russian population. Hundreds of thousands of young conscripts with no training, proper equipment or ordinance survey maps were sent into battle. Supplies failed to follow, and the food and hygiene conditions were appalling.

On 11 December 1994, the intervention was officially presented as an 'operation for restoring law and order' and for the 'protection of human rights'. It resulted in a human and political disaster. Chechnya was destroyed, its society crushed, and the Russian army also suffered heavy losses, especially among the young conscripts. It was a military failure as serious as that for the Soviet Union in Afghanistan a decade earlier. 'If by Chechnya we mean not the territory (which we can always, at the cost of thousands of lives, 'cleanse' of its 'armed gangs' but also of its entire population), but the Chechen people, then for several generations this people will be cut off from Russia, at least in their hearts and minds', wrote one Russian journalist.[13]

Instead of treating the Chechen issue as an exception—it was the only republic in the Federation that declared independence—the Kremlin claimed that the threat of contagion from the separatist virus could spread to the whole of Russia. It tried to justify the war as a preventive measure. Several leaders from the republics and the regions voiced their disapproval. In addition to the tragedy in Chechnya, the entire reconstruction of the federal concept based on consensus and democracy was compromised.[14]

Western governments and the international community showed an astonishing indulgence towards Boris Yeltsin. The conformist line revolved around the Federation's territorial integrity: Russia had already accepted the breakaway of all its satellites in Central Europe, then the Soviet republics, so its desire to consolidate its territory was understandable. Peoples' right to self-determination, especially in the case of a small nation that had battled against Moscow since the nineteenth century, and had suffered torture and deportations under Stalin in 1944, was relegated to secondary importance. The worst aspect of the West's reaction was its inability to condemn the hugely disproportionate military and physical resources used against a people that threatened no one.[15] In 1994, the Russian President still maintained his democratic credentials as the defender of the new Russia against the 'Communist backlash', standing on a tank to convince the soldiers not to fire during the attempted coup of August 1991.

We know today that Boris Yeltsin took the decision to invade and bomb Chechnya in disastrous conditions, during a late evening with his Defence Minister, the intelligence services chiefs and a few of his inner circle. Officially, it was not a war, but the 'settling of the Chechnya problem'. The result was alarming: the democratically elected president of post-Soviet Russia gave his consent for a heavy-duty attack against the civilian population of one of the republics of the Federation. Was it more legitimate to use bombs against one's own citizens than against the Afghans in the 1980s?

This recourse to blind, brutal force revealed a truth that was borne out by subsequent events: the second Chechen war that began in 1999 and the establishment of Ramzan Kadyrov's criminal regime in 2004. The fact was that Moscow did not consider the Chechens as fully-fledged citizens, their lives did not count, and even Russians living in Chechnya were not spared.

It was clear that the war aiming to 'restore constitutional law and order' in the republic had the opposite effect: it demonized a tiny territory and its population, and turned the Chechens into pariahs. In 1996, the vast majority of Russians interviewed by the Levada Centre were against this war and were of the opinion that it would be better to allow the Chechens to leave Russia.

This attitude is significant. In the mid 1990s, Russia's populations still felt committed to a non-violent culture that upheld freedoms. Even if they were already highly critical of Boris Yeltsin's economic policy and his temperamental weakness, they still resisted the lure of authoritarianism and racism. The Russian army's second war in Chechnya, begun in autumn 1999, aroused different reactions in the Russians, clearly revealing their changed attitude in favour of 'security', irrespective of violations of fundamental rights and the degree of violence used against civilian populations. Justified officially by the fight against terrorism, the goal of the new war against the Chechens was to consolidate the power of Vladimir Putin, the chief of the Federal Security Service (FSB, formerly the KGB), by creating a climate of insecurity and terrorist threat. The war was the founding moment of Putin's regime, as will be explained further below.

In 1993–1994, the use of violent armed force was not inevitable, contrary to what the Yeltsin regime claimed at the time. In both cases, the parliamentary revolt and Chechen separatism, the possibilities of compromise had not been exhausted. The Kremlin gave in to the temptation to resolve a serious problem by means of force, seeking to 'eliminate' the problems rather than deal with the deep-seated causes. The consequences of this abandonment of democracy in 1993 and 1994 have weighed very heavily on Russia's political history until now and are bound to have a strong influence in the future. The crushing of the rebel deputies in October 1993 and the military occupation of Chechnya in 1994 are key episodes which paved the way for an increasing recourse to the arbitrary exercise of power and the success of Putin's methods from 1999.

These two examples of the use of armed violence mark the beginning of a downward spiral, with the leaders in Moscow riding roughshod over the two fundamental principles of a democratic state: free voting and parliamentary representation on the one hand, and real federalism with respect for regional autonomies and minority rights on the other. At the same time, privatizations and Prime Minister Yegor Gaydar's liberal policy, unsupported by the necessary social and restructuring policies, led the economy and Russian society to the brink of collapse. Yeltsin's regime almost touched rock bottom in 1995, in the run-up to the presidential election, with the threat of a switch back to the old Communists becoming a real possibility. The elections were a very serious challenge to the existing government and revealed the mood of society and the ability of the ruling elites to salvage their position and their interests.

The Pitfalls of the New Presidentialism

A president elected by universal suffrage was a great novelty in Russia. Like his predecessors, Mikhail Gorbachev had wanted to combine the honorary post of head of state and the strategic position of Party General Secretary. But he had not dared submit to the sanction of the ballot box in 1990 and, under the revised Soviet Constitution, the president was elected by the deputies. Until 1990, the locus of power in the USSR was within the Central Committee of the Communist Party, in the Politburo and the Secretariat headed by the Party General Secretary. But this Communist power was overturned by the competition of the *Soviets*, the assemblies revitalized by Gorbachev's reforms. The main preoccupation in 1993 was to avoid any new form of dyarchy—a double system of government—and, in particular, to avoid conflict between the presidency and parliament. Instead of thinking in terms of *separating powers*, the experts reasoned in terms of a *power hierarchy*, with a presidency at the top of the pyramid. They sought to create a new institution concentrating the executive power. Clearly, in the words of Eugene Huskey, 'the Constitution of 1993 elevated the presidency above Parliament'.[16]

The Russian political analysts Lilia Shevtsova and Igor Klyamkin point out the following paradox: 'The presidency was a completely new institution in Russia's political tradition'; and yet, within the space of a few years, this system 'led right back to the autocratic tradition'.[17] They stress that from the start of the presidential system the ground was being prepared for Putin's authoritarian regime. In Russia, the tradition of a strong power has nearly always translated into despotism with a protective figure or a ruling group that accepted none but self-imposed limits to its power. However, this retrospective interpretation of the effects of presidentialism gives the impression that the lack of a democratic tradition in Russia unavoidably resulted in the corruption of its institutions. The elites must shoulder a large part of the blame and are at fault for abusing the new constitutional provisions and for showing few scruples in turning the legislative and material conditions of free elections to their advantage.

In actual fact, the architects of the Constitution did attempt to prevent the abuse of power. The president had to be powerful in order to govern effectively, but could not remain in post indefinitely. Article 81 of the Constitution stipulates a maximum of two consecutive terms. The president chooses his government, which the State Duma is bound to endorse for fear of being dissolved. The head of the government, the president of the Council of Ministers, is not the head of a parliamentary majority. He therefore has no personal legitimacy and is accountable first and foremost to the president who can dismiss him at any moment. We will see the extent to which this power system was hijacked by Vladimir Putin in 2008 when, in order to remain in power, he took on the enhanced position of Prime Minister.

At the very beginning of the 1990s Boris Yeltsin was seen as a popular reformer. He gradually established an opaque, cronyist system and abandoned the construction of a strict institutional regime that was transparent and designed to last. He did not concentrate power within his own person, but allowed his entourage to monopolize the instruments of government without being made accountable to society. He agreed to call in the army when he lost control of the situation, thus hindering the democratization of the regime.

The regime's presidentialism, as implemented by Yeltsin's entourage, led to fundamental drifts in the exercise of executive power and in the mentalities of the elites and of ordinary citizens. The supremacy of the president, who declared himself above the parties and the other state institutions, combined with the government's administrative practice and with growing corruption, produced a system of management that was unsuited to the emergence from communism. Furthermore, this presidential model was out of step with another essential development in the 1990s, the federalism of the state and the rapid autonomization of the provinces. The harsh economic climate after 1991—the economic crisis was so severe that a large proportion of the population struggled to survive with no social safety net—doubtless contributed to the emergence of a courtier regime and reinforced favours and corruption.

Disapproval of Yeltsin's Policies

Boris Yeltsin was highly unpopular in the run-up to the December 1995 legislative elections, ahead of the presidential election of June 1996. At this point, there seemed to be a very real possibility of a victory for the Communist forces, which would have marked a backward step for economic reform, but would also have been the first experience of a peaceful changeover in Russia.

In a difficult climate, universal suffrage was maintained. The Russians voted and expressed their preferences, massively rejecting the existing regime. It is important to analyze the outcome of the legislative elections of 17 December 1995 in greater depth, since, with hindsight, it proved to be the last relatively non-corrupt federal vote. The electoral geography and sociology of this vote offer an important insight into Russia's political and social situation. The presidential election of 1996, a few months later, and all the following polls gradually deteriorated in quality, impartiality and integrity.[18]

The 1995 State Duma elections were the eighth polls calling the entire Russian electorate to the ballot box since 1989 (legislative, presidential, local and regional elections and referenda). It was a major democratic obligation which until now the presidential power and the ruling elites seemed not to have been able to avoid. As they had done in the autumn of 1993, the authorities allowed doubt to be cast over the holding of the December 1995 elections. They did take place, and in acceptable conditions, with the exception of course of the sham election in war-torn Chechnya. The electorate did not shun the ballot box, and the average turnout was 63 per cent. A State Duma was elected in which nearly half the deputies were Communists or had Communist affinities, and nearly a quarter were nationalists, all critical of Yeltsin's regime.

The election of 17 December 1995 was complex. Half of the 450 deputies were elected by proportional representation, through federal lists of electoral associations and blocs, the other half by district, through a single-mandate via the system of relative majority. With the list system, 43 parties or blocs were vying for votes. Four groups exceeded the 5 per cent threshold which enabled the list to gain seats in the Duma: the Communist Party with 22.3 per cent, Vladimir Zhirinovsky's 'liberal democratic' party (LDPR) with 11.18 per cent, Chernomyrdin's Our Home Is Russia bloc with 10.13 per cent and Grigory Yavlinsky's reformist Yabloko party with 6.89 per cent. These percentages, obtained in relation to the voters and not from the number of valid votes, enable us to state that only half the votes simply translated into seats in the Duma. If we count the valid votes, the first four lists together obtained a total of 225 seats with less than half the votes. In the single-mandate system, the Communists obtained some 50 seats in addition to the 100 seats won through proportional representation. A second Communist group was listed by the Duma on 16 January 1996, Power of the People, with 37 deputies. Adding the Agrarian Party and a few pro-Communist 'independent' elected deputies, the Communist family occupied half the Chamber.

Communists and Agrarians were much more successful under the single-mandate system as their candidates were generally 'well-known figures', or rather local apparatchiks: provincial governors, former Soviet era regional Party secretaries, mayors of big cities, and bosses of large companies. A socio-professional analysis of the new members of parliament shows that 154 of them represented the various industrial sectors and 30 were 'activists' in social organizations.[19] The democrats were completely routed. Yegor Gaydar's Democratic Choice of Russia party, which in 1993 was the 'party of power', supported by Boris Yeltsin,[20] and had obtained 15 per cent of the votes at the time, only achieved 3.9 per cent in 1995. Apart from Grigory Yavlinsky's parliamentary group, with 46 deputies, the 'democrats' or 'reformers' were few. They included Sergey Kovalev, the renowned defender of human rights.

The Our Home Is Russia parliamentary group counted 55 deputies under the leadership of Sergey Belayev. While it presented itself as the only 'presidential party', it did not win many seats under the single-mandate system. The support of central government did not work in the candidates' favour. Being well established in the regions and having local connections carried more weight, showing that Communist solidarity had maintained or won back its base.

The results were all the more disastrous for the existing government if the vote is analyzed by region. The spheres of protest were either confirmed or else had grown compared with the elections of December 1993. In 1993, a large part of central Russia, to the south and west of Moscow, in particular the Black Earth regions, had voted massively for the Communist Party. The surprise was the size of the Zhirinovsky vote, unforeseen by the pollsters, which combined with the Communist vote in these regions to reject the existing government. The LDPR surpassed the national average of 22.79 per cent in the industrial regions of western Siberia, in part of the Far East and in some provinces north of Moscow. In December 1995, the Zhirinovsky vote held in all of these regions, although with lower percentages, but extended to almost the entire north of Russia. In some sparsely populated regions rich in natural resources, such as the Komi and Mari-El republics and the region of Khanty-Mansy, the high number of votes obtained by Zhirinovsky (respectively 18.8 per cent, 21.9 per cent and 15.7 per cent) can be explained by disappointed expectations in relation to the bitter power struggle between the energy sector giants and the central authorities.

The Communist Party prevailed in more than half of the regions and republics that made up the Russian Federation. It won west Siberia and south Siberia. It strengthened its positions in the so-called 'European' Russia of the north Caucasus as far as Pskov in the north, Smolensk in the west and Samara and the Bashkiria in the east.[21]

Both the Communist and the Agrarian votes seriously undermined the more 'legitimist' Russia, the Russia which, in the referendum of April 1993, had clearly affirmed its trust in Yeltsin and in reform. The only list representing the executive power, Our Home Is Russia, won in only two areas: the Kabardino-Balkaria Republic in the North Caucasus and the district of Yamalo-Nenets in north-west Siberia, with 34.2 per cent and 23.5 per cent of the vote under the list system. Elsewhere, the bloc supported by the Prime Minister, Viktor Chernomyrdin, only surpassed its national average of 10.13 per cent in ten provinces, including the cities of Moscow (19.4 per cent) and Saint Petersburg (12.9 per cent). The two big cities with federal status remained islands of reformism in a Russia that was increasingly hostile to the changes introduced since the Gorbachev years. Yavlinsky and Gaydar's parties each obtained around 15 per cent.

The fact that Our Home Is Russia did slightly better in some republics should not be interpreted as the non-Russian populations' support for the government's policy. On the contrary, by and large these votes came from Russians living in urban areas. In the majority of the Federation's national republics and autonomous districts, the territory's titular nationality was a minority and Russians sometimes made up the biggest community. And so there was no typical electoral behaviour in these territories bearing the name of a non-Russian people. The diverse populations, cultures, geographical locations and economic potential explain the voting pattern in each republic or district. By contrast, in a federal presidential election, these territories can behave similarly to the way they behaved in the referendum on the Constitution in December 1993: a high proportion of abstentions and/or a vote that is hostile to the central candidates, seen as too centralizing.

Over nearly the entire territory, the voters unequivocally penalized the men who had been in power since the major upheavals of 1991–1992. Apart from the Prime Minister's bloc, the three other parties that surpassed the 5 per cent threshold were headed by figures who had not had any governmental responsibilities since 1991 (Gennady Ziuganov for the Communist Party and Grigory Yavlinsky for the Yabloko reform movement) or who had never held any (Vladimir Zhirinovsky for the LDPR, the nationalist extremist party). These three lists won 40 per cent of the votes. If we add all the votes for small parties or groups that remained below 5 per cent but expressed an equally strong rejection of the existing government, the vote was overwhelmingly a protest vote. The voters did not seek to vote tactically. Nearly all the parties in the ring enabled the electorate to express a message of no confidence in the Kremlin, but the choice was sufficiently broad for voters not merely to protest but also to express their political preferences. Nearly 3 per cent of the electorate however chose to tick the 44th box 'against all' rather than give their vote to one of the 43 lists.[22]

Between 1993 and 1995, the Russians showed considerable consistency in rejecting the regime. The combined votes for the CP and for

Zhirinovsky, both in December 1995 and in December 1993, gave a total of around a third of the votes through the list system. There was a reversal of the number of votes obtained by the two parties, in favour of the CP. As for the so-called 'democratic' forces, they were already losing ground in 1993, but the drop was so remarkable in the December 1995 elections that only Grigory Yavlinsky could hope to play a political role within the new Duma and in the presidential campaign of 1996. In voting for the Communist and nationalist opposition parties, the Russians were protesting against the post-Soviet Yeltsin years.

The Communist Revival and the Protest Vote

The election of 17 December 1995 was dominated by the Communists in several ways. Not only did they win the list system ballot with 22.3 per cent of the votes, obtaining a total of 157 of the 450 seats in the Duma, including the deputies elected under the single-mandate system, but they were also in charge of the organization and conducting of the voting. And effectively, more so than in 1993, it was only possible to organize the election at short notice (a few weeks) with the assistance of those in charge of the polling stations and 'activists' in each locality. Overall, these men and women who devoted themselves to the election were loyal to the Soviet system; they had already been responsible for organizing elections in Communist USSR, and then under Gorbachev. They had the expertise. The Communist Party dispatched to each polling station an official observer who spent the day monitoring the voting, but there was no one from the other political parties.[23]

There are several reasons for the strength of the Communist vote nearly five years after the demise of the USSR, the chief one being the feeling of depression and helplessness which had overcome the whole of Russia since 1992. A vast majority of the population declared in the surveys that their standard of living had deteriorated.[24] Whether this decline was real or not, the main thing is that there was a perception that living standards had declined.[25] Even more significant was the increased feeling of material insecurity. People were afraid of what the future held in store; they clung to the vestiges of the Soviet system of assisted jobs, housing and public services. They rebelled against the impoverishment of the masses while 'a small minority was getting rich fast'. The issue of corruption was in fact widely invoked during the campaign, with most parties promising to eradicate the misappropriation of public funds and financial crime.

Through its powerlessness, the Yeltsin system distorted the letter and the intention of the Constitution and perverted one of the pillars of the transformation to democracy: the separation of powers and control over the executive. The Yeltsin government was perceived as more predatory than the pre-1991 Communist regime. If the changes of 1991 did not bring increased well-being and hope for the future, then why maintain the Yeltsin team in government?

As time passed, the events of 1991 aroused more feelings of hostility amongst the Russians who were both disappointed and impoverished. For the citizen who voted for the Communist groupings, the fragmentation of the USSR and the end of the Soviet system were seen as definitive breaks. Those who had set these ruptures in motion and won power stood accused. While the President and the Prime Minister called for 'stability' by maintaining the political status quo and continuing with the 'reforms', the voters replied: 'Stability won't come from you, you're the ones who disrupted everything; stability comes from security, the familiar, the predictable'. They sought to return to 'traditional values', as is clear from the opinion polls following the 17 December 1995 ballot. In his analysis of the survey, sociologist Yuri Levada, director of the VTsIOM institute, gives a profile of Communist Party voters. They are older and less well educated than average, live either in rural areas or a big city (other than Moscow), find life tough (39 per cent of respondents said that it was no longer bearable, 51 per cent that it was still bearable) and would be in favour of a return to socialism (58 per cent versus 22 per cent, 20 per cent 'don't knows').[26] The Zhirinovsky electorate was younger and slightly better educated than those who voted Communist, preponderantly male (twice as many men as women), lived mainly in medium-sized cities and comprised nearly 50 per cent manual workers. Like the Communist voters, they found life tough (90 per cent), with 39 per cent stating that it was no longer bearable.[27] On the other hand, only a third of Zhirinovsky voters supported the idea of a return to socialism. It is worth noting that a quarter of voters for the Yabloko party, headed by the reformer economist Yavlinsky, were also in favour of a return to socialism. The question is what this term meant to each person. In Russia, the word referred to aspects of the Soviet experience.

The loss of the Soviet republics does not appear to have been such a decisive factor as economic and social dissatisfaction in the Communist choice. Nearly all the parties had advocated reinforcing ties with the former republics. Some, like the Our Home Is Russia party, took a moderate, pragmatic stance; while others, like the CP and Yabloko, were more vehement, with the nationalists violently in favour, going as far as the excesses of Zhirinovsky, who was ready to conquer a large part of the European continent and Russia's southern neighbours.

It is just as hard to evaluate the impact of the war in Chechnya on the legislative elections of December 1995. Did the CP win votes as a result of its criticism of the war, and did Zhirinovsky suffer from his unconditional support for the crushing of the Chechens? The available poll findings do not provide an answer.

The disaffection with Yeltsin's policies and opposition to the changes that had come about since the Gorbachev years were indisputably the main reasons for the protest vote and for the Communists' breakthrough. However, it should also be noted that the existing government did everything within its power to encourage the vote against. There was virtually no alternative to the opposition vote, since it was not possible to vote for the existing President. There was no 'Yeltsin' party. Several times Boris Yeltsin ruled out the possibility of establishing his own party. Neither did he fully endorse his Prime Minister, Chernomyrdin, when the latter had to launch his electoral bloc within the space of just a few months.

And so only a vote for this list enabled voters to express direct support for the executive power. However, this organization was an artificial representation of the men and the networks governing Russia. It therefore had no chance of winning over the electorate in a country plunged into turmoil and suspicion by the depth of the economic and social crisis. The young deputy Vladimir Ryzhkov had agreed to manage Chernomyrdin's campaign in Moscow. He tried to believe in it and hoped that the backlash against Soviet Communism was still powerful enough in Russia to avoid a return to the Communist Party. But he did not conceal his fear that there would be a drop in the pro-Yeltsin 'legitimist' vote. The liberal reforms were rejected by the majority.[28]

Vladimir Ryzhkov reminded me much later, during one of our conversations in December 2007, that his role in the 'ruling party' in 1995 had enabled him to become well acquainted with a figure at the time unknown to the general public. One of the vice-governors of Saint Petersburg had been tasked, by the Governor Anatoly Sobchak, to manage Our Home Is Russia's campaign in Saint Petersburg. This man was Vladimir Putin. Since Putin has governed Russia as an autocrat, the two men have been diametrically opposed to each other. 'I am one of Putin's most hated enemies, because I knew him well and I can see through his lies'.[29]

In 1995, for the first time, the integrity of the elections was seriously challenged. It took ten days for the central electoral commission to announce the definitive percentages obtained by each of the 43 vying lists. Opinions are divided as to the extent of the fraud and the number of errors. According to an expert in electoral fraud Alexander Sobyanin, there was allegedly fraud in favour of the Communist Party, since he observed a correlation in some constituencies between a high Communist vote and a much higher turnout than average.[30] Sobyanin considers that overall the poll of 17 December was more or less above board. He is much more critical of the gubernatorial and mayoral elections that took place on the same day.

The Temptation to Postpone the Elections

The Kremlin's new mistrust of the electorate's vote resulted in the non-re-election of members of parliament's upper house. The members of the Council of the Federation had been elected through direct universal suffrage on 12 December 1993, exceptionally for two years, like the Duma. President Yeltsin's decision to change the way the upper house was formed fuelled a heated legal and political controversy throughout 1995. Effectively, the Constitution adopted on 12 December 1993 as a result of a referendum, stipulated that the Council of the Federation was 'formed' without specifying whether this 'formation' was through direct election or not. The president decided in favour of a council comprising two representatives from each 'subject' of the Federation, i.e. each of the republics, regions, districts and territories that made up Russia. One was to be the president of the legislative authority, the other the head of the regional executive (president of a republic or regional governor). Since many governors had been appointed rather than elected, there were provisions for all governors to be elected by the end of 1996. This effectively took place. Many Russian experts consider that because it is non-elected and has limited powers, the Council is no longer really a parliamentary authority.

President Yeltsin's attitude to the sovereignty of the people was that of a ruler who had lost his popularity. His entourage wanted him to 'freeze' the electoral process, since the election would contribute to the 'destabilization' of political and social life. On 11 January, 1996 Yeltsin announced that he might postpone all elections of local representative authorities until the presidential election scheduled for 16 June.[31] Following the poll of 17 December 1995, a clear refutation of his presidency, he stated that the results did not in any way call the executive power into question and that the Constitution did not require him to appoint a new prime minister. He did however give in to pressure from the Communists and nationalists, and in January parted company from two deputy prime ministers, Sergey Shakhrai and Anatoly Chubais, the driving force behind privatization, and from his Foreign Minister, Andrei Kozyrev, whom he had always disliked.

Boris Yeltsin's popularity was at its lowest in January 1996, with fewer than 10 per cent of people questioned expressing confidence in their president. The violence used against the Chechens, the poor image of his entourage and the lack of consistency between his economic and social policies were heavily criticized. It was not in the interests of the Communist Party, boosted by its success in the legislative elections, to form an alliance with Boris Yeltsin. Quite the opposite: distinguishing itself from the current government was a winning card. Of course a presidential election is by nature different from a legislative election as voters choose one man, the nation's representative, whose personality and image are as important as his agenda and political base. Russia lacked charismatic personalities and Boris Yeltsin was no longer the 1991 hero and 'saviour of Russia'.

In the spring of 1996, all the political and economic movers and shakers were preoccupied with the question of Yeltsin's re-election. Alexander Korzhakov, a close adviser to the President, launched an operation to try to postpone the election. The war in Chechnya could have been used as an excuse to declare a state of emergency.

The Re-election of Yeltsin and the 'Oligarchs'

At the beginning of 1996, Yeltsin's team and the most powerful business leaders had to reach agreement on the strategic issue of whether or not a change in head of state was required.

The incumbent President was already ill, unpopular and unreliable, and the possibility of rotation in office was emerging. But change would be in favour of the Communist Party, which was ahead in the polls and bolstered by its performance in the legislative elections. For all the men who were part of the Yeltsin galaxy and those who had built financial empires thanks to the reforms and privatizations, the prospect of seeing Gennady Zyuganov in the Kremlin was unbearable. It was at this point that the notion of 'oligarchs' appeared. Seven leading figures decided to support the attempts of 'the Family'—as Yeltsin's entourage was called—to get the hero of 1991 re-elected, despite his lack of popularity among ordinary Russians. They invested a great deal of money and energy in the campaign, and all their media rallied to the cause. The June-July 1996 election was the first openly corrupt post-Communist election, with a biased campaign, 'electoral gifts', and blatant fraud.

In November 1996, some months after Yeltsin's re-election, Boris Berezovsky, the financier and *éminence grise* of the Kremlin,[32] gave an interview to the *Financial Times*. He revealed that seven bankers who controlled 'half the Russian economy' had ensured that the president went on to serve a second term. At the time, there was talk of *semibankirshchina* ('the government of the seven bankers'), echoing the *semiboyarshchina* of the Time of Troubles at the beginning of the seventeenth century, when the country's fate was in the hands of seven boyars.[33] In his memoirs, Boris Yeltsin reveals the inside story:

During the elections, financial capital turned into political capital. The banks tried to influence the government unabashedly and directly. They tried to run the country behind the backs of the politicians. [...] They came to defend not Yeltsin but themselves. [...] big money had entered into the political arena. It was this 'political money' that constituted a serious threat to Russia's development.[34]

These men, and some others, benefited hugely from the system of privatization based on 'loans against shares', which enabled them to buy entire industries at rock-bottom prices, in particular a section of the raw materials extraction sector. Members of the government and the presidential administration also profited from the lucrative business of divvying up the national patrimony. Anatoly Chubais is a case in point. When he was Minister for Privatizations, then Deputy Prime Minister, he was directly involved in the privatization of Norilsk Nickel in 1994 at a ridiculous price, as well as other property transfers. Until the summer of 2008, Chubais remained one of the strong men of the Russian economy as he was head of the national electricity company, EES. Several correspondents from leading Western newspapers in Moscow have written books on the 'oligarchs' of the 1990s, and also on those of the 2000s.[35] The Putin regime has smashed several financial, industrial and oil giants to replace them with others who are loyal to the Kremlin. The common theme in all these analyses is the very close connection between financial and political interests, with the 'oligarchs' and the president's men equally to blame for Russia's slide towards an increasingly oligopolistic cronyist autocracy.

Maintaining Boris Yeltsin in power required all the energy of the entrepreneurs and men of the Kremlin in the spring of 1996. The incumbent President was only elected in the second round, on 3 July 1996, with 40 million votes, against 29 million for his Communist rival, and 4 million for the third virtual contender, the 'against all' candidate. In the first round, on 16 June, he obtained only 35 per cent of votes, compared with 32 per cent for Ziuganov, 14.5 per cent for General Lebed, 7.3 per cent for the economist Grigory Yavlinsky and 5.7 per cent for the far right leader Zhirinovsky. The five other candidates together obtained only 2 per cent of the votes. One of the five at the end of the list was Mikhail Gorbachev... with 0.5 per cent of the votes! The former General Secretary of the CPSU had wanted, for the first time, to present himself before the post-Soviet electorate, which he had not dared to do in 1990–1991, allowing himself at the time to be outflanked by the popularity and legitimacy of Boris Yeltsin, elected first president of the Russian Republic in June 1991. This humiliating defeat for the last president of the USSR showed the Russians' widespread hostility towards the man who, in their eyes, had destroyed but failed to rebuild.

The results of the first round permit a more detailed analysis of the electoral geography than those of the second, and highlight the extent of the protest vote and the shrinking of legitimist Russia that emerged from the referendum of April 1993.[36] There was a marked north-south divide. The objectors retained a strong grip on the small and medium-sized towns and the rural cantons in the Federation's south and south-western provinces. Support for legitimist Russia prevailed in the big cities and the northern and eastern regions, which were less rural and had been harder hit by de-industrialization. Some regions were divided between the two camps, like the province of Nizhni-Novgorod, where the results were closer to the national average. 'The balance of power is fifty-fifty, we are a good example of the town-country divide, the city of Nizhni is more pro-Yeltsin than our rural cantons', explained Viacheslav Bolyak, chief administrator of a canton, at the time.[37]

The battle was far from being won in the first round, and the ruling clans were seriously afraid. Exhausted by three months' campaigning,

Yeltsin vanished from public life. Nearly all the media, especially the most influential, the television channels, openly supported the incumbent President. The dirty tricks against the Communists overstepped the boundaries of campaign tactics. These abuses were more pronounced during the following electoral cycle, in 1999–2000, with the exertion of physical pressure and legal threats against Kremlin rivals. By 1996 the trend was unmistakable, and few public figures dared condemn it openly, for fear of being labelled 'pro-Soviet' and 'anti-reformist'. The political battle was artificially maintained as a clash between reform and reactionary forces. And yet, citizens had very little trust in Boris Yeltsin. From the polls it was apparent that the 40 million people who, according to the official results, supposedly voted for the ailing resident did not equal 40 million supporters of the regime; far from it.

Russians were urged not to vote for a 'break', a return to the past, and above all for the unpredictability of a change of leadership. This threat proved fairly effective.

There were other factors. Yeltsin had to commit to ending the unpopular war in Chechnya. He kept his campaign promise thanks to Alexander Lebed. This former general and the Chechen leader Aslan Maskhadov signed a ceasefire in August 1996, and the Russian troops withdrew in the following months.

Furthermore, the oligarchs' money oiled the wheels, making it possible to pay salaries and pensions. And finally, fraud had reached worrying proportions in some constituencies. In Daghestan, for example, Zyuganov obtained 66 per cent in the first round and only 42 per cent in the second, whereas Yeltsin received 26 per cent in the first and 54 per cent in the second round! It was not possible to hold elections in occupied, war-ravaged Chechnya, but results were announced there. Smaller-scale fraud was observed in most polling stations, but sometimes in favour of the Communists. In Serpukhov, an industrial city in the south of the Moscow region, I noted on 3 July 1996 that the CP monitors lacked interest and gave the impression that agreement concerning the results for the local administration had been reached in advance.[38]

During the initial post-Soviet years, profound social and geographical fault lines had appeared. Suspicion and even hostility towards the government were the result of growing inequalities, corruption and the increased wealth of the elites, and the lack of transparency of state policies. Boris Yeltsin's re-election did not resolve the major problems threatening the whole of Russian society and the economy. A series of crises led to the collapse of the political regime and the national economy in 1998–1999.

Downward Spiral

The spring of 1998 was a turbulent time for Moscow's political and financial elites. On 23 March, Boris Yeltsin dismissed his government and his Prime Minister. After a month of confrontation with the opposition in the Duma, he obtained the deputies' endorsement of his nominee for head of the government, Sergey Kiriyenko, after threatening to dissolve parliament. At the end of May, the rouble entered a stormy period. International aid helped stave off devaluation for a while; however, it did not allay the financial and monetary crisis. Finally, in June, the troubles in Kosovo once again highlighted the ambiguity of Russia, which was against intervention, but had barely any means of exerting pressure on Serbia and was not keen to be seen as an ally of Slobodan Milošević. The three crises—political, financial and international—underscored the institutions' failures and the shortcomings of a regime lacking democracy and good governance, with decisions being taken surrounded by confusion, devoid of transparency, while society looked on unable to grasp what was happening.

Russia then entered into a period of preparations for the parliamentary elections of late 1999 and for the presidential elections scheduled for June 2000. There was still uncertainty as to the legality of a third term for Boris Yeltsin[39] in the event that his health, which had been extremely precarious over the last three years, would allow him to envisage such an option.

Viktor Chernomyrdin had been Prime Minister since December 1992. There had been no major tensions in his relations with Boris Yeltsin, at least publicly, and Russian and foreign observers are agreed in praising the Prime Minister's loyalty towards the President. However, the winter of 1997–1998 witnessed some changes within the close-knit ruling elite.

The First Deputy Prime Minister, Anatoly Chubais, was demoted in October following a corruption scandal. The royalties he is alleged to have wrongfully received for an unpublished book were probably only an excuse to relieve him of the treasury portfolio. The real issue was the privatization of shares in major Russian companies where a financial group, Oneximbank, had received preferential treatment from the government at the expense of others, in particular the businessman and media tycoon Boris Berezovsky.

Viktor Chernomyrdin appeared to emerge the winner of this complicated and confusing saga, and made no secret of his satisfaction at consolidating his position as government leader, over the heads of the younger ministers Anatoly Chubais and Boris Nemtsov. He raised his media profile, took a stance on key state issues more frequently and seemed to be quietly preparing to succeed Boris Yeltsin when the time came.

These political and financial events were unfurling as the Russian President was incapacitated by a new bout of illness, with fairly long periods of absence from the Kremlin. Boris Yeltsin was clearly concerned about the positions some politicians occupied during his absence, particularly his Prime Minister whose attitude was no longer that of the number two in the shadow of the leader. That was probably the main reason for Yeltsin's snap decision to dismiss Chernomyrdin and his government. Yeltsin was ailing, weak, increasingly out of touch with what was happening on the ground, and more and more dependent on his inner circle. He wanted to remind everyone that he was there, that he was in charge and that the contest for a successor was not open yet.

And so, without warning, and catching both those concerned and the most assiduous observers of the Moscow microcosm unawares, Boris Yeltsin dismissed his government to free himself from some of the heavyweights, like Chernomyrdin. And he did so in the most extraordinary manner, apparently without having entirely understood the Constitution. He signed two decrees on 23 March and appointed himself interim Prime Minister. Some hours later, having been informed that the Constitution prohibited such a procedure, he appointed Sergei Kiriyenko, the young Energy Minister, unknown to the general public, as interim Prime Minister. For several days he remained secretive as to whom he would present as Prime Minister for the approval of the State Duma, parliament's lower house. He eventually named Kiriyenko. That was the beginning of a three-week stand-off between the president and the deputies.

The Constitution of December 1993 gave the president the right to dissolve the assembly. Article 111 stipulated that he could present a candidate for the post of prime minister before the deputies three times in succession. If the Duma rejected the president's choice for the third time, the president was duty-bound to dissolve the Assembly and appoint the new head of government by decree. Legislative elections must be held within three months. However, the new Duma was not permitted to express an opinion on the appointment of the prime minister.

In this test of strength Boris Yeltsin started out with a major advantage, since the threat of dissolution would dissuade the deputies from persisting. As the vote was secret, the party whips were not involved and many deputies preferred to save their seats, with the associated power and privileges. This disgraceful episode shows to what extent the procedure for the legislative assembly approving the prime minister was warped. By granting the president extensive powers, the present Constitution allows the use of the threat of dissolution as a sword of Damocles to force deputies to bow to the president's wishes at the last moment. The censure of parliament's freedom to express an honest opinion regarding the government has serious implications.

Because of his total dependence on the head of state, the role of prime minister is reduced to that of a steward, and the government is confined to administrative functions. Note that from his appointment at the end of 1992 to his resignation in March 1998, the former Prime Minister, Viktor Chernomyrdin, never represented a majority in the Duma. On the contrary, his parliamentary group Our Home Is Russia, formed in 1995, was always very much a minority, with a few tens of seats in an Assembly of 450 elected deputies.

One conclusion is obvious. The prime minister is not the leader of the majority, nor is his appointment the result of a consensus. It is rather the choice, by default, of a president who does not want a heavyweight politician at his side. The government as an institution was weakened as a result of this episode. The Duma had no say in the composition of the government. The ministers were technocrats rather than politicians. During the closing period of Boris Yeltsin's reign, Russian commentators pointed out ironically that the president signed numerous decrees every day, but the only ones that were applied were those in which he thanked his government.

In the 2000s, Vladimir Putin's governments would operate like a civil service, of no political stripe and with no accountability to the Duma. In 2008, Putin overturned the edifice provided for by the Constitution, without revising the Constitution, and made the presidency of the Council of Ministers the principal institution (see Chapter 7).

The Financial Crash

In 1998, the political institutions—the parliament, government, political parties, trade unions and associations—were seriously undermined by the political and economic crisis. In such a climate, the men in whose hands the country's wealth was concentrated felt as if they held the reins of power. These were the financiers, the heads of the oil and gas companies and all those who had a lucrative guaranteed income from the exploitation and sale of raw materials, the Russian economy's main resources. Their money was a political weapon in the upcoming electoral battles. No candidate could hope to win without extensive media coverage, which was very costly, or without 'campaign gifts'. All those seeking power needed the support of the financiers and major conglomerates. The political parties were almost non-existent, with the exception of the Communist Party which was better organized in the provinces, but also needed funding. The financial groups tended to support several potential candidates to avoid putting all their eggs in one basket.

Russia's financial crisis was a source of concern in business circles. There were huge losses on the stock exchange and a crash would be damaging to everyone. It was probably this uncertainty that prompted the company bosses to pull together and work with the new government to avert devaluation in May-June 1998. However, the economic and financial assets continued to remain concentrated largely in the hands of the major groups, and the government was unable to confront them head-on.

Overall, the Russians reacted to the events of the spring of 1998 with indifference and scepticism. The polls showed that they held a deep-rooted suspicion of politicians and institutions. They saw Yeltsin as a sick man, still able to bang his fist on the table but at the mercy of his entourage and the dictates of the oligarchs. They thought that power was slipping through the hands of the institutions and that the ordinary people were the losers in this clan war between politicians and financiers, in Moscow and in the provinces alike.[40]

The President and the parliament found it preferable to agree on the promotion of some senior officials who admitted to having no clear strategy for dealing with the crisis, rather than to place their fate in the hands of the voters. No one was keen to consult society in the middle of the economic storm; no one was keen to shoulder the blame for the economic disaster and social chaos. Russia was paying a high price for the derailment of an entire political system. Disenchanted and resigned, the Russian people suffered the reversals of the rulers in Moscow, whom they saw as a team of neo-Gorbachevian *apparatchik*s who had served under all the regimes since Brezhnev.

In August 1998, the Russian state was bankrupt. The currency collapsed, the state coffers were empty. The financial crash destroyed the banking system, and the government was unable to meet its financial obligations. Wages and pensions had not been paid on time for years; they were quite simply suspended. Russia was in a state of collapse: financial, political and moral collapse. The illusion of the 'democratic transition to the market economy' crumbled within a few weeks, swept away by the monetary crisis and the power vacuum that was carefully maintained by an exhausted president.

The Leaders' Responsibility

The monetary and financial collapse cannot be blamed solely on the choice of inappropriate 'liberal' or 'monetarist' strategies. Admittedly, the International Monetary Fund and the Western governments encouraged policies that failed. Were these policies the cause of the disaster, or were they simply unable to prevent the structural crisis of an economy that was unreformable? There are various different interpretations of what went wrong, and there is a great deal of controversy both internally and in the countries that supported and invested in Russia. The aim here is not to enter into this debate, but to evoke the fundamental problem which neither the Russians nor Russia's foreign partners addressed: the failure of the state, the government's inability to fulfil its duty to society. This is the key issue for Russia's short- and long-term future.

In 1991–1992, the hope was to see Russia achieve a peaceful and progressive transition towards democracy and a market economy, with increasingly active participation in global trade. It was thought that this was possible but would probably be slower than in Central Europe, for historical reasons (there was a much greater legacy of authoritarianism and weak government) and because of Russia's size. It was assumed then that the state was being rebuilt on a sound footing, the rule of law, and that the economy was becoming competitive thanks to the introduction of private property and the privatization of industry. The state therefore would no longer need to administer the economy and redistribute wealth.

The reality proved a great deal more complex and the absence of fiscal policies and public management was increasingly being felt. Paradoxically, the bureaucratic state, a legacy from the Soviet era, held up well and adapted relatively easily to new forms of entrepreneurship and local management. The administrations, both in Moscow and in the provinces, maintained close ties with company bosses, to sustain cronyist regimes and control wealth (chiefly raw materials). The influence of the administrations combined with that of the financiers and major producers averted chaos after 1991 but hampered the building of a liberal, efficient and transparent state. The state's inability to collect taxes shows how weak it was.

It is all too easy to cite the factors that allegedly 'stood in the way of reform'—from the disgruntled ordinary families worrying about day-to-day matters to the international mafias reportedly carving up Russia—in order to absolve the leaders from responsibility for the failure. To some extent, the blame should be shouldered by all those who occupied important positions in the government and the administration, the elected—head of state, deputies, regional governors, mayors of large towns—and those who remained in post after the financial and political cyclone of the summer of 1998. But none of them publicly or openly acknowledged their past role; as if it were enough, under cover of a change of government, to wipe the slate clean and redistribute the roles. The 'Yeltsin system' was a personalized and patriarchal means of exercising authority in a society torn between a new unscrupulous 'vanguard capitalism', bureaucracies with a stranglehold, and a population which was hostage to both.

The changes of government revealed the President's impotence. Twice, in March and in August 1998, Boris Yeltsin believed he could beat the economic crisis and gain a fresh impetus by summarily dismissing his prime minister. Twice, the outcome was catastrophic. The President only added to the uncertainty and worried people with his unpredictability. Teams reshuffled in a crisis have neither the legitimacy nor the authority to enforce emergency measures.[41] Yevgeny Primakov's government, appointed in September 1998, started out with a number of disadvantages and very limited room for manoeuvre.

Yevgeny Primakov, Foreign Affairs Minister since 1996, expert on the Middle East, carved out a glittering career in diplomacy and intelligence during the Soviet era, crowned by being appointed director of the Institute of World Economy and International Relations in Moscow. He was brought into the Kremlin by Gorbachev in 1989 and then won the trust of Boris Yeltsin, who made him head of the Russian Foreign Intelligence Service (SVR) from December 1991 until 1996. Primakov was considered acceptable by nearly all the political groups, since he personally did not represent any one tendency, belonged to no party and did not claim to have any presidential ambitions. He gave the impression of a faithful servant of the authorities, Soviet and then Russian. He was well acquainted with bureaucracy's mysterious ways and an old hand at diplomatic relations and the intelligence services, but he had never been in charge of economic policy. He was neither a reformer nor a Communist.

The crucial issue for the bankers and businessmen, the producers of raw materials and the bosses of major corporations who had lost a great deal in the economic turmoil of summer 1998, was for the institutional vacuum in Moscow to be filled to prevent the country from being dragged into a spiral of destruction and mistrust. The prime minister's political allegiance mattered little as his margin for manoeuvre would be so restricted, given the international constraints (in particular, donors such as the IMF) and the constraints of a social policy (the issue of liquid assets to pay wages) put in place to prevent social unrest.

One of the assets that the new team intended to defend was national industry. The new government's mantras were: encourage Russian production, pay wages and pensions, bolster the state. Save the state, in other words; but how, with what money, with what trust?

Some analysts offer a more benevolent interpretation of Primakov's few months in government and say they are convinced that the possibility of state reform of the country's industry would have put the system back on its feet. My view is that during these troubled years the Russian economy was no longer a system but a patchwork of fragmented sectors, run by oligarchic groups, along cronyist and opaque lines, all connected in one way or another to the Kremlin and to the central and regional administrations. The choice was now no longer so much between a liberal or a statist policy, but between a cronyist system and a competitive economy that accepted the rule of law.

This drawn-out end-of-an-era exacerbated the shortcomings of the political and economic system, as the financial crisis of August 1998 brutally revealed. Bureaucratic negligence, fiscal chaos and budgetary unpredictability prompted each power-wielder to deal with matters in their own way. The lack of a clear division of areas of responsibility between the federal, regional and local authorities left the field open for the local administrators. The provincial governors and the presidents of the republics developed forms of autonomous regimes more as a reaction to the central government's failure to take control than as part of a local bid for independence.

In many impoverished regions, the drop in federal subsidies was initially experienced as an economic and social disaster. At the same time, the climate was ripe for the rise of 'oligarchs'—those finance magnates, media tycoons and owners of energy and mining companies—who determined the destiny of public finance and consequently that of the government.

During this long Yeltsin reprieve, the political forces lost their traditional function of criticizing, proposing and mobilizing. The decline of the political parties and movements was linked to the weakening of public institutions. Since decisions were taken outside official channels and often outside the public sphere—as secret negotiations between the state and financial groups were outside institutional control—and politicians could only block but not drive governmental action, it was less and less productive to invest in political action through the intervention of the parties, trade unions and associations. As for the legal system, it remained the Cinderella of this post-Communist system and regularly revealed its impotence and subordination to the administrations, at both federal and local level.[42] As the Russian political analyst Lilia Shevtsova points out, 'Russia missed what Ralph Dahrendorf has called 'the hour of the lawyer' in failing to form the basis of a liberal constitutionalism'.[43] The rule of law was not being developed.

In the summer of 1999, when the electoral year began—legislative elections in December and the presidential election originally planned for June 2000—the political landscape had disintegrated, lacking in political figures and in ideas, and abandoned by Russia's citizens. The challenge for the political and business leaders was to oust Boris Yeltsin without jeopardizing the assets that had been built up. Maintaining an ailing president in post had allowed them to organize 'among themselves', with protection from above and arbitration in the shadowy area between the various political and financial networks and the countless administrations.

The issue was how to ensure the handover to a new president elect while avoiding a radical break. The legislative elections of 19 December 1999 were to prepare the ground for the presidential election. Yeltsin was persuaded by his entourage in August 1999 that now was the time to appoint a prime minister who would also be his successor, and therefore the leader of the Kremlin (the 'party of power', *partiya vlasti*) in the legislative elections. Vladimir Putin was appointed head of government on 9 August.

Yeltsin seemed to have accepted that this time frame dictated his inevitable departure from the Kremlin. So it made sense for him to choose his successor and attempt to impose him on the people. One of Boris Yeltsin's motivations was protecting his private interests and those of his associates. In actual fact, the chosen heir, the head of the FSB (federal security service, successor to the KGB), bowed to this condition. When Yeltsin announced his planned departure on 31 December 1999, Vladimir Putin immediately granted him immunity and protection by decree.

On becoming government leader, Vladimir Putin embarked on an obstacle course punctuated by the two polls, legislative and presidential. The first was to pave the way for the latter and guarantee its outcome. This meant gaining control as far as possible of the media, hindering the political campaign of his rivals and the political forces they led, convincing public opinion that the winner could be no other than the successor designated 'on high' and engineering the administrative logistics that would secure victory, in other words negotiating a winning margin for Putin with the local authorities and the electoral commissions. Resorting to political pressure and fraud were probably inevitable outcomes after the autumn of 1999, even if trust in the new Prime Minister rapidly peaked as a result of the start of a second war in Chechnya.

War Again

In the summer of 1999, the Yeltsin family and their entourage were mired in a financial scandal. Furthermore, tension was growing in the north Caucasus and there were clashes in Daghestan, bordering on Chechnya. Terrorist attacks, for which no one claimed responsibility, were immediately blamed on the Chechens, whereas some insiders accused the FSB of being behind the operation.[44] This was a convenient pretext for dragging the army into a new war, presented officially as a 'fight against terrorism'.

Since the humiliation of military and political defeat of the first war (1994–1996), the Russian leadership had not sought to progress negotiations on the status of the republic with the Chechen government, and the situation in Chechnya had deteriorated to such an extent that the tiniest provocation was enough to spark things off again. This new war in the Caucasus was a political gamble that was won, in the short term, by the Kremlin and Yeltsin's heir. It offered a poor, anxious and disoriented population an issue that united them in adversity. The material insecurity in their day-to-day lives was interwoven with the threat of random attacks, and Putin's hard-line speeches on restoring order in the Caucasus were given a favourable reception. After years of uncertainty, the Prime Minister's resolve and tough stance were assets, as attested by the high level of trust that Putin enjoyed.[45] His determination in the early months of the conflict unquestionably boosted his popularity by creating, in the public mind, the image of a man of order, a statesman with no qualms. The government clamped down on access to information on the war and swamped the media with 'anti-terrorist' and national-patriotic propaganda defending Russia's integrity and security. In such a climate, public opinion was not alienated by Vladimir Putin's KGB past. After all, as Russian commentators underscore, it was the *apparatchik*s who were in power; and those trained by the KGB were not necessarily the worst.

The war also enabled those who 'made' Putin to hastily construct a political persona presenting him as the 'saviour of the nation' and defender of state power, so as to marginalize the other forces in the battle for deputies' seats in December 1999. Later, during the winter, opinions changed. The war which, once again, was likely to be protracted and fruitless was no longer an advantage, and even threatened to become a handicap. It was used much less as an argument in the campaign for the presidential election in February and March 2000. This second Chechen war was another failure of Russian military and political strategy. It would take five years of destruction, fighting and corruption to break the Chechen resistance and impose Ramzan Kadyrov's horrendous regime. The conflict begun in September 1999 very soon became mired, and remained so for a long time. History was repeating itself with a disturbing exactness. Once again, bombings and military occupation resulted in an impasse. How can the repetition of such a huge tragedy within an interval of just a few years be explained?

The Russian sociologist Yuri Levada, director of the VTsIOM research centre, was disconcerted and horrified by the reactions of the Russian elites and society as a whole to this second horrendously brutal war. For this man who had been analyzing Russian opinion for more than ten years, the lack of public opposition to the war was a painful observation. He explained it by the lack of any real democratic instinct in his country. Whereas in 1994–1996 resorting to force still provoked condemnation, in 1999–2000 the public's critical faculty had disappeared. Even the intellectuals 'went with the flow'. Despite the intense propaganda, the Russians were aware that the war had become bogged down and wanted negotiations, a 'political solution' in their words, but they became resigned, and anti-Chechen feeling increased. For Levada, the gradual disappearance of democratic referents introduced under Gorbachev, making it possible to articulate criticism, was one of the reasons for Russian society's change of heart. The changes in people's outlook and behaviour had not had time to become rooted and would remain fragile, 'superficial' phenomena that were easy to manipulate. On the other hand, pointed out the sociologist,[46] if the new President Putin had decided to halt the war in Chechnya, society would just as readily have supported him! And they would easily have become reconciled to the idea of an independent Chechnya.

The Legislative Elections of 1999: Choosing Yeltsin's Successor

Boris Yeltsin never formed a party. Each time the electoral calendar required it, he left it to his henchmen to set up a 'bloc' or a 'movement' flying the presidential flag. In October 1999, the team tasked with preparing Putin's victory created the Edinstvo (Unity) movement led by a minister lacking in charisma, a firefighter by training.

Edinstvo was created in the purest bureaucratic mould. Most of the names on the list were unknown to the general public; they were mainly civil servants. In each province, the authorities were tasked with finding the candidates, giving them the resources and campaigning on their behalf. Edinstvo's real rival was the Otechestvo-Vsia Rossiya or OVR (Fatherland-All Russia) party, led by the mayor of Moscow, Yuri Luzhkov, and the former Prime Minister, Yevgeny Primakov. Both blocs effectively drew their votes from the same catchment area: those who did not want to vote Communist, those who wanted to vote tactically by ruling out the small, marginal lists, those who preferred to avoid any major political change by choosing rather a 'legitimist' movement close to the existing government, but those who also expected improved social protection, more security, less liberalism. The tendency to vote for the Kremlin's candidate proved a powerful asset for the re-election of Yeltsin in 1996 and for Putin in the December 1999 and March 2000 polls.

And so, despite its solid social base (around a quarter of the electorate), the Communist Party no longer played the part of enemy number one in a two-party contest, as it had done in the elections of 1995 and 1996. The Communists' attitude was striking in its obvious defeatism, from the legislative elections onwards. Their campaign was weak and they did not appear to be attempting to win over new voters, confining themselves merely to consolidating their achievements. They settled into the role of peaceful opposition, negotiating their votes with the government. And so in the autumn of 1999 the media unleashed their venom solely against Yuri Luzhkov and his movement. Every dirty trick in the book was permissible in order to crush the mayor of Moscow, who still nurtured presidential ambitions. The two leading television channels constituted the Kremlin's strategic weapons, as the majority of Russians chiefly watched these two channels. This campaign will certainly remain in the annals of the early history of free elections in Russia as being outrageously unfair.

For a movement that had not even existed a few weeks earlier, Edinstvo achieved a remarkable and suspicious number of votes on 19 December 1999, in the list votes:[47] 23.3 per cent of votes as against 24.3 per cent for the Communist Party, 13.3 per cent for Fatherland-All Russia, 8.5 per cent for the new Union of Right Forces (SPS) bloc, 6 per cent for Zhirinovsky's movement and 5.9 per cent for Yabloko.[48]

Those past years, the Duma had continually lost prestige and trust in the eyes of the population. Depending on the situation and the mood, it was seen either as an authority that obstructed government policy, or as a chamber for recording the government's decisions. The interviews conducted in the provinces confirm the lack of trust in the deputies, who were suspected of being more interested in perks and trips to Moscow or abroad than in defending the interests of their constituency.[49] There was doubt as to the very existence of an organized parliamentary opposition. Votes were negotiated, and, with a few rare exceptions, there was no voting whip within a parliamentary group.

Following the legislative elections of 19 December 1999, the kingmakers in the Kremlin had cause to celebrate the effectiveness of their methods. No political formation opposed the 'government party'. The only movement properly organized as a political party, the CP, opted for constructive opposition to parliament. It upheld the candidature of its leader, Gennady Ziuganov, for the presidency, but it was perfectly prepared not to win.

Putin's Guaranteed Victory

From the beginning of 2000, there was no longer any doubt that Putin would win the presidential election of 26 March. Putin did not campaign. He published an 'open letter to Russian voters' in February, made some declarations during the exercise of his duties as interim President, and refused to take part in any public debate with the other candidates. Posters were rare, leaflets non-existent. On the other hand, there was an active drive to convince administrations, businesses and farming collectives. Rural sectors were subject to more pressure from the local authorities than the big cities. There were numerous eye-witness accounts of fraud, which gave a fairly coherent overall picture. Naturally they were refuted en bloc by the Central Electoral Commission and the presidential administration. From my own observations of the December 1999 and March 2000 elections, I am inclined to accept the accounts of fraud which corroborate each other. The report published in September 2000 by the *Moscow Times* describes the different forms of falsification and names the republics and regions most affected.[50] The main falsifications were the registration of fictitious voters, the stuffing of large packets of ballots into the boxes, the rewriting of the *protokoly* (voting counts signed by the officials in charge of the polling stations after they had closed) in the absence of any observers. After the closing of the polling stations, at 8 p.m., in principle, observers are entitled to monitor the entire counting process until the transmission of an official *protokol* to the territorial electoral commission, which covers several dozen polling stations. It is at this stage that the opportunity to falsify the results arises, away from the scrutiny of outsiders. Despite their 'independent' status, the territorial commissions are mere annexes of local government (town hall, district or administration of the regional governor).[51]

However, a high number of complaints were lodged, often by Communists, but most of them were buried or dismissed 'for lack of evidence'. We learn from existing accounts that names were added to the list of registered voters, that the turnout figure (68 per cent) was inflated and that, if there had not been fraud, Vladimir Putin would probably not have been elected in the first round (with more than 52 per cent of the votes), but only after a second round that would have pitted him against the Communist Zyuganov.

The question then is why the provincial governors, civil servants and members of the electoral commissions as a whole so easily agreed to play the Putin card, even going so far, in some constituencies, as to resort to organized fraud. There are several factors that explain this rallying behind Putin under cover of a national pseudo-consensus that stifled any public debate.

The first reason is precisely that Putin was the Kremlin's candidate, the man already at the helm. His advantage was power, because the fact that he occupied the highest post showed that he was stronger than the others. His promises rang truer since he was supposed to be running the country and to be acquainted with the problems. Moreover, he proved this to be the case with numerous 'campaign gifts', like the payment of wage arrears in some professions and regions, and the granting of tax concessions or other forms of incentive (Yeltsin had not stinted on such electoral gifts in the run-up to the 1996 election either). The candidate Putin did not produce a manifesto; being in the Kremlin was enough. It should not be suggested that he was in competition with others; he was above the others and should not be expected to have to convince through ideas or well-defined policies. His motto was to rebuild a strong state, a task which he claimed was already underway.

A second factor was of a material and budgetary order. Most provincial leaders were loyal to the central government candidate. It was vital for a governor not to be marginalized in the incessant budgetary and fiscal bargaining. It was also important to have good relations with the federal officials (FSB, taxes, finance) working in the region, and with the major industrial groups established there. For the leaders of the republics and the regions, ensuring that Putin was elected meant preserving the status quo and choosing the devil they knew rather than uncertainty.

At this time, they too were elected through direct suffrage, and some had no hesitation in assuring themselves of a favourable outcome. Moscow elites and provincial elites played along similar lines and had similar interests to protect, each at their own level: their power sphere.

Thirdly, Vladimir Putin did not fear any serious rival. The battle of the legislative elections had reduced political competition solely to the Communist candidate, who acknowledged that he could not command the majority of votes in a second round. Yuri Luzhkov and Yevgeny Primakov, who might have stood a chance in succeeding Boris Yeltsin if the presidential election had taken place before the summer of 1999, had abandoned the contest. General Lebed had left the forefront of the political stage. On the eve of the election, the polls all showed that Vladimir Putin was way ahead in the voting intentions. The population rallied to the choice made at the top, not out of enthusiasm, but because of the lack of a credible alternative and out of fear of the uncertainty associated with real political change.

In these circumstances, if it was a foregone conclusion, why did the administration resort to fraud? The experts all agree that Vladimir Putin would easily have won the second-round duel. But he wanted a landslide victory from the first round, a form of plebiscite. The Soviet mindset left a legacy of universal consensus that made people particularly rebellious against the tyranny of the majority and the unpredictability of the ballot box. The rejection of pluralism, fair competition and opposition was, together with resorting to violence in Chechnya, one of Vladimir Putin's policy instruments for consolidating his power and gradually transforming the post-Soviet regime into an authoritarian system. From then on, order and control became the Kremlin's catchwords.

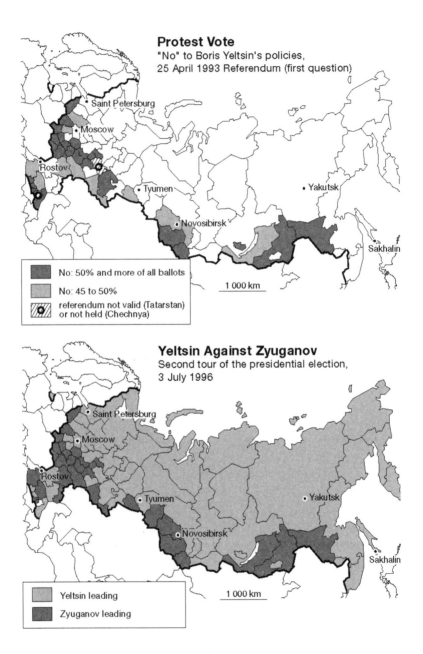

Protest Vote
"No" to Boris Yeltsin's policies,
25 April 1993 Referendum (first question)

- Saint Petersburg
- Moscow
- Rostov
- Tyumen
- Yakutsk
- Novosibirsk
- Sakhalin

No: 50% and more of all ballots
No: 45 to 50%
referendum not valid (Tatarstan) or not held (Chechnya)

1 000 km

Yeltsin Against Zyuganov
Second tour of the presidential election,
3 July 1996

- Saint Petersburg
- Moscow
- Rostov
- Tyumen
- Yakutsk
- Novosibirsk
- Sakhalin

Yeltsin leading
Zyuganov leading

1 000 km

4

THE POWER OF BUREAUCRACIES

'For even if the old way of life vanished, there were some signs that in dying, it poisoned the new with its venom, and that despite the apparent change in social relations, their essence remained intact'.

Mikhail Saltykov-Shchedrin[1]

Since 1991, Russia has undergone two major cycles of administrative transformation of the state, the economy, and the role of the bureaucracies. During the Yeltsin years, the administrations battled to survive and prevent the state from breaking up completely, which by 1991–1993 was looking likely. They did so for a variety of reasons, depending on their nature, their purpose and their resources, but most of them did not allow themselves to be eliminated by the exit from Communism. On the contrary, they took advantage of the removal of the Communist Party structures to regain full possession of their administrative powers, reliant until then on the Party. Throughout the 1990s, the weakness of the central state and of Yeltsin's government did not pose a threat to the administrations but instead enabled them to consolidate themselves while adapting to the market economy. While political life was in the throes of change, the resilience of the administrations and their chiefs is impressive.

From 2000 onwards, these 'public-sector' political and administrative elites were brought back under the control of the Kremlin machine, the intelligence services and other 'power ministries' (the infamous *siloviki*,

121

men from the KGB, Interior Ministry, army and police, who regained power under Vladimir Putin), with the collusion of a significant proportion of judges and media bosses. However, the system was not an exact replica of the good old Soviet system. The situation had changed considerably, and leaders at all levels were materially affected by the new balance of power; each person's powers and pay were defined according to new codes. During the years which they described as 'destructive chaos', the men of the KGB and Putin's personal networks, Sergey Ivanov, Igor Sechin, Gennady Timchenko[2] and others, realized that the new yardstick of power was money. Furthermore, the leaders who had been struggling to keep their region, municipality or *kolkhoz* (collective farm) on its feet after 1991 did not remain in the mould of Soviet officials but invaded the spheres of politics and, directly or indirectly, the new world of business. Furthermore, at the close of the Yeltsin era, dozens of men built up economic and financial empires that largely escaped the Kremlin's control.

The previous chapter analyzed the rapid decline of the representative institutions designed to hold rulers accountable, namely universal suffrage and parliament. The following sections focus on the operation of the state bodies, their responsibility or lack of responsibility, and the role of the administrations at the various territorial levels. The central hypothesis is based on the observation of events on the ground—the amazing survival, in a time of crisis, of administrative bodies cut loose from Communist party supervision—and on a paradigm (the preference for fluid and unclear rules of the game) which saw both the rulers and the ruled complicit in the same avoidance of law and accountability. This chapter looks at how the bureaucracies operated, the sway they held over a vast country in the process of transformation, and attempts to show why Russians tolerated their bureaucrats, the infringements of the law, small-scale corruption and, ultimately, their leaders' autocratic behaviour. The issues discussed here will provide some of the keys to understanding the Putin state model analyzed in subsequent chapters.

Survival of the Administrative Elites

The ruling elites—administrative and economic, local and national—held out astonishingly well after 1991. The rulers' and officials' survival was more striking in Russia's provinces than in Moscow. They sometimes changed jobs: the head of a *kolkhoz* became mayor, a former Party secretary became manager of a restructured company, an ex-KGB operative acted as an intermediary between the administrations and industrial and finance groups. But the vast majority retained a role in the country's governing and operating structures. Few institutions were dismantled, the great exception of course being the Communist Party's supervisory organs.

After the failed coup d'Etat of August 1991, when the regime collapsed and the ruling party was neutralized by Boris Yeltsin, one might have expected the worst scenarios of breakdown and chaos across the USSR. However, neither the breakaway of the independent republics—the Baltic states, Belarus, Ukraine, Moldova, the countries of the Caucasus and Central Asia—nor even the disappearance of the Party hierarchy in Russia led to the collapse of society. Armed conflicts were confined to some regions of the Caucasus, Central Asia and Moldova.

The main events were played out in 1989–1993, during the transition from *perestroika*, instigated by Gorbachev, and the start of the era of Yeltsin. The reformers abolished the formal Soviet unitarism which took the form of a single owner, the state; a single decision-maker, the Party; a single producer, the big state-owned corporations; and a single legitimate interest, that of the political leaders.

With the end of the USSR, the very essence of the state, whose omnipotence and arbitrary nature had been criticized within and beyond Russia, was brought into disrepute. Had not the Soviet state-party paralyzed national development, made people apathetic and corrupted people's outlook? 'Soviet public administration is one-party administration', wrote the historian Merle Fainsod in 1953. 'Every field of administration, however technical, is regarded as a channel for the propagation of the Party line and the directives of the top leadership'.[3] Until 1989, the entire running of the country depended on the Communist Party, with the KGB as an active force. The exit from Communism initially resulted in the various Soviet republics and their national governing authorities seizing autonomy and shaking off the rule of Moscow—followed by a bid by actors within Russia to emancipate themselves *from the state* and its central structures.

The state was and remains unpopular with Russians as they do not associate it with the positive aspects of government that exist in Western European societies. Having suffered from arbitrariness, repression and a system of privileges reserved for the rulers, they were instinctively wary of political power and the authority of the law. The notion of political society, where citizens are actively involved in debating and shaping public policy, remained embryonic. People still, and above all, expected that the state would increase pensions and the minimum wage, and provide free social services.

The Soviet state was valued mainly as a world power and guarantor of the country's security. The population accepted a great deal of deprivation in order to strengthen the means of defence against an outside world perceived, under the influence of propaganda, as highly hostile and aggressive. The collapse of the Communist regime spelled the end of the Cold War; the fortress-state locked in implacable conflict with the capitalist West disintegrated. However, from the mid 2000s onwards, Vladimir Putin endeavoured to build a new form of besieged fortress (see chapter 9).

In any case, it is not surprising that the reorganization of the state did not arouse the Russians' interest in the early years of the post-Communist regime, which were very difficult materially. The survivors of the Soviet collapse were primarily worried about maintaining local power, and the local administrations did indeed prove indispensable for day-to-day survival in this uncertain situation.

At the time it seemed surprising that the political class in Moscow did not pay more attention to the reconstruction of the state and the re-establishment of a legitimate public sphere—*res publica*. But the priority of the ruling elites was reforming the economy and privatization. The rulers were preoccupied with dividing up wealth and increasing the value of commodities, thereby neglecting political and social issues, even though these were of fundamental importance; as if the choice of society depended mainly on economic and financial factors and the running of the country were above all a matter of 'management' and 'business'.

Political leaders in Moscow did not explicitly integrate economic reform into a social project where public institutions would be given a vital role and, above all, would be explained to citizens and businesses. The profound transformations of the political, economic and social systems were not backed up by a coherent, well-defined strategy for building a new federal state, a new public administration or a new conception of the relations between government and citizens. Once the 1993 Constitution was adopted, there was less reflection on the nature and organization of the political regime, even if the law-making machinery was operating at full throttle.[4] The Yeltsin system was the result of numerous uncoordinated developments. Each power-wielder redefined their own interests and tried to adapt to the new conditions as best they could.

Complexity and Diversity

In 1991–1993, the country entered into a regime of multiplicity and complexity surrounding the devolution of economic and political power, which had developed within an extraordinarily short time. No protagonist, no institution could now determine any issue on their own. Boris Yeltsin was aware of the limitations both of his power and of the authority of the law. Negotiation and compromise were not simply methods, but became a system of government where plasticity and ad hoc accommodation prevailed over law and regulations. Corruption and rule-bending both by those who made the rules—the rulers—and by those who were supposed to follow them, the citizens. Paradoxically, the lack of rigorous institutional order, and individuals taking matters into their own hands, created a flexibility that made it possible to avoid violent armed clashes until 1993. The political class as well as Russian society experienced the assault on parliament in October 1993 and the war in Chechnya begun in December 1994 as traumas and failures.

Abuse and the settling of scores were part of the risks of a system where central government did not have the ability to control and centralize, nor the will to enter into direct conflict with the regional authorities, the new company bosses and the godfathers of organized crime.

Fragmented into increasingly autonomous and diverse spaces, Russia saw the pace of lives of its inhabitants begin to vary enormously from one part of the country to another. The weakening of the central authorities after 1988–1989 created a power vacuum that was quickly occupied, through force of circumstance, by the protagonists present on the local and regional scene. Administration chiefs, company bosses, influential figures (a deputy, a writer, a university dean) imbued their role with a political dimension that they would not have claimed previously. In the absence of a strategy defined by Moscow, local leaders faced with the huge unpredictability of the political orientations at the top naturally moved into the political sphere and affirmed their positions of power by entering simultaneously into economic and financial milieus.

Overall, the leaders in Russia's provinces maintained their positions, adjusting remarkably well to the disappearance of the Communist institutions and to the new constraints of democracy, particularly free elections and the necessary endorsement of the ballot box. The administrations and their leadership controlled the electoral process, as described in Chapters 3 and 5.

There was never any question of making a clean sweep and removing the elites of the Soviet era. The local and regional administration chiefs became political leaders as a matter of course. With the election of provincial governors and mayors in most cities, from 1993 to 1995 the former positions of high-up administrative officials subject to directives from Moscow became elected posts, giving a local leader the same legitimacy as the president of the Russian Federation. Furthermore, some of these chiefs of the regional or municipal executive also became bosses of the local economy by controlling or signing agreements with businesses, financiers and investors. Political scientist Igor Klyamkin explains this clearly: 'Public office became a sort of private business. Entrepreneurs saw themselves forced to buy their constitutional rights from the bureaucrats. These legitimate rights (including the right to own property) were precisely the merchandise whose supply was guaranteed by the officials'.[5] Small and medium-sized businesses soon found themselves caught in a 'corrupt alliance with bureaucracy',[6] an alliance that potentially jeopardized the economic success of enterprise and the region. This was exactly how Vladimir Putin operated as a municipal official in Saint Petersburg in the early 1990s.

At the beginning of the 2000s, Igor Klyamkin thought that this scheming between business and local politicians and their administrations would encourage both sides to reinforce the rule of law, in other words to adhere to and apply the law, so as to avoid the unforeseen, the arbitrariness of an unpredictable regime rife with corruption. His theory was that the stakeholders in the new market economy in a decentralized situation would lobby for the kind of clear legal rules that facilitate economic contracts and exchange. The sociologist later had to revise his predictions. Under cover of the slogan 'the dictatorship of the law', Putin's policies resulted in the law of the jungle and interfered with the life of big and small businesses in the provinces by reducing the regional administrations' margin for manoeuvre, both budgetary-wise and politically. Meanwhile the fate of small businesses depended essentially on maintaining good relations with the local authorities, or at least being able to count on their indifference.

Throughout the 1990s, the regions' and the republics' new-found autonomy and their leaders' increasing power caused considerable anxiety among Moscow's ruling elite, which was still traumatized by the USSR's fragmentation into 15 independent states. This created a sense of the precariousness of the state and of the nation. While declaring their support for a federation, the Moscow leaders had not grasped the fact that the regional capitals were living their own political lives, with their electoral issues, their *nomenklatura*s and business corporations, and running their own economic and financial affairs. They clung to the reassuring premise that Moscow retained authority over the entire country, that the provinces lived off the central state, that the governors were 'under supervision' as they were incapable of governing alone. This illusion concerning the degree of subordination of the local political elites stemmed from the Muscovites' ignorance and disdain for the Russia 'of the lower orders'. By insisting on treating the governors as deputy administrators, tasked with implementing directives from Moscow, and by using subsidies as a blackmail weapon, Yeltsin's government was hoist with its own petard: the blackmail backfired and the governors bartered their political loyalty to the 'centre' for economic concessions. They consolidated their administrative apparatus' hold on their territory's resources and developed their own methods of governance, which varied from one region to another.[7] This was the phenomenon that, starting in 2000, Vladimir Putin attempted to tackle by reasserting the Kremlin's control over these local networks.

Federal Governance

As the 89 subunits that made up the Russian Federation (a territorial division directly inherited from Soviet history)[8] increasingly eluded central control, the Kremlin began worrying about the possible break-up of Russia. And yet Boris Yeltsin's government did not put forward a strategy for a federalism adapted to the country's inevitable regionalization and decentralization. The solutions were makeshift. For example, the provinces signed agreements (*dogovory*) with the federal state, sharing out areas of responsibility in order to fill the constitutional and legislative vacuum on the crucial issue of the respective powers of national and regional institutions.

Unlike the Republic of Sakha (Yakutia) and Tatarstan, which were battling for sovereignty within a form of confederation, the tiny Republic of Chechnya was the only one to declare its independence unilaterally in October 1991. It was an exception, but the leaders in the Kremlin considered it a dangerous precedent which was likely to be replicated. As a result, their analysis of the regionalization sweeping through Russia was misguided. In a domino theory nightmare, they saw the threat of political and territorial breakdown. The idea that decentralization was fundamentally a positive development could not take root in a country where 'strong state' remained synonymous with centralization and control. In actual fact, the phenomenon taking place in the 1990s was, apart from the north Caucasus, the fragmentation of the economic, social and cultural spheres into more autonomous spheres, and not the break-up of Russia into independent political entities.

The provincial leaders had never demanded real independence from the federation. They filled the ideological and political vacuum left by the disappearance of the Communist Party, which for decades had maintained close and hierarchical relations between the many territories and between the elites. They continued to run the country's day-to-day affairs, a task that no one in Moscow wished to take on. Autonomy was thus forced, and not won as a result of a hard struggle. Autonomy was thrust upon the local authorities as the only option, since they no longer received any regular subsidies from the 'centre', had no instructions and had to tackle urgent situations, especially public provision, paying wages and attempting to maintain essential infrastructures.[9]

Moscow's understanding of events was muddled as it was highly politicized. Governors, mayors of big cities and private entrepreneurs were accused of seeking to undermine central government further and trying to destroy Russia. The question of Russia's integrity and power was a highly emotive issue for the Moscow elites. Any freedom displayed by local protagonists was deemed an attack on national cohesion and, of course, on the central government.

My many interviews with Moscow leaders and provincial rulers during the 1990s convinced me that the Achilles heel in the relationship between the centre and the provinces was the lack of reliable information about each other. The Kremlin and the government had no idea what was going on among the Federation's 89 subjects, neither in the heart of the municipality of Moscow nor in the remote territory of Primorie in Vladivostok. Ill-informed and fuelled by national prejudice against the provinces and above all the republics, the 'reformers' in Moscow defined their policies without taking serious account of the varied and complex realities of the different provinces.

President Yeltsin and his Prime Minister, Chernomyrdin, rarely travelled to the provinces, except during the election campaign period of 1995–1996. They juggled between macroeconomic data provided by the ministries and the International Monetary Fund, and reports and rumours from their personal local sources and reports made by the governors when they met in Moscow. There was no rigorous, systematic gathering of information on the Federation's republics and regions. That was the most tragic flaw of the Yeltsin era: tragic because the war against Chechens and Russians living in the tiny Caucasian republic was primarily the result of an incredible disinformation campaign by the intelligence services and the army regarding the situation in Chechnya (see Chapter 3). This lack of information and understanding was also tragic for the future of Russia's transformation. Society's disillusionment and its rejection of democratization set in as early as 1993–1994, when ordinary Russians realized that the President and his government had no idea about the crisis in which they were embroiled and had no concern for their material survival.

It should be emphasized that, in the USSR, the hierarchy of the Communist Party and the KGB extended deep into the heart of impoverished rural areas and remote little towns which were sometimes completely cut off during the winter. Information wound its way through this labyrinthine, hierarchical organization in an undoubtedly limited, biased and random manner, to reach the capital of the republic and eventually the supreme authorities in Moscow. This information piled up in a vast data store which some leaders and some experts were supposed to monitor to inform the Central Committee of the 'general mood'. In short, some monitoring, however low-level, was necessary in order not to be caught out by ad hoc crises (mainly shortages of essential commodities such as bread or milk), social discontent and possible *bunt*s (the peasant revolts that were the bane of the administrators of the Tsarist empire).[10]

During the Soviet era, the Politburo and the central ministries were also at fault for failing to acquire precise, reliable knowledge of the situations in the vast country under their leadership. The mediocrity of the reports drawn up by the administrations of the republics and the central departments, in particular the KGB, could be explained by the widespread system of corruption and lies. To head off problems, high-up and lowly officials alike excelled in the art of ignoring and embellishing the facts.

They exaggerated achievements, covered up production shortfalls and accidents, and glossed over disasters big and small, as is illustrated by the horrendous example of Chernobyl in 1986. The knee-jerk reaction of the leaders—Gorbachev at their head—was to hush up the affair by refusing to talk about it, and then, after a few days, to release watered-down information in dribs and drabs, preferring to save face rather than evacuate millions of people and thus save thousands of lives.[11] Another example is the infant mortality rate that had risen to such a high level, over 25 per thousand, that it was simply omitted from official statistics after 1974.[12]

In his *Memoirs*, Mikhail Gorbachev mentions this refusal to take responsibility as a weakness of the system of which he was head from 1985. Trivial matters would land on his General Secretary's desk, for no *apparatchik* had wanted to make a decision.[13] He was well placed to appreciate the scale of the reform that needed to be undertaken, since he had been in charge of the Stavropol region (bordering the North Caucasus) for several years as First Secretary of the Party. For him, the empowerment of chiefs, deputy chiefs and officials, together with compulsory transparency and real accountability, was the key to modernization. However, he had massively underestimated the republican elites' desire for autonomy, which pushed him into a top-down reform scenario that was impracticable, as outlined in Chapter 2.

Since the collapse of the Soviet state in 1991, the leaders in Moscow continually blamed the problems of governance and the undermining of the state on the local and provincial elites. In their view, these elites selfishly defended their own domains at the expense of Russia as a whole. They were accused of jeopardizing the country's integrity and its chances of rising out of the economic and social abyss into which it had sunk.

Consolidation of the Regional Systems under Yeltsin

Observation and post-hoc analysis of the developments of the 1990s suggest a different, indeed contradictory interpretation. The local administrative bodies and their leaders proved to be the guarantors of the state's existence. They maintained an organizational structure and fulfilled most of their functions without being paralyzed by the upheavals 'at the top'. During the crisis years, 1990–1993 and then 1998–1999 (financial crash and the end of Yeltsin's rule), subnational bureaucracies were the pillars of the state edifice. It is thanks to them that Russia existed as a public sphere. The ailing President Yeltsin left his entourage to run things and no longer embodied the country's unity. The Russians ended up hating him. The economy was in turmoil and the gulf between rich and poor was widening (the spectrum between the poorest categories and the wealthy had expanded considerably). Economic wealth had been hijacked by some circles of the *nomenklatura*, Russia's heritage had been broken up and distributed among private individuals, and the ordinary citizen felt betrayed.

In these circumstances, day-to-day continuity and security acquired a great deal of importance. There remained at least one constant in the changing public and social landscape: local administrations, schools, and sometimes factories. This is what allowed the transition to be made relatively smoothly. The principal coordinators of this adaptation were the administrative structures inherited from the former regime.

And so, paradoxically, it was by becoming independent from Moscow that the provincial leaders were able to weather the storm and preserve the state edifice, for they were all officials, elected or otherwise, of the state. I had the opportunity to make a close case study of the Sverdlovsk region and its capital Yekaterinburg, in the Urals. This region was industrialized at a rapid rate in the 1930s and 1940s. The emergency relocation of the weapons factories from the western part of the USSR to the Urals in 1941, after the German invasion, created an industrial, pioneering spirit.

Sverdlovsk and its population developed as a mining community to meet an industrial challenge. The balance between mining, industrial output and food production, which was the secret of sustainable growth in previous centuries when survival was a daily anxiety, was no longer an issue. Central Russia and the Caucasus were to feed the Urals, Siberia and the big cities. In actual fact, food dependency was a heavy handicap throughout the Soviet period, and the industrial regions suffered greatly from erratic distribution and shortages of everyday provisions and consumer goods.

For the population of the Sverdlovsk region in the mid-1990s, the priority was the restructuring of factories which worked almost exclusively for the military-industrial complex. The post-Soviet state no longer bought the entire output of military and civil factories as the Soviet state had done, by juggling the books and paying very low salaries in cash. The economic shock created by the end of the Communist system therefore hit this type of region even harder than the others. Unemployment and under-employment in particular leaped, even though the factories simply stopped paying their workers if they had no cash. Most factories were no longer able to fulfil their obligation to provide social protection. And the public services, neglected by the central budget, found themselves unable to meet social demand: support for the unemployed, for unpaid workers, housing, management of day-care centres and schools, maintaining hospitals, payment of healthcare professionals and teachers. Those I interviewed in the Sverdlovsk regional administration in 1994 spoke openly of their distress: 'We have no other option, we absolutely have to get on with the factory bosses, privatized or not, because we at the governor's office produce no wealth! We have to protect the company bosses to bring in money, otherwise the rope will snap'.[14]

The regional governor, Eduard Rossel, was a regional and national figure. He stood up to the Moscow *apparatchik*s and to the *ukases* (decrees) of President Yeltsin, who had been in charge of the region in the 1980s as Party First Secretary. 'A crucial problem is the sharing of authority between the centre and the region. Of course, Moscow finds it hard to let go of power', Rossel explained. With no financial resources, the federal authorities had no chance of imposing measures and policies on the governors. Eduard Rossel concluded that Moscow would have no option but to sign a *dogovor* with him—an agreement similar to the one signed with Tatarstan in February 1994.[15]

In another major industrial city on the Volga, Saratov, located some two thousand kilometres south of Moscow, the municipal and regional authorities openly expressed their annoyance with Yeltsin's government. Some of them made no secret of their intention to vote for Gennady Zyuganov, the Communist candidate, in the presidential elections of June 1996, against Boris Yeltsin.[16] Saratov had also found itself deprived of 'state orders' to buy products, which came automatically from central ministries. And the region had no raw materials to provide temporary revenue during the necessary industrial restructuring. In 1996, the simple word 'reforms' provoked an angry response. These men illustrated the extent to which personal contacts and deals between the economic and administrative players were the only way to save the region from disaster.

In other provinces, the demise of Communism was experienced with more optimism. The regions close to Moscow, such as Tver, Kostroma, Kaluga and Vladimir, had for a long time lived under the oppressive shadow of the capital and aspired to a greater degree of self-rule. They barely had the financial means in the 1990s, but even so they tried to develop new activities in the agricultural and food processing sectors, generally with the help of foreign firms. The chiefly rural regions, which had not been a priority in Soviet times, had less to lose than the industrial areas hard hit by de-industrialization. The region of Kostroma, in the north, was successful in salvaging some and restructuring other industries under difficult conditions: a sausage factory was set up on the basis of a *kolkhoz* (collective farm) as a joint venture with a German company; a mink farming *sovkhoz* (Soviet state farm) set up a fur-coat factory to maintain jobs and add value.[17]

Unbridled decentralization of the state boosted the autonomy of the regional and local authorities which consolidated their administrative grip on resources and on individuals. So, for example, a mayor might be tempted to levy a new tax to top up the municipal coffers, and line his pockets. This was completely illegal (such cases were referred to the Constitutional Court) but, at home, in his town, if the apparatus and the local police were with him, he assured himself of an easy income for a period. The regional governors were past masters at exploiting loopholes in the federal justice system. They took advantage of the ambiguities and lack of clarity in the law and the powerlessness of federal bodies over their regional territory to develop their own political and administrative regime. During the 1990s, the federal ministries were increasingly struggling to pay their officials stationed in the provinces. There were sometimes more 'federals' than there were local officials, and it was not uncommon for them to end up being paid, late, from the regional budget.

If the balance of power on the ground was favourable, the provincial governors made unstinting use of their power, with no fear of opposition from the provincial assemblies or the courts. To ensure a certain control over the rural areas, which in general did not interest them, they relied on the chiefs of the cantons and rural councils whose subordination was guaranteed.

In some cases, the governors did not hesitate to reshape local institutions to suit themselves, judging them inferior and dependent on the provincial administration. In Bryansk for example, in spring 1999, the Governor dismissed the town's mayor, even though the latter had been elected through direct universal suffrage two years earlier. The Governor acted with the agreement of the municipal assembly and then, subsequently, he dismissed all the administrative chiefs of the rural districts, also elected through universal suffrage. He instigated a strange recruitment system 'by competition' for the new mayor of Bryansk.[18] In other provinces, competition between the two main prominent figures, the Governor and the mayor of the regional capital, often resulted in a fierce battle from which the mayor could emerge the winner, by taking the place of the incumbent governor after an electoral victory.

In the 1990s, weak central institutions were unable to implement either a recentralization or a decentralization policy. They attempted to assert their authority by appointing presidential representatives in the regions or by issuing more and more decrees. But instructions from above went unheeded because they were not backed by adequate financial and economic resources. In these conditions, measuring the costs and benefits of centralization versus decentralization was only of limited value; political and economic actors behaved opportunistically and myopically.

Research carried out in the Russian provinces confirms this.[19] Local elites sought rather to protect themselves against the vagaries of central policy and to consolidate their position in a regulatory system specific to the city, region or business. One important observation is the rootedness and autonomization of the political and administrative elites at regional and municipal level.[20] From 1991 to 1995, the situation was more fluid and new protagonists entered the hitherto hermetic arena of the ruling elites. Market forces, institutional democratization and the opening up of the country changed the behaviour of the elites. Then, things gradually slid towards a restriction of economic and political competition, and favoured those who were already in place. In the regional capitals, the elites tended to close ranks and protect their 'political regime' from outside interference.

Meanwhile, ordinary citizens remained spectators. They exercised an arbitrating role when they elected their federal, regional or municipal representatives. Their choice, however, was often little more than a sideshow to the game of musical chairs between two or three members of the local elite. In this respect, the behaviour of regional and national politicians was similar. The population was always treated as if it were causing an economic burden (the standard of living had to be maintained) and a political constraint (universal suffrage was mandatory). This is one of the explanations for the regional leaders' acquiescence to the Putin system post 2000. Putin invited them to submit to his loyalty system, which we shall analyze in the following chapters, thus saving them from the unpredictability of elections and the restriction to two terms in office.[21]

At the time when they were elected by universal suffrage, the governors were not necessarily seeking legitimacy or authority at federal level. They appreciated having a seat in parliament's upper house and thus enjoying 'national' status, and also being able to lobby on behalf of their region, or for a particular local enterprise, and for their own interests. And yet, bar a few exceptions, they devoted little effort to building a federal legislative system. In this sense, the loss of their seats on the Federation Council as a result of the reform instigated by Putin in 2000 did not greatly affect their function in the Russian political system.[22] On the other hand, this reform further weakened the parliamentary institution in Russia, with a loss of the upper house's legitimacy and influence.

Experts on budgetary matters and public policy were right to emphasize the pre-eminence of economic and financial variables in the conflicts between central and regional government. All the groups in power tried to gain as much freedom of action as possible, which requires revenue. From this point of view, Putin's control strategy of reducing the share of resources allocated to the regions in favour of the federal budget was more effective than his overhaul of the administrative system.[23] However, some financial resources were outside the public fisc, in private or corporatist and 'semi-public' funds, and in the shadow economy.[24] Negotiation took place behind the institutional veil, between the powerful networks of bureaucrats, financiers, company bosses and politicians.

Administrative 'Paternalism'

Soviet administrative bodies were able to adapt after 1991 since they already operated as networks during the Soviet era, in a way that was much more flexible than the centralizing doctrine of the Communist regime suggested.[25]

Already in the early 1960s, Merle Fainsod offered a sober analysis of party rule:

In practice, this picture of monolithic unity is only imperfectly realized; the struggle of the elite formations of Soviet society for power and influence continues to find expression. The Party apparatus, the police, the army, and the administrative bureaucracy vie with one another for preferment, and the local and departmental interests of different sections of the bureaucracy exercise their counterinfluence on the Party. […] The pressure from above is ruthless and unremitting, and evasion from below is resourceful and not unavailing.[26]

Private property, the market and the liberalization of trade allowed these systems of network governance to flourish as they tightened the links between the local administration and business, individuals and in some cases organized crime. Public bodies however remained anchored in their administrative function, the legacy of a long history of managing people and resources. What is most interesting in the case of Russia is precisely this combination of bureaucratic traditions with a long undemocratic history, which was able to adapt easily to the new post-Soviet situation, especially to privatization. Mikhail Gorbachev's 1987–1990 reforms received the support of the majority of the elites that had been hamstrung by the Soviet regime and wanted to line their pockets, travel, and broaden their horizons.[27]

Russia has the reputation of suffering from an excessive bureaucracy. The few serious studies of the administrations carried out in Russia provide evidence that puts the size of the civil service into perspective. National figures for 2002 record 1,140,600 civil servants working in public administration—federal, regional and municipal—in three categories, A, B and C. The civil service therefore accounts for around 0.8 per cent of Russia's population, and 1.8 per cent of the working population.[28] This goes against the idea that Russia is and always has been a country with a bloated bureaucracy. Already in the Tsarist era administrative officials were far fewer in number than in Germany or France.

Paradoxically, the number of Russian civil servants has increased steadily since the early 1990s, in other words, as the economy has been opening up. It rose officially from 1,004,300 in 1994 to 1,140,600 in 2001, and then to 1,578,000 in 2006.[29] Even more interesting is the following observation: in the 1990s, it was the number of regional and local officials that rose, whereas the number of federal civil servants dropped; in the 2000s, the trend was reversed, as Putin's regime relied on a growing class of federal civil servants based in Moscow or in the provinces. Vladimir Gimpelson notes that the bureaucrats from pre-1991 remained bureaucrats, whereas today's young people spend only a few years in the civil service and then leave, as it is not very attractive to those at the start of their working life.[30] But the trend seems to have changed in recent years as civil servants are now better paid and receive important perks.

Some administrative agencies now offer relatively attractive career prospects, which was not at all the case after the collapse of 1991.

The Russian civil service was seen as top-heavy. One reason could be that in the public mind the term 'civil servant' also encompassed a number of people doing jobs such as 'consultant', 'expert', 'assistant' or 'intern' that were not officially classified as part of the civil service and were paid for by an administration or by a company that had an interest in having dedicated people inside the administration.

Another, more essential, reason was that the implicit criterion in establishing the right number is efficiency, the profitability of each civil servant taken individually or of an administrative body as a whole. They 'oversaw' and 'extracted', but what did they contribute? So the perception of a surfeit of civil servants was confused with a perception of the superfluity of their activity compared with productive activities. Here the Communist legacy made itself felt, since only production activities were valued. Anecdotes from the Brezhnev era on the failings of the system made a laughing stock of politicians, the Party, the *apparatchiks* and the technocrats, but not the engineers or the workers.

The notion of public service, provided by hundreds of thousands of civil servants and therefore productive for society—health, education, infrastructure management, the legal system, public order—did not exist. Firstly, the big state-owned corporations fulfilled the role of a social service. It was at a person's workplace and through their job that they obtained a place for their children in nursery school, access to hospital and food supplies. Secondly, the control and distribution roles of the state administration and the Party organs were closely interlinked, making it impossible to recognize a 'public service' in the sense of a pact between society and the rulers governing the redistribution of national resources, particularly through the collection of taxes. Strictly speaking, the Soviet individual and company did not pay taxes, but received wages and subsidies to meet their minimum consumption needs or enable them to operate from day to day.

The sociology of organizations has shown that an organization tends to expand, since it seeks to protect itself from the external environment and from the competition by growing in size, becoming more complex and less transparent.[31] This phenomenon is particularly striking in Russia. The advantages of a light, versatile, fast-responding organization where each person can take the initiative and duplication is avoided do not seem to be taken into account. Even in private companies, the management structure is often very top-heavy.

An administration's apparent rigidity may hide flexibility and adaptability. No organization, public or private, works in a strictly hierarchical manner. Despite precise organizational charts, the division of responsibilities and power relationships depend on the people in place and evolve through practice. So the civil servant finds his margin of autonomy, albeit small, and can influence the resolution of a problem, either by facilitating things or by hampering them, sometimes by demanding payment for his service. The most serious problems arise when several administrative agencies produce contradictory regulations and companies must find a solution amid a maze of technical norms.

'Bureaucracy' is a convenient concept that allows politicians in particular to separate the spheres of politics and administration artificially. It is tempting to make a distinction between a good political decision and its failed implementation. That enables the Russian government to avoid taking responsibility for its failures. Blaming the incompetent and reactionary bureaucracy increases political leaders' room for manoeuvre and allows them to shrug off their responsibility for the poor outcome of governmental policy.[32] The method was widely used in 1998–1999, when the government and the Russian economy were undergoing a major crisis. But even in more prosperous times, Vladimir Putin has been unable to resist the classic trick. In each of his annual speeches to parliament, he criticized the bureaucrats' corruption and shortcomings, and President Medvedev chose the same scapegoat in 2009 and 2010. According to all Russian and international assessments, corruption has constantly increased in recent years.

Local Powers

The reality of the situation in Russia is always more complex than is conveyed by a general overview, which does not take account of variations in individual situations and behaviours. In some cases, the sluggishness and complexity of administrative channels hinders reform or renders it meaningless. In other cases, a municipal administration or a ministry's resources and contacts can guarantee a project's success. And so it would be reductive to focus only on the traditional failings, the pen-pushers doing their utmost to complicate matters in order to assert their petty bureaucratic power, and to line their pockets in the process.

The transformation of the Russian system was not effected against the administrative bodies, but with them. They participated directly in defining the country's political and economic direction. We have pointed out the key role played by the governors, the mayors and their administrations. Simple observation of the situations in the Russian provinces from the early 1990s indicates that a certain economic and social order at local level prevailed over the chaos. In all my research trips, which excluded Chechnya and the areas of armed conflict, I observed numerous cases of poverty, distress, injustice, archaic infrastructures and inappropriate production tools, but I never encountered a situation of total chaos, where the population of a town or village was left entirely to its own devices without being able to rely on any local organization. The people were not abandoned in an economic and social jungle, but continued to live in a relatively ordered world where authority was present, the main services provided, even if they were extremely insufficient: the trains ran irregularly but they ran, the schools remained open despite considerable difficulties, water was supplied even if it was not drinkable.

The landscape was very grim and day-to-day life very difficult, especially between 1991 and 1994 when there was a shortage of food products combined with inflation and the importation of foreign goods. By comparison with the Soviet era, there was a very real decline in the standard of living for the worst-off and those on a low income whose purchasing power decreased along with access to healthcare and free services. But the local authorities acted as a bulwark against humanitarian disaster. Epidemics of diphtheria and tuberculosis were not curbed in time, but were more or less contained. On the other hand, what can be said today of the growing number of AIDS cases when the Putin government has the financial and organizational resources to check and prevent the spread of the virus? The shortcomings of the healthcare system have not been seriously and efficiently remedied since the 1990s.

Local societies' resilience developed from the staying power of the former Soviet administrations and enterprises. Most Soviet bodies remained in place and tried to do their job, sometimes in very difficult conditions, without sufficient resources. And so there was a marked discrepancy between the new institutional and political structure on the one hand, and the realities of day-to-day life marked by the strong grip of local and regional administrations on the other, a relationship to the law and to institutions that had not become 'Europeanized' and which still display a preference for fluid rules and ad hoc interpretations.

In an economic and social context where individuals and small communities increasingly depend on their 'immediate protectors', in other words the local administration and the company that employs them, the power of bureaucracies is not likely to wane. The dependency created by a survival economy encourages forms of bureaucratic arbitrariness and cronyism. The failure of the law and the ineffectiveness of public policies are all the more tragic in a situation where the market is not capable of regulating trade or the commitments entered into by multiple contracting parties.

During the Soviet period, the local power represented by the factory, the *kolkhoz* and the Party leaders was already extensive, but it was exercised in a pyramid system which, even though corrupt and cronyist, curbed personal ambition and bids for autonomy. The work of the leading Russian sociologists, in particular Tatyana Zaslavskaya, points out that from the 1970s, the system that encouraged workers to do as little as possible was counter-productive. 'They pretend to pay us, we pretend to work', went the adage. French sociologist Basile Kerblay's *La société soviétique contemporaine* is one of the best analyses ever published on the subject.[33]

Thirty years later, the opportunities for growing rich and circumventing the law were incomparably greater, and cronyism and networks flourished. For wheeler-dealers, the miracle was money! However, the less privileged half of the population was still caught in the stranglehold of material dependency. Owing to the lack of geographical, professional and social mobility, this sector barely counted in the political game. It assessed the risks and did not revolt against those who held the reins of survival. And it remained extremely wary of government leaders and institutions. The habits of self-protection are not so easily shrugged off. Society was characterized by a very low level of social participation and by the quasi-monopoly of public life by the economic and administrative elites.[34]

Disparities

Although economic indicators showed an improvement in median income from 2000 onwards, this should not be allowed to mask economic and social disparities or the uneven distribution of growth outside the most dynamic regions and boom-sectors. A vast proportion of the population across the many and diverse provinces lives in a precarious situation. Precariousness creates a dependency on local authorities and employers. These sub-systems of management of day-to-day existence are outside federal state policy and guarantee a minimum stability threshold as well as protection against too violent an upheaval of the economic and social order. Thus, the governors and mayors, with their administrations and networks, whether they were honest or corrupt, held a structurally essential place in their constituency. Which explains why even corrupt state representatives who were weak managers sometimes remained in office, whether they were elected by their constituents or appointed by the Kremlin.

In Tver, a town north-west of Moscow, the situation improved between 1994 and 2004.[35] This region was hit hard by the industrial crisis and had a low agricultural output, so life was very tough after the collapse of the USSR in 1991. In 1994, there were no well-stocked shops in Tver, no quality service industries. The buildings and infrastructures were in a worrying state of decay. There did not seem to be any impetus coming from local leaders.

Nowadays, the town has emerged from its torpor and money is circulating. Various shops, hotels, cafés, hairdressers and Internet cafés make the city centre a lively hub. Some local people have launched services, small businesses have started up, some foreign investments have financed the renovation of the truck factory and the food industry. The first private banks appeared in the mid 1990s, and several insurance companies are well established.

On the other hand, the urban infrastructures remain deficient, the streets and roads are in a poor condition. As the Tverians would say, the mayor's changed but the potholes have not been filled. There is still evident poverty, both in the town and in the region's rural cantons. The regional capital is out of the mire, but the region is still poorly developed. For many young people, the only way out is to leave for Moscow. There is work to be found in the province of Tver, but pay is a pittance. Often people work in Moscow, or in the Moscow region, while continuing to live in Tver. That means sub-letting a room in the suburbs of the federal capital as the 170-kilometre train journey takes two and a half hours.

The population is angry with their leaders, but only 'around the kitchen table', amongst themselves, as people do not see what they can do. This example is typical of a general drift in Russia: the political class is not developing in a climate of transparency or competition, but in a closed world. It is increasingly rare for candidates to present an agenda or ideas;

generally they refrain from criticizing the Kremlin and pledge loyalty to Putin. Furthermore, money is required to get elected. So the choice is becoming increasingly restricted to a particular type of candidate where the criteria of money, financial networks, contacts inside the administration, and ties with the FSB are more important in the battle than reputation, political ideas or a track record in good management.

The contrasts are salient, from one small town to another, from one company to another. The big city of Vladivostok has often gone without water or heating. Other cities like Perm have managed to develop infrastructure. The key to success is largely linked to resources. Producing hydrocarbons or other raw materials brings in high revenue which a town like Ulyanovsk, for example, will never have.

The embryonic development of private property—in the sense of property guaranteed by the law and the public authorities—is closely bound up with the low level of public participation. In a democratic society, property owners and entrepreneurs are powerful stakeholders. They define their role and their interests themselves and are concerned about the way their country, region and town are run. They express their preferences in the political arena. Private property and its defence are the cornerstones of the history of the capitalist economy and of modern democracies. The vast majority of Russians care about ownership in the sense that they like to be assured of a place to live and a plot of land. But they are less concerned about seeking legal guarantees or accepting the obligations that come with owning property.

Lack of clarity and stability in the definition of private property, and therefore of the private sphere, goes hand in hand with a similar confusion over the definition of the public arena, of what is related to property and the state's responsibility at local or national level. Local individuals and businesses have consolidated their power by embracing this fluidity.

The Preference for Unclear and Unsettled Rules

Adaptation can have untoward effects. In Russia it has reinforced a permissive conception of the rules and the exercise of authority, which was already pervasive in the Soviet era. One indirect and unforeseen effect of free elections and institutional competition in the 1990s filled one of the vacuums left by the disintegration of the Soviet single-party system: hierarchical organization.

Money and political competition did not construct a new power pyramid but built new reference points around which allegiances and subordinations re-coalesced. More than ever before, cronyism was rife and needed to mould itself into an institutional configuration. Furthermore, the elites had the means to shape the institutions' organization and practice, thanks in particular to the administrative bodies which retained a central role. Their power over society was all the greater since individuals were trapped in a strong relationship of dependency on their local administrators. The day-to-day problems, big and small (from simple enrolment in a school to a company obtaining tax relief) depended on the quasi-discretionary power of the local civil servants and their networks. So the Russians were not so much preoccupied with knowing whether the administrative bodies in their vicinity were legitimate and honest, as whether they had the means to resolve material problems which, for many of them, were questions of day-to-day survival. Authorities and citizens both preferred the status quo, or a slow drift, to a major leap, a great effort, a major reform that could usher in sweeping change.

During the Yeltsin years, Russia lived in a state of permanent imbalance, but did not tip over into chaos and anarchy as far as most of the population was concerned. Nothing was well organized, the future was not planned, but people adapted as best they could to this incredible hotchpotch of imbalances and irrational situations. The Russians had been so critical of Gorbachev for having caused the USSR to totter by striving to reform some of the workings of the great Soviet machine that ultimately what they wanted from Yeltsin was for him not to disrupt their day-to-day arrangements. They felt too poor to change and replace, and were not incensed enough by their low standard of living to lose patience and attack the authorities head-on.[36] It was a matter of making do and reworking what was already there.

Fluidity offers more instant comfort than clear, rigid rules laying out each person's duties and obligations. The memory of the Soviet era carried with it the continual struggle of ordinary individuals and organizations to prevent the rules and punishment coming down on their heads rather than on someone else's. They fought the insecurity that arbitrary power injected into society by creating networks and doing deals. Even the bureaucratic organs, all in a state of uncertainty, had to protect themselves. The interstices of any totalitarian regime contain concealed pockets of effective bureaucratic resistance. The Soviet rulers engaged in a ceaseless effort to stamp out this resistance and forge the bureaucracy into a pliable instrument of their will', wrote Merle Fainsod in 1953. He was analyzing the chaos of the Soviet administrative system resulting from arbitrariness and people's need to come to 'understandings', to find a 'haven of peace', contradicting Hobbes' idea of the war of all against all (*bellum omnium contra omnes*).[37]

In Russia, rulers and citizens speak more readily of order (*poryadok*) than of the norm, contracts and responsibility, which involve numerous constraints: applying the same rule to oneself as to others, keeping to what has been agreed, paying off debts on time, fearing legal sanctions. In other words, the rule of law means enshrining the rules of the game in laws and ensuring these laws are followed thanks to social consensus and effective punishment. But, in Russia, the vast legislative and regulatory corpus did not produce a democratic, consensual and efficient system of government.

The vast number of laws—adopted by the republican, federal and regional institutions and municipal bodies—were mainly treated as norms linked to the economic climate, eminently temporary since they had been devised to help a ruling circle manage an immediate situation, with no great consideration for legal cohesion or long-term social planning. Everything was likely to be modified, circumvented and interpreted according to expediency. Even if some people did use their new rights and prosecute the state or one of its officials, the body of citizens as a whole saw the cumbersome legal and regulatory edifice primarily as a rulebook for the elites. Furthermore, since they often owned only a tiny home or a minuscule plot of land, Russians did not feel an imperative need for the law to guarantee a status and protect their heritage.

An attachment to vagueness and shifting interpretations was not so much a symptom of drift as an expression of preference. And this preference was shared equally by the population and the elites whether they liked it or not. For even if Russian citizens despised their leaders and did not feel protected by the law, or perhaps precisely because of this innate suspicion, they also had a preference for a lack of legal certainty. A decision could be revised or simply not applied: 'We'll come to an arrangement'. The impression that the door remained open and that it was possible to slip through, renegotiate, postpone or forget an obligation governed relations between people, and between institutions and businesses. And this suited everyone in a way that is incomprehensible for a Swedish or Swiss citizen.

Naturally, behaviour patterns often bore the imprint of Soviet methods. Brezhnev's USSR was already a world where loose interpretations and bending the rules were prevalent. Repression was, in a way, the tip of the iceberg which gave a mistaken impression of a rigid and perfectly controlled system. Although the Communist government was merciless towards the rare dissidents who dared openly to confront it, over the years it had lost its grip on the 300 million Soviet people.[38] The Brezhnev years saw a relaxing of central control and of direct control of businesses, administrations and individuals. The local elites in the many republics and regions that made up the USSR had partly broken away from the Moscow hierarchy. Making the most of their margin for manoeuvre, they devised their own system of government, only providing the central authorities with carefully selected 'tweaked' information that fed a chain of false statistics and inaccurate or incomplete reports. A company manager inflated his annual production figures not only to 'fulfil the plan' or surpass it, but above all to obtain from central government more 'transfers' or subsidies and more supplies of raw materials, machines and consumer goods (the economy was not accountable, costs and profitability were not rigorously calculated). Conversely, another might report lower output than the actual figures so as to sell some of the goods produced by his factory on the black market. If such trading was reported, punishment followed; but laws against black-market dealings were not always applied. The *nomenklatura* was not monolithic but plural, not united but competing, and rife with corruption. A network involved in shady dealings could be bailed out by a Moscow 'big shot'.[39] Leaders at all levels had learned to operate in networks, corporations, 'living on their wits' and, above all, with as little transparency as they could manage. In an excellent work on the disintegration of the hierarchical system in the 1980s, Steven Solnick starts from the observation that 'mid- and lower-level bureaucrats were not simply instruments of the top elite but were able to pursue their own agendas'.[40] He endeavours to show that 'Soviet organizations collapsed not because they were too rigid but because they were too flexible'.[41] Mikhail Gorbachev's reforms accelerated a process, already well underway, of loss of control of the hierarchical system. Opportunism, cronyism and the pursuit of personal and corporatist interests were not born of economic and political reforms.

Society as a whole had weighed up which risks were not worth taking and which opportunities should be seized. It had, in a way, internalized the permissible and the forbidden, which were not enshrined in law but determined by custom. And so anyone who thought that the Russians would diligently obey a democratic law, in a country rid of Communism, because they were used to obeying the rules, was wrong from the outset. The Soviet citizens did not 'obey the rules', but were subject to a complex system of authority and subordination, often very individualized, whose workings were outside the principle of shared obligations.

And yet, the Soviet Union produced a considerable number of regulations, laws and Party resolutions, declarations and speeches framing official programmes. Each administration, each business was sagging under the weight of paperwork and had to devote a disproportionate amount of time to writing, signing and stamping vast quantities of documents, and to receiving the many orders and resolutions that came to them from other institutions.

It was concluded that Soviet society was profoundly legalistic, even if its law did not fulfil democratic criteria. 'Legalistic' is not, in my view, the right word. Russia's administrative bodies were, and still are today, highly interventionist, cluttered with red tape. A top elite liked and still likes to have its authority enshrined and constantly reinforced by the production of laws, regulations and authorizations. The civil service has retained its appeal. A businessman as powerful as Boris Berezovsky held an important position—secretary of the Security Council—under President Yeltsin. After propelling Vladimir Putin to the leadership, he fell out with him, sought exile in London and became the Kremlin's enemy number one. Business, even the most underhand, could not be done outside the bureaucratic arena, but on the contrary only with the involvement of the administrative and political machinery.

Bending the Rules

Red tape and officialdom have traditionally been very much in evidence since the Tsarist era. In a way they occupy the arena for negotiation, the search for a compromise and consensus which, in societies governed by the rule of law, form a vast public sphere. In Russia, the laws and their interpretation end up fulfilling a role of communication and arbitration within the political elite, according to complex methods that are inaccessible to grassroots citizens. The leaders take the time to read and analyze the laws, decrees and regulations. The struggle for power is played out around them. No leader, no civil servant can disregard the written norms; he must manipulate them and circumvent them, but cannot simply ignore them. He also aspires to putting in place his own system of norms, in the sphere in which he exercises his authority. And so it is not surprising that Russian bureaucrats were, and still are, sticklers for rules. Law-abiding behaviour, however, is a different story. Abuse of power is part of day-to-day life. There is no culture of trust, of keeping contractual obligations.

A classic example is obtaining a residence permit or official authorization to start up a small business in a large town. The applicant is faced with an obstacle course and a number of palms to be greased before he is able to obtain the documents, duly signed and stamped, required by the municipal regulations. But outwardly, the procedure is followed, the law is applied. I encountered another illustration of the particular relationship the authorities have with the law during my stays in various Russian provinces. Nearly all the senior leaders I met—governors, mayors, regional assembly presidents and presidential representatives—had a copy of the Federal Constitution sitting on their desk. They are part of a power system and are connected to other institutions and other leaders by a basic law. And yet they have no hesitation in exempting themselves from it to assert their own powers, which are not explicitly spelled out in any federal laws.

This 'legalistic' mindset explains why Vladimir Putin was so strongly against revising the Constitution to his advantage in order to obtain a third term. He wants to appear as the custodian of the law, even if his remaining in power in 2008, as the new President Medvedev's 'regent', is an amazing circumvention of the Constitution and its spirit, as well as of the principles of democracy and pluralism. A striking example of disregard for the law and fundamental freedoms was the war in Chechnya, first under Yeltsin and then under Putin.

The power of the state continues to be synonymous with coercion, and it does not seem so shocking that the state defines its own security at the expense of society and outside any democratic control. There is a huge gulf between this conception and the liberal definition of the state. In a democratic society, the state's 'strength' depends on the legitimacy of its authority and its ability to maintain a stable and continuous relationship between citizens and government. The state reflects society's idea of itself as much as the public power exercised by its representatives. As the philosopher and constitutionalist Stephen Holmes points out, 'democratic procedures are of value only if they establish some sort of dependency of public officials on ordinary citizens.[42]

The testimonies gathered from numerous regions of Russia and opinion polls express profound suspicion towards governing institutions and leaders, both elected and appointed. In all the opinion polls we have analyzed over the last fifteen years, most political leaders, with the exception of Putin and Medvedev in recent years, garner approval ratings no higher than 10 to 20 per cent, whereas unfavourable opinions are as high as over 70 per cent. Mistrust of parliament and the legal system is even more pronounced.[43] Overall, citizens are poorly informed of their rights and do not trust the courts, which are just as bureaucratic as the administration but with fewer resources, and are powerless to enforce their judgments. Their sluggishness, lack of resources and sometimes their corruption deter people from resorting to legal action.[44] At the beginning of the 2000s, Vladimir Putin led the country to hope for a reform of the legal system, but judicial independence decreased during his two presidential terms.

The Russians' suspicion of those in power is widespread. They see them as exempt from any accountability or legal liability, and as interested primarily in feathering their own nests and that of their corporation. The building of personal fortunes, a result of monopolizing national resources, has exacerbated the antagonism between the men in power and society.

Russians express no more trust in their municipal and regional authorities than in central government even though they urgently need them. The local authorities consolidate their influence through their proximity and their detailed knowledge. The mayors and administrative chiefs know very well what is going on in their own area. Furthermore, they treat their little society (commune, canton, urban neighbourhood) as their personal fiefdom. The shops, the modest little town museum and the new local radio station are 'their babies' in a way. Each person's life remains partially 'under the protection' of the local administration. The omission of a stamp on a document can lead to all kinds of inconvenience, and it is essential that everything should be 'in order' for the sake of bureaucracy, be it that of a municipality, a regional administration or a district court.

The former Soviet elites, and more particularly today the KGB/FSB networks, largely controlled the division of spoils and the distribution of income. They also ensured they had a stranglehold on resources while consolidating their administrative grip. More in the provinces than in Moscow, senior and middle-ranking members of the *nomenklatura* remained in office, with the same duties or with a new hat. The links between the political and administrative sphere and the economic sphere are still very close, and local officials now have a financial stake that was unheard of in Soviet times. The persistent blurring of the boundaries between the public arena and the private (from lack of appropriate laws and obedience to them as well as from lack of habit) is a corollary to and bolsters the elites' corporatism.

Through their doggedness in maintaining their strategic position in a period of economic and social change, administrative bodies have managed to impose their own order. This order is shape-shifting, but it guarantees protection for the bureaucrats, entrepreneurs and businessmen loyal to the Kremlin. It imposes itself too on a local society as the only safeguard against chaos. The administrative machine consolidates itself through the need for arbitration, for a hierarchy amid this vagueness. From 2003–2004, Putin challenged this equilibrium by gradually establishing a new model for administering resources (see Chapters 5 and 8).

The growing power of the provincial capitals was the major hallmark of developments in Russia in the 1990s. In the uncertainty that followed 1991, and faced with the dismantling of the state pyramid, the regional elites exercised a growing influence that was essential for the day-to-day running of the country. The leaders in Moscow actively sought their support and cooperation. The 'pact between the elites', which still provides the underlying framework of the political regime, became more complex, less hierarchical and less rigid.

One of the most consequential trends in the decade starting in 2000, however, was the decline of the provinces as political subjects. When Vladimir Putin took the helm, he wanted to reverse the movement and streamline the system's complexity. He tried to weaken the provincial leaders and control their public arenas and their economies. In Moscow and in the provinces alike, he attacked the bureaucracies and the 'oligarchs', labelling them 'enemies' of the state and of reform. He hollowed out the new institutions born of democratization, consolidated the 'traditional' organizations like the FSB and built systems of government through personal, quasi monopolistic networks. What kind of state did he thus forge by turning his back on both federalism and public involvement in political life?

5

THE HOLLOWING OUT
OF PUBLIC INSTITUTIONS

'It is not possible to construct the state and at the same time to destroy society'.

Yuri Olesha, dramatist[1]

When Vladimir Putin took over control of the state in 2000, he endeavoured to restore its authority and efficiency. He also promised security, but stoked the conflict in Chechnya, thus encouraging terrorist attacks. Ten years later, the public institutions were all weakened and subject to the arbitrariness of the 'Kremlin system'. Universal suffrage, the flagship institution of the transition to democracy launched by Mikhail Gorbachev, was now no more than a ritual submission to the choice of the ruling elite, as was clearly demonstrated by the legislative and presidential elections of 2007–2008.

The most striking feature of this systematic hollowing out of the institutions of state and society is that it now took place openly, in broad daylight, with no pretence of keeping up appearances. Until 2003, Putin's regime attempted to maintain a semblance of democracy and still courted the approval of Western democracies. The fundamental difference between Vladimir Putin's first and second terms is the abandonment of civil liberties, competition, and self-government specific to liberal-democratic societies.

The Kremlin's new credo, 'sovereign democracy', can be summed up as follows: Russia is big and powerful, its economy is in good shape, Russians support their leaders and there is stability; under these conditions, we should no longer follow the injunctions, the influence or even the advice of foreign governments, who rejoiced at our weakness under Yeltsin (and were partly the cause of it); they are wrong and we are right, we are choosing the path of Russian sovereignty, a model that suits us and which is the best. Since the ordinary Russians are not complaining, this model is democratic.

The chief ideologist of the new doctrine, Vladislav Surkov, proudly revealed the ingenuity of the formula in 2005.[2] In a nutshell, he summed up the essence of domestic and foreign policy and the close link between them: sovereignty is national independence and no-holds-barred protection against outside interference, while avoiding multilateral or international obligations as far as possible; democracy is political and social consensus between the government, the elites and the people, with no opposition or protest. Consensus, as we shall see, is ideally anti-pluralist and unanimous.

The political history of Vladimir Putin's two terms unfolded according to a scenario which, viewed with hindsight, reveals its full meaning, the main goal having been achieved, i.e. a loyal society and elites prepared to accept cohabitation with an autocratic and oligopolistic regime, in a robust economic climate. This chapter outlines the key moments and main trends of the years 2000–2008. The following two chapters offer an interpretation of the power system and of the elites that serve it, in a Russia that is still under Putin.

The Break with Yeltsin

In order to understand the mood and methods that have prevailed since the beginning of Putin's presidency in 2000, it is important to remind ourselves how a lieutenant-colonel who became head of the FSB and was unknown to the public was propelled to the position of Head of State.

During Boris Yeltsin's first term, Russia experienced a remarkable opening up and a real democratization of public life, in particular through the introduction of pluralism in the media and competitive elections. However, at the same time, the democratic institutions were slowly being eroded, albeit in a sporadic manner, a tendency that accelerated during Yeltsin's second term, from the summer of 1996 to Christmas 1999. Re-elected thanks to the financial backing of the oligarchs and the zeal of some administrations, the ailing Boris Yeltsin was rarely seen in the Kremlin, which permitted the creation of a 'courtier regime'; corruption and scandals were rife at the very highest levels of the state. The financial crash of August 1998 caused the Moscow bubble to burst and revealed the government's shortcomings.

Boris Yeltsin's presidency can be divided into two distinct periods. The first Yeltsin regime still rode the wave of democratization associated with the exit from Communism, but aberrations were already apparent, particularly the war in Chechnya. The second regime allowed the institutions to decay. The gulf between the clans in power and society widened.

It is against this end-of-an-era backdrop that Vladimir Putin was selected as the heir apparent. He had to fulfil some commitments in very particular circumstances. Boris Yeltsin's entourage was corrupt and divided. Vladimir Putin, recently appointed head of the FSB (the internal intelligence service, successor to the KGB), had worked within the presidential machine from 1996 to 1998 and seemed to be the man best placed to give assurances to 'the Family' and to the oligarchs close to the government. He benefited from the conflicts within the ruling group, which prevented any consensus emerging on the choice of another politician to take over.

The FSB chief was not a member of Yeltsin's inner circle; no one expected that someone who was an outsider in political spheres and unknown to the public would be launched into orbit. In 1999 the head of the FSB was shrouded in secrecy and few observers followed his activities. Putin became the man of the moment, then played his hand very shrewdly. Over the months and years, he established himself in the Kremlin, at the centre of powerful networks, and his personality as well as his method of exercising power increasingly influenced Russia's political history. But initially, in 1999, Putin was not chosen for his personality or for his leadership skills.

Contrary to what was commonly accepted at the time, Vladimir Putin was not installed in the Kremlin to prolong the Yeltsin regime, but to bury it. His role was to break with the previous decade, to transform the means of government and to hand back control over resources, people and the territories to the administrations and 'structures of force': the army, the FSB and the Ministry of the Interior. Two major conditions were set: Putin was to guarantee Yeltsin and his family immunity from any legal proceedings, particularly resulting from the Bank of New York scandal;[3] his remit was also to crush the Chechen separatists, at any price, thereby giving the 'power ministries' and their numerous men—the *siloviki*—the opportunity to take their revenge after the terrible military rout of 1996.

Most Russian and foreign analysts failed to grasp the nature of the change underway since they quite simply had not envisaged the re-establishment of an autocratic system. On the face of it, there seemed to be a certain continuity, since Putin was careful not to tread on the toes of Yeltsin's entourage too quickly. Chief of Staff Alexander Voloshin remained in post until October 2003, when the arrest of Mikhail Khodorkovsky, the boss of the Yukos oil company, forced him to step down. In the early months of Putin's leadership, only a handful of extraordinarily perceptive observers guessed to what extent it boded a return to authoritarianism, among them the brilliant journalist and reporter Anna Politkovskaya.[4]

Even the savviest Russian politicians were mistaken in their predictions. Perhaps they were afraid to voice their concerns, perhaps they were unaware in 1999 of how badly the public institutions and the economy had deteriorated already and of society's low morale. After all, these politicians were at the hub of the political machine and belonged to the first, second or third inner circles of the Kremlin. They were dependent on this machine and its problems, and sometimes they profited from it too. We have seen the extent to which opaqueness and bending the rules suited the ruling elites in the Yeltsin years. The preference for fluidity, a legacy of the Soviet era, permeated mentalities and behaviour in the post-Soviet period even more profoundly. Many protagonists in this political history probably did not envisage the major aberrations that this preference would end up creating within the state institutions and big corporations. Gradually, it became routine for people to operate without scrupulously adhering to the law or conventions, convincing themselves that 'this is how it has always been', 'you have to oil the wheels'. However, it is all a matter of degree. When the margin of accommodation and circumvention of the rules takes on considerable proportions, when favours and privileges become common currency, arbitrary power and impunity increase, and autocracy takes hold.

Although Boris Yeltsin had made him his heir, under pressure from 'the Family', Putin continually criticized the chaos and neglect inherited from his predecessor. As Yuri Levada wrote, 'each changing of the guard at the top echelons of government turns out to be the negation of the actions conducted by the politicians of the preceding period'.[5] The new leader's quest for legitimacy spontaneously set about undermining the legitimacy of the former leader. Since 2000, the entire rhetoric of 'order' has been built around condemnation of the previous government. The minute there is the slightest criticism of the drift towards authoritarianism, the defenders of the regime reply: anything is better than the chaos of the past. This behaviour is symptomatic of a regime in which authority is vested in the person rather than the position. And it naturally led to the personalization of presidential power, which Putin exploited brilliantly, to the point where he was unable and unwilling to relinquish power in 2008 and stayed on in the position of Prime Minister, wielding extensive authority.

Violence and the Chechen Foe

Vladimir Putin came to power thanks to the new war in Chechnya and the September 1999 bombings. It is through extreme violence that Russia's second president elect won his position. The destruction of Chechnya is the political regime's original sin. Even Vladimir Putin's closest advisers recognize that the climate of insecurity created by the 1999 attacks and the re-igniting of the war provided the vital ingredient for the FSB chief's ascent to the top position. Of course, they vehemently refute the theory of a destabilization strategy carefully orchestrated by the 'structures of force' and the kingmakers in the Kremlin in 1999. But they do not deny that, without this extreme violence, the succession to Boris Yeltsin was far from certain.[6]

The decision to resume hostilities against the Chechens was taken in the spring of 1999. This period is absolutely crucial: it marks a break with the 'exit from Communism' period when, despite all the mistakes and abuses described above, the elites remained faithful to a spirit of experimentation and openness and were not seeking to revert to Soviet modes of thought and action.

At the start of 1999, several significant events took place. NATO's strikes against Serbia in March were seized on by the presidential advisers, paving the way for Putin's rise, to launch an anti-Western, mainly anti-American spiral both in official diatribes and in the media. Those few weeks were extremely tense and the West was taken to task. Some Russian experts returned to a Cold War discourse and announced that the mask had fallen. 'The USA wants to weaken Russia, the proof is there, and you Europeans slavishly follow American policy'.[7]

This crisis of confidence was exploited by the authorities to prepare the Russians for other events. The military leadership echoed the politicians in denouncing American unilateralism and reminding people of their priority: defending national interests, the security and integrity of the Russian Federation. They prepared the ground for a resumption of the war in Chechnya. If Washington trampled on the integrity of the Federation born of the former Yugoslavia, and NATO took the liberty of bombing that territory without a UN resolution, then Moscow was entitled to protect its territorial integrity against the Chechen terrorists! Confusion soon set in, thanks to an intensive media campaign on a scale the Russians had not seen since pre-Gorbachev days. The second Chechen War was accepted by the majority of Russians, thanks to the series of attacks in September 1999. Relations with America were dented by the confrontation over Kosovo. Some weeks after the anti-NATO hysteria, the polls showed that society's attitude towards the United States and Europe in particular had calmed down, but it never regained the level of cordiality that had existed before the Kosovo war.[8] Even the compassion felt for America after 11 September 2001 did not make it possible to regain the trust that had been lost.

Furthermore, the end of Boris Yeltsin's pernicious rule, the scandals and corruption and the changes of prime minister also helped develop in the Russians feelings of insecurity and therefore of growing xenophobia against the Chechens, and all those suspected of supporting the 'terrorists'. From 1999 to 2000, thanks to the war in the north Caucasus, Putin was able to count on his citizens' worried and nervous attitude and started building an inward-looking policy based on the idea of a Russian order and the rejection of foreign influence. We shall see the extremes to which the image of the enemy has pushed the Kremlin, in particular against the Georgians since 2006, without society protesting.

The second Chechen War gave a clear signal to the army and the police. The ruling elite became increasingly militarized after 2000. The men in uniform felt as though they were getting their revenge after a decade of humiliations when they were treated as inferior state officials. In 2001, two years after the resumption of the war, the situation was disastrous in Chechnya and was rapidly deteriorating in the neighbouring republics where the populations were impoverished and vulnerable. Ingushetia, which took in large numbers of Chechen refugees, Daghestan, Kabar-dino-Balkaria found themselves swept up in the storm of violence and poverty. But an unforeseen event provided Vladimir Putin with an extraordinary opportunity to obtain endorsement for the conflict as one of the battlefronts against international terrorism: Al-Qaeda's attacks on New York on 11 September 2001. The confusion between the Chechens and international terrorism was accepted by George Bush, then by all the Western governments. Vladimir Putin no longer met with any strong resistance from Europe. The international community's tolerance of the violence in the Caucasus had very serious consequences. Indirectly, Russia's foreign partners recognized Putin's right to national exceptionalism: national exceptionalism of repression, national exceptionalism of the lack of political control over the army, national exceptionalism of minorities who had to bow to the central government's *diktat*. From 11 September 2001, democratization was no longer seen as possible in Russia, and the authorities made it known. Security was the priority; freedoms and civil rights could wait.

Today, nobody wants to discuss the Chechnya question, or that of the north Caucasus more generally. No politician would take the risk of criticizing the war that raged from 1999 to 2004, and even less the daily exactions of the regime led by Ramzan Kadyrov, placed at the head of the Republic by Putin.[9] The elites preferred to 'close their eyes and ears' and were content with the official media's silence or disinformation on the violence in the Caucasus. No one was even prepared to raise the question of blame. The worst crime, that of a war waged by the army of a huge state against the population of a tiny territory that belongs to it, was not the fault of any institution, any elected politician, only that of the 'terrorists'.

The brutality of the men in uniform against a civilian population, and not only against fighters, lasted long enough for the conviction to become rooted in people's minds that it was necessary to 'put an end to it', that eradicating resistance through armed force was the only possible response to the threat. The more the Chechen War was rewritten by propagandists and the official historians as an inevitability, or, worse, as an heroic episode in the defence of the fatherland, the more ordinary Russians bowed to a selective and falsified memory of their present and recent past. The war corrupted people's minds.

Putin I and Putin II

Vladimir Putin's image in Russia and abroad came not from the man himself, who was relatively unknown, but from the contrast with the ailing and impotent incumbent President. Putin benefited from an astonishing social capital of trust for a former head of the secret services and KGB agent in East Germany. He was young, and therefore modern; active, a reformer; spoke German, and was consequently open towards Europe. His years at the side of the 'democratic' mayor of Saint Petersburg, Anatoly Sobchak, gave him the reputation of being a reformer. And yet, it was enough to look at his track record, the nature of his activities in Dresden, then in Saint Petersburg, and finally in Moscow from 1996, to understand that the man was not a 'young reformer' with a democratic and open spirit.[10]

The density of his personal network shows the man's ability to weave his own web. By 2010, Putin was surrounded by men who for the most part had worked in Saint Petersburg in the early 1990s and/or had belonged to the various intelligence services which, at the time, were still grouped together in a state body, the Committee for State Security (KGB).[11]

Putin I is the character who, from 1999 to 2003, took refuge behind a smooth, expressionless face, and a young wolf image, both hard and without charisma. And yet, the targets to be shot down had already been identified by the new President: the Chechens, the oligarchs, the provincial governors, as well as any journalists and opponents who were too vociferous. However, commentators in Moscow and outside Russia tended not to recognize that he was the driving force behind these decisions, seeing him rather as carrying on the Yeltsin heritage, battling behind the scenes of a hostile Kremlin. The tragic episode of the *Kursk* submarine in August 2000 perhaps boosted this image of a young political greenhorn, unable to react and virtually manipulated by the senior military hierarchy. However, in retrospect, it seems that Putin's failure to react, his inability to express the slightest sympathy for the families of the 118 submarine personnel abandoned in their fortress on the sea bed, and his refusal to punish those responsible revealed the methods of the spy turned king: a frigid monster devoid of emotion, whose role was not to sympathize with mere mortals and who was not responsible for the fortunes and misfortunes of his administration or his armed forces.

His reaction had been the same following the bombings of September 1999, but at that time he was Yeltsin's Prime Minister and played the part of custodian. The Russians praised his 'calm' and believed him when he stated that the 'Chechen terrorists' had blown up the two Moscow buildings in September 1999.[12] Putin's response was identical in the wake of the Beslan school tragedy in September 2004. He accepted no blame, did not dismiss any of his close associates, and accused 'outside agents who want to undermine Russia'.

Putin II is the man who was re-elected in 2004 and has grasped power with both hands. He must protect the formidable networks and interests which he relied on for support, and he thinks that the credit for Russia's regained international prestige is due exclusively to him. The country's economic growth, guaranteed in part by the rise in the price of hydrocarbons, gave him a renewed confidence and a new mission: to re-establish Russian power and gain world recognition for it. We shall see how the Beslan tragedy and particularly Ukraine's Orange Revolution at the end of 2004, which caught the Kremlin completely off guard, were a shock and a humiliation for Putin which he sought to overcome by exercising his power in an even more authoritarian manner, rejecting the idea of putting a time limit on his tenure. Putin was resolved not to suffer the same ordeal as Boris Yeltsin. Once his second term began in 1996, Yeltsin had already entered the fragile pre-succession phase, since he had neither the constitutional right nor the physical capacity to remain in power after 2000.

Spurred by this experience of presidential impotence, from 2003 Putin started planning possible scenarios for 2008, not unveiling any precise strategy until the last minute. He intended to remain the supreme leader with his power unchanged throughout the duration of his second four-year term. To do this, he needed to maintain the suspense regarding his desire and his capacity to stay in power beyond 2008. The Yeltsin model was therefore to be avoided at all costs. By 2008, Putin's system made rotation in office and placing a time limit on the leader's term impossible. Putin ensured the presidency was in the hands of his protégé and occupied the role of a very powerful prime minister (see Chapters 7 and 9).

The journalist Elena Tregubova had grasped the real nature of Putin's plans from very early on. She regularly rubbed shoulders with the new President since she was one of the pool of Kremlin-accredited journalists up until 2001, and had attracted the attention of Putin in person.

After cutting loose, she took the risk of writing two highly critical books, the first on her years in the Kremlin, the second on the harassment she suffered.[13] The first title is worth a close read. Tregubova emphasizes Putin's predilection for secrecy, corruption scandals and *kompromaty* (compromising files) against rivals and potential mischief-makers. Long before anyone else, she wrote that Putin's men would stop at nothing and that they resorted to violent methods to 'solve problems'. When the book came out in 2003, the Russian public and foreign observers were probably not ready to hear the message, for Vladimir Putin still had a dual reputation, a mix of hardness and modernity. Within a few months, the forcefulness of Tregubova's testimony could no longer be ignored; with the pillorying of Khodorkovsky and the series of dramatic episodes in 2004—bombings, hostage-taking in the Beslan school, Orange Revolution—the Russian President revealed his true colours as an autocrat who would not tolerate any argument and repressed those who stood in his way, his 'foes'.

In an interview given in September 2004 after the Beslan disaster, the President's First Deputy Chief of Staff and chief ideologist, Vladislav Surkov, had no compunction in saying: 'Faced with a threat to the integrity of the state, the President is forced to apply the constitutional principle of unity of the executive power'.[14] The fight against terrorism meant the rejection of federalism and concentration of all the executive powers in the hands of the Kremlin.

Putin Consolidates his Power

For Russian experts independent of the government, the presidential election of March 2000 was a mere formality (*formal'nost'*). Nikolay Petrov considers that the cycle of free elections that opened in 1989, closed in 2000: 'The 2000 presidential election marked the end of political figures and public life as such. The political class succeeded in avoiding an open bid for succession, through controlled elections. Power was passed on "through heritage" and the vote simply endorsed it'.[15]

We stated earlier that Putin obtained 52 per cent of the votes in the first round, but this result would not have been achieved without significant vote rigging, both in the number of votes cast and in the number of votes for the man designated by the Kremlin.[16] The fact is that society was not interested. Faced with this drift away from the free vote and the rules of democracy, citizens were resigned: 'In any case, Putin would have won'. Or: 'It doesn't make any difference who's in power at the Kremlin. It is the bureaucrats, the oligarchs and the mafia who decide'. People did not reason in terms of principles, law and fair competition. They sought first and foremost to reduce the risks, protecting themselves against the unknown, often remaining highly dependent on the local administrations for their material survival. Yuri Levada emphasizes that, in 2000 and again in 2004, the presidential elections were a 'transition' that met no external resistance, 'either from political forces, or from public opinion, or from the influential media'. A 'mechanism guaranteeing the continuity of the institutions and representatives of government with no alternative'[17] had been formed.

The mantra of Putin's new team was 'we are the state'; in other words, the 'restoration' of state authority meant the affirmation of the central executive's powers, concentrated in the various political and federal administrative bodies. From the moment he took up his position, Vladimir Putin focused his efforts on crushing those he saw as an obstacle to the exercise of his presidential authority: the oligarchs, the governors and the critical media.

In 2000, the team gathered around Putin was a mix of civil servants anxious to serve the leader, former members of 'the Family', men from the intelligence services, especially those of Saint Petersburg where Putin had worked for many years, and some 'advisers', such as the propagandist Gleb Pavlovsky and the economist Andrey Illarionov. Some 'liberals', for example Grigory Yavlinsky and Boris Nemtsov, did not range themselves against the regime. They acted as if they thought they could mollify the President and influence policy. They were wrong about the nature of government, which was fundamentally a bureaucratic power, devoid of ideology and conviction, but well constructed to convince, win over and impose its views.

Very early on, the Putin team launched the attack against some powerful financiers, company bosses and media magnates. Vladimir Gusinsky and Boris Berezovsky were forced into exile. At the same time, central government sought to undermine the provincial governors, whose powers were felt to be excessive. Above all, the Kremlin wanted those regional leaders, elected through universal suffrage, to apply the directives emanating from the centre and to be part of a 'power vertical'. There is no doubt about the determination of Putin's team and central administrations to rein in the elites. However, implementation of this resolve brought them into conflict with the habits, patronage politics and 'local systems' that governed the localities and the regions more assuredly than laws and federal decrees. The functioning of the Russian territorial administrations was more flexible than might have been expected. Local bureaucracies were able to adapt to the market economy and negotiate with local businesses. They provided the population with skeleton public services and social welfare which federal authorities struggled to ensure. They chose to display their political loyalty to President Putin so as to guarantee the support of the centre, and above all to avoid conflicts and meddling from Moscow. By declaring themselves pro-Putin, they gave themselves room for manoeuvre without necessarily obeying the injunctions of the federal government.

The Putin administration's control policy brought results when it came to regulating tax revenue, harmonizing the legislative bodies and laws of the Federation's different regions and republics, and strengthening the role of the intelligence services, the Interior Ministry and the police forces. On the other hand, the local and regional authorities remained the principal protagonists in the economic and social arena. One of the negative consequences of this control strategy was the loss of accountability. The central administrations passed off their responsibilities onto the regional and local administrations. Meanwhile it was easy for the latter to say that the central bureaucracies were hindering them from working, particularly by curbing their budgets.

The local and regional civilians' capacity for resisting central government policy and the ability to protect themselves against interference from above is one of the main explanations for why the Putin system, authoritarian in its design and in its methods, was unable to impose a centralized, interventionist regime at the level of day-to-day life. The best bulwarks against autocracy are undoubtedly the strength of the local networks, the adaptability of private interests, the elites' lack of transparency and their habit of hiding behind a façade of obedience.

Antifederalism

The 'power vertical' began in Moscow and descended to the regional or republican level through a reinforced presence of the federal administrative bodies in the provinces. Tax authorities, courts, security services, the police and the army had to be wrenched from the control of the regional governors and mayors of large towns and brought back under the direct control of central government. To do this, Putin's government tried to ensure the regular payment of civil servants' salaries so that they would be less dependent on the goodwill of the local administrations.

However, experience showed that prosperity or simple survival in Russia demanded benefits in kind and income over and above a person's official salary. A judge or tax inspector remained reliant on the goodwill of the local bureaucracy, the governor's or the mayor's system for his home, car, the upkeep of the building where he worked—in other words the entirety of day-to-day logistics. Moreover, each person's situation was determined not simply by their formal status, but by networks and cronyism.

In the spring of 2000, the institutional responses that Putin's team came up with to counter the governors' autonomy were the establishment of seven superdistricts (*okrug*) each covering ten to fifteen provinces, as well as the reorganization of the Federation Council and the right to dismiss governors elected by universal suffrage. For each *ukase* the Russian President introduced a new bureaucratic level, that of 'plenipotentiary representatives' (*polnomochnye predstaviteli* or *polpredy*), spread over seven major districts, and in charge of supervizing the territorial federal agencies and sanctioning the governors' activities. The former regional 'representatives of the president' appointed by Boris Yeltsin, who had proved ineffective, were dismissed.

The country was now divided into seven vast administrative districts: Central, North-West, South, Volga, the Urals, Siberia, and Far Eastern Russia. These districts were organized in bureaucratic systems which in principle had extended powers of control. Public administrations started to reflect this division into seven large regions, such as the Federal *Prokuratura* (the Russian equivalent of, but not exactly the same as, the public prosecutor's office), the Justice Ministry, the natural monopolies (like gas and electricity) and all the other territorial federal department outposts—which opened 'offices' in each of the seven administrative centres of these new administrative apparatuses. A 'federal inspector' was appointed in each province.

Five of the seven 'super-representatives' appointed at the time were army or FSB officers. The message was thus clear: the police and army had the authority to act at the centre of the country's system of government, to supervise the proper application of central directives and to ensure compliance with federal laws. The reform also provided for regaining control of the regional *prokuratura* and the judicial bodies to reduce their subordination to the leaders of the regional executives, a subordination linked to their material dependency and patronage politics.

A preliminary review of the achievements of the seven plenipotentiary representatives was modest given the ambitions announced in the spring of 2000 for the creation of the new institution in the service of the president.[18] The discourse on regaining control over the regional authorities was cleverly countered by a number of governors. These governors had chosen to affirm their loyalty to Putin's government vociferously with ostentatious declarations. Thus they thwarted the Kremlin's tactic of entering into a test of strength with the regions deemed recalcitrant in order to assert the power of the federal executive more effectively. The 'strong arm' tactics could not be justified since the majority of the *oblast* governors and presidents of the republics declared their allegiance to the new president and even agreed to some of the proposed reforms (particularly the new composition of the Federation Council where representatives of the executive and legislative powers of each province now sat, whereas previously it had been the governors and presidents of the regional assemblies). In a number of cases, the governors even succeeded in pressuring the *polpred* to have one of their men appointed as the new 'federal inspector' of their region, responsible for briefing the *polpred* on the local situation.

The President's representative had to find common ground with the governors, some of whom had just been re-elected for four years. As in the whole of Russia, the most powerful economic players (the mining, gas and oil and raw materials industries) did not need to negotiate with the new bureaucracies of Putin's seven representatives. Putin himself had to clarify matters during a television interview on 25 December 2000 stating that 'the *polpredy* should never intervene in the local leaders' sphere', adding that their task 'was not to govern, but to coordinate the activities of the federal districts'.

The regional elections of the autumn and winter of 2000 were a reminder of the strength of the local systems and of the Kremlin's feeble ability to interfere. Bar a few exceptions, the presidency did not want to become involved in the ballot.[19] The rallying of most governors and presidents of the republics in support of Putin at the beginning of 2000 should be interpreted with caution. When the die is cast and there is no viable alternative, it is always wiser to position oneself favourably in negotiations with the future holder of the executive power. Relations between Moscow and the provinces involved constant bargaining over budgets and taxation, sometimes with political compensation. The Russian President tried to reduce the regional administrations' capacity for action by tangibly cutting the share of tax resources allocated to them.

By not obstructing the election of Vladimir Putin and by not refusing the reforms concerning them *en bloc*, the bosses of the provinces obtained from the new administration guarantees of non-interference in their local affairs. They also won the option of standing for a third term, which enabled the President of Tatarstan to hold on to his position. As for the right Vladimir Putin gave himself to dismiss a regional leader elected by universal suffrage, it proved very difficult to put into practice. Yevgeny Nazdratenko, Governor of Primorsky province (Vladivostok), was ousted from his post at the beginning of 2001, but through 'voluntary resignation' and appointment to a high ministerial post in Moscow.[20]

The corollary of the policy of 'restoring the state' was the weakening of powers other than the federal executive. In seeking to strengthen the central executive's powers, the President undermined the representative and legislative authorities, seen as obstacles to the efficiency of the government, and likewise the independent and critical media. This tendency pleased the regional and republican executive powers whose base was founded on a bureaucratic omnipotence that assured them control over vital economic resources and restricted the independence of the assemblies and the courts.

The 'power vertical' primarily meant less interference from individuals outside the administrative sphere and a rejection of checks and balances and parliamentary oversight, which satisfied most leaders of regions and big cities, especially since the hierarchical control that Moscow sought to impose on them proved largely ineffective. Most mayors and governors followed Putin's example in trying to strengthen their grip on the local media.

The decline of the provincial and municipal assemblies echoed the decline of the State Duma and the Federation Council. With no separation of powers, the authority of parliament's lower house diminished constantly. Nowadays it is a chamber for recording decisions of the administration. The interviews conducted in the provinces confirm the lack of trust in the deputies, suspected of being more interested in the privileges associated with their status, like trips to Moscow or abroad, than in defending the interests of their constituency. The very existence of a parliamentary opposition is questionable among the Duma elected in December 2007. Only the Communist deputies still sometimes vote against proposed laws.

By conceiving government in a spirit of control and curbing local and individual initiatives, Putin's team betrayed a defensive attitude. Instead of unifying the public and the economic spheres, an ill-conceived centralization of decision-making carried the risk of increased circumvention of the rules. The experience of other countries shows that a top-down battle to combat corruption in the administration can exacerbate the phenomenon and weaken the state. Vladimir Putin was not happy about the level of autonomy retained by the regional chiefs and took advantage of the Beslan school tragedy in September 2004 to undermine their power.

Increased Authoritarianism

From 2000 to 2004, managed elections, pressure on the media and the Yukos affair revealed a growing intolerance of political competition, independent criticism and private economic power. The pursuit of the military occupation in Chechnya, under increasingly intolerable conditions, was closely bound up with this general tendency to control and the refusal to negotiate. A charade of polls was organized in Chechnya in 2003: a referendum in March, then presidential and legislative elections in the autumn.

Against this backdrop of monopolization of the public sphere by the President and his cronies, the leaders of the administrations and even the bosses of the major private groups, the disintegration of democratic movements and of the independent media, society's weariness and the abdication of intellectuals was exacerbated. The so-called 'oligarchs' contributed to the creation of this political desert, even if some of them are now its victims. The boomerang effect of 'doing deals' with the politicians struck with full force in 2003: Yukos was a prime target. These battles by Putin's team were spearheaded by the intelligence services and the Interior ministry.

Mikhail Khodorkovsky's arrest at the end of October 2003 set alarm bells ringing in a relatively calm climate. Admittedly, the attack against the oil giant Yukos had begun in the spring and one of the shareholders and directors, Platon Lebedev, had been behind bars since July. However, the brutality of Khodorkovsky's arrest (his plane was stormed by an anti-terrorist unit at Novosibirsk airport), the flouting of legal procedures, and the spiteful rage of the government and a section of the media against the oligarch showed that this affair was both a settling of scores and a crack-down to serve as an example to other over-ambitious businessmen.

Finally, Putin's chief of staff, Alexander Voloshin, resigned in protest at Khodorkovsky's arrest. The man who had been appointed by 'the Family' left the Kremlin. For some observers, securing the departure of the last pillar of the Yeltsin era was the true goal of Putin's team. For others, this exit was the price to be paid for crushing Khodorkovsky, considered a rival by Putin. Controversy over this issue still rumbles on in Russia. There was reason for other big bosses, like Roman Abramovich, to be worried about the new methods of pressure being applied to powerful economic players. The treatment of the Khodorkovsky case exposed all the flaws in the Russian legal system, and its subordination to the government. Having attended the trial in Moscow on several occasions and having followed the case closely, I can testify that the investigation was biased and both the first and the second trials were a parody of justice.[21]

The entrepreneur aroused the enmity of the President, who saw in him a political rival and a powerful industrialist capable of challenging the Kremlin's desire to control the hydrocarbons industry. His arrest some months before the presidential election of 14 March 2004 was no coincidence. The Kremlin, with the help of the judges at its disposal, quite simply stole Yukos from its shareholders.[22] The minority shareholders in Europe and the USA sued the Russian state and the companies that bought up the assets of Yukos. The company managed by Mikhail Khodorkovsky was, unquestionably, the country's most profitable oil production, exploitation and sales company. The state-owned company Rosneft lagged behind considerably in the fields of management and productivity.

On 24 February 2004, two and a half weeks before the presidential election, Vladimir Putin disbanded his government without any official reason other than: 'The Kasyanov government worked hard, but the voter is entitled to know who the president will govern with after his re-election'. This move ran counter to all democratic practice. The Russian president should have waited to be re-elected before forming a new government. There was no urgency. On 2 March, Vladimir Putin put forward the name of his future Prime Minister, Mikhail Fradkov, a bureaucrat unknown to the general public. Fradkov was chosen precisely because he was of no political stripe, because his sole purpose would be to serve the president. Russians questioned by the Levada Centre research organization expressed their indifference (45 per cent) or their astonishment (22 per cent) with regard to this sudden change of prime minister; only 17 per cent stated they were 'satisfied'.[23]

One theory frequently heard in Moscow was that there were hidden conflicts between the presidential administration, the financial and oil interest groups and the pillars of 'the Family', in other words Boris Yeltsin's inner circle. Prime Minister Mikhail Kasyanov had been critical of Khodorkovsky's arrest. He openly opposed Putin, but was prevented from standing for the presidential election of 2 March 2008, like all the other true opponents of the regime (see Chapter 7).

However, the Putin regime was bolstered by the strong economic situation. The rise in oil prices and the tax reform implemented in 2001–2003 gave the government a tremendous boost and played a decisive role in consolidating Putin's power and in distancing Russia from its Western partners.

Dropping the Mask

By the end of Putin's first term, the workings of the state had become increasingly opaque and social problems were piling up, but the country's leadership refused to do any soul-searching. It claimed to have regained control of the entire 'power vertical'. And yet it deplored corruption and inefficiency in the administrations, the Interior Ministry's inability to combat terrorism and the insubordination of the provincial governors.[24]

Additionally, the leaders in Moscow were dragging Chechnya into a political and security deadlock. They forced on the Chechens a referendum on the status of the tiny Caucasus republic (which had to remain part of the Russian Federation) and the election of a 'President' of Chechnya. The polls took place in appalling conditions, with the population under military and police occupation. Vote-rigging to try and demonstrate that Chechnya was becoming 'normalized' resulted in the assassination of the pro-Russian leader, Akhmad Kadyrov, in an attack that left dozens of people dead on 9 May 2004. From that date on, there was a rapid succession of attacks and assassination attempts both in the north Caucasus and Moscow. The 'Chechenization' of the local authorities, in parallel with the arbitrary actions of the Russian troops, exacerbated the tensions, prevented any real negotiation between Moscow and the independence movement, and resulted in the proliferation of terrorist networks.

The years 2003 and 2004 also witnessed deteriorating conditions in the run-up to and during the elections. International observers criticized the unfairness of the electoral campaigns and the irregularities in the legislative elections of December 2003 and the presidential election of March 2004.[25] They finally put down in black-and-white the failings which Russia experts had already pointed out in the previous elections, in 1999 and 2000. The electoral campaigns were outrageously biased towards the Kremlin candidates. Access to the media was not balanced, threats were used against undesirable candidates and overly critical journalists, and fraud during the vote count complete the picture, when the result was not a *fait accompli*.[26]

Putin's team was aiming to stifle pluralism, competition and criticism in the political arena as well as in economic affairs. Yukos, Chechnya and the elections were three closely interwoven strands of the same phenomenon: the concentration of power within a small leadership circle, the desertification of the public sphere and wresting control of the country's resources. The results attest to the effectiveness of arbitrary methods and the fear they instil in the heart of society. There were few intellectuals, independent deputies or human rights activists who dared challenge the regime outright.

The corrosion of universal suffrage and representation, and therefore of popular sovereignty, precisely mirrored the chronology of the conflict waged by the Kremlin and the military in Chechnya. The years 1999 to 2003, during which the conflict was particularly violent and bloody, were also the years of intense pressure on opponents of the regime and of direct intimidation to prevent political figures from taking a stance on the war.

Grigory Yavlinsky had been virtually a lone voice in condemning the war during the electoral campaign of autumn 1999. He did not speak out again and gradually aligned himself with the consensus imposed by the Kremlin; criticism was permitted as long as some questions remained taboo: Chechnya, Putin's share of blame for the war, Putin's growing personal wealth. Grigory Yavlinsky allowed himself to be drawn into a fatal spiral of compromise with the regime concerning its most reprehensible actions. Chechnya recurs at every stage. For example, in the campaign for the regional elections of 2006, his Yabloko party agreed to head a list in this republic that was occupied by the army and sacked by Ramzan Kadyrov's militia.

Another liberal party, the Union of Right Forces (SPS), which brought together some of Boris Yeltsin's former ministers and advisers, did likewise. This attitude is explained by the tacit arrangement that these opposition parties entered into with the Kremlin. By giving in over Chechnya, which they considered a lost cause and therefore politically of no importance, they hoped to obtain assurances of high percentages of votes in the constituencies where they were well established. Their calculation did not pay off and none of the so-called 'democratic' parties sat in the Duma.[27]

Putin's Re-election in 2004

The presidential election of 14 March 2004 confirmed that the political sphere in Russia had been eroded and that the leadership around Vladimir Putin was no longer even bothering to maintain a democratic façade. The Kremlin's only concern over the vote of 14 March was a predictably high level of abstention. The same applied to the polls of 2 December 2007 and 2 March 2008. If more than 50 per cent of those on the electoral register abstained, the vote would be nullified. By mobilizing the administrations and the electoral commissions, and probably with the help of fraud in some territorial electoral commissions, the turnout was guaranteed; officially, 64 per cent of voters placed their voting cards in the ballot boxes. According to the Golos Association and experts from the Moscow Carnegie Centre, the authorities initially used the electoral registers and voting authorizations in polling stations other than the ones where people were registered. Effectively, registers were amended after the legislative elections of 7 December 2003 and the total number of voters registered in Russia fell considerably: from 108,906,244 in December 2003 to 108,064,281 in March 2004.[28] What happened to those 900,000 voters? Deaths were more than compensated for by the number of young people reaching voting age (demographers point out that there had been a minor baby boom in 1985–1986), but it is not known how many of these young people had been added to the electoral register. And the many 'absence slips' that allowed people to vote elsewhere than at their official polling station added to the opaqueness. The experts explained that, faced with the threat of high levels of abstention, the authorities wanted to round down the number of voters to mitigate the impact of the abstentions.[29]

Furthermore, all the independent observers who have monitored voting in Russia in recent years are clear that the 'administrative resource', as the Russians call it (i.e. the ability of political candidates, and parties, to use their official positions or connections to government institutions to influence the outcome of elections), is functioning well. Once the count in the polling stations is finished, it is easy for the territorial electoral commissions and the central electoral commission to engage in fraud; not forgetting cases of overt vote rigging, as in Chechnya, where ballot box stuffing was barely concealed in some constituencies.

It is impossible to evaluate the extent of the fraud with any accuracy. We can only note that the incumbent President was in no danger of having to run a second round against the few hand-picked candidates, and that only a low turnout could jeopardize Putin's re-election. Putin needed a fairly comfortable turnout, barely lower than that of his initial election (64 per cent in 2004 compared with 68 per cent in 2000), to consolidate his authority for a second term.

The legislative elections had prepared the ground. The reform movements, Yabloko and SPS (Union of Right Forces), had not withstood the steamroller of Putin's power. The Communist Party presented a candidate unknown to the rank and file, Nikolay Kharitonov, who was not allowed to appear on television. As Kharitonov pointed out after the voting, with six minutes' broadcast time in total compared with the many hours of daily programming devoted to the President's candidacy, his 9.5 million votes (13.7 per cent) were all the more significant! None of the other candidates permitted to run obtained more than 4 per cent of the votes.[30] It is striking the extent to which the candidates tolerated by the Kremlin, with the exception perhaps of Irina Khakamada,[31] did not speak out loudly against Putin; 3.5 per cent of the voters ticked the last box 'against-all', the additional box on the voting slip—the ideal protest vote.

The results of the 2004 presidential election nevertheless showed that, despite the partiality of the campaign and interference by the administrations, the plebiscite was not a landslide. For, according to the official figures, Vladimir Putin obtained 71 per cent of the votes of the 64 per cent of voters who turned out. So nearly 30 per cent of the citizens who went to the polls voted against him. Expressing protest was still possible. Moreover the President declared his satisfaction without enthusiasm. On election day, the Chairman of the Electoral Commission, the grand master of ceremonies, did not disguise his weariness from television viewers. All those in charge and commentators alike seemed relieved that the inescapable exercise was over.

In 2004, Russia did not follow the anti-pluralism electoral model of the dictatorships of Central Asia, but it certainly took a backwards step with regard to political openness, transparency and freedoms, separation of powers and the exercise of traditional counterbalances to the Executive.

The following argument was frequently heard: of course, Putin made sure of the rules of the game and sidelined any serious contender in the race. Yes, the administration played its part in averting any nasty surprises. But, even without these pressures, the Russians would have voted for Putin, so why worry so much about anti-democratic abuses?

I feel that such a superficial approach is questionable on two counts. Firstly, the legitimacy and authority of an elected politician depend on the quality of the political situation and the impeccable conduct of the election. And perhaps the stern expression on the victors' faces can be explained by the fact that they knew their victory was not entirely theirs, but that of an administrative machine. Secondly, society expressed its preference for the incumbent President who had enjoyed the support of the majority of Russians for four years. Sociologists have explained the significance of this support: Putin was the only known alternative in a non-competitive regime; he represented the lesser evil since no one knew what use a politician, who was not part of the existing power system, would make of his executive powers. The more closed the competition, the more Russians accepted the status quo as a matter of course. Voting for Putin was also reassuring because his regime had brought more material security than that of Yeltsin.

Beslan: Exploiting Terrorism Politically

Six months after Putin's re-election, the Beslan school tragedy was a stark reminder that violence and terrorism had taken root in the north Caucasus. North Ossetia, along with Chechnya and Ingushetia, were part of the patchwork of tiny republics in the south-west of the Russian Federation that had been destabilized by the military occupation of Chechnya. The bombings, the destruction and the daily acts of violence by the Russian army and the militia caused tens of thousands of deaths in Chechnya and resulted in destitution. The spiral of violence accelerated. There was much greater insecurity in Russia in 2004 , when the second military campaign in Chechnya was getting underway, than at the time when Vladimir Putin began his ascent towards the Kremlin in the summer of 1999.

I was actually in Russia at the time of the Beslan siege, and am still deeply shocked by the barbarity of the hostage-taking and the other terrorist acts that preceded it: the two planes blown up in mid-air on 24 August 2004 and the bomb attack in front of a Moscow Metro station on 31 August. Having been in direct contact with senior Russian politicians, deputies, experts and journalists while following the Beslan crisis, I am alarmed at the contradictions between the official discourse and the censorship imposed on the Russian media.

On receiving us on 6 September 2004—some thirty Western experts on Russia—the Russian President stated from the outset that it was not appropriate to discuss the events but that he would reply to our questions as best he could. And he replied at length, but of course it was impossible to challenge his assertions.

Speaking about the unfolding tragedy, Vladimir Putin defended the special forces who 'bravely went in to attack, showing disregard for their own lives'; he had no reservations about the conduct of the operation, a line that was out of step with his more critical televised speech of 4 September. And yet, the lack of preparation was blatant, the confusion unbelievable, given that the authorities had had more than 48 hours to plan the rescue operation. The presence of families, some armed, around the school added to the panic and the carnage that followed. There was no safety cordon preventing the population from crowding around the scene of the drama. Armed civilians took part in the battle.

During our meeting on 6 September 2004, Vladimir Putin's position was to deny all links between this latest tragedy and the conflict in Chechnya. Furthermore, the President reprimanded one of us who questioned him about the worrying prolongation of the war: 'The war is not ongoing, there are no more offensives'. He added that the policy of transferring power to the Chechens was progressing satisfactorily. Asked about his refusal to negotiate with the Chechen leaders, he replied that he had reached agreement with 'President' Akhmad Kadyrov, even though the latter had fought the Russian Army in 1994–1996. Vladimir Putin took care not to pursue this upbeat story or point out that this violent man, catapulted to power by Moscow following an electoral charade six months earlier, had been assassinated during a deadly attack on 9 May 2004 and that, since then, the violence had worsened.

The greatest hole in the President's argument related to the cause of the attacks and the identity of the terrorists. Rather than say 'we don't know yet', both the President and his Defence Minister declared that none of the hostage-takers was Chechen and that there were 'Arabs' among them. Two days later, the President's statement was corrected by the FSB, then by the Public Prosecutor, who established the identity of some of the hostage-takers: Chechens, some of whom were alleged to have taken part in previous attacks. Finally, the FSB put a price on the head of Shamil Basayev, the extremist Chechen leader, and Aslan Maskhadov, elected President of Chechnya in 1997. Then Basayev claimed responsibility for the hostage-taking and other earlier terrorist acts.

In denying the link between cause and effect between the war begun in 1994 and the many attacks that followed, some carried out by female Chechen suicide bombers, the Russian President was seeking to impose his interpretation of events. According to him, Russia had become the target of international terrorism, like other countries. 'Russia did not create terrorism and nor was the USSR the first to produce nuclear weapons. Who was behind the rebels in Afghanistan in the 1980s? The USSR was not an angel, but the genie of terrorism came out of that bottle. [...] International terrorism has chosen Russia, to weaken us'. Thus, according to Putin, there was no difference in kind between 11 September 2001 in the United States of America and 3 September 2004 in Beslan. But he did not say that the commandos that occupied the school in Ossetia had demanded, during the aborted negotiations, the end of military occupation of Chechnya. Nor did he mention the mediation of the former President of the Republic of Ingushetia, Ruslan Aushev, who succeeded in liberating 26 hostages the day before the attack (the Kremlin had forced Aushev to resign in 2001). Putin's administration refused to acknowledge the failings of its own policies. I am referring to the police's lack of preparation during the hostage-taking in the Dubrovka theatre in Moscow in October 2002, which should have been the starting point for an overhaul of the police force. I am also referring to the stubborn-ness with which the Russian leaders presented Chechnya as a situation 'where normality was in the process of being restored'.

Vladimir Putin was leading the country, he was head of the armed forces and had launched the resumption of hostilities in Chechnya in 1999. How could he still be seeking to convince us that Russia was sim-ply the new victim of international terrorism led by Al-Qaeda? This per-sistent refusal to recognize that the state of war and desolation in Chechnya was the reason for terrorism prevented the Russian President from dealing with the root causes of the violence—even if this violence was also used and exploited by foreign Islamist networks. Since 11 Sep-tember 2001, Putin hijacked the American discourse on the international war on terror to deny the causes of terrorism in Russia.

Russia was no longer the Soviet fortress with impermeable frontiers, locked in around its own propaganda. Foreign media were present, and independent journalists from the Russian print media were doing an extraordinary job in a climate of heavy censorship. In addition to the regime's stranglehold on information and its increasingly hardline stance, its most worrying aspect was the lack of initiative applied to breaking the spiral of violence. The measures announced by Vladimir Putin on 13 September 2004, designed to undermine federalism and universal suf-frage even further, had no connection with the fight against terrorism.

The 'Constitutional Coup' of 13 September 2004

Ten days after the fatal hostage-taking, on 13 September 2004, Vladi-mir Putin announced a series of measures designed to 'step up the fight against terrorism'. In addition to anti-terrorist measures, particularly the security cordon around the north Caucasus region, he proposed two major reforms that had nothing to do with security policy. Firstly, even though they had been elected by direct universal suffrage since the mid 1990s, the regional governors and presidents of the republics were henceforth to be nominated by the President of Russia and 'elected' by the provin-cial assemblies—in other words, appointed de facto.

Secondly, Putin demanded a revision of the electoral laws which would further weaken an opponent of the regime's chances of sitting in the Duma. Since 1993, half the deputies in the lower house were elected through proportional representation and half through the single-mandate system. Putin wanted to eliminate the single-mandate system, which allowed an independent candidate to stand in their constituency. In the Duma that sat from 2004 to 2007, the few liberal or independent deputies had been elected through the single-mandate system. In the legislative elections of December 2003, only the parties close to the Kremlin and the Communist Party had broken through the 5 per cent barrier, subsequently raised to 7 per cent. The Communists did not behave as an active opposition party and often voted for government-proposed projects. The 'pro-presidential party', United Russia, was a vast elitist organization, membership of which political leaders and administrative officials felt was essential. After the presidential announcement of 13 September 2004, the provincial governors rushed to become card-carrying members to demonstrate their loyalty, outwardly at least, to the Putin regime.[32]

The Constitutional Court refused to express an opinion on the presidential proposals of 13 September 2004, thus confirming that it had abdicated its role as an independent means of control years earlier. As a matter of fact, the Constitution did not specify how the Parliament should be formed or how the representatives should be elected. Nor did it lay down how the regional governors and presidents of the republics should be elected. The President's advisers therefore stated that the reforms did not require the Constitution to be changed. But the key democratic and federal principles enshrined in the Basic Law, particularly popular representation, were being flouted.[33]

Furthermore, Putin also took advantage of the wave of terrorism to subordinate the judges further. Supreme Court judges were appointed by the Supreme Qualification Collegium. The members of this Collegium were henceforth to be chosen by the Head of State or by the President of the Federation Council. Judges were to become a minority in this college.[34]

At the same time, all the media were subjected to increasingly stringent controls by the Kremlin, controls justified, again, by the 'war on terrorism'. The war in Chechnya and the attacks it had provoked provided Putin with the opportunity to impose a bill that had been in the pipeline for months. Despite increased censorship, very heated discussions took place on Internet forums and in some Moscow newspapers criticizing the counter-liberalization moves. Even the former Presidents Gorbachev and Yeltsin broke their silence and voiced their hostility to this hijacking of the Constitution.[35]

Another historic development took Vladimir Putin and his close advisers by surprise: the Orange Revolution in Ukraine in December 2004. The rigged presidential elections and Viktor Yanukovich's declared 'victory' were contested by millions of Ukrainians. In a few weeks, Ukrainian society, mobilized day and night in the centre of Kiev, with the opposition led by Viktor Yushchenko and Yulia Timoshenko, succeeded in ousting Leonid Kuchma's regime. The Russian President alone congratulated Yanukovich on his election, and stubbornly clung to a position of denial of the massive peaceful social movement that overwhelmed Ukraine. He was clearly scared of similar developments in Russia and decided to exert even more control and repression over free speech and opposition rallies.

Stranglehold on Information and the Media

Putin's iron grip on the Russian media, especially on television channels and most major newspapers, was tightening. The President and his team could no longer bear to hear or read the slightest criticism. The witch-hunt against any form of public opposition was intensified in the run-up to the legislative elections of 2 December 2007. Vsevolod Bogdanov, Chairman of the Russian Union of Journalists, stressed the fact that the media were no longer produced by journalists, but by *apparatchik*s and spin doctors (*polittekhnologi*) who worked directly for the administration. 'In the media, less than 12 per cent of the programmes and publications can be described as "journalism" and all the rest is propaganda and "public relations" [PR in Russian], grey propaganda used in information warfare against opponents in business and politics [*kompromat*] and advertising', and of course entertainment.[36] In an in-depth study, Oleg Panfilov gave an alarming appraisal of the press and television in Russia.[37] As the media expert Floriana Fossato stressed, since the two government television channels, ORT and RTR, toed the line completely, this gave the Putin regime control over political and social information reaching 80 per cent of Russians. The crushing majority of Russia's population were hostages to the official television stations as they did not have access to the Internet, or to satellite channels, or to Moscow's critical press.[38]

The persecution of the independent media intensified in 2003–2004 with the Yukos affair and the imprisonment of Mikhail Khodorkovsky, then the Beslan crisis of September 2004, and the Orange Revolution in

Ukraine in December 2004. For example, the daily *Izvestia*, even though it rarely steps out of line, published photos of the hostage-taking. The editor was immediately fired and reading that newspaper became pointless.

Between 2000 and 2007, 22 journalists were murdered. Anna Politkovskaya was killed in the lift of her block of flats on 7 October 2006. The investigation will never produce results, except perhaps to end in a sham trial of one or two underlings. Those behind the atrocity have nothing to fear in an authoritarian system where the judiciary is at the service of the executive in political matters.

Another journalist, Manana Aslamazian, head of Internews Russia was trapped by the Russian authorities in 2006. She could not return to her country, where she was falsely accused of money-laundering and risked several years in prison. Internews, an organization that did a remarkable job in training regional journalists, was shut down. It took eighteen months of proceedings to obtain from the Constitutional Court in 2008 a judgment condemning the abuse of power by the customs administration and pointing out that the Aslamazian case did not come within the scope of penal justice. There are many ways in which the Kremlin continues to wage war on its critics, exaggerate the threat of the enemy within, and instil a vague anxiety among the elites and society in general. The legislative elections of December 2007 and the presidential election of 2 March 2008 were conducted in a climate of intense pressure, while the administrations had the 'electoral machine' well in hand and objectively did not have anything to worry about with regard to obtaining the desired electoral results. How then do we explain the behaviour of an authoritarian power that stoked uncertainty and anxiety among those it ruled with no heed for democracy?

Creating an atmosphere of uncertainty before a poll was a tried-and-tested tactic. It was a matter of making the Russians believe that something was perhaps at stake, that they still had a small part to play in the regime's great drama. Political life was resuscitated for a while, the few weeks when people feared losing Putin, the father of the nation. And what a relief when the father announced, after so much prevarication, that he was not going to abandon his people and would remain in the government to ensure its stability and prosperity!

This ploy was double-edged, for Russia was no longer the USSR, shut in behind its high Communist walls. The polls showed that Russians as a whole were worried, even if Putin stayed, and they did not buy the official line that society was perfectly stable and cohesive. On the one hand, the tensions at the top of the power structure were visible. For a start there was the incredible letter, published in the daily *Kommersant* by General Cherkesov, Director of the federal anti-narcotics service, which leaked news of the bitter infighting between the FSB and other internal intelligence organizations against his men;[39] then the murder of Alexander Litvinenko in November 2006, which was made public and revealed that violent settlings of scores were taking place.

Ordinary Russians were aware of tensions at the top, particularly since these tensions were echoed in regional and local political life. We have already mentioned the pressures and accusations to which mayors and governors were subjected, not to mention journalists and regional deputies in a number of provinces.

Several provincial governors and mayors of large cities were deposed or even prosecuted in 2006–2007. When a mayor or governor was a thorn in the Putin administration's side, it was easy to prosecute him for some spurious offence. The mayors of Togliatti (a large industrial city in the Samara region), Arkhangelsk and Khanty-Mansysk, to name but a few, were all prosecuted. The second trial against Mikhail Khodorkovsky and Platon Lebedev, instigated in 2008 under conditions that were just as controversial as those surrounding the 2005–2006 case, and the second iniquitous sentence of December 2010 (see chapter 9) invite speculation on the failure of the judicial reform initiated at the beginning of the 1990s, and which was one of the main planks for building a state governed by the rule of law.

Subverting Judicial Independence

In 1991, still during the Soviet era, the Russian parliament introduced a 'Conception of Judicial Reform': this indicated a will to establish a judiciary that was independent of the government and would safeguard human rights. Very quickly, the reform focused on the necessities of the transition towards a market economy, which was the priority for Yeltsin's leadership. At the same time, the development of private law was given precedence over public law.

Unlike the countries of central Europe which were keen to become part of the European Union and abandoned the socialist system of law and justice quickly and completely, Russia did not break radically from the Soviet system. And, as Anne Gazier notes, 'development in this area remained hamstrung by the authoritarian tendencies of the political leaders and the conservatism of the administration'.[40] She emphasizes that Russia's present judicial system remains 'a judicial system in the process of change'; remnants of the Soviet system persist, particularly in the specific instance of 'judicial surveillance', which the new programme, 'The Development of Russia's Judicial System for 2007–2011', does not plan to abolish.[41] European and independent Russian experts are all agreed on one point: attempts to reform the Russian judicial system are hindered by the way the law is enforced or rather, twisted. The judges are biased when cases referred to them have important political and/or financial implications, as was apparent in the Yukos case, that of the media bosses and the Aslamazian case where it was a question of 'setting an example' to encourage self-censorship. The most outrageous denials of justice apply to the victims of violence in Chechnya. No Russian court has ever convicted an individual or a state authority, despite the thousands of complaints lodged, even though some trials have actually taken place.[42] Many Russian citizens turned to the European Court of Human Rights. In all the cases judged, the Russian state was found guilty and paid the victims compensation.

The contrast between Russian justice and European justice is evidence of the denial of justice in post-Communist Russia. In a Russian poll carried out in June 2007, the majority of respondents answered that an ordinary citizen has more chance of obtaining justice at the European Court of Human Rights (60 per cent) than in a Russian court (26 per cent). Only 14 per cent had no opinion, which shows that Russians are fully aware of the problem with their justice system.[43]

The weakness of the judicial authorities is the principal reason why some crimes go unpunished, and therefore why they were committed. It is blatantly obvious that if the judiciary were independent, and if Anna Politkovskaya's murderers and the authors of racist crimes were to be severely punished, the rising violence would be stemmed. In the absence of punishment, and often even of a trial, unruliness will continue to flourish. The political, administrative, military and police chiefs are not accountable to anyone, except to their leader. Vladimir Putin has not acknowledged the state's responsibility for the tragic outcome of the Beslan school hostage crisis of September 2004. No Moscow leader was punished, and only a few 'local' officials in North Ossetia were penalized.[44]

Putin claims to be the guarantor of a strong state. In reality, he has weakened and undermined the credibility of public institutions. Even the military has been affected by the general erosion of the state. The subordination of military men to civilian leaders is neither structured nor controlled by any public institution. The impact on the operation of the armed forces and on relations between the civil and military authorities is criticized by experts and by the Russian opposition.[45]

While most democratic institutions were declining before the arrival of Putin at the helm, they are clearly in danger today. In elevating the cult of personality and authoritarianism to new heights, Putin has transformed the political regime. When he sweeps away the machinery of competition and changeover, the leader takes on a particular role that is disproportionate and increasingly ill-suited to the challenge posed by major crises. A leader who is subject to no institutional controls thus finds himself open to behind-the-scenes manoeuvring and battles between private and corporatist interests, in a world of patronage politics.

With perfect composure, Vladimir Putin replied to the journalists from the French newspaper Le Monde who were concerned about the institutional abuse caused by his remaining in power as head of government, and the planned succession of Dmitry Medvedev: 'The way in which the roles and ambitions are divided is of secondary importance'. He treated these institutional questions as minor details given that 'Russia is facing a number of challenges' and 'has to modernize'. 'If we succeed', he added, 'the organization of the highest echelons of government will not matter so much'.[46]

Thus, the man who had been President of Russia for eight years, and who finally decided to retain his grip on power by appointing himself Prime Minister interpreted at his will the Fundamental Law. Why wish for increased pluralism and democracy at a time when the regime had a tight hold on the reins and the state was rich? Might this be the 'Russian system' disparaged by academics and experts such as Yuri Pivorarov, Lilia Shevtsova or Igor Klyamkin? A power system that leaders can mould to their needs? A class of men above institutional rules, parliamentary oversight and accountability to citizens? What do the Russians think of this system?

6

A DISTRUSTFUL SOCIETY

'At every difficult turning point in Russia's history, authoritarian models of change have prevailed. And that is not because they are effective [...], but because they are easier and more accessible both to the population and the elites. Being dragged down requires less effort than rising to create more complex models of social organization'.

Yuri Levada, sociologist[1]

In the mid 1990s, one fact was clear: for the Russians democracy was not a priority. Ten years on, the reality was even more stark: the Russians were denied democracy. Those in power had become more repressive, and the government media were spreading an anti-democratic ideology that was hostile to everything not Russian. Democracy and openness, respect for human rights and fundamental freedoms, tolerance of others and of difference, free competition between ideas and projects, were all unattainable since democracy had vanished from the television screen and from everyday language.

There is a striking difference between the first post-Soviet period, when democracy was valued and seen as possible but difficult, and the second, after 1999–2000, during which democratic culture gradually disappeared from the political landscape.

This distinction between the two eras is vital. It discredits Putin's line which stigmatizes the entire Yeltsin period as being ravaged by chaos, corruption and the power of the oligarchs who feared neither God nor man. In earlier chapters we analyzed the abuses committed by Yeltsin: the storming of parliament in October 1993 and above all the war in Chechnya launched in December 1994. We also pointed out the consequences of rough-and-ready privatizations and the creation of an oligarchy of entrepreneurs and financiers. However, freedoms were never so alive as during the period from 1989 to 1995. And even after the acrobatic re-election of Boris Yeltsin in 1996, freedom of opinion and pluralism still drove public life. Most of those who wished to express themselves and act publicly could exercise their free will without fear of repression.

And so when Vladimir Putin propounds his theory of a backward people unprepared for the disruption of democracy, the memory of the years of freedom and burgeoning civil society should provide the ammunition to counter this new dogma. Many Russians were in favour of opening up their country, and valued freedom of information, freedom of expression, freedom of movement and free trade.

Withdrawing the Democratic Promise

To quell the burgeoning civil society, Putin's team reawakened the Soviet reflexes of withdrawal into the private sphere and fear of political life. In acting thus, the government successfully muzzled the citizens and is reaping the pernicious effects of controlling individuals—effects already well known during the Soviet era: diverse forms of passive resistance, rule-bending, and individualism as self-defence against servility.

For the Communist-era leaders, one of the pitfalls of the Party's dictatorship was that individuals had learned to evade control and subservience. They developed hidden modes of thinking and clandestine behaviour. They lived in a bind of internal captivity and private rebellion which made them dissatisfied and often aggressive and disrespectful towards others. The Soviet citizens, in people's minds, were less simple than the stereotype portrayed by propaganda.[2] Their forced obedience went hand-in-hand with the art of circumvention and putting on a façade.

Russians who had lived through the trauma of the Soviet system, then the trauma of the collapse of that system and the loss of all their bearings, were also psychologically and culturally complex and contradictory social beings. The studies and sophisticated analyses carried out by the sociologist Yuri Levada and his colleagues have shown that the Soviet citizens of the 1980s had lost faith in the Communist system, whose negligence they experienced in their day-to-day lives. They had a gloomy outlook and hoped for change in their bleak routine, without however being prepared to join forces and take action or take personal risks.[3] And so they welcomed the beginning of the top-down reforms and were delighted at the possibility of openly criticizing the Communist regime and the leaders for whom they had no respect. They thus behaved reasonably and there was nothing to support Vladimir Putin's view that this population was incapable of coping with change or opening up to other values and other models of government.

Those who still dare oppose Putin's regime reject the myth of *dikiy narod*, the 'savages' unsuited to democracy, which was the justification for the return to authoritarianism. In an interview, Vladimir Putin's former economic adviser, Andrey Illarionov, broke ranks and made a scathing attack on the propaganda: 'It is this same pro-Putin, nationalist government that presents itself as the 'only European' in an Asian country, forced to act as go-between for the 'enlightened West' and the 'savages''. Illarionov spoke out against the bad faith of the leaders who, deep down, turned their backs not only on economic liberalism, but also on fundamental freedoms and human rights.[4]

And indeed, during the meetings of the Valdai Club, where Western Russia experts came face to face with Vladimir Putin, the Russian leader had no compunction, even in front of academics, in asserting his position: 'The Russian people are backward. They cannot adapt to democracy overnight, as they have done in your countries, they need time, otherwise the effects will be destabilizing, and you do not wish to see the destabilization of our country'.[5] This reveals the contempt, and perhaps also the fear, of the political class towards the grassroots Russian, the *mujik*. But it is they, the leaders, who, via the television channels they control almost entirely, feed the *mujik* with hostile images of the outside world and create a nebulous fear, a xenophobia that is not borne out by any real threat.

Freedoms

According to opinion polls, Russian society was engaging with the issue of democracy and felt that post-Soviet Russia was neither democratic nor on the road to democratization, but it did not reject the European model. In December 2006, questioned about democracy and Western culture, 45 per cent of Russians responded that these could benefit Russia, as opposed to 30 per cent who thought that they 'were not appropriate to Russia'; 12 per cent stated that they would have a damaging and pernicious effect; only 3 per cent thought that Western democracy was necessary; 10 per cent had no opinion. The same question had been asked six years earlier, and the outcome was markedly more pro-Western democracy. In 2000, 55 per cent of those questioned thought that their country could benefit from the Western model, against 25 per cent who thought that it was inappropriate.[6] In 2008, asked whether Russia was going along a specific historical course, with its own culture and traditions, 80 per cent agreed and 15 per cent disagreed. Only 34 per cent believed that relations between Russia and the West could become really friendly (down from 60 per cent in 1994).[7]

Democracy remained an ideal, but one so far removed from everyday life, and foreign to Russian history, that it seemed unattainable. The abuses and failures of the 1990s made the Russians hostile to reform and free competition, which they considered to be a lottery. Their resentment towards *perestroika* and the very difficult economic and social transformations of the 1990s turned into a fear of change and a high degree of political conservatism. Asked about their present situation compared with their situation fifteen years earlier, a small majority stated that they had adapted to the new political, economic and social conditions.

The Russians clearly know what political freedoms are, since these are not just concepts for them, but very concrete rights of which they have experience. To be able to choose between several television news programmes broadcasting different opinions, buy a government newspaper or an independent paper, travel freely, speak freely without worrying about being overheard and reported by a KGB informer, all these freedoms were valued, even by the poorest sections of society, in the 1990s. And these freedoms have been seriously eroded by the Putin administration. Free consumption however remains unaffected: people still have the choice between Russian and imported goods, but more than half of the population cannot afford to choose. When Russians answer 'I feel I am a free person', they mean that their private life cannot be dictated by others. They clearly state their preference on the question of political rights: it is better to have less political freedom and more security. Of those interviewed in June 2007, 57 per cent thought that there was sufficient freedom in Russia, 24 per cent that there was too much, and 12 per cent not enough (6 per cent 'don't knows'). What does this suggest? More detailed questions in the surveys show that security for them means day-to-day needs: a guaranteed salary, medical care, reasonable water, gas and electricity bills, plus protection against crime. And in exchange for these 'economic and social rights', they are prepared to accept some conditions laid down by the government, in particular increased state control over their work life, the media and public life in general, but not over their private lives. To the question 'can most people live without continual state support', 21 per cent replied 'yes, it is possible', but 74 per cent said 'no, it is not possible' (5 per cent 'don't knows').[8] Asked in 2009 to define what they mean by 'Human Rights', 68 per cent answered 'the right to free education, health care and pensioners' care', 51 per cent 'the right to a good job', 28 per cent 'free speech', and 14 per cent 'the right to information' (several answers possible).[9]

As the Russian journalist Natalya Gevorkyan writes, the Putin-controlled media have made the Russians more closed, xenophobic, and fearful. Perhaps they do not naïvely believe everything they see on television, but they have become 'sponges'; they live in an atmosphere that they soak up.[10] Russian media analysts say that the television channels have been 'Putinized'.[11] The journalist and political expert Georgy Bovt points out that 'only around 12 per cent of Russians have a passport to travel abroad'.[12] This shows the extent of the differences between a comfortably-off, relatively open Russia and a modest, inward-looking Russia. This differentiation and segmentation of Russian society has been part of the government's strategy since the beginning of the 2000s. As soon as the state's financial situation improved with the rise in the price of hydrocarbons, the Kremlin stimulated some economic sectors, opened up vast opportunities for growth and enrichment to some major groups and industrialists, and enabled a small middle class to benefit from the positive effects of this economic upturn. For this well-off, dynamic class, it was important for the standard of living and working conditions to keep pace with their aspirations. And the regime provided them with the freedom to travel, invest their money, build and buy out companies, i.e. to be real capitalists and real consumers. On the communications front, these people had the means of connecting to the Internet, of communicating freely, of obtaining information from any source.

In actual fact, Putin's approach differentiates between the Russia that counts, and which cannot be totally subordinated, and the Russia that does not count but which can easily be controlled. Russia is an open economy for those who are rich, informed and loyal to the regime, and a 'strong power' for all the others.

The positions of Russians on the Yukos affair were indicative of the climate created by the Kremlin in the mid-2000s. Most of them believed Mikhail Khodorkovsky to be guilty and that the government was right to have him arrested. And yet, they thought his trial was unfair.[13] Numerous intellectuals and commentators had an ambiguous position. Meanwhile, fellow oligarchs, who could just as easily have been tried for tax fraud and misuse of company assets, kept quiet and refrained from expressing solidarity with the Yukos boss. Worse, in 2005, several of them signed a letter condemning Khodorkovsky. Only former dissidents—dissidents again under Putin—like Lyudmila Alexeeva and Sergey Kovalev defended the Yukos boss with no ulterior motive. Their prime concern was the injustice to which he was subjected, and the fraudulence of the investigation and the trial. They maintained that progress could not be made on the rule of law without independent courts. The trial was an absolute sham, as was obvious to anyone who attended. The fact that Khodorkovsky was an oligarch who had grown rich as a result of the privatizations of the 1990s cannot justify the violence of the attack or the arbitrariness of the judiciary.

The second trial in 2009–2010 was analyzed much more negatively by those Russians who knew about it, i.e. only about a third of the respondents. A consensus emerged over the fact that the harassment of Khodorkovsky and Lebedev was politically motivated, mainly nurtured by Putin's personal vendetta. The second sentence delivered in the very last days of the year 2010 caused almost an outcry against the judiciary on the Internet and in some more independent media (see chapter 8).

By creating controversy, by waging battle against an oligarch, against the tiny Georgian nation, against 'American imperialism', Putin's regime built up an image of the enemy. By fomenting a mood of threat and suspicion, it was able to convince a deeply conservative society, traumatized by the changes, to accept a form of hierarchy of freedoms.

At the same time, Russians are worried about the unpredictability of a system where the state is no longer the sole provider of jobs, housing and essential public services, but has allowed other players to emerge: private companies and services (bodyguards, private hospitals and schools, etc.). For the majority of them, these players are unreliable, corrupt, safeguarding their own interests rather than those of their employees, fellow citizens and customers. Why do they have this image of the 'privatization' of public and economic life? Why do they continue to invest their expectations in the state, when the state has generally betrayed them and the bureaucracies have not become any more efficient or trustworthy in recent years? Are they even more wary of organizations that do not depend directly on the central state? Or do they have the same distrust of any institution on which they depend and over which they have no control?

The second explanation seems the more likely. The polls conducted in the 2000s reveal a mistrust of all institutions, except towards Vladimir Putin, whose rating has not waned after he handed over the presidency to Dmitri Medvedev and took over the leadership of the government and the ruling party, United Russia. Medvedev saw a lightning rise in public support when he was chosen as successor with the aim of maintaining Putin at the summit of power. Both men experienced a reversal of fortune in the autumn of 2011 after they bluntly announced that they would 'swap seats' in 2012 (see Conclusion).

The criteria according to which people evaluate the actions of the government, of companies and of other individuals depend of course on their own experience. The disastrous perception of the exit from Communism and of the privatizations can be explained not only by the economic crisis that lasted from 1991 to 1999, but also by the fact that Russians judged events by Soviet standards. So they were caught between two matrices of understanding, that of Soviet values and that—still imprecise and hazy—of post-Soviet values. Social scientists have highlighted the contradictions produced by this antagonism: between the values of the Soviet way of life, which still had great resonance, and the very real desire for openness and progress.[14] Putin's regime built its method of control on this antagonism, this 'neo-Soviet schizophrenia', and one of the key components of this schizophrenia is fear.

Why distil fear and nervousness among Russians when they need to have confidence in the modernization of their country and participate actively in the process? Why did the Russian leaders—whose own finances like those of the state were more than healthy, and who consolidated their power system virtually unhindered—need to push their population back into a world of fear and mistrust? This contradiction reveals the authoritarian and closed nature of the regime governing Russia for the benefit of private, corporatist interests.

Fears

In *The Spirit of the Laws*, Montesquieu distinguishes three regimes: democracy (on the Athenian model), monarchy and despotism. He underscores the need for fear, anticipating the analyses of twentieth-century authoritarian regimes and totalitarianism. 'Just as there must be *virtue* in a republic, and *honour* in a monarchy, there must be FEAR in a despotic government. Virtue is not at all necessary to it, and honour would be dangerous'.[15] For the sociologist Vladimir Shlapentokh, fear was the pillar of the Soviet system, which he suffered until he emigrated to the United States in 1980. He defines fear (*strakh*) as 'a feeling of anxiety caused by the presence of a danger, real or imaginary'.[16]

Nadezhda Mandelstam, the wife of the great Russian poet who died in the Gulag, tells of a conversation with the poet Anna Akhmatova: 'Akhmatova [...] and I once confessed to each other that the strongest feelings [...] stronger than love and jealousy, stronger than anything which is human [...] were fear and its derivations: the heinous awareness of shame, restrictions, and full helplessness'.[17] Traditionally, in Soviet Russia and Tsarist Russia alike, fear was inseparable from physical violence and suffering. A massive reduction in the level of repression was required for freedoms to take on meaning, to become real in the day-to-day sense. And it is thanks to this end to fear that constitutionalism was able to progress in Russia at two crucial points in its reformist history: at the start of the twentieth century, and during *perestroika* and the liberalization of the Gorbachev era. The Baltic populations would not have taken the risk of demonstrating and standing up to Moscow in 1987–1991 if they had felt under threat of massive repression. The survival reflex in these little nations, part of whose populations had been deported in 1944, depended on the refusal of direct physical confrontation.

After de-Stalinization and the thaw during the Khrushchev and Brezhnev years, there was still marked repression of dissidents and rebels against the system. It softened towards the rest of the population and took on dissuasive forms.[18] However, violence remained a constant in discourse, in the means of communication between bosses and managers, between managers and employees, and of the Party with everything outside its control, especially its aggressiveness towards 'Westerners' and the 'capitalist foe'. It is clear that the spectre of the enemy shaped Russians' vision of themselves and of the outside world. Fear was used both as a government resource and as an instrument of mobilization. The leaders explained to the Soviet people that they had to be wary of everything and everyone, other than the 'Guide', the Party, and that consequently they had to mobilize against the threat. Until the mid 1980s, the Party and its enforcers, like the KGB, had a right over individuals, the right to lock up, refuse access to medical care and deprive of freedom and dignity any person who roused a leader's anger.[19]

In recent years fear, still nebulous and sometimes intangible, has resurfaced in Russia. If a person is in trouble with the authorities, their friends no longer telephone them and often sever all relations with them. It is also this form of servitude fuelled by fear that Anna Politkovskaya criticized in her books and articles. She testified tirelessly to the violence, abuses of power, injustice and human distress. She was one of the very rare journalists in Russia to meet young Russian conscripts returned from Chechnya, wounded and mentally broken, left utterly destitute by the army and the administration. Anna Politkovskaya was appalled that in the twenty-first century Russia continued to live in medieval conditions of indifference in the face of suffering and death. She fought the arbitrariness of the powerful.

This great journalist and opponent had few friends left in the last years of her life; especially after September 2004, when she tried to go to Beslan during the hostage-taking in the school in North Ossetia: she was poisoned on the plane and had to be taken back to Moscow urgently for hospital treatment. Shortly afterwards, she said to me: 'My telephone remained completely silent for three days when I returned home from hospital. Only the American ambassador called me to find out how I was'. The reflex of colleagues and friends was that of the Soviet era: keep away from anyone in trouble, because the machine is likely to also destroy those who express their support for the victim.

The Russians have learned not to cross swords with those in power. They are prepared to keep quiet in order to defend their benefits and some form of stability, as long as they do not feel 'cheated' by the system. In her last book, Anna Politkovskaya expresses a mixture of compassion and exasperation towards her compatriots. 'This whole system […] can operate only if nobody protests. This is the Kremlin's secret weapon and the most striking feature of life in Russia today. […] People react only when something affects them personally'.[20] Her revolt against Vladimir Putin stemmed from this observation. She was convinced, and most free thinkers in Russia agreed with her on this point, that Russian society was not culturally servile, that it could have been transformed intellectually, morally and socially if the ruling elites had not reactivated those mental shackles.

The radical break that made possible the end of Communism and an attempt to establish the rule of law was the end of the arbitrary role of the state-Party in shaping the fate of individuals. The state can no longer send a man or a woman to their death and admit it publicly. If the Kremlin wishes to eliminate a thorn in its side, a political adversary, an independent journalist, it can of course do so, as we have seen with the Putin regime's spiralling authoritarianism since 2003, but it does not admit it. The Kremlin hides behind the judges who allegedly condemned Mikhail Khodorkovsky 'completely independently', or the 'mafias' and the 'Chechens' who allegedly murdered Anna Politkovskaya on 7 October 2006. Five years later, no progress had been made in the Politkovskaya case.

The Putin regime is a more violent and more belligerent regime than the post-Gorbachev governments that preceded it. The level of violence in Chechnya and the north Caucasus, army and prison brutality, day-to-day criminal activity, the attempts to destabilize neighbouring countries such as Ukraine, Georgia and even Estonia, demonstrate the regime's non-peaceful nature. Russia's bombing of Georgia in August 2008 was a resounding reminder of this.

But, while instilling a high level of violence, Vladimir Putin deprived Russian political and social life of any public conflict. Debate, criticism and negotiation were in practice prohibited. Putin's conception of 'sovereign democracy' is a society with no differences of opinion and no discussion, but one which is violent. The negative consequences of the lack of public confrontation also extend to the economic and social sphere.

A Low-Conflict Society?

From the point of view of the ruling elites, democracy is an intolerable constraint and a source of disorder: institutional constraints, constraint vis-à-vis foreigners, constraints of free competition, and constraints coming from society and citizens. Playing on the Russian people's fears, the leaders stated that the main objective of the transition was to ensure a low-conflict public life, which would constitute, in their view, a success in itself.

Western democracies on the other hand open up the way to 'disorder', with the freedom to demonstrate, and dismiss a government through parliamentary procedures or the will of the electorate. But, explain the ideologists and practitioners of the restoration, while the old democracies can afford the luxury of these crises, Russia, on the other hand, cannot. So people must accept the Russian way, the specific nature of its 'democracy'.

The stated ideal, and the rolling out of this society without conflict, is one of the most worrying aspects of Putin's enterprise. For to refuse any dissension is tantamount to refusing any dialogue, any negotiation. Montesquieu underlines the virtues of good governance in a moderate monarchy: 'In these circumstances, people of wisdom and authority intervene; temperings are proposed, agreements are reached, corrections are made; the laws become vigorous again and make themselves heard'.[21] Such is the spirit of the laws. In the Russia presided over by Putin, if there is a spirit of the laws, it is officially the 'dictatorship of the law', akin to the 'democratic centralism' of the 1920s: once the line has been laid down by the leadership, no dissidence is acceptable. In an interview in *Le Monde* in 2008, Putin alluded to it in covert language that would have been clearly understood by an ex-Soviet citizen. He defended the multi-party system and claimed that a genuine political battle had been fought during the electoral campaign, that 'one side won', and it was he who was in power.[22] In a health study, Debra Javeline highlights the dangers of such a stance:

Given the extent and nature of the grievances in a country, what are the implications of a low-conflict public? [...] It is a relief when the public is inactive and conflict is minimal. But this perspective on conflict reveals only one side of the story. [...] A low level of conflict allows the interests of some politically disadvantaged groups to be ignored. It is also possible [...] that there might be negative health implications for a low-conflict public.[23]

The statistics on contagious diseases (AIDS and tuberculosis in particular) and on life expectancy, which is still very low in Russia, confirm this conclusion.[24]

In the Soviet era, public debate was unthinkable. Western Kremlinologists did their utmost to read between the lines to find the chinks in the ruling elite's front. Any acknowledgment of disagreement would have betrayed a weakness within the state. Anyone causing unrest was severely punished. The system covered up any conflicts, like the social unrest in 1962, and above all disasters, such as Chernobyl in 1986.

This culture of secrecy and prohibition of dissent created a mindset. Officially surrounded by foes, the Soviet state could not reveal any internal disagreement to the outside world, and so it was natural for the authorities to window-dress the truth. Lying was integral to the day-to-day life of the state, society and the economy. Seeing political conflict as a sign of weakness is a major obstacle to democratization. The Russians' reluctance to engage with public life, to vote against the Kremlin's man or read critical journalists stems from this attitude, and not from a love of the arbitrary and of force, as some commentators would have us believe.

The fact is that 'low conflict' ideology is an ideology that encourages violence. The public's silence is achieved by intimidating people, by creating enemies for them. The relentless hounding of the Caucasians, the rise of racist violence and fascistic movements like the Nashi (the Putin Youth) testify to this tendency. In Saint Petersburg, in 2005, an eight-year-old girl was murdered: 'Yes, those foreigners have to be punished and that girl deserved it. She was dealing drugs at school, that Tajik'.[25] The government sits back and does nothing. In most cases, no proper investigation is carried out. In September 2006, in Kondopoga in Karelia, the incidents reached such a level of violence and created such a panic among the Caucasian and non-Russian communities that the police eventually stepped in. The general mood is summed up by the slogan shouted freely in the streets and on television: 'Russia for the Russians'.

A brutal fight took place on 11 December 2010, near Red Square in Moscow. Several thousand youths gathered after the killing of a football fan and attacked non-Russian groups, shouting 'Russia for the Russians'. Several were wounded and 800 arrested, but the police were slow in intervening. Another demonstration of the police's incapacity, and even their complicity in crime, was the brutal killing of a whole family (12 killed and set on fire, including four children) by a rival clan in Kushchevskaya in southern Russia (Krasnodar region) in November 2010. Most commentators presented this barbaric act as yet another example of lawlessness, the collusion of bandits and corrupt bureaucrats.

Racist attacks are claiming an increasing number of victims each year. The support given by the authorities to the Putin Youth, who are trained in military camps and organize xenophobic demonstrations, does not offer much hope of an improvement in the climate. If the government does not issue the order to crack down severely on these brutal, racist actions, it is because it wants to keep these groups of young people, neo-Nazi movements, Chechnya veterans and other armed groups in reserve, within easy reach.

As these men have a troubled past and could easily be prosecuted, the government can potentially use them for very specific purposes. First of all, they help maintain a climate of anxiety and obsessive fear of the enemy within. 'We are only happy among our own, among Russians', say some inhabitants of Kondopoga. 'We want to be rid of these foreigners'. And yet, most victims are former Soviet citizens, Azeris, Tajiks, Chechens, Ingush and other representatives of the former nationalities of the USSR. The Russians who defend the murder of these 'others' (*chuzhiye*) have lived side by side with these people from a different ethnic group and religion for decades. Nearly all the cities of the USSR were multi-ethnic; now we see proof again, as if that were necessary, that the glorious Soviet family of nations and nationalities was nothing but a slogan.

Submission or Consent?

Officially, the executive power no longer assumes the right of life or death over its subjects. Fear then takes on a different, more insidious and more commonplace dimension, as it is less dramatic. It remains a resource that guarantees the attitude so essential to the Putin regime—'loyalty' (*loyalnost'*), which is a form of submission stemming from the fear of trouble. Trouble has different guises: losing one's job, having one's home searched, not being able to enrol one's child at university, being subjected to a tax inspection or, (for company bosses) a health and safety inspection, losing benefits in kind, or even being attacked by strangers in the street. And so the government can still make people feel that it can exert direct pressure on them, on their physical person. But, unlike the Soviet system, it can also be completely uninterested in their lifestyle and way of thinking if they keep a low profile.

The obsession with controlling individuals is gone, but on the other hand, a vague sense of insecurity is carefully maintained. And in the absence of an independent, non-corrupt legal system, this insecurity eventually seeps into everyone's lives and changes behaviours. The political leaders have also used another source of fear, officially external to the state: economic competition, social non-interventionism.

In my view, it is in these terms that the major crisis of 2005 over the 'monetization of social benefits' should be understood. This measure put an end to the free services enjoyed by tens of millions of Russians: invalids, the retired, single women, Chernobyl heroes and other categories who benefited from free transport, medical care and often housing too.

The authorities tasked with implementing this project were fully aware of the specificities inherited from the Soviet era. Everything was free, all essential services were a 'right', and the Soviet citizens therefore earned a pittance. Incorporating the notion of charging for a public service that tens of millions of Russians had become accustomed to considering as free (in other words, costing nothing) was an impossible gamble. World Bank experts organized colloquium after colloquium to explain that 'monetization' would be the answer in what was now a capitalist economy. And, effectively, the exit from Communism involved an evaluation of costs, the empowerment of individuals and an increase in earnings. But simply to seek the economic rationale for the reform is to ignore the facts.[26]

The Russians affected by this reform saw it as a betrayal. They were being asked to pay for things they had never paid for, in exchange for a tiny increase in salary at the end of the month. Is it possible that the authorities had not foreseen their reaction? It seems to me that their thinking was to show the population that nothing should be taken for granted, that the government had the power to change the rules of the game, and that they should not get on the wrong side of the ruling powers. Even if the government had to climb down over some of its plans, it succeeded in getting across this message of insecurity. And what did it matter if people expressed their dissatisfaction, since its target was the bureaucracies, the petty local officials, not the president. Vladimir Putin saw his popularity dip in the months following the proposed reform, but it soon rose again, after the summer of 2005.

It is worth considering this strange particularity of a Head of State considered as absolutely blameless, in other words never held liable for poor decisions and crises. The Beslan school tragedy in September 2004 was a prime example. Putin barely suffered as a result of the disastrous management of the hostage-taking. On the other hand, the citizens' distrust of the administrations and the police increased. And this mistrust further bolstered the ruler's blameless image. 'The President is not to blame, he couldn't deal with the problem directly. He would have wanted everything to end well'. This is how the vast majority of Russians try to reassure themselves. The ruler is strong and good, but he is poorly served by his administrations and police force in the Caucasus.

Putin's Image as Leader

The Russians are suspicious of nearly all public institutions; they put their faith in the leader. President Putin has enjoyed a high level of support, which he has transferred to his new role as Prime Minister. His protégé Dmitri Medvedev has even benefited directly from this popular support because he was the leader's other self.

What does a level of 'contentment' mean? A high *rating* (the word used by the Russians themselves), when there is no other credible choice on offer, when Putin has eliminated all other dominant figures who might appeal to the population from the national political arena? The concept of popularity does not apply in a non-pluralist and quasi-unanimous situation. And yet, it cannot be disputed that in the eyes of the Russians the political legitimacy of the Head of State rests on universal suffrage, even if the election is neither fair nor competitive. Vladimir Putin succeeded in capturing the ballot boxes for himself alone. He abolished the elections of the provincial governors and the presidents of the federal republics; the legislative elections are a lottery decided in advance between a handful of parties, and, in December 2007, he managed to transform the election of the State Duma into a referendum on his name, in order to justify his remaining in power a few months later.

With this increasing unanimity, what is the relationship of the Russians to Vladimir Putin? In surveys conducted in Russia, the question is asked as follows: 'Do you trust Vladimir Putin?' or 'Do you agree with his action?' The hollowing out of public institutions in recent years makes the relationship to the leader, the father of the nation, increasingly primitive. The vacuum in public life has to be filled by emotions. Nationalism and concerns over violence are also instruments to fill the void and wean ordinary citizens off the taste for freedom. The discourse accusing the West of seeking to control or destabilize Russia is another means of stirring up political emotion. And this emotion works in favour of the leaders who then set themselves up as guarantors of the country's integrity and power.

The sociologist Boris Dubin analyzes the Russians' astonishing relationship with the President as a quest for a figurehead, a father of the nation, which the seriously ailing and impotent Boris Yeltsin had profoundly damaged. The Russians are not attached to Putin as a person, but to what he represents, and they are capable of transferring their 'submissive trust' onto another statesman, as long as he is in good health, has a tough image, and never admits to having been wrong.[27]

As soon as the questions become more concrete and touch on specific aspects of day-to-day life, the Russians' opinion of their government is much more critical. They are convinced that Russia is badly governed, that corruption is on the rise, and that the leaders do not prioritize the needs of the people; 80 per cent of the people interviewed in 2008 would like the state to give more consideration to the needs of the population.[28] Conversely, they find it easier to buy into the Russian state's 'strong Russia' foreign policy. They feel themselves to be outside European norms, but do not really have any alternative values that enable them to locate themselves in the outside world. Deep down, what they respect in Putin is power, and power is what they want for Russia, without entering into a reflection on what that power means.

So the Russians display a highly ambivalent attitude towards Putin's regime. They tolerate the methods of the government and the administrations while distrusting them, and they support Putin in his role as leader of the nation. The various opinion polls already cited show clearly that, as soon as the questions became more specific about the government's achievements, the respondents seemed sceptical of the wisdom of the policies in place.

Willing Hostages?

In an authoritarian system, society is always in a hostage role. But to what extent did the Russians who had lived through the exit from Communism in 1988–1993 agree to accept the rules of the game, and did they become enmeshed in this system consciously and sometimes actively? This is the crucial question at this point in our analysis. The replies inside Russia vary enormously.

At one extreme, the official doctrine states that society is satisfied with the regime and hostile to anything that hinders government policy. This assertion is justified by two diametrically opposed arguments. The first contends that since the Russians are lagging behind the other industrialized countries, it is natural for the enlightened elites to lead them by the hand towards a more 'modern' and democratic culture, but not too fast, 'the time isn't ripe' (this has been Putin's stance since 2000). In contrast, the second argument is based on the assertion that Russia is as developed as European countries, and as powerful as the United States, a country where the 'sovereign' citizens freely choose their leaders and their political orientations, and live in harmony with the government.[29] Is Russian society retarded and primitive, or at the cutting edge of progress? Articles and books by the regime's advisers, the political parties emanating from the Kremlin, and 'loyal' journalists argue for one or the other theory, depending on the occasion and the target audience.

Opinion polls and testimonies that we have gathered in Russia indicate that the problem is posed by the government in a way that is inaccurate and biased. Why evaluate the disposition of Russians according to a normative behaviour scale in relation to Western societies? Ironically, the bias comes from the leaders themselves who continue to use the Western referent to 'hitch' their population to a 'universal' scenario even though they are spearheading a policy that cuts Russians off from democratic Europe.

For the political analyst Lilia Shevtsova, there is a form of consensus between society and the elites since they all want to uphold the status quo through fear of change. Unlike the Soviet era, the government does not require the population to mobilize.[30] Nervousness was meant to keep people on their guard and stop them from acting. The government certainly did not want it to be necessary to send millions of demonstrators into the street to defend its ideology. It does not want people demonstrating in support of major causes. Above all it wants them to stay at home watching television and be content with a more comfortable material life. This is far from the Soviet discourse of 'Come on, comrades!' that filled people's heads, even if the 'fight' was rarely followed by concrete actions. It was important for the Soviet citizens to feel as if they were 'on the bridge', for them not to be 'left to their own devices', to their thoughts and their personal ambitions.[31]

The government's priority since 2004 has been to ensure that an Orange Revolution would be impossible in Russia. Vladimir Putin and his advisers failed to anticipate the major events that shook Ukraine in the autumn of 2004. They were convinced that the Ukrainians were even less developed than the Russians and that President Leonid Kuchma had his administration well in hand and would ensure the electoral outcome that suited him. The Ukrainian voters occupied Kiev for several weeks in protest against corruption and fraud, and rejected the election of Kuchma's man, Prime Minister Viktor Yanukovych. The second round of the presidential election was invalidated and reorganized on 26 December 2004, returning Viktor Yushchenko, a pro-Western reformer. For Putin, who had campaigned in Ukraine for the candidate endorsed by Moscow, the humiliation was unbearable. He refused to accept the facts and embraced the conspiracy theory: foreign 'interests', American undoubtedly, bribed the Ukrainians to take control of Ukraine and undermine Russia. This line, that the Orange Revolution is a complete fabrication, is repeated in all official and unofficial Kremlin communications. It is possible that some people in Moscow believe it. No one in high places dares contradict it.

The fact is, Vladimir Putin was afraid of the repercussions of the Orange Revolution on his own regime. If the democratic gap between Ukraine and Russia widened, Russia would find itself increasingly isolated in its authoritarian Russian 'specificity'. And democratic contagion might encourage people to rebel against the ruling powers. To curb such developments, Putin chose to bring the lid down harder on society, which above all must not become 'civil' and active. Civil society only exists formally, or cosmetically, through specially established bodies, like the Public Chamber or the NGOs supported by the administrations. The Russians derisively call them GNGOs—*governmental* non-governmental organizations.[32]

Putin's government imposes an ideological framework by carrying out a strategy of occupying the public and media spheres, in defiance of freedom of information and expression. This policy is dangerous because it beguiles the leaders with the assurance that, whatever they do, they will not be punished, either by the population or by the media, or by their peers. And this lack of blame, of accountability, creates a deceptive stability. For there are conflicts, of course, and they are becoming more marked, especially in this post-2000 context of 'predatory state capitalism'. And these conflicts find their outlet in explosive cases, like relations with Georgia or Ukraine, or again the disputes between the Russian state and foreign shareholders in an oil giant such as TNK-BP.

The power of this self-righteous rhetoric is that it offers explanations of the past and the present that free the ordinary Russian from all blame, and the leaders even more. Thus the fault lies elsewhere, abroad, or in a dark period of history (the transformation period under Yeltsin and not the years of the Stalinist terror), and also with the enemy within, the fifth column which is increasingly evoked in the rhetoric of the Kremlin and the state-controlled media.

This negative, withdrawn vision contains absolutely nothing of the Utopian, which makes it very different from Marxist-Leninist ideology adapted to Krushchev's, then Brezhnev's methods: no goal to be attained, no achievement that would make it possible to crush the West, no plans to change the system in favour of more equality.

The Russians are becoming used to this discourse of threat and conflict with 'the other', and are unable to articulate another vision, that of a modern state that is accustomed to its frontiers and its boundaries, and organizes itself so that it can have normal relations with its neighbours on an equal basis.[33] Putin stirs up in his fellow Russians the wish to humiliate and debase their neighbours, who were formerly united in the Russian and Soviet empires. They do not want the Georgians or the Ukrainians to succeed any better than the Russians, either economically or politically—that is the line. And they do not want them to go over 'to the West' by becoming members of NATO or the European Union.

Russian society's connivance with this aggressive attitude and contempt for other communities has been analyzed by sociologists. The government draws on the Russians' cruder feelings; it does not call on noble sentiments or speak to them of a future. It convinces Russians that the situation is worse elsewhere, especially in the former Soviet republics. Television channels regularly carry out massive disinformation campaigns on the chaos in Ukraine, corruption in Georgia and fascism in Estonia. While the high price of hydrocarbons enables the leaders to maintain a healthy growth rate and to provide Russians with a slight improvement in their standard of living each year, Putin's ideology of the superiority of the 'Russian way' over others will maintain its impact. The armed conflict with Georgia in the summer of 2008 received the approval of 70 per cent of Russians, on the basis of information controlled by the government media.[34]

The problem with the present Russian regime is that it is not accountable to a society which, for its part, shields itself behind a stance of not taking any responsibility. The historian and political analyst Igor Klyamkin defines this society as 'uncivil' (*negrazhdanskoe*).[35] Russians are increasingly indifferent to everything that is not related to their own personal life and interests. They also tend to be complacent with regard to their dependency on the state. On the one hand, they ask the state to look after them, and on the other, they do not participate in the construction of public institutions that are representative and effective. A minority, however, is determined to contest Putin's rule.

Young people's attitudes are ambivalent with regard to the democratization of Russia. The majority express opinions that are conservative and hostile to change, as they are worried about the future. Opinion polls indicate that young Russians are utterly uninterested in political and social questions, and are ignorant of international problems. Born during the Gorbachev era or in the early Yeltsin years, they did not experience life under the Soviet state and know about it only through the accounts of their elders. They do not really know where today's Russia comes from and have no interest in finding out. For them, personal and social success naturally involves having a good income and being materially comfortable. But for half of them, the situation is tough, with limited job prospects if their parents have not been able to afford higher education. They are attracted by the Western world, but the vast majority of them have never been outside Russia and have no passport or the money to holiday in Europe.[36] In the elections of 2007 and 2008, most 18–25-year-olds voted for Putin or abstained. The presidential election of 2012 will be a test.

It would be too easy to explain today's Russia solely through the paradigm of authoritarianism and the arbitrariness of the executive power as if the former KGB chief, Vladimir Putin, had come to power via a coup d'Etat, crushing freedoms and a flourishing civil society. We have seen that democratic values and customs were still embryonic in Russia. A change of leadership at the highest level will not be enough to set Russian politics back on the road to democracy. The next two chapters describe the mechanisms of the power system in place which, despite the many imbalances and abuses, have guaranteed the continuity of Putinism until 2011. The team that has been ruling Russia since May 2008, barely different from the previous one, has based its authority on its ability to continue providing the majority of Russians with a decent standard of living and a feeling of security.

7

THE PUTIN SYSTEM

UNANIMITY AND AUTOCRACY

Mr Fox: 'Mr Crow, will you vote for Putin?'
Mr Crow did not answer.
Mr Fox asked again, 'So tell me, Mr Crow, will you vote for Putin?'
Mr Crow did not answer.
Mr Fox persists, 'Come on, don't be sore, Mr Crow, tell me if you'll vote for Putin.'
Mr Crow finally opened his beak: 'Yesssss.'
The piece of cheese fell to the ground; Mr Fox snapped it up and ran away.
Mr Crow wondered to himself, 'And if I'd said no, would it have made a difference?'[1]

The Putin system consists of the authoritarian exercise of political and economic power. It is not a constitutional regime given that, according to the definition adopted earlier in this book, a Constitution is the foundation of a political regime when it is respected, protected and interpreted in accordance with democratic rules and behaviour. It made little sense to study the constitutional regime of the USSR. Nor does it make much sense to look into the constitutional nature of the Turkmen or Belarus regimes, as authoritarianism and personality cults, the subjection of the security forces to the President with no political control other than that of the President himself, and the lack of a separation of powers all leave the Constitution devoid of any sovereign authority.

In the case of Russia, the Constitution was approved by referendum in conditions open to criticism, but at a time when civic liberties and citizens' free will were not fettered in the way they are today. Since that time, the Constitution has inexorably lost the meaning and the spirit of a basic law, and truly retains only the considerable powers of the executive branch. It was battered once again in 2008 to install the Putin-Medvedev duo at the head of the state. Thus, even the hyper-presidentialism of the post-Soviet regime has been altered to accommodate the will of the most powerful men.

The comparison between the Russian and Belarusian situations in terms of violation of civil rights and basic freedoms, and the dominance of a core executive is meaningful, even if the scales are different.[2] Both regimes reject pluralism and opposition. But Russia is an economic, energy and military power. It is therefore spared the criticism the West directs at Belarus for regressing into authoritarianism.

The system is closely associated with one man, Vladimir Putin. And this man has decided to remain in power with no time limit, even if a close friend whom he picked and trained has been President since May 2008. In 2012, he plans to regain his presidential post. Mounting protest in the autumn of 2011 will make it more difficult to rig elections and give Putin a landslide victory.

Rotation in Office Refused: A Sure Sign of Autocracy

The Constitution of 1993 endows the president with considerable powers and at the same time sets an eight-year limit on the exercise of these powers by a single person.[3] In the minds of legal and political advisers in 1993, these two axioms were inseparable: a powerful president, but for a limited time. Those who drafted the final version of the Basic Law in October and November 1993, amid considerable tension, wanted to prevent the personalization of power and the arbitrary rule of a single person or group. *The Yeltsin Epoch*, a work by former Boris Yeltsin advisers, as well as the research of Lilia Shevtsova and Igor Klyamkin,[4] emphasize this genuine political concern among Russian experts and leaders in the early 1990s: 'No more totalitarianism' was the motto. The strategy went off the rails because the safeguards were not strong enough and the constitutional framework was barely outlined.[5]

The absence of a changeover in power is a distinctive feature of author-itarian regimes. Russia's case is emblematic. Vladimir Putin chose not to leave power and thus brought an end to the regime's constitutional façade once and for all. While claiming to abide by the Constitution and the law, he freely interprets the texts, twists rights and freedoms, and stifles pluralism and competition. He presents his devotion to the fatherland as an act of courage to ensure his country's 'stability'.

The Putin system is well established and can last so long as no major change reverses the situation. But the continuity of individuals and their methods does not guarantee a system's stability. On the contrary, by imposing personal power with no time limit, Putin has radically altered the nature of political and social life in Russia. He has not merely renewed a mode of government and an elite, he has caused the degeneracy of the state that no opposition can counterbalance or stop. The refusal to allow an open succession and the rejection of any changeover in power signal the end of constitutional and political opposition, at least in the years to come.

The official 'stability' paradigm should be countered with the paradigm of concentration and merger of powers and the irresponsibility of those in office. Maintaining Putin and his close associates at the summit of political and economic power with no democratic means to counteract them is another point of rupture in post-Communist history.

According to the terms of the Constitution of 1993, the President of Russia can hold two consecutive four-year terms. The incumbent Presi-dent thus knew he would have to leave his post in March 2008 unless the Constitution was amended. Putin chose not to engage the constitu-tional amendment procedure, to amend article 81 of the Basic Law, even though it would not have presented any difficulty given that the Duma very largely marched to the orders of the Executive.

There are several interpretations for this. The most relevant would seem to be Putin's wish not to behave in the same way as dictators in Central Asia and Belarus, who extend their terms as they please and can remain in power so long as no one prevents them from doing so. Putin has no desire to be compared to Islam Karimov, Nursultan Nazarbayev or Alex-ander Lukashenko. He, to some extent, prides himself on maintaining the appearance of respecting the letter of the Constitution. The Editor-in-Chief of *Echo of Moscow* Radio, Aleksey Venediktov, offers his own interpretation: 'Putin doesn't want the Western leaders at the next G8 summit to make him an outcast! He likes to be able to say he does not touch the monument known as "Constitution," even if he basically does what he likes with this Constitution. And his Western partners will be only too happy to have a good excuse provided directly by the Kremlin not to have to think any further about the next Russian president'.[6]

Yet, while claiming that he would not seek a third term, Putin fostered the formation of a popular 'movement', orchestrated by a few loyal *apparatchik*s, that begged him to stay. 'Vladimir Vladimirovich, don't forsake us! How can we live without you? Please, remain our President'. The 'conversation with the people' that Putin conducts each year was an opportunity for pre-selected Russians to express their dismay.[7] Several provincial assemblies were encouraged to pass resolutions asking for a constitutional amendment to allow the President to run for a third term, and popular referenda were held. These initiatives took place particularly in the republics of the Caucasus, where the 'directed vote' studied by Dmitry Oreshkin has long held sway.[8] In the legislative election of 2 December 2007, official figures gave a voter turnout of 99 per cent, with 98 per cent of the vote for the United Russia party in several districts!

On Russian radio and television, every morning and every evening, the same programmes on the 'succession' were aired. How could Putin be persuaded to stay, given that it was too late to amend the Constitution? Listeners asked questions, they expressed their concern: if Putin went and preparations were not made for his succession, what would happen?

A perfect illustration of the trend toward unanimity was the drift taken by institutes and think tanks close to the Kremlin. Beginning in late 2006, these spin doctors (*polittekhnologi*) were no longer talking about the 2008 'elections'. They referred only to the 'succession' (*preemstvennost'*). A round-table discussion held in March 2006 was edifying.[9] Russian experts managed to talk for a whole hour about the presidential succession in March 2008 without ever mentioning the issue of elections. They explained that the Russians feared chaos if Putin left, but they had to be told to prepare for a succession, and that everything would work out fine; not a word about the other candidates or voters' behaviour. The experts had not only to scare ordinary Russians by telling them there was no future without Putin, but also to convince them that Putin had to leave the presidency. At the time, the scenario of the President slipping naturally into the post of Prime Minister was not announced.

During the years 2006 and 2007, Russian politics was dominated by the 'Problem of 2008'. The most fervent Putin supporters were labelled the 'Third-Term Party'. Sergey Mironov, Speaker of the upper house of parliament, vociferously worked to obtain this additional term even as he agreed to preside over the new official party, Fair Russia, founded in 2006 to pick up the electorate from the Fatherland (Rodina) party, whose leader Dmitry Rogozin had begun to occupy too much space in the political landscape.[10] Igor Sechin, Putin's *éminence grise*, who did not make public appearances, also preferred the third-term option.

Sechin and Medvedev belong to two different cliques in the Putin galaxy. In the spring of 2008, just before Medvedev took office, Sechin was still Chairman of the Board of Directors of Rosneft, the oil giant, and occupied the position of Deputy-Chief of Presidential Administration, while Medvedev still chaired the Board of Directors of gas giant Gazprom. Much more was therefore at stake in the succession than state interests alone. The financial and personal future of these men depended on their place in the Putin galaxy. The ministers appointed by Putin and the officials nominated to Medvedev's presidential administration in May 2008 showed that the galaxy was playing musical chairs at the top without restraint. All important posts were occupied by men who had long been loyal to Putin (see below).

Contrary to what the propaganda had suggested, Putin was not 'weary of power' but wanted to continue to exercise considerable authority. During his meetings with foreign Russia specialists at the Valdai Club, the Russian President had always remained ambiguous. In September 2005, then again in September 2006, he was asked the question very clearly several times. After a few rhetorical detours, he finally said that he would not 'revise the Constitution to his advantage', but that he 'would not lose interest in the fate of his country'.[11] Participants could interpret the President's answers as they saw fit or in the ways they found the most realistic. The main thing for Vladimir Putin was to remain vague about the crucial issue of his own succession, as if it depended entirely on him. He held the joker in his hand up to the last moment, perturbing the other players' game. With respect to his foreign partners, the carefully sustained suspense made foreign embassies and financial markets jittery. When the doubt was lifted, relief finally took precedence over criticism. If Putin had truly decided to leave power, the West would have greeted his move as a democratic one. Although he chose to maintain his control over the country, his move was not deemed anti-democratic.[12]

The Medvedev Scenario

So as not to 'revise the Constitution to his advantage', Vladimir Putin had to come up with other scenarios, which were the object of endless discussions among the intellectual and political elite. The scenario finally hit upon took shape in September. Putin made an unexpected change in Prime Minister on 12 September 2007. He dismissed Mikhail Fradkov, 'who had done a good job, but reforms weren't moving fast enough', and installed one of his close associates, unknown to the public at large, Viktor Zubkov. There was nothing to account for the urgency of forming a 'new government', and indeed most ministers kept their posts after the 24 September cabinet reshuffle. Why would a President planning to leave office six months later undertake such manoeuvres? One explanation could lurk in the personal finances of regime officials and their need for protection. Viktor Zubkov, the new head of government, was in charge of the Financial Monitoring Service, officially an organization to clamp down on money-laundering. In such conditions, he was the person best informed of individual fortunes and the situation of private and public companies. It is easy to imagine the importance of the immunity issue to these men who all built personal fortunes and little economic empires in clientelistic and uncompetitive conditions.

The nomination of a 66-year-old man as head of government made plausible a scenario in which Viktor Zubkov would be the presidential candidate in March 2008 and then leave his post after a few months to enable Putin to run again after this short interval without breaching article 81 of the Constitution, which bars anyone from holding more than two *consecutive* terms. This option seemed at first to be confirmed with Vladimir Putin's formal announcement that he would remain in the game. On 1 October 2007, before the United Russia party congress, the incumbent President agreed to run as head of the list of the 'party in power', without becoming a member. He led this list of *apparatchik*s to a definite victory in the legislative elections held on 2 December 2007.

But his heir apparent turned out to be Dmitry Medvedev, 42 years old, with a different profile: he had worked with Vladimir Putin since the age of 25, when he was starting a legal career in Saint Petersburg, in particular at the city hall where Putin was Deputy Mayor. For Russia specialists, he is 'Putin's son', trained by him and perfectly loyal: Medvedev owes him everything.

After his party won by an overwhelming majority on 2 December 2007, Putin could then announce that he was considering becoming the Prime Minister under his protégé, Dmitry Medvedev. After months of prevarications about the succession, the 'Putin III' scenario was played out in a matter of days in December 2007. All of Russia stood by as onlookers.

The plebiscite process thus continued into the presidential election of 2 March 2008 which established an unprecedented tandem, consisting of the President and Prime Minister but with the head of government being higher than the head of state. Putin knew he could recover his position for many years after Medvedev's departure if he undertook a 'minor' revision of the Constitution that would fix the presidential term limit at six years instead of four. As early as October 2008, President Medvedev proposed this revision of the Constitution, approved by Parliament in November. In 2012, Putin can in principle recover the supreme office for twelve years. It is unlikely that he will be President until 2024, but what matters is that the possibility exists. In the model he has set up, his authority depends on a virtually limitless prolonged existence.

The Medvedev scenario posed a few political and technical problems, particularly that of the temporarily designated successor's total 'loyalty'. Given that the Constitution grants the President extensive powers, the 'loyal friend' could be tempted to eliminate his mentor. However, in the current Russian system, in which the intelligence services and the security forces play a preponderant role, with the help of the judges in cahoots with the Executive, the young successor's rapid emancipation from his mentor's supervision is highly unlikely. And we will see that in the spring of 2008 Vladimir Putin was careful to shift a number of presidential powers over to the government.

Medvedev arrived at the top through Putin's networks and the Saint Petersburg cliques. He is in the service of a clientelistic system and cannot do what he pleases. The financial and political stakes are too high. Power is in the hands of Putin, his close associates and the intelligence services; it remains concentrated wherever Putin happens to be.[13] The most obvious choice seemed to him to be the post of Prime Minister, which formally remains an executive position, but subject to the President's authority and with no responsibility to members of the Duma since the government does not answer to the Parliament. The Prime Minister is not bound by elected mandate; he can remain in power indefinitely if such is the President's will.

The benevolent interpretation that some Western commentators gave Putin's intention to shift from the presidency to the cabinet, thus giving the Parliament greater influence, was not based on serious political analysis. If the Parliament is a body made up of *apparatchik*s from the *nomenklatura*, controlled by the executive branch, how can one speak of 'parliamentarianism'?[14]

The legal and institutional interpretation of the scenario no longer interests anyone but foreign constitutional experts.[15] Vladimir Putin was able to pull off this political feat simply because he is the head of an all-powerful organization and because he holds all the levers needed to command obedience. He moves in a complex and opaque milieu made up of personal ties, economic paternalism and corporatism. However, I do not subscribe to the opinion that Putin is the unwilling hostage of cliques that force him to remain in power to guarantee their positions and their gains. The operation to keep Putin in power could only succeed with the active participation of the person directly involved. Moreover, independent Russian analysts did not hesitate to call the 2 December 2007 vote a *Spetsoperatsiya*! (Special Operation!),[16] thereby emphasizing that the methods used to obtain the desired outcome from the ballot boxes were typical of the intelligence services.

The Plebiscite of 2 December, 2007

Vladimir Putin's 1 October 2007 declaration that he would head the list of the 'governing party' turned the State Duma elections into a plebiscite for himself and his regime. Who would take any interest in the presidential election three months later, given that Putin remained in control and that voters would automatically approve his protégé by at least two-thirds?

Vladimir Putin demanded an incontestable victory on 2 December 2007. The administrative machine thus worked zealously and without external control throughout the campaign until late into the night of 2 December. The authorities thwarted any long observation mission by independent experts. After a battle that lasted months, the Organisation for Security and Co-operation in Europe (OSCE) election observation department sent only a few dozen people to monitor the vote on election day. Its Director expressed regret that the 70 observers scheduled to oversee preparations for the legislative elections as of 7 November were unable to obtain visas. Usually, the OSCE conducts missions several weeks long to assess the fairness of an election campaign.[17] The aggressiveness of the remarks made by Russian officials denouncing this 'attempt to interfere' in Russian domestic affairs surprised no one, because the tone had already been set by Putin's famous speech in Munich in February 2007 that had echoes of the Cold War.[18] The Kremlin's anti-Western stance was part of the Putin system's rhetorical and strategic arsenal. The ideology of 'sovereign democracy'[19] was clearly translated into policy.

Everything leading up to this election, planned over three years at least, aimed to control the names that would finally appear on the list of the 450 members of the State Duma, the lower house of Parliament. There was little doubt that this list, give or take a few names, had been drawn up months beforehand. Precise measures were taken in assigning percentages to each party in order to reach the desired number of members for each of the four lists entitled to sit in the Duma.

Thanks to years of experience monitoring elections in Russia, and in view of declarations made by Putin, his close advisers, and the chairman of the Central Election Commission (TsIK), Vladimir Churov, there was no need to look into a crystal ball to guess the results in advance: 64.30 per cent for United Russia, 7.74 per cent for Fair Russia (the second largest 'governing party'), 8.14 per cent for Zhirinovsky's LDPR (a vassal of the Kremlin) and 11.57 per cent for the Communist Party, the only true political party, which still occasionally dares to vote against a government bill.[20]

Voter turnout was rounded up to 63 per cent. It would have been difficult to inflate this figure any further, given that abstention was actually high for a vote that was supposed to be a resounding triumph for the President. Analyses made by independent experts evaluated actual voter abstention at about half the electorate.

During the run-up to the vote, the government deliberately cultivated doubt and uncertainty and created a false sense of anticipation to make commentators talk and generate the illusion of a real contest with an uncertain outcome. It was good form among well-placed Russian experts to 'fall into the trap' and play the role they were supposed to play—guessing at Putin's fears, the possible 'surprises', thereby fuelling the Kremlin's rhetoric that 'it's up to the people to make their voice heard!' As if the control was not tight enough to ensure an outcome according to plan. In fact, it is revealing that the platform of the official party, United Russia, was entitled 'Plan Putina' or Putin's Plan. Soviet-style banners slung across the avenues from one building to another all touted the same slogans: 'For Putin, for Russia', 'For stability, for United Russia', 'Vote for a United Russia, vote for Putin'. There were a few posters and pamphlets for the CP and the LDPR, but almost no sign of the other parties in the running. Eleven parties took part in the election, but only the first four could hope to reach the 7 per cent mark, below which votes are redistributed to the winning parties.[21]

The campaign was organized in such a way as to convince the Russians that only one choice was possible. The alternative to the legitimist vote was the protest vote, but abstaining or voting for a little party that had no chance of winning more than the 7 per cent required to sit in the Duma, such as the liberal SPS party or the Union of Rightwing Forces, would have no effect on the make-up of the Duma. Until the eve of the election, the authorities used the most humiliating and brutal methods to prevent opponents from expressing themselves and thus proving to voters that they would sideline themselves by voting for a loser. Arrests and imprisonment, confiscation of pamphlets, banning from the airwaves, physical threats and slander were the government's everyday tactics for months on end. Garry Kasparov, a fierce adversary of Putin, was sentenced to five days in prison the week before the legislative elections. Such methods were the culmination of years of pressure on the active representatives of civil society. Today they are even more repressive, demonstrating the impunity of men in uniform and the judges' partiality.

For ordinary Russians, everything was quiet on the eve of the legislative elections, to the extent that one would not know that an election was taking place. In the city of Tver, north-west of Moscow, the only place with a semblance of political activity was the Communist Party headquarters. In a humble basement, between photographs of Lenin and Gennady Zyuganov, again running for President in March 2008, CP officials explained, 'the social situation in Russia is dramatic, disparities are widening', but they could do nothing without approval from the local authorities. It was the Vice President of the Tver municipal assembly, a United Russia party official, who had accompanied me to CP headquarters. Sergey Golubev is a historian who joined the governing party and owes his political career to it. 'Our party is destined to be the dominant party, the party that governs', he explained to me openly. When questioned about the return to Soviet practices, he assured me that the single-party regime would not be reinstituted, but that 'the other political forces are not designed to lead, they are merely associated with the government in the various assemblies'.[22] Decorative pluralism, or imitation democracy, seems to me the notion conveyed by these remarks.

The End of the Free and Pluralist Vote

The conditions under which election campaigns and voting take place in Russia have deteriorated continuously since 1996: the first acceleration occurring in 1999–2000 to impose Yeltsin's chosen successor; the second in 2003–2004 to sideline opponents and ensure that Putin was re-elected with a comfortable margin; and finally, the outcome in 2007–2008 in which the results were decided beforehand and no independent candidate was able to stand.

During those 12 years, all the indicators of democratization gradually began flashing red: political party status and funding, conduct of election campaigns, the media, preference given to 'incumbents' or candidates close to the executive. Election laws were revised thoroughly and decisively after the Beslan tragedy in 2004. Moreover, neither the opposition forces, nor the citizens, nor even the judges could stop the Putin machine careering out of control or curb the passage of anti-constitutional laws that ran counter to the spirit of freedom and competition. As for the application of constitutional and legislative laws and the interpretation of regulatory texts, they depend on the Kremlin's goodwill.

The latest amendments made since 2000 aim to strengthen the 'governing party', block small parties and prevent the rise of politicians. In 1993, 1995, 1999 and 2003, the Duma was elected in two distinct halves: 225 members were elected by the single-mandate system, 225 by the list system. To be eligible to enter Parliament, a party had to garner 5 per cent of the votes cast. The law of 2005 vastly altered the situation. The 450 members of the Duma are now elected by the list system, and the threshold was upped to 7 per cent. If the results of December 2003 are used as a gauge, the scope of this change is perfectly clear. In 2003, several parties had secured between 3 and 6 per cent of the vote.

The third legislature, 2003–2007, still included a few opposition members elected by the single-mandate system. Either they were independent candidates or they belonged to a party that did not have the right to form a group in the Duma, or belonged to the Communist Party, which had its own group in the lower house. These members vanished from the fourth legislature, elected in December 2007. Vladimir Ryzhkov was a victim of the revision of the electoral procedure code. Popular in his home republic of Altay, constantly re-elected since 1993 by single-mandate vote, he was co-President of the Republican Party. This party was shut down by an arbitrary administrative decision in the spring of 2007. Nearly all opposition parties were dissolved by force or banned from seeking election: the National Bolshevik Party, the Republican Party, Rodina and others.

As Dmitry Oreshkin has written and a few brave journalists have stated, the election campaign was highly unfair and the outcome of the 2 December 2007 vote was 'directed' with a firm hand.[23] The presidential election of 2 March 2008, in which only the hand-picked successor was likely to become President, was also perfectly orchestrated. The pre-set goal had to be achieved; the authorities could not waver.

Two dress rehearsals had taken place in October 2006 and March 2007. Many provinces had organized the renewal of their regional assemblies and sometimes held local elections. The task of sidelining political figures and forces that were not loyal to the Kremlin was carried out without concern for keeping up appearances. Mikhail Sokolov analyzed many situations in detail and denounced arbitrary, sometimes brutal procedures, such as a candidate's arrest on a trumped-up charge. He already identified all the abuses noted in autumn 2007, particularly the stranglehold on the media, the countless administrative hurdles to prevent a candidate or a list from registering, the preference given to those who clearly indicated their pro-Kremlin stance, and financial pressures.[24]

In the legislative elections of 2 December 2007, universal suffrage was abused to such an extent that voters were invited to express themselves on something other than the choice of members who would sit in the State Duma. They did not go to the polls to make sure that Ivan Ivanovich instead of Platon Platonovich would 'represent' their district in a Duma devoid of any authority. They turned out to offer their support for a system, or on the contrary protest against it. If they voted for United Russia, they would be giving Putin a blank cheque, even when he had not revealed his entire plan (the choice of Medvedev had not yet been announced). They could also decide not to vote as a way of indicating their indifference or opposition to the election charade. However, if they abstained, they knew their votes could be used to stuff ballot boxes. A Levada Centre poll conducted some ten days before the election showed that two-thirds of the people interviewed believed that the election would not be fair.[25] Russian voters understood that their ballot had no impact on political, economic and social decisions.

Legalizing the Designated Successor

The 2 March 2008 election was not a free and plural election, but the ratification of a selection that was already set in stone. Two out of the three candidates authorized to run against Medvedev were election veterans. Gennady Zyuganov had already represented the Communist Party in the 1996 presidential election. He did not expect to win, but he nevertheless lamented that in the end he only garnered 17.72 per cent of the vote on 2 March. Vladimir Zhirinovsky, who had perfectly toed the Kremlin line for years, took part in each election as leader of his nationalist party, the LDPR. He officially won 9.35 per cent of the vote. Lastly, the third 'contestant' was a figure drawn out of the hat at the last minute to occupy the place refused to all 'independent' candidates. Andrey Bogdanov had actively participated in establishing the Putin party, United Russia. Then he was entrusted with capturing the little Democratic Party, presided over until 2005 by former Prime Minister Kasyanov, who went over to the opposition after being ousted in 2004. The Central Electoral Commission only granted Bogdanov 1.3 per cent.

Dmitry Medvedev won 70.28 per cent of the vote, a remarkable outcome for a young Deputy Prime Minister who remained in Putin's shadow until he was thrust onto the media stage as Chairman of the Board of Directors of Gazprom, then in connection with his mission as head of 'major national projects'. National projects are a facet of the policy to distribute a portion of hydrocarbon revenues to develop certain industrial sectors and improve infrastructure and public services, particularly by increasing civil servants' wages.

According to independent Russia experts who monitored the 2 March 2008 election, the authorities once again largely inflated voter turnout. The 65 per cent officially announced would appear to exceed real turnout by at least 10 percentage points. The regional aberrations in 2 December 2007 voting patterns were repeated. The republics of the Caucasus and some republics of the Volga were claimed to have had a turnout of over 90 per cent with over 80 per cent of votes for Medvedev. The most extreme cases, and the most unlikely, are Ingushetia with 91.66 per cent for Medvedev, Dagestan 91.92 per cent, the Republic of Karachaevo-Cherkessia 90.35 per cent, Mordovia 90.31 per cent, Kabardino-Balkaria 88.80 per cent, Bashkortostan 88 per cent. Tatarstan was in the vicinity of 80 per cent. In the Chukotka and Yamalo-Nenets autonomous districts, turnouts of 81.41 per cent and 83.86 per cent were announced respectively.

This geography of mandatory unanimity is highly revealing of the control exercised by local authorities at Moscow's request in the most sensitive areas of the Federation. The provinces of Krasnodar and Rostov on the north Caucasus border show a vote of 75 per cent and 77 per cent for Medvedev. The capital was surprisingly pro-Medvedev on 2 March 2008 (71.52 per cent), whereas at the legislative elections only 55 per cent had voted for the United Russia list led by Putin. The scope of the fraud organized in the city of Moscow itself was unprecedented.[26]

Independent experts point out that the official figures produced by the election board were inconsistent and in themselves revealed some of the methods used to falsify results. For instance, they attest to the difficulty of obtaining from local election commissions the number of registered voters by polling station on the day of the vote; the commissions only give a turnout percentage, and the polling stations commissions often get their figures mixed up. Everything gets 'fixed' at the territorial level, then at the central commission in Moscow.

Similarly, all point out the irregularity of the drop in the number of registered voters (174,000 fewer voters) in the Moscow polling stations between December 2007 and March 2008. Out of 3,281 polling stations in the capital, 209 were set up in closed locations (hospitals, prisons), 8 in places of transit such as train stations and the Vnukovo airport. Some documents attest to the falsification of voter turnout, particularly in 182 polling stations where it was 100 per cent (where half the voters supposedly voted during the last hour of the election).

The Kremlin had no qualms about resorting to methods still unthinkable a few years earlier. Polling stations were set up in Abkhazia and South Ossetia, two separatist provinces that are part of Georgia, and in Transnistria, a self-proclaimed republic within the state of Moldavia. The votes of all the 'citizens' residing outside Russia's borders were recorded in a single column of the Central Election Commission table, and supposedly amounted to 85.8 per cent for Putin's chosen successor.

As in the autumn of 2007, the OSCE mission was asked not to monitor the presidential election. Only a handful of observers from the Parliamentary Assembly of the Council of Europe were issued visas. Their criticism was immediately discredited by the authorities. Loyal observers chosen by the Commission on the other hand applauded the fairness of the campaign and the vote. According to the Union of Russian Journalists, candidate Medvedev was given a total of seventeen times more air time than the three other candidates together. In these circumstances, the opponents called for a boycott of the polls. All peaceful demonstrations in major Russian cities were once again banned and quashed, and several opposition figures were arrested. Many foreign governments and heads of state congratulated Dmitry Medvedev without expressing any clear reservations regarding the conditions in which the campaign, the vote and the counting of the ballots had taken place.

Why Keep Holding Elections?

Elections are a crucial instrument in the Kremlin's hands, even more than the constitutional provisions regarding the powers of the executive and the legislative branches. It is therefore essential to control them, as Russia's leaders have no formal plans to end universal suffrage. On the contrary, once the regime obtained the population's support/compliance, expression of this support, however distorted and manipulated, is considered useful. The regime has constructed its own legitimacy criteria, and one of these criteria is the popular, quasi-unanimous vote lightly veiled as pluralism with 'loyal' contestants. On election day, everything was all set.

The polling stations were clean and brightened up with flowers, a 'buffet' (a refreshment stand with food for sale), and sometimes games and lotteries. Several anomalies were to be noted, however: lower and poorly isolated voting booths; still no envelope in which to place the ballot; police presence at the polling station; and greater vigilance than before by the polling officials checking who went in and out.[27]

The function and meaning of universal suffrage are at the heart of the question of representative democracy and popular sovereignty. By corrupting the free vote, the government distorts the crucial link between citizens and those who govern them in a lasting and profound manner. This link had begun to take shape under Gorbachev and the early days of the Yeltsin presidency, but for too short a time and too superficially. The relation between voting citizens and the political, economic and social system has deteriorated, once again characterized by formality, force and wariness. It is mainly geared towards support for the president as a person. This personalization of power is a symptom of the regime's authoritarian tendencies.

It is difficult for Europeans to understand the advantage of maintaining a non-democratic vote. Indeed, in the society in which they live and vote, they hope that the vote they cast will have an effect on the way in which the country is governed. In a democracy, the relationship citizens have to elections should ideally involve trust and the guarantee of respect for the vote and the messages conveyed by this vote.

In Russia, the aim is the opposite. The system must be organized in such a way as to exclude political forces that are not loyal, not only to parliament but to other institutions as well. Adversaries become illegitimate and dangerous. The Public Chamber offers the best illustration of the strategy of distorting the principle of representation of popular sovereignty. It was created by Putin in 2005 to act in lieu of Parliament as a place for civil society to debate and express itself. 'Competent' figures are appointed to it, people who belong to the circle of power and agree to play this servile role of unelected representatives. In this way, the representatives elected to the Duma act with virtual unanimity in representing the people and framing the people's will. The people have not formally been excluded; they have been tamed. And other organizations that are under the government's thumb supervise the legislative assembly and claim to be the vanguard of society. The parody of public debate played outside the parliament is the most visible mark of a return to Soviet practices, reminiscent of the iron rule of 'democratic centralism': once a decision is made at the top, it brooks no discussion.

The authorities are eager to show that a national consensus exists and that they have built a Russia without conflict. They are obsessed with the danger of an Orange Revolution. The historic events of November and December 2004 in Ukraine took Putin and his advisers entirely by surprise. Having failed to anticipate them, they could find only one explanation: subversion by the United States, which was supposedly pulling the strings via NGOs and covert funding. The Americans even allegedly paid people to protest in the streets. It should be remembered that over one million Ukrainians demonstrated night and day in bitter cold weather to defend their rights. Three weeks of peaceful rebellion brought down the Kuchma regime and prompted a new presidential election guaranteed by the presence of a host of Ukrainian and foreign observers.

The trauma was so great among Russian leaders that they still cannot analyze Ukrainian politics calmly, and they systematically make disparaging remarks about the Ukrainians. In September 2006, when I asked about relations with the Ukrainian government, one of President Putin's advisers replied: 'How do you expect us to get along with the Ukrainians? It's impossible to do business with them. They lie and cheat, they can't be trusted! I speak from experience, I did my military service in Ukraine! You can't expect anything out of them'. And yet the question was asked at a time when relations seemed to be improving, given that Leonid Kuchma's former Prime Minister, Viktor Yanukovich, had got the job after Yulia Timoshenko was ousted. The hostility of the remark was surprizing coming from a pillar of Putin's team in answer to a question from Western experts in Moscow. Angry spite against President Yushchenko and the 'Oranges' was customary in the government media and so, as I witnessed, the leaders had no compunction about adopting the same tone. In slightly less offensive but equally contemptuous terms, the Russian President reiterated the same position the next day.[28]

The calculated emotion and patent aggressiveness offered stark confirmation that Vladimir Putin could not bear the affront Kiev had inflicted on him. The Orange Revolution first of all proved that Ukrainian politics was moving in an independent direction from Moscow. And especially, it showed the Kremlin that leaders who had little respect for the rule of law and democratic principles could lose in the face of a multitude of ordinary individuals. This example of an undemocratic regime being overturned at the polls convinced Putin of the need for virtually total control over the organization of elections and firm repression of any political opposition. Minimizing the risk of situations eluding its control has been the Kremlin's main concern since 2004, and all means are justified so long as the danger of 'instability' is averted.

Currently the authorities have strained relations with this former Soviet republic of 47 million inhabitants. Ukraine's plans for partnerships with the European Union and NATO with a view to possible membership are the nemesis of Russian propaganda, while the main aim of the lightning war waged by the Russian Army against Georgia in August 2008 was essentially to discredit Tbilisi.

The Russians thus turned a page in March 2008. To a certain extent they relinquished their right to elect their representatives freely and fairly, although this right is enshrined in the 1993 Constitution. They accepted, whether they liked it or not, the strengthening of the Putin system without having any direct influence on this system of government. They renounced choosing their leaders from among several alternatives and turned their backs on any form of political activity. They no longer participated in public institutions, entrusting them to the most powerful groups. They withdrew into their private lives and professional careers, and on the whole felt relieved. They have gradually been led to this by the systematic bleeding of all public institutions and the encouragement to retreat to the private sphere. The Russians have reverted to the habits under Soviet rule: criticize the authorities as they please *na kukhne*—'in the kitchen'. Repeated electoral fraud and blatant ballot box stuffing, however, will drive more and more Russians to express their distrust and to protest.

Imitating or Downgrading Democracy?

Putin, Medvedev and their peers are not concerned with imitating Western customs or respecting propriety and, as we saw in Chapter 5, since 2004 no effort has been made to keep up appearances. The crushing of opponents is shown on television. Attacks against NGOs and the British Council, for instance, or, much more serious, the murder of Alexander Litvinenko by polonium 210 poisoning in London are intended to be forcefully exposed. People are not killed behind closed doors but out in the open; adversaries such as Garry Kasparov and Maxim Reznik are not arrested in the early hours in their homes but in the middle of a peaceful demonstration in the centre of Moscow or Saint Petersburg. The law on extremism passed in 2006 aimed to give a very broad interpretation of the extremist threat and to make it easy to sentence any individual or organization that the courts consider dangerous because they encourage hatred and destabilization of the state. Some terms of this law are reminiscent of the notorious laws of the Soviet era. The spirit is clearly one of repression.

How should this two-sided behaviour—displays of authoritarian methods while claiming to be a people's 'democracy'—be construed? Putin could have flouted the institution of universal suffrage with multiple candidates and moved closer to the Soviet or Chinese system. He could have assumed the choice of a non-representative but populist regime, a non-democratic but 'orderly' and predictable system. He chose to run with the hare and hunt with the hounds, leaving room for interpretation in describing the system he heads.

His achievement is twofold. First, no cast-iron definition of the regime has been established, and the controversy as to what Putinism truly is continues both in Russia and abroad. This plays into the hands of the Russian leaders who draw public attention and can blow hot and cold; they build strong support in the West, in business and government circles as well as in intellectual and political milieux. They thus manage to undermine political and moral criticism of their system and deflect arguments pointing to the violation of public freedoms and human rights. Second, this margin of uncertainty is part of the system itself. It helps maintain doubt about the deep-seated nature of the regime, the intentions of its leaders and their long-term goals, and prevents the crystallization of harsh, systematic criticism of the regime, its intrinsic weaknesses and the danger it poses for Russia's future.

Therefore, holding 'directed' elections takes on its full meaning in this context of fuzziness and uncertainty consciously sustained by the leaders. In the weeks following the dubbing of Medvedev as heir apparent by the voters, nearly all the foreign and Russian media held forth at length on the probability of a 'thaw', a 'liberal' turn, or on the contrary an unfortunate tightening of the screws if the 'young Medvedev' did not manage to shake off his mentor and 'kill the father'. In my opinion, we were in the midst of a fairy tale, one orchestrated by the Kremlin's contradictory little remarks and the smiles and smirks of the main players. A few weeks prior to the 2 March presidential election, Putin, in all seriousness, reiterated that he would be the one to decide if he took the post of Prime Minister and that he would not 'hang the new President's photo on his wall'. Many Russian civil servants and officials ended up hanging a picture of Putin and Medvedev together!

The day of the election, 2 March 2008, the two protagonists were lunching in a restaurant in the capital in the company of numbers 2, 3 and 4 of the regime: the President of the upper house of parliament, Sergey Mironov; the President of the State Duma, Boris Gryzlov; and the head of government, Viktor Zubkov. The camera remained for a long time focused on an unfamiliar Putin, his face beaming, dressed in a white polo shirt, and his protégé in a business suit, more reserved but very cheerful. The footage conveyed the message of a little group of cronies noisily celebrating the clever trick they were playing on the Russian population and the media the world over. Putin has shown considerable talent for PR these last years after having corrected the errors of his early days (particularly his disastrous handling of the *Kursk* submarine tragedy in August 2000). Each image is calculated, every word, whether benevolent or brutal, is weighed. When Putin 'fluffs' his choice of words, is it not a way of demonstrating his power? The leader need not bother with mincing words on strategic topics such as Georgia, foreign 'interference', or adversaries labelled 'foes of Russia'.

Interpretation of Russian leaders' behaviour thus carries us beyond the mere theory of imitation democracy or keeping up democratic appearances. The Russian leaders no longer pretend to strive towards democracy as an ultimate goal after a phase that will be long and difficult. They vehemently assert their refusal to follow the Western path. Putin is not seeking to copy, he wants to discredit 'Western' democracy. The best proof of this is the spring 2008 creation of an agency to promote Russian democracy with offices in Paris and in New York. Natalya Narochnits-kaya, appointed to head the Paris office, even found a French publisher to translate her ideological and anti-Western book, with an afterword by a French academic to boot![29]

It is interesting to note that during the heated debates of the winter of 2007–2008, the argument of Russian traditions was often used. But just what traditions were meant? Soviet history was not an extension of the Tsarist 'father of the nation' tradition. Stalin's dictatorship in the 1930s and 1940s was a tragedy. Neither Khrushchev, nor Brezhnev, nor Andropov fully played the role of a 'tsar' above institutions. The political leadership was theoretically collegial in nature, with a Communist Party leader, a head of state and a head of government. Brezhnev endeavoured to personalize power by concurrently holding the positions of Party Secretary-General and Head of State. But the prevailing notion of a 'number one' was in fact fairly depersonalized. Mikhail Gorbachev attempted to reform the USSR around his name and his central idea—*perestroika*—but he did not succeed. His presidentialization of the USSR came too late. Boris Yeltsin had already taken the presidency of the Republic of Russia, and other men occupied the head of the other Soviet republics.

In such conditions, 'Russian tradition' is mentioned for lack of anything better. And I find it disturbing to see this cultural and misguided neo-Tsarist explanation of power echoed over and over again, particularly in Europe. The last Tsar abdicated nearly a century ago, discredited and hated by both the people and the elites. There is no monarchic romanticism in people's minds, and it is unsubtly manufactured by certain media in order to convince Russians that constitutional and legal rules are worth nothing compared to the wisdom and magnanimity of the providential man who restored their 'dignity and power': Vladimir Putin.

It is important for European societies to understand this challenge now that they are open to political, cultural, economic and financial influences from Russia, which was not the case when Russia was a closed, Soviet republic. To dismiss the theory of imitation, I will review a few fundamental aspects of Putinism, which are at odds with western democracies.

Since 2000, the aim of Putin's team has been to curb pluralism, competition and criticism in both the political and the economic spheres. Yukos, Chechnya and elections form the three pillars of a general undertaking: to concentrate power in the hands of a small circle of leadership by provoking the desertification of the political sphere and wresting control of the country's resources.

Putin's Power and the Cult of Personality

Putin has been very lucky and has cleverly used the propitious combination of circumstances that have presented themselves since 1999. He has also managed to bounce back from disaster, sometimes even managing to portray it as a test of Russia's new-found power.

His first stroke of luck, as noted in Chapter 5, resulted from the collapse of the Yeltsin regime in 1998–1999. Other candidates had been sounded out as Boris Yeltsin's successors to no avail, and the urgency of the situation led to appointing as Director of the FSB a man who at least would ensure continuity within the intelligence services, and would attract support from the military with an iron-fisted discourse and, especially in the case of the war against the Chechens.

Putin's second stroke of luck was the lack of preparation among the Russian political and economic elite in 1999. The main actors were taken by surprise by the rise of a man who was stronger and more determined than they expected. The Berezovsky affair was a good illustration of this: the man who promoted Putin so as to remain the *éminence grise* and the most powerful oligarch made his descent into hell as early as May 2000, two months after the successor he had chosen was elected. Perhaps Boris Berezovsky was naïve and lacked awareness of the corporatist, virtually sectarian nature of the post-Soviet intelligence services.

The events of 11 September 2001 were obviously the Russian President's greatest opportunity, as he immediately offered an outstretched hand to George W. Bush. The entire world noted that the new President of the United States had acquired in that tragedy a stature that he would never otherwise have attained. At the same time, Putin imposed himself as the indispensable partner in the 'war on terror', to use the official American terminology. The facile confusion between Chechens and Islamist terrorists had taken root.

Lastly, the continual rise in hydrocarbon prices until 2008 provided increasing revenue that gave the Putin administration an exceptional ability to turn the economic and social situation around. Without the oil and natural gas windfall, it is unlikely that Putin would have consolidated his power.

The Russian President did not hesitate, either, to take advantage of serious crises or to enact brutal measures. The 2003–2004 period was a major moment for him. In 2003, Putin entered into direct confrontation with Mikhail Khodorkovsky and had him arrested in October, rather than attempting to strike a bargain. Putin came out on top, but at the cost of considerable injustice: a sham trial, the carving up of the Yukos oil company and the sentencing of its CEO to eight years in a labour camp.[30] Putin would concentrate energy resources in the hands of a few men who were loyal to the Kremlin and established the oligopolistic autocracy on this basis. On 3 September 2004, the Beslan massacre gave him a pretext to enact authoritarian reforms: the submission of Chechnya to Ramzan Kadyrov's dictatorship, provincial governors placed under supervision, the reform of the electoral system and the weakening of the Duma and the creation of the Public Chamber made up of appointed rather than elected members. It was starting with this rebound in 2004 that Putin intensified his move to place men and organizations loyal to the Kremlin at the head of all institutions and major companies.

Power is personified in Putin. The government's power is equated to Putin's power, even under the presidency of Dmitry Medvedev. Putin worship differs from the cult of Leonid Brezhnev, who established himself as a structural feature of government propaganda and uniformity: the leader is above the others, he is infallible as long as he leads, for the Communist Party is infallible. At the time of 'consolidated socialism', the cult had no echo among the population other than scathing irony. People remember the anecdotes making fun of an ageing and ailing

Brezhnev better than the millions of copies of his speeches and 'writings' distributed in all offices and classrooms throughout the USSR, along with his picture that had been airbrushed to such an extent that the man looked ageless and expressionless.

Putin worship is not similar to Stalin worship either, even if its underpinnings liken it more to the people's attachment to the leader. Stalin exercised total power in a closed country held hostage. For many years, absolute terror was a daily fact and life a total sham. No one, from the lowliest worker to Stalin's close associates, could sleep entirely peacefully. Today, ordinary Russians give politicians little thought and have little remorse about losing interest in politics. They are free not to think about politics. This detachment is what affords them their peace of mind.

Voluntary Servitude?

Vladimir Putin is certainly unfamiliar with Étienne de La Boétie, a friend of Montaigne in sixteenth-century France. Yet *Discourse on Voluntary Servitude* is probably the most convincing expression of the very complex relations between rulers and the ruled in a country dominated by the will of a powerful figure. La Boétie built his thinking on the following observation:

For the present I should like merely to understand how it happens that so many men, so many villages, so many cities, so many nations, sometimes suffer under a single tyrant who has no other power than the power they give him; who is able to harm them only to the extent to which they have the willingness to bear with him; who could do them absolutely no injury unless they preferred to put up with him rather than contradict him.[31] [...]

It is therefore the inhabitants themselves who permit, or, rather, bring about, their own subjection, since by ceasing to submit they would put an end to their servitude. A people enslaves itself, cuts its own throat, when, having a choice between being vassals and being free men, it deserts its liberties and takes on the yoke, gives consent to its own misery, or, rather, apparently welcomes it'.[32]

And La Boétie sharply and sarcastically addresses these millions of individuals who accept all the misfortune that comes 'from the one enemy whom you yourselves render as powerful as he is'.[33] He emphasizes the facility with which people allow themselves to be taken in by words and promises. For instance, as soon as the tyrant is called 'lord' or 'master' or 'people's tribune', his authority becomes greater among those subservient to him. And in 2000, the title of 'President-elect of the Russian Federation' probably lent Vladimir Putin much greater legitimacy than the actual representation Russians granted him. It is for this reason that his succession is so tricky.

The ruling elite, as well as the population, share the same vision of the personalization of power. In a study conducted by the Levada Centre in 2006 among representatives of the ruling class, 86 per cent considered beyond a shadow of a doubt that the only political actor defining the main orientations and state policy was President Putin.[34] The respondents did not mention political parties, institutions, or social groups, but Vladimir Putin in person. On the other hand, the 'intellectual' and financial elites were less convinced that ideas and strategies were concentrated in the person of the President alone. As Lev Gudkov notes, this tends to reinforce the hypothesis that the elites in the broad sense have no authority and hardly any influence over public opinion. They do not fulfil their role. At the same time, the sociologist points out, representatives of the establishment as well as the population 'give a fairly modest assessment of the true achievements of the President's policy action'.[35] Hence, personalization does not lead to success in managing the country. It demonstrates a less rational and more subservient attitude of ordinary Russians who leave things up to the leader since they cannot, or do not wish to, take part in the nation's choices.

Putin has forged his personal and authoritarian system in an open country where money is king and the elites are, on the whole, well settled into their condition of obligatory loyalty to the regime, but rewarded by previously-unheard-of financial comfort. These factors thus make the current system a real innovation in Russia. And a comparison with China, or Chile under Pinochet, or even Saudi Arabia quickly reaches a limit and does not take away the particular and novel characteristics of the Putin system in a Russian context still imbued with Sovietism.

Thus, the system is neither a Communist dictatorship, nor a military dictatorship, nor an oil power headed by a clan-like dynasty. It indisputably shares some of their features but not all of them, and has its own specificities.

What is unusual is this combination of openness and withdrawal, of oligopolistic power and messy capitalism, brutal repression of political opponents and tolerance for criticism broadcast over the Internet, intense state nationalism and society's ideological and political indifference. One of the driving forces of the regime is what I call 'biscuit baiting'. On the strength of their financial capacity, the leaders and their many intermediaries attract foreign individuals, companies, municipalities and partners according to an immediate quid pro quo mode of exchange: 'We offer you an advantage today, take it with no questions asked, nothing is set in stone; if you demand other conditions, for instance legal or political, in the middle or long term, then you risk losing everything, that's your tough luck'. The relation is established on a mode of diffuse blackmail, that gets tougher when big interests are at stake. It is absolutely not based on trust or institutional guarantees. It is a relationship between citizens and the government that is deeply marked by this preference for fluidity and vagueness analyzed in Chapter 4. It is asymmetrical and unstable by nature, and this is what gives the ruling class its strength. For, in Russia, the notion of a ruling class is more appropriate than a middle class or elite in the sociological and political sense of the term as understood in older democracies.

The personalization of the system by the leader himself is the inevitable flipside of the weakening of institutions. For individuals to submit to the will of on high, they must distrust institutions and view these public organizations as both abstract and burdensome. Institutions are abstract because their ways of functioning remain impenetrable to ordinary Russians, but they weigh heavily in each person's life because bureaucracies have consolidated very strong positions in all areas of social, economic and cultural life.

It was essential to Putin's strategy to undermine provincial governors and big city mayors because these men had a face, a personality and hence a personal authority over those they governed. They had established local, sometimes authoritarian, sometimes fairly liberal, personalized systems that defied the Kremlin's will to concentrate power around a single man and his direct networks. They thus enjoyed a potential for autonomy and contradiction that presented an obstacle to sanctifying power around a single figure. They taught the Russians, consciously or not, to view their space differently, to free themselves from the weight of an all-powerful sovereign who was above institutions and the population. For even a paternalistic and clientelistic president such as Tatarstan's Mintimer Shaymiyev could not close his republic in on itself, the autocratic model being more difficult to impose. Contrary to the alarming discourse coming from Moscow, I do not believe that Russia in the 1990s was facing the danger of being broken up into dictatorial and primitive subsystems.

With regard to these conflicts on high and the battles at the heart of the political machinery, Russians have gradually developed a nebulous fear: a fear of others, a fear of the future, a fear of losing what they have. And we have seen the extent to which disinformation via increasingly controlled media wore down the Russians' critical reflexes. Two-thirds of them ended up giving up any ambition to participate in building society and the state in which they live. 'The state is them, so is society' is one way of summing up their state of mind. The most important thing is to make a living.

Naturally Putin took advantage of the lack of rooted democratic values, which requires abstraction, as Igor Klyamkin explains.[36] The state is abstract, power is concrete. The character that Putin has constructed corresponds to this mindset. The man falls outside of the categories into which other political officials fit. He has something more, and this is what the propaganda must create in people's minds through television. His physical appearance has changed over the years from 1999 to 2008. Official photographs of summer 2007 struck all observers: bulging muscles, chest thrown out, the President had 'taken on substance'. He represents the return of Russia's power, the return of the uniform as well, and the illusion of appearance in a country where images strike people directly, without being filtered through critical analysis.

The new structure invented in 2008, with two men at the head of the Executive, poses several problems in an authoritarian and personalized regime. The first question is precisely who is the person who should symbolize Russia and personify power. Only a single individual can fulfil this symbolic role, which is all the more important since the other institutions have been undermined and are not representative. Vladimir Putin's preponderance is the key to this temporary construction, the 'tandem'.

Putin III: The Unlikely Dyarchy

In 2008, Vladimir Putin can be considered to have granted himself a third term, a term with no limit in time. The argument claiming that he acted in accordance with the Constitution is made in truly bad faith given the regime's drift towards authoritarianism in recent years.

The Russians are deeply wary of a double-headed authority. The dyarchy (*dvoevlastie*) harks back to dark periods in their history, the Time of Troubles in the early seventeenth century, 1917 and 1989–1993. Power shared equally by two men is simply inconceivable. A few months after Putin and Medvedev switched functions, the ascendancy of the former left no doubt. Both men's entourages are made up almost exclusively of people loyal to the former President.

Those very close to Putin, and therefore very powerful, went with him into the Cabinet. First of all the seven deputy prime ministers: Viktor Zubkov, the former Prime Minister who became Chairman of the board of the giant Gazprom on 27 June 2008; Igor Shuvalov, his aide for the G8 in the Kremlin; Aleksander Zhukov, former Deputy Prime Minister; Sergey Ivanov, FSB officer and Minister of Defence until 2007; Aleksey Kudrin, who retained his post of Minister of Finance; Sergey Sobyanin, former Chief of Presidential Administration who also heads the Prime Minister's office; and especially Igor Sechin, the *éminence grise*, formerly of the KGB and President of the Rosneft oil company (until April 2011), who also followed Putin from the Kremlin to the White House. Former FSB chief Nikolay Patrushev, another long-time follower, took the Secretariat of the Security Council. This institution would end up taking on more weight to enable Putin to remain a central figure in the foreign policy system.

Even more revealing is the choice of men Putin installed around his successor in the Kremlin in 2008. This team is totally loyal to Putin, starting with the new Chief of Presidential Administration, Sergey Naryshkin, and his deputy Vladislav Surkov, chief ideologue at the Kremlin for years, down to the President's advisers, such as Arkady Dvorkovich. None of them owes his career to Medvedev. Their loyalty goes first to Putin and, for most of them, to the FSB and/or the Saint Petersburg networks.

In the 1993 Constitution and the ensuing legislation, the position of head of government was designed to be an administrative function coming under the presidency. Articles 111 and 112 outline the procedures by which the head of government is chosen by the president, and then must obtain from the Duma a vote regarding the formation of his government. He need not be the leader of a parliamentary majority. Putin decided, in order to remain very powerful, to convert the prime minister into the head of the parliamentary majority. He restated this forcefully in the above-mentioned interview in *Le Monde*. In that regard, he radically altered the spirit of the 1993 Constitution, which was designed to avoid any duality in the Executive by fostering a strong presidency.

In his speech to the Duma on 8 May 2008, Putin covered the entire political, social and economic terrain. Medvedev once again played second fiddle. He listened to his Prime Minister, whereas Putin did not attend Viktor Zubkov's inaugural address to the Kremlin when the latter was sworn in as Prime Minister in September 2007. Even more significant, the new President of the Russian Federation was deprived of the chance, during that spring of 2008, to give a big speech before Parliament. Putin stole the show from him with his 8 May speech. He also formed a new institution, the Government Presidium, which meets weekly and deals with all issues. This Presidium is made up of the seven deputy prime ministers and seven other ministers, three of whom hold 'sovereign' portfolios (Foreign Affairs, Defence and Interior) which constitutionally should report to the President.[37] It should be remembered that a Presidium of the Council of Ministers existed under the Soviet system; the power ritual is thus fairly close to the Soviet ritual.

Putin has not really changed his presidential habits, as he usually lives and works in the presidential residence of Novo-Ogarevo. In early 2008, he announced he would keep this residence after the succession. He also occupies an office in Old Square, very near the Kremlin, in his capacity of President of the dominant party, United Russia.

Officially, Medvedev has direct authority over the ministries of Foreign Affairs, Defence, and Emergency Situations, as well as the Federal Migratory Service and the new Federal Agency of CIS Affairs. In actual fact, Vladimir Putin retains the upper hand over 'structures of force', i.e. the army and the police. He ordered and coordinated the military intervention against Georgia in August 2008. Dmitry Medvedev is Head of State and represents Russia at all the major international meetings and during state visits, but Putin remains the leader. The years 2008–2011 confirm this simple fact (see chapter 9).

A nice Russian joke being told in the summer of 2008 perfectly illustrates the way the Russians see the President-Prime Minister duo: 'Putin wakes up a bit foggy one morning, as he'd gone to bed late. He suddenly has a doubt about an important issue. He goes to see Medvedev and asks, "Dima, tell me, 2 plus 2 equals 4, right?" Medvedev rubs his eyes, as he hasn't slept very well, and answers, "Of course, Volodya, you're right, 2 plus 2 equals 4; making 3 for you and 1 for me!"

8

THE PUTIN SYSTEM

PATRONAGE AND THE ENRICHMENT OF THE ELITES

Russians have become consumers, the elites have grown rich and those who hold the reins of political power control a large swathe of the economy. Money has redefined social relations and the nature of state power. Affluence gives leaders personal comfort and power to manage the country, often inducing them to prefer arbitrariness and preferential treatment to the practice of negotiation and application of the law.

But the system is unstable, for it is made up of a number of imbalances that temporarily offset one another. Russia's economy is one of growth and not development.[1] When international turbulence—for instance a drop in oil prices or the resumption of armed conflict in the Caucasus—or domestic political and social crises occur, the Russian economy is likely to find itself exposed and vulnerable. Domestic destabilization can arise from poorly arbitrated sectarian conflicts, uncontrolled violence or endemic social malaise that can upset current arrangements.

The Putin galaxy holds together thanks to the continuity of political power, which remains centred on Vladimir Putin. Dmitry Medvedev is part of it and could not free himself from it if he wanted to. He exists only through this constellation of clans, networks and corporations that ensure the movement and exercise of power. The iron rule of this system is member loyalty and elite submission to both written and unwritten rules. Loyalty is expressed in the negative—do not criticize or hinder the centre of the constellation—and in the positive: take action against disloyal actors who are stigmatized as 'enemies' and jeopardize the system. The dominant ideology and necessary conformism produce protectionist attitudes and siege mentalities. Will the opening up of Russia, key to the 1987–1993 transformation, be called into question?

Economic Growth, the Key to Consolidating the Political Regime

Since the start of the 2000s, the Russian economy has undeniably experienced remarkable growth and has recovered from the 2008 world crisis more promptly than expected. Living standards increased until 2007, and again in 2010.

Average GDP growth was 7 per cent between 2001 and 2007, there was a trade surplus, public debt was paid off and inward foreign direct investment doubled between 2005 and 2007.[2] Russia was severely hit by the world economic crisis in the autumn of 2008 and through the year 2009, but it returned to growth quickly. Thanks to the devaluation of the rouble in late 2008, and the rebound in commodities prices in 2010, the growth rate in 2010 is officially assessed at about 4 per cent, and imports growth at 10 per cent. However, 'while quick in international comparison, future growth will not reach the speed seen in the long growth spurt of 2000–2008'.[3]

During the years of growth, household income has increased steadily and better access to credit has stimulated consumption. Most Russians have become consumers, except for the poorest quarter. Income disparities remain high, with the wealthiest 20 per cent averaging an income six times greater than the income of the poorest 20 per cent in 2008.[4]

In these favourable conditions, the Kremlin conducted a strategy of rebuilding the instruments of government, once the authorities had monopolized them. It concentrated economic resources in a few large state corporations, carried out effective fiscal reform, undertook 'major national projects' using stabilization funds fed by hydrocarbon revenues. It imposed rules of unfailing loyalty on the oligarchs and placed provincial governors and local officials under supervision.

Economists generally agree that the continual rise in the prices of hydrocarbons has been the driver for growth since 2000, with the exception of the sharp fall in prices in 2008–2009, but they differ over how well the leadership has managed the oil and gas windfall. In particular, Vladimir Putin and his government designed a tax reform in the summer of 2000 that offered the state budget the means to exit the financial crisis of 1998–1999. A flat income tax was set at the relatively low rate of 13 per cent, and a direct deposit system was set up to deter large companies from continuing their practice of tax evasion. The government also undertook structural reforms, some of which improved the situation—for instance, the reorganization of customs and the legislation for small and medium-sized businesses. Others, such as reform of the judicial system and revision of social welfare, came to nothing. All in all, short-term measures were appropriate, but long-term reforms did not follow suit.

It should be noted as well that the bankruptcy of the Russian state in August 1998 provided a springboard for economic stimulus measures and gave Russian producers a new impetus; the collapse of the rouble had in fact brought nearly all foreign imports to a halt and stimulated domestic supply. Vladimir Putin was thus able to turn this disastrous legacy around and also take advantage of an incredible stroke of good fortune: the rise in oil prices as soon as he acceded to the Kremlin in 2000. Andrei Illarionov, an adviser to the President until his sudden departure in 2005, admits that Putin was very lucky, but used this luck skilfully by listening to the advice of liberal economists in the early years of his presidency.[5] He explains how Putin's economic policy took a wrong turn in 2003–2004, with Mikhail Khodorkovsky's arrest and the dismantling of the very successful oil firm Yukos. From this dramatic point on, the leadership conducted a strategy of systematically taking control of the major raw materials producing companies, the arms industry, aviation and gradually the metallurgical industry.

For the Finnish economist Pekka Sutela, there is no doubt about Russia's economic success, but it could have been much better if the political authorities had not acted in such a clientelistic, monopolistic and opaque manner. Basically, the success is striking if one compares 2007 to 1998, but more mixed if one reasons in terms of potential—in other words the use that could have been made of the extraordinary resources and opportunities available to Russia. Sutela points out that the price of oil rose tenfold between 1998 and early 2008, and that the incredible windfall that hit Russian producers and the state represented a sizeable economic and political challenge. Putin's government could have met it differently and ensured a far more solid foundation for Russian economic development. Russian leaders were alarmed when hydrocarbon prices fell in 2008, and struggled to see what options they had in case of a prolonged reduction in state revenue. Vladimir Milov relates with irony his unofficial conversations with former colleagues from the Energy Ministry who are very concerned with the curve of the price of hydrocarbons: 'What's your forecast? How long will it last?'[6]

Russia is also rich in other minerals, such as bauxite and nickel, which have all been pushed up because of the rise in hydrocarbon prices. Russian officials have only half managed to avoid the well-known Dutch disease, or the 'oil curse', by which easy money anaesthetizes a country's leaders, consolidates a rentier economy and impedes modernization. Reforms in nearly all areas have been blocked since 2003. On the other hand, following the positive Norwegian example, a stabilization fund was created in 2004, into which about 10 per cent of sales revenue is paid. The fund played a critical role in keeping the state budget afloat during the crisis of 2008–2009.

Altogether, energy (hydrocarbons, coal, electricity) provides Russia with about two-thirds of its export revenue, approximately one-third of its GDP and nearly half its public-sector revenue. This sector, however, employs only 2 per cent of the nation's work force and does not automatically diffuse dynamism into the whole economy.

Various issues threaten the future of the oil and gas sector. For one, prices will eventually drop. Secondly, investment remains insufficient and the authorities block large-scale foreign acquisitions. Long-term prospects depend on investments in future production, in order to exploit new oil reserves at competitive world prices. Management of the major state industries is opaque. Furthermore, domestic energy consumption in Russia is on the rise, which may lead to a decrease in exports. Until 2008, the rouble was relatively strong and inflation remained controllable (7 per cent in 2007 according to official statistics). Russian consumers took advantage of this upturn. Renewed inflation currently presents the government with a real challenge, given that the poorest population segments, as well as the still vulnerable part of the new middle class, are directly hit by the rise in the prices of food and services. The productivity of the Russian economy is growing less steadily than before, and labour is comparatively expensive. This is one of the reasons why Russia is not as competitive as other emerging economies such as India and China.

Economists believe that three essential factors are decisive for the future: the price of raw materials, the rule of law (and action against corruption) and the internationalization of Russia. The future will only be prosperous if consumers take an interest in public life and assume their duties as citizens, and if entrepreneurs go international and hence European. Pekka Sutela summarizes the economic challenge as follows:

The true source of Russian growth since the collapse of the Soviet Union has been the shift of resources from inefficient heavy industries to modern services sectors. For this catch-up growth to continue, Russia does not need to innovate but to imitate; it can import technology, know-how and institutions from richer countries. However, successful catch-up growth requires a sound business environment, the rule of law, open markets, and good infrastructure. The Russian authorities should focus on these things rather than top-down attempts to encourage innovation.[7]

Julian Cooper reinforces the argument:

The structure of the Russian economy, dominated by resource-based sectors, is not conducive to vibrant innovation as the demand for new technologies and goods is not strong, and is focused on a limited range of activities. To make matters worse, as underlined by international rankings, such as that of the World Economic Forum, the Russian economy exhibits only weak competition, for which the structure of the economy is clearly a determining factor. There is an unhelpful circularity: Russia needs a more diversified economy and for this needs change and innovation, as the leadership appreciates, but a precondition for innovation is the existence of a more competitive and diversified economy.[8]

William Tompson believes that the most serious problem is the shaky form of clientelistic state capitalism.[9] This OECD economist shows that the expansion of state ownership and control has diminished Russia's economic performance. For Yevgeny Yasin, liberal economist and former Minister of the Economy, the abrupt arrest of Mikhail Khodorkovsky in October 2003 and the legal action against Yukos marked a turn towards a predatory 'state corporatism'.[10] The succession of scandals in recent years confirms the appalling nature of the predatory practices employed by groups in power. In July 2008, Prime Minister Putin personally took in hand the attack against Mechel, the large coal and steel company, and accused its CEO, Igor Zyuzin, of tax evasion. Mechel stocks plummeted within days.[11] Sergey Aleksashenko, former Deputy Minister of Finance, is one of the most vocal critics of the Putin government's policies.[12]

Yet, it is not rare for Russian and European experts to claim that Putin did the right thing and that only a strong form of 'state capitalism' is appropriate for Russia. State capitalism or clan capitalism? The oligarchic phenomenon has developed within the very heart of the state apparatus insofar as the loyal business establishment is very close and sometimes even part of the political sphere.

The Resources of Oligarchy

The Russian power system today stands on three major pillars: considerable financial and material resources, a few powerful organizations and networks, and a group of people that form the galaxy of power at the summit. The oligarchic phenomenon is the keystone. It creates a strong link between financial power and political power, between the country's economic resources and established networks. These networks are not a mafia, strictly speaking, because they were spawned within the 'state' machine itself, i.e. the intelligence services, federal and regional administrations, the Tax Bureau, the Interior Ministry, etc. They all exist publicly and develop within institutions that 'cover' them. It has become dangerous in Russia to conduct investigations into economic, political and media power networks and leaders' private fortunes.

All financial experts are confronted with the same opacity of the system. Who are the shareholders of Gazprom, the industrial giant and natural gas company that also owns banks, large media concerns and a considerable amount of real estate? Who controls Rosneft, the state oil company? How is one to go about deciphering the empire that is the city of Moscow, built under the reign of its mayor Yuri Luzhkov and his wife Yelena Baturina, a wealthy businesswoman who figured in the *Forbes* magazine list of billionaires, when most large companies are headquartered in the Russian capital, causing real estate prices in the 2000s to skyrocket? Luzhkov's forced resignation in September 2010 shook the edifice but did not bring it down.

This book does not claim to analyze this world that is at once closed, clientelistic, wealthy and violent. The tycoons of the 1990s have been featured in a number of good works already mentioned. Those of the 2000s have also aroused the curiosity of journalists and experts.[13] The big difference is that today the latter are discouraged from investigating behind the screens set up by the authorities. Threats are explicit and certain examples have sufficed to dry up the source of any information on the major groups and their managers and owners.

The 2003–2004 period marks a turning point towards more systematic use of repression and arbitrary measures to the detriment of the law in the strategy of acquiring the most lucrative sectors of the economy. *Novaya Gazeta* journalist Yuri Shchekochikhin was poisoned on 17 June 2003 and died on 3 July. He was reporting on Chechnya and arms sales, in particular illegal sales of weapons to Syria. Mikhail Khodorkovsky was arrested on 25 October 2003.[14] Paul Khlebnikov, Editor of *Forbes Russia* magazine, was murdered in 2004. He was investigating corruption and personal enrichment among Russian oligarchs. Andrey Kozlov, Deputy Chairman of the Central Bank, who was fighting cases of corruption at a very high level, was killed in September 2006. Anna Politkovskaya, gunned down on 7 October 2006, wrote extensively on the Northern Caucasus but was also investigating power networks and criminality within them.

Politics and business are so tightly enmeshed that it is difficult to distinguish, for example, Igor Sechin's role as the most powerful man in Putin's government from his role as Chairman of the Board of Directors of Rosneft. The oligarchic phenomenon embraces political circles, administrations and the business world, all tightly interlocked. It makes no sense to separate an oligarchic class from the political world.

Contesting the leadership is nearly impossible for a politician, a regional administrator businessman in today's Russia. The Yukos affair is emblematic. It marks a pivotal moment in bringing the Russian judiciary to heel, which took place in a context of increasing pressure on the media. Even Mikhail Khodorkovsky, in the early years of his imprisonment before his appeal was rejected, tried to 'negotiate' with Putin, saying he agreed with certain facets of his strategy to modernize Russia. How can this be explained? He was probably led to believe that an arrangement with the Kremlin was possible. This reveals another contradiction of the intellectual and economic elites towards those who govern them. They are convinced, rightly, that the 'tsar' decides and has the power to settle matters. At the same time, they want to believe that the Russian courts can defend their rights and recognize that the accusations are groundless. Khodorkovsky's parents were hoping for a fair trial.[15]

Mikhail Khodorkovsky spoke fairly reassuring words with regard to Russian justice in the months preceding his arrest. To friends advising him not to return from Europe, where he sojourned in the summer of 2003, he replied that if the political authorities attacked him, he could defend himself. In the weeks following his arrest, his lawyers, both Russian and foreign, said they were confident that he would be released on bail and an arrangement would be worked out. Robert Amsterdam, one of Khodorkovsky's international lawyers, believed that the case would be settled quickly. 'He'll be home for Christmas!'[16] Yet it seemed perfectly clear to seasoned Moscow-watchers at the time that if such means had been deployed to arrest the powerful businessman *manu militari* on the tarmac of an airport in Siberia, the intention was to lock him away for a long time, to erase him from the Russian political and economic landscape for good.

Another member of his defence team, the famous Russian lawyer Yuri Schmidt, admitted that his client at first was far too optimistic about the probability of receiving a fair trial. In January 2005, over a year after Khodorkovsky was imprisoned, when asked about the line of defence, he explained that they had adopted the wrong strategy. Their client wanted to leave a chance open for an amicable settlement, trusting that coming to an arrangement was in the Kremlin's and Yukos' mutual interest. He did not envisage the case as a life or death battle, a ferocious settling of scores. He decided to take his trial and his defence seriously. Schmidt added, 'We, old hands at Soviet and Russian justice, knew that the judges obeyed orders when the Kremlin took a personal interest in the case. But we were unable to convince our client, or we didn't go about it properly. We probably should have protested against the partiality of the investigation and the trial right from the start, refused to cooperate and accused the government of locking up a political prisoner'.[17] Yuri Schmidt, like his father before him, defended political cases in the Soviet era. He built his reputation on the trial of an officer, Aleksandr Nikitin, who in the 1990s blew the whistle on the environmental disaster of the nuclear armed forces in the Baltic Sea. He won the trial hands down, in public, against the Yeltsin administration, the intelligence services and the military. 'But', he explains, 'in the Yeltsin era, the Kremlin did not control the media, and the courts still operated more or less with integrity. The judges, prosecutors and attorneys still cared about their dignity. I should have realized the full extent of the change that had occurred since Putin's arrival'.[18]

Putin's policy to do away with republican sovereignty and regional autonomy also implied head-on attacks against individuals. But observers at first analyzed it in institutional terms, as dictated by the rationality exhibited by the Kremlin. 'We have to rationalize', Putin said afterwards, 'control, prevent corruption and personalized systems'.[19] As N. Varlamova aptly explains, the Russian President showed his determination to impose a 'vertical of power' which had three objectives: bringing the legislation of the subjects into line with the law of the Russian federation, strengthening responsibility towards federal power, and weakening the influence of leaders of the regions on the activities of federal authorities.[20] In actual fact, the argument of institutional rationality was used to denounce the personal faults of men in positions of power. In 2000, Putin's attack against oligarchs, provincial governors, and republics' presidents had become the main weapon in his battle to deprive both the economic and the political spheres of personalities of any stature. In the mind of the Russian President, there was no reason to distinguish between businessmen and super-administrators. All had to serve the state, in other words they served Putin. The European governments, especially the French, saw it as a strengthening of the state, and considered it a good thing. But they stopped short of admitting that the state *is* the Putin system.

The French philosopher Montesquieu offers a useful key to analyze the corporatist authoritarianism of the Putin regime that the elites support. He notes that a despot is not attended by intermediate powers and figures of authority; in a despotic regime he notes a lack of the tribunes that exist in a monarchy, a regime he defends as being the least undesirable of known forms of government, the republic remaining for him epitomized by small communities, as in the *polis* of classical antiquity.

The prince's immense power passes intact to those to whom he entrusts it. People capable of much self-esteem would be in a position to cause revolutions. Therefore, *fear* must beat down everyone's courage and extinguish even the slightest feeling of ambition.

A moderate government can, as much as it wants and without peril, relax its springs. It maintains itself by its laws and even by its force. But when in despotic government the prince ceases for a moment to raise his arm, when he cannot instantly destroy those in the highest places, all is lost, for when the spring of the government, which is *fear*, no longer exists, the people no longer have a protector'.[21]

'Cicero believes that the establishment of tribunes in Rome saved the republic. [...] One can apply this reflection to a despotic state, where the people have no tribunes, and to a monarchy, where the people do, in a way, have tribunes'.[22]

From 2000 to 2010, Vladimir Putin has managed to marginalize in public life nearly all tribunes—politicians, intellectuals, journalists, businessmen—who openly express disagreement with him and insist that there is an alternative to his rule.

The legitimacy of political power is usually assessed primarily by the population's support for it. In the case of Russia, this correlation is deceptive. The Russians may offer the president their support, but display great wariness towards all institutions. They therefore do not fully back the political system. And yet, they do not find it lacking legitimacy either. During his last major press conference at the Kremlin as President, Putin was asked the following question by a German journalist: 'Why has the candidate Medvedev refused to participate in any televized debate before the 2 March 2008 election?' After claiming at length that the campaign was fair and discounting debates as 'disruptive', Vladimir Putin ended by tellingly sidestepping the issue: 'Wages rose by over 16 per cent this year. There's the answer to your question'.[23]

The Loyalty Paradigm

In the face of such complexity, the attitude of the elites warrants particular attention, because it offers a yardstick by which to judge the degree of consensus that reigns among the leading classes, whether they empathize or not with society regarding major issues and their way of envisioning the future. A system is sustainable if it is designed to last. If the elites see it as temporary and unstable, the regime is unlikely to be consolidated. All the more so if society remains cut off from the ruling classes.[24] After analyzing the institutional drift since 1993, my aim here is to study the behaviour of both intellectual and professional elites as well as the political establishment. Some fine studies on the Russian elites have been published in recent years and contribute to the analysis presented here.[25]

My argument hinges on an observation: Russians in the upper social strata who have positions of responsibility in their fields of competence, who have an above-average standard of living, demonstrate a growing reluctance to criticize, oppose, build solid alternative structures or become involved in existing structures such as unions, voluntary associations, universities, foundations and so on. Why has the establishment tended to withdraw in this fashion, abandoning the political sphere and submitting to the central authorities? Why such a fear of free competition and an open society?

My answer is built on three propositions. First of all, in the current Russian system, 'the people that count', i.e. the establishment, have allowed themselves to become entangled in a relationship of subordination to the political authorities. They could have acted with more independence and determination.

Second, deep down, their attitude towards Putin's regime is far more critical than is suggested by their public behaviour, the obligation of loyalty concealing clear-sightedness with respect to the system and the means of reconciling themselves to it. They do not feel bound to the power system by a strong sense of shared values or a common ideology, but by some degree of *shared interests*.

Third, society is not out of step with the establishment as regards the nature of the regime and its inherent defects, of which most Russians are fully aware. There is no significant gap between the *mentalities* of the citizens and those who govern them. The same wariness towards norms and responsibility to one another, as well as to institutions, induces citizens and the government to exploit the system's fluidity and to work around it. On the other hand, the gap is widening between the *interests* of citizens and the perceived vested interests of the ruling elites, which are seen as predatory and devoid of any sense of public service.

For all powerful and ambitious people in Russia, success requires 'loyal' behaviour to the commanding authorities and dominating networks. The reason for this is the desire and need for recognition. Success cannot be achieved discreetly, outside the channels of power, unless one is to remain a bit player in the big economic game. In a country where the power of money and of political administration matters most, access to the ruling classes goes through the circles that wield both financial and political power. A man as powerful as Mikhail Khodorkovsky thought himself entitled to believe that the Putin leadership would prefer a 'reasonable' agreement and would order the courts to seek one. He believed that he had already crossed the threshold and that his economic clout made him untouchable. But the Kremlin gave the general instruction to go ahead, suggesting that the man has stepped outside the system and is a traitor, hence the rules of cohabitation with business no longer apply to him.

Ambitious individuals have to work with the people in power. Since there are no actors independent of the ruling circles, nor any alternative society, the economic, intellectual, scientific and political elites cannot operate effectively outside the system and what is 'in line'. Once someone becomes a pariah, access is difficult—all doors close.

Consequently, the mere desire to survive economically is a good incentive to play by the rules of the game. In a system where the powers-that-be can socially make or break an individual as they see fit, keeping one's job and income can require compromising with the powerful.

Another factor that encourages loyalty is the general wariness of everyone towards everyone else, which the government turns to its advantage because it ends up being the only one to arbitrate in disputes, as seen with the battle of interests between oligarchs and the conflicts pitting corporations against the administration. This power of arbitration is an essential element of the Putin system and the administrations in its service. To consolidate it, the government needs obedient judges when it comes to cases deemed to be strategic, such as the Yukos case, or complaints of electoral fraud, or the murder of an outstanding journalist.

Lastly, the willing servility can be explained by Russia's long isolation from the rest of the world. It is difficult for a businessman or a public figure to ensure him- or herself a comfortable future elsewhere than in Russia. If one plans to continue to live in Russia, one cannot disregard the rules of the game laid down by the Russian government. And no one has total confidence in international law, the protection of foreigners' rights or free trade. If an entrepreneur wishes to carry on his activities successfully in his country, he must comply with the tacit rules of behaviour.

There is no firmly settled Russian diaspora in the West that supports the new economy from abroad, unlike in the case of the Ukrainians, the Armenians, and the Estonians in North America. Russian émigrés in the West arrived well before Gorbachev's reforms and the exit from Communism. But they have not formed a 'second Russia' taking over the official culture and contributing to financing some of the reforms. As for the 'new Russians' established at great expense in London, Berlin, Paris or Nice, they distinguish between their activities in Europe and those they conduct in Russia under the watchful eye of the government and networks involved.

No Russian businessman or figure will take the risk of directly criticizing the government about specific issues if he or she hopes to continue to lead a prosperous life in Russia as well as abroad. And they will ardently defend the political regime to foreign rulers, which will induce the latter to advocate entente with the regime despite its authoritarian and xenophobic tendencies.

In 2006, some French officials expressed surprise that one of the rare independent members of Parliament, Vladimir Ryzhkov, who was critical of the regime, was invited to the Sciences Po University in Paris, on the grounds that he carried no weight and was not a figure of much importance. 'Wouldn't it be better to invest in those who matter?' a senior French official asked. We are thus caught in the trap of authoritarian regimes that marginalize their adversaries and induce their foreign partners to do the same on the pretence that they are too weak to overturn the system. Often, in Europe, discussions about Russia end up becoming falsely nostalgic of a great history, that of 'eternal Russia', the 'Slavic soul', Pushkin and Dostoyevsky, thus circumventing the fundamental issue: should Russians be treated as a separate civilization, or as a society that is destined to get along with Europeans?

Lastly, another reason for submission to the authorities, which flows from those that precede, is fear, be it diffuse or direct. The incarceration of Mikhail Khodorkovsky and his partners, the murder of Anna Politkovskaya and other journalists, the murder of Alexander Litvinenko by polonium poisoning, the open threats against remaining opponents are intended to maintain this fear and the self-censorship it produces.

Clientelism and Corruption

The corporatism of the Russian state has very negative effects on the behaviour of individuals at the head of institutions and large companies. The exercise of power is becoming increasingly personalized and clientelist. Patronage is a product of clan relations around a chief who can escape from the obligations supposedly attendant to his position. The boss of a federal or regional administration, like the boss of a state company, has immense power. The weakening of institutions releases him from the application of the law as well as any legal, financial and political responsibility before the citizens under his jurisdiction or towards his employees. The only rule imposed on him is total loyalty to the Putin system at the top of the ladder and in its provincial representations.

Corruption has reached astonishing proportions, because money flows freely and it is difficult for a person who works in the administrative machinery or in a large company not to get sucked into this system of bribery. Studies by the INDEM Institute in Moscow show that the strengthening of Putin's networks, which belong as much to the public as the private sphere, is the framework for a system of authoritarian patronage in which money and gift-exchange are the currency of business and power.[26] In Russia, the considerable increase in the amount of money in circulation occurred in a society in which *blat* long reigned. This word refers to a mode of relations based on arrangements and gifts in kind and in services that bind individuals together. *Blat* is the 'economy of favours' so aptly described by Alena Ledeneva,[27] involving the combination of Soviet customs of bribes and privileges, and the weaknesses of the new capitalist and corporatist system.

The Russian leadership fuels corruption and criminality through its policy of concentrating wealth, the retreat of free competition and its control over society. Institutional rules no longer apply, safeguards do not exist and clientelism prevails in power struggles. This is why action against corruption, the eternal promise made by successive presidents, from Yeltsin to Medvedev, is so devoid of meaning. Bureaucrats and entrepreneurs are in the line of fire, whereas the problem is mainly one of a lack of political will at the top to change behaviours by imposing legal sanctions that apply to all, big or small, and would hold in check and rein in the Putin oligarchy.

In their seminal study,[28] three great Russian sociologists, Levada, Gudkov and Dubin, attempted to define the mentality and behaviour of the elites under Putin, whether they are political, administrative, economic or 'security-related'. Their observations are particularly enlightening.

The aim of the Putin government is to reduce the elite to only the 'faithful' *nomenklatura* and the circles close to the Kremlin. All the others—intellectuals, journalists, businessmen eager to maintain their independence and freedom of thought—are cast out of the public sphere, which is more and more controlled. They have become 'strangers', *chuzhie*, and the most vocal among them are stigmatized as being Russia's 'enemies', the fifth column. The book published by Kremlin propaganda adviser Gleb Pavlovsky, *Putin's Enemies*,[29] provides a stark illustration of how a few major figures have been victims of Putin's purification. The strategy of exclusion involves exaggerating the image of an external enemy.

The elite must no longer exist from a functional standpoint, that is, it must not justify its power and privileges by its effectiveness, its merit or its political impartiality, but on the contrary solely by its proximity to the political authorities. 'The Russian elite is not a meritocracy', points out Lev Gudkov, who stresses the mediocrity of political officials.[30] Proximity is crucial for the senior officials in the capital or the provinces: nothing is accomplished without direct access to the chiefs or one of their close associates. For lower-level provincial officials, they are connected to the powers on high through a 'vertical' tie of loyalty and often corruption that rises towards Moscow. Loyalty is expressed in various ways depending on the area of activity in which the civil servant, member of a regional assembly or company head is involved. Politically speaking, the first obligation is to 'serve up a good result' in the elections and to control channels of information and the media.

In the economic sphere, the task is to strengthen the monopoly over resources in the hands of big bosses within 'public' groups such as the natural gas, oil and industrial conglomerates. From a financial standpoint, the objectives set are intended to enrich both individuals and corporations approved by the government, and to channel tax revenues and corporate profits into projects decided by the President's office and the government. As regards social policy, it is mandatory to obey instructions, for instance wage increases for *byudzhetniki* (health, education and community services staff), but there remains more or less room to manoeuvre depending on the resources of the city, province, administrative office or company, to implement specific projects.

The exercise of power is archaic, in the sense that it is not fettered by the rule of law or administrative directives. As discussed when analyzing the 'preference for fluidity', Russian tradition is hyper-legalistic, as authoritarian regimes often are, especially communist regimes. Official texts overrun the public sphere as well as the economic sphere, but application of them is often arbitrary. Some Anglo-Saxon analysts use the concept of a dual state, one that is both legalistic and 'illiberal'. I prefer the simple notion of circumventing the rules, the ultimate arbitrator being the supreme office. As long as leaders use decrees and regulations as they please, and interpret the law according to their immediate needs, the famous 'dictatorship of the law' announced by Vladimir Putin in 2000 will continue to protect networks of corruption and organized crime that go all the way up to the highest circles of the oligarchic galaxy.

The ruling elite is no longer an efficient player in state modernization. The change is clear with respect to the 1980s and the early 1990s, when the reformers exercised great influence through the dissemination of their ideas and their ability to project themselves into the future and propose new forms of economic, social and political government.

Which 'Elites'?

Officials in government structures are increasingly cut off from other elites, those who strive to keep their independence from the political authorities. The latter have been steadily weakening since 2000. The groups in power have moved closer to the Soviet-era definition of *nomenklatura*, where an individual derives his authority, and his income, from his relationship to the hierarchy and the 'dominant party'. They are thus moving away from the Western conception and practice of accountability, which is based on political competition and effectiveness sanctioned by the electorate and its representatives in elected office. Nor do they embody values or symbols, because they are 'bureaucratized' in a hierarchy cut off from society.

Lev Gudkov has coined a very eloquent term in Russian: *okolopoliticheskaya elita*, the elite 'surrounding politics', which lives clinging to the circles of leadership and does not feel responsible for the proper government of the country. 'The post-Soviet Russian state is thus fundamentally ineffective and the elite "surrounding politics" is corrupt and amoral'.[31] The new administrative elites are not required to earn their positions by demonstrating management skills; they must consolidate structures, and impose the political authority's priorities without worrying about being accountable to or meeting the needs of those they govern. One example is the behaviour of election commission presidents at both the local and national level who are mainly concerned with producing results that conform to wishes from on high.[32]

The meaning of the term 'elite' or 'elites' is highly specific in Putin's Russia. It has to do at once with the neo-Soviet *nomenklatura* and the new classes created by state capitalism, enrichment and 'recovered power' thanks to the extraordinary raw material windfall. It is clearly different from the more varied and freer elite that began to emerge in the early 1990s in the liberal context of the early post-Communist reforms. The turning point took place in the years 1994–1999, when the Yeltsin regime entered into turmoil and the 'former' elites—people in the intelligence services and civil servants held at a distance from politics and enrichment stemming from privatization—began to hold their heads up high once more and gradually take on strategic positions in the heart of the administrative and economic power structures.

It is not by chance or mistake that in Russia the 'elites' are perceived only as circles of power or close to power. It therefore only makes sense to speak of an 'elite by position', i.e. the *nomenklatura*. In all events, they are people appointed to influential positions by superiors, and thus people who are dependent on the government and indulgent towards it.

'Belonging to the post-Soviet 'elite' has nothing to do with *the productivity, originality or exemplarity* of the achievements made by any individual or social class whatsoever. [...] The Russian 'elites' have nothing to do with the objective of *symbolically representing the values* of society as a whole. They are neither tribunes nor demagogues adored by the masses'.[33] The study conducted by the Levada Centre shows that the members of these 'elites' do not believe in the modernization of Russia. In their answers to the investigators' questions, they express a negative opinion of those who hold power, finding them both incompetent and 'reactionary', because their aim is to 'ensure the preservation of the political system as it stands and specific government interests'.[34] They believe modernization is necessary, but unlikely in the near future.

A major innovation in recent sociological studies conducted in Russia is to suggest that the game played between the government and society does not involve two players but rather three: the leaders, the 'elites' and the people. The elites are 'loyal' by obligation but often critical deep down, because they are sceptical about their country's economic and social future. They nevertheless do not have the ability, or perhaps the desire, to move closer to ordinary Russians. For Russians, the term that speaks to them is *vlast*, power, i.e. those who dominate, those who are in possession of the instruments of power and can therefore bring others into subjection. To the vast majority of people interviewed, the word *vlast* calls to mind the leader. And in 2008–11 the real leader remains Vladimir Putin, not Dmitry Medvedev.

The sociologists who authored the study emphasize civil servant mediocrity. 'Advancement and personal success in such a system of an 'ersatz elite' depend less on individual qualities and achievements than on the opinion of one's superiors. [...] They are oblique forms of nomenklatura, a group of people the government has placed in influential positions, [...] and who are thus dependent on the government and obey it'.[35]

The understanding of the new, post-communist notion of public affairs, *res publica*, remains primitive, as was argued in earlier chapters. The 'elites' are partly responsible for the archaism of Russian society, for they prefer connivance with the government and do not fulfil their role of intermediary between the rulers and the ruled. This power-elite-society triangle is not dynamic in the present situation, but it could begin to function differently in the future and then pose a challenge to the government's authoritarianism. Elite 'loyalty' is not in fact monolithic. Conflicts of interest and contradictory aspirations can rise to the surface in the event of an economic crisis or political upheaval. We shall see the extent to which the new anti-Georgian and anti-Western nationalism is orchestrated by the Kremlin to cement a national consensus that is probably more fragile than it seems.

The elites have various attitudes towards the conception and implementation of modernization. For 35 per cent of respondents, the European model of modernization would be preferable: rapid progress towards a market economy and democracy as well as the rule of law. Nearly as many (31 per cent) are more in favour of a slow evolution towards a market economy framed by a centralized state drawing on national values. Only 18 per cent believe it is better not to emulate foreign experiences, but to follow Russia's own 'unique path' (*osobyi put*). In other words, 'ideas about the country's future development are imprecise and not very well thought out. Despite the strengthening of elites around Putin, there is no consensus about the country's future, nor a preference for well-defined political objectives'. The idea of modernization is 'a factor in legitimizing beliefs about Russian (and even Soviet) power, part of its legend'.[36]

A majority of the elites who have been sidelined from Russian politics in recent years express interest in modernizing their country along Western lines, i.e. the development of democratic institutions and a market economy. They are mainly company executives, journalists and some members of regional political elites (particularly representatives in provincial assemblies). According to the survey, a more sceptical line is endorsed by the *siloviki* (those who work in 'power ministries': the army, the Interior, the FSB and other bodies) who are wary of a pro-Western alignment which inevitably would impose more transparency, accountability, and respect for the rule of law.

In April-May 2008, another survey demonstrated the ambivalence and anxiety among rich young elites. About 1,000 representatives of the upper middle class between the ages of 24 and 39, having well above average incomes,[37] were interviewed by Levada Centre sociologists. The findings are striking. Half of the respondents believe there is no real stability in Russia, and 60 per cent do not foresee it in the near future. A majority is convinced that Russia would modernize faster if the rule of law were respected; 50 per cent admit that if their rights were violated, they would be unable to defend themselves; 74 per cent add that they do not feel protected by the authorities and police forces. Approximately two-thirds would like their children to study and work in Europe. Lastly, the majority of respondents are pleased that Russia has regained its strength, but see in this renewal of strength an impediment to the establishment of good relations with Europe. Russia is feared, but not trusted.

Russian society is fraught with anxiety about the future and prefers to display its loyalty to its leaders, but that does not mean it is firmly controlled. It remains wary and unenterprising in a state of uncertainty. The horizon is short-term, pushing forecasts way into the future. The vast majority of Russians are proud to live in Russia, but are more reserved when it comes to the future. They are pleased that Russia has become stronger and respected, but doubt that this achievement will be consolidated. Over half the upper young elites would prefer their children to live and work both in Russia and in the West; they do not wish a life for them only in Russia. The economic crisis of 2008–2009 has confirmed this attitude.

This feeling of being hemmed in, rooted in the limitations of a personal trajectory in Russia, puts the upper middle classes in an uncomfortable position with regard to their previous geographical space and the new space open to them, in Europe. Russia and the ex-Soviet countries belong to the near and familiar domain that is well-charted and naturally offers opportunities, but they are limited. The Western and Asian universes are perceived as distant, more competitive, but also more promising in the long run.[38] And yet, these upper strata of Russian society are incapable of reacting to the increasingly intrusive policies that their leaders are conducting in neighbouring countries, in particular the lightning war against Georgia in August 2008. They have the means to obtain information freely, thanks to the Internet and satellites, but they remain prisoners of the official version: the Georgians were at fault, not the Russians, and military action was necessary.[39]

More generally speaking, regardless of income level, the attitude of young Russians does not reflect a greater inclination towards the rule of law, but they find being locked into a compartmentalized system burdensome.

Despite the weight of a legacy of obedience handed down from the former Tsarist and Soviet regimes, attitudes have changed. Russian political culture is evolving, but in a private, hidden manner, because Russians know the virtues of caution. Loyalty without trust is a more appropriate notion today than that of obedience or servility. But fear remains one of the indispensable instruments used by leaders. It is a more diffuse fear and one that does not affect an individual's private sphere. It harbours a general wariness: citizens are wary of civil servants and their chiefs, voters are wary of the 'dominant party', employees are wary of supervisors. This distrust among individuals, and between institutions and individuals, serves the current system. Russia's leaders shrewdly cultivate this state of mind and the behaviour it engenders. They do not want a confident and optimistic society, because it would be strong and dynamic and would necessarily have a critical and independent attitude towards the political authorities.

Despite his early speeches on justice and the law, President Medvedev did not gain the trust of ordinary citizens. He implicitly acknowledged that the rules dictated by him and his peers must be imposed firmly from on high. Only strength imposed by the will of the rulers, often on the basis of misleading information, can ensure economic and social order as it is envisaged at the top. In Russia, the law has always been dictated from the top down. It is virtually synonymous with force and absolutist power. In Europe we are often mistaken about the uses of the words 'rights' or 'law' or 'rule' by the Russians. Asked in the late summer of 2008 about the fate of Mikhail Khodorkovsky, who was to be brought to trial again a few months later, Medvedev answered, 'Let's trust in the courts; politicians should not be involved'. The cynicism of the reply was not lost on the defence team, which had largely proved the unfairness of the first trial.[40] Medvedev's powerlessness in the Khodorkovsy case was starkly demonstrated in 2010 when Putin hinted on 16 December, days before Judge Danilkin's guilty verdict, that the defendant's place was in prison.[41] In the current context, the debate on judicial reform and respect for law will not go far because the leaders find it too comfortable to be able to blame things on the judges.

Opinion polls indicate the clear-sightedness of ordinary Russians. They know that the leaders curb freedoms and civil rights out of convenience. Regarding the nature of government in their country, 83 per cent of respondents answer that the country is governed by a small circle of people, compared with only 6 per cent who believe that the people control the government.[42]

Unstable Equilibrium

Analyses made by Russian experts are instructive as to the terms in which these essential problems of government are debated. Political scientists and *polittekhnologi* each have their own interpretation of the Putin phenomenon. Although they vary considerably, nearly all agree on one observation: Vladimir Putin, together with Dmitry Medvedev at his side, is fairly suited to Russia today. Some deplore this statement of fact, others are pleased with it and see in it the strength of the 'sovereign democracy' ideology, i.e. the specificity of Russia and hence of the type of governance that suits it, with its own values that differ from those of the West.

For Stanislav Belkovsky, a provocative figure at odds with the Kremlin after having once served it, Putin's *modus operandi* is primarily oriented towards the ruling elite. He made a pact with these political and financial groups, a 'corrupt' pact, by which the financial interests of people loyal to the Kremlin are taken care of. After having eliminated those who were not quick to adhere to this pact, he consolidated his authority around the more powerful networks. Putin's accomplishment may thus have given these elites stability, but certainly not the country.[43]

According to Dmitry Oreshkin, Belkovsky's interpretation of a mafia in power is simplistic. Putin is recognized by the population, and thus has a form of 'legitimacy'. If society recognizes itself to a certain extent in its leader, then Putin is not all that different from Russia. More precisely, Putin's media manufacture a virtual reality that ends up infusing public consciousness, or at least what Russians believe to be true. The leader and society are thus bound up together in a virtual Russia that looks less and less like the reality, but which provides a simple and convenient understanding of the context in which they are immersed.

For the sociologist Olga Kryshtanovskaya, the nature of the Putin regime is mainly conveyed by the considerable scope given to various armed forces, the intelligence services and the Interior Ministry's special corps. Other individuals have gradually been eliminated as Vladimir Putin formed a team made up mainly of *siloviki*, men from the former KGB and other 'power structures'; a number of them worked in Saint Petersburg with Putin in the early 1990s. Halfway through Vladimir Putin's first term in office, a quarter of the leading class came from 'power ministries'. In 2008, Kryshtanovskaya estimated this proportion had reached more than half. She includes in her definition members of government, heads of provincial administrations, governors and speakers of regional parliaments as well as their representatives. The elite thus defined amounts to 1,100 people. She maintains that, politically speaking, membership in structures and networks is a sign of loyalty. The figure below illustrates this obligation; Duma members and governors are obliged to join the party in power, United Russia. On the other hand, an employee of the Presidential Administration does not feel obliged to take out a party card. The Soviet system therefore cannot be said to have returned, because in the USSR it was virtually impossible to pursue a career in the administration without being a member of the Communist Party. Kryshtanovskaya made the following assessment in early 2008:

Position held	Percentage of United Russia party members
Kremlin civil servants	2.5%
Members of the government	7%
Members of the lower house (State Duma)	70%
Governors	85%

In 2011, almost all regional heads of administration, in regions and republics, are members of United Russia.[44]

Business people must be careful not to back social projects independently unless they want to be perceived as potential political rivals seeking to improve their image. They are, moreover, subjected to 'government racketeering', the proceeds of which go mainly to fill civil servant 'envelopes' (cash payments).

These 'envelopes' constitute the better part of a civil servant's pay. Business people in Russia are obliged to pay this unofficial business tax. For the most powerful, the alternative is to move to London. For small businesses, these illegal levies can compromise their future. In such a system, there is no truly private company, because ownership requires real guarantees without the interference of political considerations. The various interest groups in the business world are more akin to an upper layer of the *nomenklatura* where no one can be richer than Vladimir Putin's followers. The top leadership is the ultimate arbitration force when groups fight one another. There is an attraction to the Chinese model, which makes a clear distinction between economic and political liberalization and only liberalizes the economy.[45]

Most analysts emphasize the inherent risk of this type of clientelist and opaque system in which colossal sums are involved, given that each protagonist controls a segment of the national economy. Internecine battles take place in the wings. Sometimes they are revealed by one of the protagonists, such as the one that pitted former FSB chief Nikolai Patrushev against the Head of the State Anti Money-Laundering Committee, General Viktor Cherkessov, in September 2007. Since institutional arbitrage does not function and Putin probably did not want to settle the issue, a scandal broke out. Purely formal subordination of the *siloviki* to President Dmitry Medvedev could carry risks for the continuity of the regime.[46] This is one of the reasons why Medvedev could not hope for re-election in 2012.

Another contradiction that experts point out lies in the relationship to the central authorities. The Kremlin and the Moscow elite remain contemptuous of the provinces and local elites. Outside the Kremlin, authority is never entirely assured. Yet despite this ideology being focused on Moscow, provincial Russia lives more and more detached from the capital. And Moscow remains more ignorant than ever of the provinces. Putin's policy of control and recentralization has failed to unify the political, economic, social and cultural space of the Federation.

When a government is at once too administrative and clientelist, it can no longer operate effectively along a well-oiled vertical. Each segment of this hierarchy is defective because there is no trust to guide relations from the top down and from the bottom up to the top of the territorial pyramid. And impunity is even greater than it was under Brezhnev. Only major political and financial scandals lead to sanctioning of a powerful figure. At the level immediately below, which no longer interests the bigwigs in Moscow, settling conflicts of competence or interest necessitates the use of other channels and depends on other criteria that are incomprehensible for anyone who does not live in the city involved. For Dmitry Oreshkin, Putin's government is taking a 'Yugoslavia-style' risk. He is inflating a centre that is unable and unwilling to manage day-to-day business and which no one at the local level really needs.[47] But the central government has weakened the regional administrations and local societies, thereby weakening provincial Russia on the whole.

According to Lilia Shevtsova, society at large and the elite want to maintain the status quo because all are afraid of change. This attitude is dangerous because it lulls the leaders with the assurance that whatever they do, they will go unpunished, either by the population or their peers. And this lack of responsibility and accountability creates an illusion of stability. Conflicts naturally exist, and are heightened, all the more so in the context of 'predatory state capitalism' that has reigned since the early 2000s.

Analysts close to the Kremlin, or anxious not to rankle Putin, have taken ambiguous stands since the legislative elections of December 2007. For instance, Igor Bunin, Director of the Centre of Political Technologies, expressed concern at the fragility of a system that no longer has 'any political, legal or social institution that can ensure stability and prosperity'. Even the Kremlin's Communication Adviser, Gleb Pavlovsky, made jokes and talked on the radio and television about the Russian 'political theatre' and the danger of a '*coup de théâtre*'.[48] Do the people responsible for the official agit-prop perchance have instructions to maintain the uncertainty and fear of change? How should the game be interpreted? The goal may simply be not to let society be reassured by a well-organized and predictable scenario, because it might become demanding and not accept measures of economic recession if inflation or the drop in hydrocarbon prices required them. It might also challenge the grounds for repressive measures against independent media and the Internet, the harassment of the dissenters and dissidents who still attempt to make their voices heard, and be concerned about the deterioration of relations with neighbouring countries.

In actual fact, society and elites alike worry about 'stability' becoming 'stagnation' (*zastoi*) as in the 1970s. They understand that Putin's prolonged reign will not bring positive change. Experts and journalists, spin doctors and Kremlin advisers have devoted much energy, in 2010–2011, to the inside story of the 'tandem', the alleged ups and downs or the relationship between Putin and Medvedev. Some of them have built romantic narratives about the 'Medvedev alternative', the young President winning over his mentor and opening a new era. They have rekindled a stifled public debate, stirring up expectations of unpredictable developments. When Putin declared on 24 September 2011 that he would run for the presidency, the game was over. Many felt betrayed and discouraged. The lack of political prospects was a disappointment to those who had hoped for some changes in the Putin system.

Population decline is another cause for pessimism. Mortality remains too high and the birth rate hovers at the threshold of industrialized societies. Infant mortality is double that of Europe (10 per cent). Life expectancy is age 60 for men and 73 for women. Institutional responses are inappropriate, as demographers have explained for years. The Russian anomaly is the high rate of mortality among men between ages 40 and 55, unknown in developed countries. But the authorities target their measures on increasing the birth rate with financial incentives for young mothers.[49]

Only an active immigration policy could curb the decline (a fall of half a million people every year) in the population, which in 2007 reached about 142 million inhabitants. But Putin's regime did not want to legalize the millions of clandestine foreigners. Many Azeris, Georgians, Moldavians and other former Soviet citizens work in Russia without a residence permit. This situation is reinforced by a protectionist and xenophobic attitude fuelled by the official media and the Orthodox Church, a faithful Putin supporter. Fearful and anxious about the future, Russians are intolerant towards the presence of non-Russians, who are often more mobile and more flexible on the job market. They are also afraid of an even more serious housing shortage, an endemic problem since the Soviet era.[50]

Moreover, as a consequence of the conflicts of 1991–1993 in the Caucasus and Moldova, millions of people have been displaced and have not been able to return home. The two wars in Chechnya caused massive population displacement, with refugees in neighbouring republics in the north Caucasus, such as Ingushetia. Clashes in Georgia have caused new forced evacuation of villages. Human realities are darker than the smooth chart of macroeconomic achievements.

The government has not shown any determination to meet these considerable challenges, which supports the theory that the leadership is concerned most of all with the upper social strata. The gap is growing between the very wealthy top of the pyramid and the middle part that is trying to consolidate its standard of living and 'middle-class' status. This mid-level Russia is, in turn, cut off from poor Russia, which sees no means of gaining access to the middle classes. Depending on how calculations are made, an estimated 15 to 20 per cent of the population sits at the top of the pyramid (a minute fraction of which is made up of billionaires and millionaires); the middle classes make up about 50 per cent (which are subdivided by income level); and 30 per cent are underprivileged Russians who are treated as a burden by the government and the elites and do not take part in the economic dynamics.

Society is socially, geographically and culturally fragmented. The leaders thus look for rallying themes to forge 'common values' and strengthen adhesion to the regime. The image of the enemy and the vision of a threatening outside world, as well as Russian specificity and recovered power, are the pillars of a new ideology that must distinguish itself from the West and even oppose it. The confrontation between Them and Us once again occupies a strategic place in the Russian system. The countries in between, especially Ukraine and Georgia which have broken away from the autocratic model, are caught up in a dangerous facedown between the Russian and the Western worlds.

9

NATIONAL EXCEPTIONALISM

The year 2008 marked a turn in Russia's domestic politics and external policies. In May, Dmitry Medvedev was elected President of Russia and appointed his mentor, Vladimir Putin, head of government, in a phoney succession scenario. The executive 'tandem' was set up for a period of four years. A second trial of Mikhail Khodorkovsky and Platon Lebedev was being actively prepared. In August 2008, Russia and Georgia waged a short war with far-reaching consequences. In September-October, the Russian economy was hit by the international financial crisis and abrupt fall in the prices of commodities. At the end of December, Russia once more cut off natural gas deliveries to Europe via Ukraine.

The military conflict of August 2008 is a milestone. It took place in a country which, in the eyes of Russian rulers, is neither inside nor outside Russia. Georgia belongs to the 'near abroad' (*blizhnee zarubezhe*) and is not treated as a fully sovereign country. A first consequence of the war in Georgia and subsequent occupation of significant parts of the territory was to question the legality of interstate borders and claim Moscow's right to secure a sphere of influence in former Soviet republics. A second major effect of the dismantling of the Georgian state was to discredit the Saakashvili government and freeze the prospect of NATO and European Union membership. A third pernicious consequence was to shed doubt on the capacity of Russia's neighbours to become democratic countries.

The Putin-Medvedev 'tandem' is another key development in 2008. It was presented and promoted as a benign adjustment of the inner workings of the Putin system, a clever invention to circumvent the Constitution and leave the regime unchanged. Russian society wished for Putin to stay on as leader, and would not object to a convenient and apparently 'legal' solution. But the coexistence of two heads for one political body, one single power, could not be of no consequence. To be more than a stand-in, the new elected President had to exist. His works and deeds could not be mere acting. And the real boss, Prime Minister and former President, also had to find his own role in the new formal organization. Towards the end of the tandem's four-year term, it looks clear that the main objective was to consolidate Putin's power system and ensure his re-election in 2012, but at a political cost that will be underlined below.

This final chapter aims at analyzing the 2008–2011 period in the light of the key thesis of this book: the hollowing out of public institutions, the Russian power-wielders' claim to a specific mode of rule, and the propensity to protect the regime from outside influence.[1] National exceptionalism is becoming the new doctrine and pattern of conduct, in a fragile combination of political protectionism and necessary adjustment to economic globalization and the Internet.

The War in Georgia: A Turning Point

The armed conflict between Russia and Georgia in August 2008 did not break out by chance. The powder keg was full; all that was needed was the spark. The most important thing to explore is not the spark but the powder keg, carefully tended over the years. And the rise in tension did not concern only the Caucasus, but Ukraine and Moldova as well, and even the Baltic states, although they are members of the European Union and NATO.

One of Russia's goals was for the West to accept that these 'in-between' countries, squeezed between East and West, should stay under some form of Russian control, by the use of military force or the threat to use it, and by economic pressures thanks to the oil and gas resources and the financial capacity of Russian companies to conquer parts of the former republics' economies.

History accelerated in 2004. On 3 September, the hostage taking at the Beslan school ended in bloodshed: over 330 inhabitants of North Ossetia were killed, mostly children. South Ossetians in Georgia showed solidarity. Against a backdrop of Russian military occupation in Chechnya, all the small nations in the Caucasus felt threatened. Every man owned at least one weapon, and Russian soldiers and policemen carrying sub-machine guns were trigger-happy. Putin took advantage of the tragedy to declare that such disasters did not occur in the Soviet era and that 1991 was the biggest geopolitical catastrophe of the twentieth century.

In November-December 2004, the Orange Revolution triumphed in Ukraine, the citizens managing to bring down a corrupt regime with affinities to the Kremlin. Vladimir Putin experienced this historic moment as a terrible humiliation and was bent on wreaking vengeance at all costs. He thus decided to deploy all possible means to undermine the process of democratization and Westernization of the former Soviet republics adjacent to Russia, especially Ukraine, Georgia and Moldavia.

It should be remembered that the 'Rose Revolution' in Georgia in October 2003 did not provoke such a hostile reaction from the Kremlin. It was Kiev's display of independence a year later, greeted with enthusiasm by the West, that infuriated the Russian leaders. If the younger 'Slavic brother' in Ukraine took flight, how could the Russians be kept locked up in Putin's authoritarian straightjacket? The Kremlin is familiar with the domino theory.

The other neighbours still in the Russian sphere of influence did not pose an immediate danger. Belarus was held by an isolated dictator, Azerbaijan by an authoritarian regime buoyed by oil resources, Armenia had very little room for manoeuvre with respect to Moscow (particularly because of the problem of the Armenian enclave of Upper Karabakh in Azerbaijan) and the Central Asian republics did not put themselves in the position of having to choose between the West and Russia.

Georgian territory fell prey to the fierce battle raging between Russian troops and Chechen separatists during the two Chechnya wars. The rebels organized a rear base in neighbouring Georgia. Moscow's distrust of Tbilissi never abated, from Gamsakhurdia's short and disastrous presidency and throughout Shevardnadze's unstable years. Mikheil Saakashvili hardly benefited from days of grace after he was elected president in January 2004. The fate of Georgia remains closely intertwined with the current tragic history of neighbouring Chechnya, Daghestan, and the entire North Caucasian region. Violence, destitution, unemployment and corruption ravage these small republics which are part of the Russian federation. Terrorism is not receding, as the many blasts and suicide bombings of the years 2007–2011 illustrate.

In Autumn 2006, another escalation occurred. Putin decreed a total embargo on Georgia: Georgian mineral waters and wines were banned, and communications (air, postal, banking) were severed. This was also the time when several adversaries who were very knowledgeable about the situation in the Caucasus were killed. The famous investigative journalist and government opponent Anna Politkovskaya was murdered on 7 October in her apartment building in central Moscow in broad daylight. Alexander Litvinenko was poisoned with polonium on 1 November in a hotel bar in central London. Putin publicly protected Litvinenko's suspected murderers (one of them even landed a seat in the December 2007 legislative elections and now enjoys parliamentary immunity). In the winter of 2006–2007, anti-Western rhetoric reached heights that were unknown since the worst moments of the Cold War. In his infamous 'Munich speech' of February 2007, Vladimir Putin adopted a surprisingly aggressive tone to recite a long list of complaints against the USA, 'the unipolar power' and NATO whose actions were, he said, 'unilateral' and 'illegitimate': 'They bring us to the abyss of one conflict after another'.[2]

In August 2008, for the first time since the invasion of Afghanistan in December 1979, Russia sent its army into foreign territory to interfere with domestic developments. Georgian troops launched an offensive in South Ossetia on the night of 7–8 August, but they had been repeatedly submitted to Russian provocations in preceding weeks and months. What must not be overlooked is the result: the Russian military did not waver in its strategy of invading and bombarding Georgian towns and ports, beyond the two secessionist territories of Abkhazia and Ossetia.

Whatever tragic errors may have been committed on the Georgian side, most seasoned experts who monitored the region in recent years have little doubt about Moscow's intent to draw Georgia into a conflict.[3] Russian propaganda gradually managed to dominate the media space and win the propaganda battle during the first days, to the point of sowing doubt among Western governments and in public opinion in many countries.

However, once again Putin's team was too cocksure. It had hoped that the display of strength and bluff would paralyze Western diplomats who were presumably tired of problematic small countries, impossible enlargement issues (NATO and the EU), and were eager not to annoy the great Russian nuclear and oil power. But the European Union took a united stand. French President Nicolas Sarkozy flew to Moscow and Tbilisi on 12 August and, in the name of the European Union—in which France held the presidency in the second half of 2008—brokered a six-point plan which helped stop the fighting but was never fully implemented. Sarkozy did not hide the difficulty he encountered with Vladimir Putin, very tense and uncompromising, and welcomed the presence of Dmitry Medevev who adopted a less emotional tone and worked on building his presidential image in the heat of his first major international challenge. The French President was well aware that his new Russian counterpart was not the decision-maker, but his presence smoothed up the process of talks.[4]

The following step came as a surprise to most: the Russian state recognized the independence of Abkhazia and South Ossetia only two weeks after the ceasefire. On 25 August, the state Duma unanimously voted in favour of recognition. The next day, President Medvedev signed a decree recognizing the two self-proclaimed republics. Only three other states, Venezuela, Nicaragua and Nauru, followed suit, to Moscow's dismay. Neither Belarus nor any other member state of the CIS gave in to Russia's insistent pressure.

An independent international fact-finding mission on the conflict in Georgia, led by Heidi Tavigliani, was asked to investigate and write a report on the causes and conduct of the conflict. The report was presented to the Council of the European Union, the Organization for Security and Cooperation in Europe (OSCE), the United Nations, and the parties to the conflict on 30 September 2009.[5] The conclusions reveal the ambiguities and lack of transparency on all sides. Georgia's decision to resort to force on the night of 7–8 August is criticized, but Russia's relentless harassment of Georgia is also denounced. Tavigliani emphasizes that all parties bear a heavy responsibility in the souring of relations and failure to seek negotiated settlements to the disputes.

The legitimate question to pose is who gained from the conflict and subsequent separatism of Abkhazia and South Ossetia, with the blessing and full support of the Kremlin. Georgia lost a lot more than Russia did; its state sovereignty and territorial integrity are now shattered so gravely that a reversal of fortune in the near future seems highly unlikely. Unruly South Ossetia and Abkhazia, more dependent on Russian subsidies and security than ever, remain in an unstable situation domestically and illegitimate position internationally. Mikheil Saakashvili still heads his country, despite constant pressure from Moscow and unconcealed attempts to further damage his reputation and force him out of office. Vladimir Putin openly speaks in favour of a change of leadership in Tbilisi, as he did about the Yushchenko regime in Ukraine from 2005. He celebrated Viktor Yanukovich's election in January 2010 as a major victory against the Orange movement and its leading figures, Viktor Yushchenko and Yulia Timoshenko. He probably believes that the two former Soviet republics followed, and will follow, similar patterns: a short period of aborted attempt to 'go West' by toppling neo-Soviet leaderships and seeking to join NATO and the European Union, then a swing of the pendulum and a return to the Russian sphere of interests. The Rose Revolution took place one year before the Orange Revolution in Ukraine; Saakashvili suffered a military defeat two years before Yushchenko suffered a political defeat; in Putin's view, he should share the fate of his Ukrainian counterpart and disappear. By and large, ordinary Russians agree with him.

The Image of the Enemy

Opinion polls in 2008 demonstrated the overwhelming support of Russian people for the armed conflict, perceived as a military and strategic victory. Again, the quasi-monopoly over television and radio news allowed the authorities to give a one-sided explanation of the reasons for the war against the 'Georgian threat' embodied in the villain, harebrained Mikheil Saakashvili. The Russian public nevertheless became increasingly hostile to the Georgians, and not only to their Head of State. In 2009, more than a third (37 per cent) said that they have a bad, or very bad, opinion of Georgians. Their attitude to the Georgian state is overwhelmingly negative: 69 per cent in 2009, doubled from 36 per cent negative opinions in 2004.[6] War provided a means of further rallying loyalty, all the more so in a context of further destabilization of the North Caucasus. The armed operation in Georgia in August 2008 occurred at a time when the regime was looking for a new impetus. Putin's non-succession and Medvedev's installation created a climate of tension and uncertainty in society and among the various ruling groups. The operation was a slick one, but staging it was complicated. Then the time came to return to simple images. Reactivation of the outside enemy and Russia's military and political display of strength were necessary.

The leadership's public stance and the government-controlled media served classic disinformation about Georgia's actions and the relation with Russia. They unscrupulously clung to biased explanations and even unverified facts, and they masked important parts of the story, like the effects of the Russian embargo since 2006 or the role of the highly criminalized Ossetian ruling groups. They dared tell blatant lies, such as the accusation of 'genocide' of Ossetians by Georgians, when the number of Ossetians killed during the five-day conflict was probably about a hundred. Dmitry Medvedev himself claimed that a genocide was planned by Tbilisi. Undoubtedly, Mikhel Saakashvili did not tell the whole truth either, but it was not quite on the same scale, and Georgia clearly lost the 'communication war' in August 2008. The Russian media and public relations establishment showed more dexterity and ruthlessness.

Russians end up relying on Putin, Medvedev, Lavrov and the military command to decide whether they should be friends with Georgia, or crush Georgia. They are relieved to let their leaders decide, thereby escaping responsibility as a national community. Paradoxically, August 2008 disclosed Russia's intrinsic vulnerability as a nation. The xenophobic fervour expressed during these fatal days is worked-up emotion and goes against a true commitment to the construction of a modern state.

The military conflict that broke out in August 2008 was a high point in a long war of attrition between Russia and Georgia, coupled with a steady deterioration of everyday security in the Caucasus. It enabled Putin to make progress along two strategic lines. The first was to turn his neighbours into states with weak sovereignty which thwarted national capacity to devise an independent foreign policy. The second was to curb democratization and Europeanization of the former Soviet republics and strengthen the dominant nationalistic spirit and anti-Western attitude in Russia itself. A significant drawback of Putin's strategy, however, is the drastic increase in military expenditure in almost all these countries. According to the military analyst Vladimir Mukin, in 2010 the 11 member countries of the Commonwealth of Independent States (CIS) plus Georgia 'as a group have increased military spending by almost 25 per cent, a growth six times that of their economies as they have emerged from the recent crisis and one that raises serious questions about stability in many parts of that enormous region'.[7] The Russian military budget is also on the rise.

In the case of both Chechnya and Georgia, the decision to rely on military force to deal with a difficult neighbour, which once upon a time was part of the Soviet motherland, signalled with striking clarity the dismissal of public institutions whose reason to exist is to negotiate and provide peaceful, political solutions to internal disputes as well as external conflicts. Neither the State Duma nor the Federation Council was asked to approve the resorts to military force in 1994, 1999 and 2008.

The years 2005–2009 also witnessed several disturbing gas crises between Russia and Ukraine. The Russian company Gazprom decided to cut off Ukraine's gas supply, and the main importers in Europe were affected by the pipeline shutdown. Putin placed himself at the forefront of the battle and, in a bellicose tone, emphasized Russian domination over the energy supply of neighbours and Europe. For the first time, Western countries realized the bluntness of Russian methods. Another crisis involving Moscow and Minsk over oil in January 2006, led to the interruption of oil deliveries via Belarus.

Putin wants selective globalization, bridled competition and discretionary room to manoeuvre in the former Soviet countries. The supremacy of hydrocarbons has given him the means to develop this ideology of a partial opening-up of the Russian economy to the international market and specific rules of the game in the energy field. But Russia cannot live cut off from Europe for geographical, economic, energy and human reasons. Short of rebuilding unassailable walls around its fortress, which is impossible in a world where instant communication is indispensable to economies, the Russian leaders cannot choose total isolation.

The regime mobilized Russians against the Georgians, then against the Ukrainians and against all former Soviet citizens who try to keep Russia at a distance. But could it mobilize them to cross swords with the Germans or the Chinese? The army is not all that strong, and the national economy has its weak points.

Deep down, Russians know that Russia is less developed and less prosperous than Europe. They are also aware of their leaders' shortcomings and the media's lack of objectivity. They tend to submit to government rituals and subscribe to a facile ideology that offers them a positive vision of Russia as a major power that is feared if not loved. They are anxious to protect their private lives and keep their distance from politics. Their support for a nationalist rhetoric does not subdue their deep-seated distrust of the authorities and the system that governs them.

The Democratic Threat

The Russian Federation is not threatened by Georgian rifles or international terrorists, but by damaged social relations, elites' mismanagement, corruption, and terrorists from Russia's northern Caucasian republics. Insecurity stems from problems at home rather than outside.

Moscow has perceived the democratization of its former vassal states as a real danger; and it undoubtedly is. If Ukraine, Georgia, Moldavia and Belarus simultaneously worked towards the consolidation of constitutional states and were preparing to join Europe—both in their political and economic practices and in the advancement of European Union and NATO accession talks—Putin's regime would find itself besieged, because the considerable gap between political systems would destroy the legitimacy and authority of the Russian regime.[8]

It is therefore in Moscow's interest to make sure societies and political regimes in these countries do not radically change and do not move closer to the West. At the same time, in Russia, people's minds must be mobilized on domestic issues and drawn away from European attraction. They must be prevented from imagining an alternative to the present system.[9]

Starting in 2004, Putin sought to shape this discourse and spread it throughout the population. He probably had no deep convictions or very elaborate concepts, but he pursued a strategy whose success depended on his rhetorical and media performance. The Russians have to be kept on their guard, wary of a looming confrontation with unfriendly foreign actors. They are encouraged into a form of patriotic self-defence, a mentality of national exceptionalism according to which their history, geography and traditions make them different and justify the necessity for a 'specific path' to modernization instead of following in Europeans' footsteps.

Such a strategy is doubly useful. First, any criticism of state policies towards the outside world is labelled 'anti-patriotic' or 'extremist', thereby discrediting political adversaries and independent news reports; second, the Russians easily go along with the Kremlin's historical revisionism which, by presenting the past as dramatic and the present as threatening, puts them in a position of passivity and dependence via-à-vis the regime, and cuts short their expectations for better and more peaceful relations with foreign partners.

The content of the 'new ideology' is fairly meagre and straightforward. The recurrent motifs are 'sovereign democracy', 'Russia's specific path', 'innovation policy', the 'grandeur' of the fatherland in the absolute and the infinite, the victory of 1945 over Nazism and Stalin's historic role, 'enemies' seeking to fragilize Russia, and 'revenge' to be taken for the years of collapse in the 1990s.

In substance, the narrative endlessly repeats the theme of yesterday's humiliation and today's power, with very few big promises for the future. In that respect, the leitmotif of 'modernization', calling for a hightech leap forward and innovative strategies, sounds too general and virtual to form the backbone of a political doctrine. The rhetoric about the past outweighs the promises about the future. From that standpoint, Putin's propaganda has not revived the utopian vision that was one of the foundations for the Bolshevik ideology of the 1920s and 1930s. Nor does it lapse into Mussolini-style voluntarism. Putin has not sponsored any major architectural project or written a landmark doctrinal 'Red Book' to be read by all school pupils. He does not seek to mobilize the masses in gigantic rallies. He clearly has no personal inclination for such rituals, and is probably even afraid of large and loud gatherings. He also knows that the Russians had to submit to such exercises of popular enthusiasm for so long that they are reluctant to involve themselves in any mass movement.

Putin is a man of networks and inner circles, of closed deals and well-guarded plans. Russians seem to appreciate his cold and sharp manners, those of a leader who goes about his business and makes decisions. Their support for the Putin regime is a new paradoxical combination of 'affectless' relation to the man, and emotional embracing of his determination and patriotic leanings. They see in him an adequate representation of the stronger and richer Russia they would like to see consolidated. They also adopt the given ideological mould because it suits them and requires little effort on their part. By and large, they find it fairly comfortable and risk free. One major exception is insecurity in the Caucasus, which hits local populations and neighbouring regions, families of military and police men, and at times Moscow when a terrorist attack occurs. The majority of Russians, however, have grown accustomed to this danger. After the Domodedovo airport suicide bombing that killed 36 and injured more than a hundred, polls showed that society was less emotionally affected than in 1999–2004.[10]

The Russians' current attitude towards authority and state policies can be better understood if one takes the full measure of the decay of public institutions since the late 1990s. The weakening of public institutions analyzed in previous chapters places the Russians in an anxiety-ridden relation to the state. What, and who, is the state? Where is authority and what can be expected in the future? The Putin-Medvedev duo established in May 2008 made the puzzle more tricky. Vladimir Putin continued to exalt political authority and embody the Russian nation, but Dmitry Medvedev represented the Russian state, thereby demonstrating that the state is weak compared to the powerful system that Putin controls.

Terrorism and 'Extremism'

The form of nationalism that came out in Russian attitudes after the 'victory over Georgia' seems to bear revanchist and negative sentiments rather than pure patriotism in defence of the motherland. The same was true during the two wars in Chechnya, when ordinary Russians could not seriously buy the official argument according to which powerful Russia was threatened by tiny Chechnya. But the 'PR machine' effectively convinced many Russians that small Muslim peoples in the North Caucasus are hostile, unruly, and bring havoc to their country.

The ultimate consequence of anti-Caucasian propaganda, and of terrorist acts, is to reshape the national community as conceived by the average Russian. For the latter, the imagined community does not include the North Caucasus. Terrorism and extreme violence have two powerful effects on the Russian polity: they heighten the role of the security services and all men in uniform (*siloviki*), and fragment the Russian space into regions that do not communicate and do not share a sense of belonging to one and the same community.

Thanks to official and effective propaganda, the majority of Russians believe that terrorism comes from the outside, as one of the many negative consequences of globalization. Islam, the Caucasus, Al-Qaeda, 9/11 in America, blasts in Madrid and London, are all mixed up in one major world danger. Gennady Gudkov, Deputy Chair of the Committee on Foreign Affairs of the State Duma, builds a convincing counter-argument. Firstly, terrorism is not a North Caucasus problem, it is 'the problem of Russia and its region'; in the Caucasian republics, the situation is similar to that of many other provinces of Russia, but aggravated and more acute. Secondly, conflicts in the Caucasus have one origin: separatism, and terrorists today act 'in the continuity of the extremist methods of struggle for separatism in Chechnya'. At the start, terrorism was an extreme form of pressure on the powers that be to give in to an independent Chechnya. Later, when that goal was no longer attainable, Chechnya and the rest of the North Caucasus drifted away from Russia.[11] A number of Russian intellectuals and experts point at the negative influence of the Church hierarchy on issues of national identity, Russianness, and the Islamist threat. Patriach Kirill is as powerful as his predecessor Aleksei and works very closely with the political power and its leaders.[12]

Since 2007, numerous terrorist attacks, often suicide bombings, have taken a heavy toll in Moscow, in the Russian provinces and in the North Caucasus. On 29 March 2010, two explosions in the Moscow Metro killed dozens and injured hundreds. On 24 January 2011, another suicide bombing hit the international terminal of Moscow Domodedovo airport. The Moscow-St Petersburg train has twice been the target of terrorists. In Daghestan, Kabardino-Balkaria, Ingushetia and Chechnya, since 2007 hardly a day passes without a violent incident. Investigations rarely lead to any serious conclusion, very few independent observers and journalists can report on the situation in these countries, and the Russian authorities have not devised an appropriate counter-terrorism strategy. Tanya Lokshina's reporting on the most dreadful events in Daghestan, Ingushetia, Kabardino-Balkaria, Chechnya leave little doubt as to the inefficiency and lack of political will of local authorities. Corruption and impunity of the police, government departments and the justice system are major causes of terrorism and of the failure of counter-terrorism led by the FSB and special units.[13]

Terrorism threatens populations in the North Caucasus and in other parts of Russia, including the capital Moscow. Commanding authorities, however, emphasize the threat against *the state*, its infrastructures, and business climate, not against *the people*. On 26 January 2011 at the world economic forum in Davos, President Medvedev's leading point was that the suicide bombing in Domodedovo airport was meant to destabilize the regime and 'prevent him from coming to Davos'.[14]

In Putin's system, security means, first and foremost, security of the state, and its leadership, not human security. A major task of counter-terrorism agencies is to protect public buildings, state borders, and to defend the regime against any threat of destabilization. In their work on the FSB, Andrei Soldatov and Irina Borogan underline that 'Putin gave the FSB a new, even riskier role. The FSB was charged with protecting the stability of the political regime—Putin's own rule—and the country'.[15] They also explain that a new definition of terrorism has emerged in 2006 and a new definition of 'extremism' in 2008: counter-terrorism aims also at fighting against individuals or groups that oppose the regime.

'In 2006 a new antiterrorism law called "On Countering Terrorism" replaced the 1998 version and offered a quite different definition of terrorism: "Terrorism is an ideology of violence and practice of influence on decision-making by bodies of the government, institutions of local government, or international organizations, by means of intimidation of the population and (or) other forms of illegal violent actions. (…)"' Russian officials also seem to have shifted their definition of terrorism quite markedly in recent years, so that the effort to combat it is geared less towards preventing acts of violence aimed at civilians and more towards preserving the state against external threats.[16]

The close correlation between counter-terrorism policies and disregard for human rights and public liberties needs to be emphasized. The more the commanding authorities, in Moscow and in the North Caucasian republics, accept the use of exceptional measures to combat terrorists, separatists and opponents, the more civil society is held hostage to the 'Save the Nation' order. Instability and violence in the southern part of Russia are used to justify a policy of vigilance and extraordinary means of enforcing law and order. It explains why no one is truly interested in solving the very roots of the conflicts. Keeping the Caucasian peoples in a situation of no rule and no development has become part of Moscow's policy.

The Russian political and economic leadership are very closely connected to the security structures and the FSB. Many of them have worked in these structures and value the networks and loyalty. Andrei Soldatov and Irina Borogan have given a thorough assessment of the role of the FSB in Russia's ruling system. They argue in their book that since Putin came to power,

the Federal Security Service (FSB), the modern successor of the Soviet secret police (KGB), has been granted the role of the new elite, enjoying expanded responsibilities and immunity from public oversight or parliamentary control. For eight years, a veteran of its own ranks, Vladimir Putin, held power in the Kremlin as the Russian President, and in the years following, his influence was felt as Prime Minister. The FSB's budget is not published; the total number of officers is undisclosed. But according to even cautious estimates, FSB personnel total more than 200,000. Putin made the FSB the main security service in Russia, permitting it to absorb many of the former parts of the KGB and granting it the right to operate abroad, collect information, and carry out special operations. Under Putin, former and current security service agents permeated the ranks of business and government structures, and the FSB resurrected as models old KGB idols: the founder of the early Soviet secret police, the Cheka, Felix Dzerzhinsky; and the most prominent of the KGB bosses, Yuri Andropov.[17]

The spiral of violence and repression is conducive to more arbitrary behaviour and impunity on the part of administrative, police and military commanding organs in Moscow and in the provinces. Russia is not a state under siege, but the leadership more often than not creates a climate of emergency. Foreign and domestic policies belong to one whole strategy which I define as 'national exceptionalism' whereby the resort to force and repression, inside and outside Russia, is justified by the duty to protect national specificity and state sovereignty against potential dangers.

Since 2008, the fight against 'extremism' marks a new level of repressive policies against critical media and opponents. Soldatov and Borogan underline that the FSB and the police have begun an ambitious surveillance program to control "extremism," which has come to include, among other things, political protest against the regime, writings critical of the Kremlin or security services, and participation in independent trade unions and informal youth groups. This broad definition of extremism, embracing participation in activity that challenges the existing political order in Russia, was put in place when the Kremlin was worried that the 2008 financial crisis might ignite popular protests. On September 6, 2008, Dmitry Medvedev, the newly elected Russian President, made a key change in the structure of the Interior Ministry, which acts as a national police force. Under Medvedev, the department dedicated to fighting organized crime and terrorism was disbanded and a new department established, charged with countering extremism. Similar changes were made through all regional departments. Thousands of experienced police officers accustomed to dealing with bandits and terrorists were redirected to hunt down a new enemy.[18]

A rising number of journalists and human rights defenders have been victims of violence and harassment. In November 2009, the attorney Sergey Magnitsky died in prison for lack of medical care, after almost a year in police custody. In July 2009, Natalya Esterimova, head of the Memorial office in Grozny, was abducted and killed. In January 2010, Stanislav Markelov and Anastasia Baburova were murdered in central Moscow in broad daylight after a press conference. In October and November 2010, several journalists suffered brutal aggressions, most notably the *Kommersant* newspaper's Oleg Kashin and the *Khimkinskaya Pravda* editor Mikhail Beketov who were severely beaten, as well as Konstantin Fetisov, environmentalist and defender of Khimki Forest. Many other cases of abuse occurred in recent years. This spiral of repression goes unimpeded because of the *de facto* impunity of the police and special units, and more generally the *siloviki*. The new law on the police, adopted in 2010, will not improve civilian control over police action. Are Russia and Human Rights 'incompatible opposites', asks Bill Bowring in a question that summarizes the general sense of helplessness amongst Russia specialists and democracy advocates.[19]

Khodorkovsky: Second Act

The former head of the Yukos oil company had been in jail since 2003 and had already been sentenced to eight years in 2005 for tax evasion. Then the judgment of 30 December 2010 condemned him and his former associate Platon Lebedev to fourteen years' imprisonment, from which the eight years already purged are subtracted. The two men can thus be kept in jail until the end of the year 2017. Khodorkovsky should have been released in late 2011, after serving his full sentence of eight years; an application for his parole was denied in 2008. The second trial therefore aimed to obtain a new conviction extending the imprisonment by several years. Judge Danilkin punctuated the reading of his judgment on December 30, 2010 by a famous phrase that will be remembered: 'The guilty can only make amends in jail'.

The outcome of the second trial confirms the lessons of the first one but reveals new subjects of concern. In such a sensitive case for the political power, judges are placed under pressure and they have been chosen for their susceptibility.. A compromising file may have been held against them, in order to dissuade them from following their consciences. Ask any journalist or Russian jurist, critical of the regime or not, and even an adviser of President Medvedev and they will answer that the judges 'have instructions'. The best proof is the incredible statement made by Judge Viktor Danilkin's court assistant in February 2011. In an interview with the online site *gazeta.ru* and *Dozhd* television, Natalya Vassilyeva revealed that the long sentence read by Danilkin in the last days of December had not been written by him but imposed on him. She also gave an account of the numerous pressures that they underwent after the beginning of the second trial in 2009. Danilkin denied the accusation and Vassilyeva persisted and resigned from the court in March. For those who attended the trial and listened to the reading of the sentence, there was no doubt that judge Danilkin read a text he had not written himself.[20] It is now conventional knowledge that the Khodorkovsky case is political.

The second trial is similar, in large part, to the revision of the *res judicata* five years earlier, made worse by adding to the sentence. To the defence lawyers, it was a rougher experience than the first trial because they had more opportunities to express themselves and assert their arguments. They were able to bring evidence that would have exonerated their client in an honest court, but they were duped, and the sense of injustice felt was even greater than in 2005. As one of his lawyers sadly admitted, at least the 22-month-long trial had the advantage of keeping Khodorkovsky out of his prison in Chita in Siberia, 6,000 miles away from home, where it was a violation of the prisoner's rights to hold him.[21]

This second trial aroused more criticism in Russian society than the first one. Indeed, the arrest of the managers of Yukos in 2003 took place in the context of a campaign to control large companies that had benefited from the favourable privatization in the 1990s and which were reluctant to pay their taxes. And even if Yukos behaved better than the others, and other powerful entrepreneurs were not disturbed, the political climate pitted President Putin against the 'oligarch' Khodorkovsky. Few Russians took the side of the entrepreneur.

No institution protects anyone caught in Putin's line of fire. In his ultimate and remarkable speech at his trial on 2 November 2010, Mikhail Khodorkovsky summarized the nature of the "lawless system" (*bezzakonie*) that prevails in Russia: 'Even enshrined in law, rights are not defended by the court. Maybe the court is afraid, or is it a simple cog in the 'system'?' This criticism is broadly shared by informed Russians who have followed the Yukos case since 2003 and who express themselves on the Internet, in the few media still critical, such as radio *Echo of Moscow*, and in the newspapers *Novaya Gazeta* and *Kommersant*. They are convinced that Khodorkovsky is the victim of a personal vendetta and that, as long as Vladimir Putin rules, he is unlikely to regain his freedom.

Why did Vladimir Putin and his government choose to make public such a non-credible judicial case? Was it a spectacle intended to show that the courts will continue to serve the regime? Was it meant to deter other oligarchs from contesting Putin's authority? The absurdity of the charges and the aberration of the judicial process put this case far outside the boundaries of what is reasonable, outside the 'normal' functioning of institutions. The charge against Khodorkovsky was not designed to be true or believable, but implacable: both extraordinary and uncontested. It proved that the will of the political power is more important than the authority of judges.

And yet, even reconvicted and confined, Khodorkovsky remains a concern. Foreign governments which have expressed doubts about the fairness of the trial were asked not to 'interfere in the work of Russian justice'. Pressures continue against his defenders, particularly by attacks against the site *Khodorkovsky.com*. Will the relentlessness against him make him a hero in national history, one day? This is the contradiction of Putin's power. This fear of the enemy already on the ground could indicate that leaders do not totally trust their own system and that they are aware of its limits and flaws better than anyone.

Vladimir Putin is a man who takes no risks. He chose not to have to deal with a troublemaker in the upcoming political events: the legislative elections in December 2011 and the presidential election in March 2012. The best way to control Khodorkovsky is to keep him behind bars, while maintaining the idea that he must be a little guilty of something. On several occasions in recent years, Vladimir Putin implied that Mikhail Khodorkovsky was involved in a murder, and that Russian justice was pretty lenient with him. In an interview in February 2011, Igor Sechin, Putin's *alter ego*, Deputy Prime Minister, repeated these brutal attacks.[22] This attitude is all the more shocking since the former head of Yukos has never been prosecuted for anything other than economic crime.

Khodorkovsky's punishment is a way to increase pressure on businessmen, heads of administration, and policymakers who are reminded of the golden rule: get rich, pay taxes, but never go against the interests of the ruling groups. It is worth remembering that the defendant was charged with stealing oil—black gold for Putin's Russia. The symbolic impact is obvious: oil and gas and other commodities are the national wealth that sustained the Russian state since the beginning of the 2000s. To exploit and export part of this wealth outside the channels of Putin's state may be a crime in itself.

The Imagined Community: A More and More Fragmented Russia

Is the Russian state today more whole, united and cohesive? Do orders from the top reach all levels of the hierarchy and regional/local pyramid?

Are they implemented? In a system lacking transparency and a culture of open 'reporting', it is nearly impossible to measure the effective implementation of defined tasks. One may only approximately assess the overall product of the national economy, the level of welfare amongst various social strata, and the success or failure of middle-sized and big companies.[23]

Alena Ledeneva makes a convincing demonstration that networks and loyalties are what keeps the system together.[24] The give-and-take is so tentacular that everyone is hostage to it. Masha Lipman writes of a *no-participation pact* between the leadership and society:

Putin's model of state-society relations looks like a divorce, or at least a separation: each side minds its own business and doesn't interfere with the other's sphere. It is a model best described as a no-participation pact. The Kremlin may have monopolized decision making, but it is largely nonintrusive and enables citizens to live their own lives and pursue their own interests—as long as they do not encroach on the government realm.[...] For now, at least, provincial Russians and the new urban class alike have accepted Putin's no-participation pact. In fact, should events turn out badly, critically-minded and well-informed urban achievers would be most likely to embrace the ultimate form of nonparticipation: emigration. In the current political climate, the more enlightened Russians would rather use their skills and talents for self-fulfilment abroad than be the driving force of Russia's modernization.[25]

Since 2000, Vladimir Putin has been dismantling republics' sovereignty and weakening federalism. The official justification for making republics and regions more obedient and less autonomous was the need to restore a 'vertical of power' (*vertikal vlasti*). Recent developments have shown that the political and administrative hierarchy has not worked as efficiently as publicly claimed by the powers that be. Ruling elites in the provinces have undoubtedly suffered more arbitrary decisions from Moscow, but central authorities do not seem to have gained better control and more productive management of regional resources, administrations and populations.

By trying to weaken ethnic-national identities, as well as local-regional specificities, the Putin regime is making more fragile the sense of willingly 'living together' that makes a strong national community. Mentalities are drifting apart because people who live in the Irkutsk region have fewer and fewer occasions to share views and projects with people living in Krasnodar territory near the Caucasus or Karelia next to Finland.

There is less and less communication between Vladivostok and Voronezh, between Ingushes and Yakuts, between a young Muscovite and a young rural worker in the Urals. Their only potential locus of encounter would be on the Internet, but the poor youth living in a rural district may not have access to a computer and Internet, and if he does he probably does not look at the same sites and blogs. The Internet is the new mode of communication, but it is an individual mode, not an institutionalized social link that may forge alternative public organizations. Discrepancies are still huge between the many diverse universes that coexist without ever sharing common experiences. Social and geographical mobility is much less dynamic than in Soviet times. And demographic trends point not only to a further national population decline, but also to more significant demographic disparities between regions and between rural and urban areas. The 2010 national census results are to be published at the end of 2011.

Opinion polls disclose a growing indifference to big national ambitions. In the future, economic fragmentation, lack of political cohesiveness, and growing indifference to central politics will weigh more heavily than historical legacy and mythical representations of the Russian nation. The image of the enemy cannot replace a positive image of Russia as a state organization and a human community.

Emphasis on the 'vertical of power' has undermined the horizontal links and communication between regions, between communities, and put at odds ethnic groups and minorities. Russia is fragmented into many local societies, with their own cultures and interests. The Kremlin's policy to control appointments of regional heads of administration does not reinforce the cohesiveness of the state. From 2008 to 2010, some twenty governors and presidents of republics were asked to step down, at the end of their term, or before the end, as in the case of Yuri Luzhkov, Mayor of Moscow, and head of a 'subject' of the Federation (Moscow and Saint Petersburg have a status similar to a region and are two of the 83 'subjects' composing the federal state).

The Luzhkov system was corrupt and ruthless. It served its own interests, but also the interests of the central government and the Kremlin networks. And it ruled the capital as a police state within the state, silencing dissent and opposition with all the traditional authoritarian means: selecting friendly demonstrations and denying authorization to independent movements, repressing 'illegal' rallies, harassing journalists, activists and alleged 'extremists', imposing intrusive administrative controls on nongovernmental organizations and associations, etc. After Luzhkov's dismissal and Sergey Sobyanin's appointment, not much has changed.

Putin's government and *siloviki* have relied on the Mayor of Moscow to keep the capital quiet and interest groups under control. They were closely connected with the Luzhkov system, and undoubtedly continue to work hand in hand with Sobyanin and his team. Boris Nemtsov and Vladimir Milov wrote a devastating criticism of the Luzhkov system in September 2009.[26] It was circulated widely in Moscow and on the Internet, and life became even more difficult for the two opposition politicians and their movement, *Solidarity*. Ironically, Putin's opponents gave him ammunition to speed up the offensive against Luzhkov in 2009–2010. For as early as 2007, it was clear to many observers that Luzhkov's immense power and fortune provoked irritation and conflicts amongst the elite, and in Putin's circles. But the mayor-oligarch could not be easily replaced and Putin needed him in the elections of December 2007 and March 2008. Like almost all heads of regions and republics, Yuri Luzhkov had joined the dominant party, United Russia, and even became Vice-Chairman of the party, next to Chairman Putin. The latter could not hide his ambivalence about Luzhkov; he needed him for his power, but was concerned with the extent of his power that nobody could control.

Dmitry Medvedev finally signed the Mayor's dismissal on 28 September 2010. He did not hide his satisfaction at getting rid of Luzhkov who had bluntly stated that he did not take Medvedev seriously. The President has the prerogative to appoint and dismiss governors, but he does it with the Prime Minister's approval or even at his request. The Moscow crisis, and the Khodorkosvky trial three months later, have shown that Putin remained the boss.

The President appeared powerless to stop the parody of justice against Khodorkovsky and Lebedev. On 24 December 2010 he implicitly criticized Vladimir Putin for asserting on 16 December, before the sentence was known, his belief that Khodorkovsky was guilty. Seasoned observers knew, since the establishment of the famous 'duo' in 2008, that one of the conditions of the extraordinary promotion of Dmitry Medvedev was to leave the Khodorkovsky case untouched. But the second trial lasted from March 2009 to December 2010, a long test for Medvedev who had to make new promises on the 'modernization' of Russia, and at the same time avoid questions about an unfair trial against a former entrepreneur and personal enemy of Vladimir Putin.

The Unequal Tandem

The tandem did not mark the advent of a new constitutional system, but it certainly stressed one more aspect of Vladimir Putin's 'national exceptionalism'. It was neither a constitutional revision, nor the institutionalization of a forced coexistence, like the 'French cohabitation' where the elected president must appoint a prime minister from the opposition after the latter has conquered the majority of seats in the National Assembly.[27] The Putin-Medvedev temporary arrangement has sown confusion amongst observers in Russia and abroad. Spin doctors in Moscow offered complicated explanations of why Putin's 'stepping aside' was democratic, implying that he could have mastered a last-minute constitutional revision and stayed in the Kremlin. Embarrassed partners abroad preferred to underline Putin's restraint, although they knew that he remained at the helm. And Russian citizens who voted for Medvedev in March 2008 wanted to believe that they had followed lawful instructions and saved the status quo.

The tandem innovation did not result from institutional reforms and was not discussed in Parliament. Only the Constitutional Court could have stopped the scenario by declaring it unconstitutional, but judges thought it was better not to jeopardize their position in Putin's personalized powerweb. As a result, the constitutional judges have finally relinquished their independent mission and lost all authority.

To prepare his transfer from the presidency of the state to the Council of Ministers, Vladimir Putin took the precaution of getting himself elected chairman of the dominant party, United Russia, two months before the Duma elections of December 2007 gave a large majority to his party's list, a list he conducted. He was keen to secure the legitimacy of his staying in power by a vote. The executive duo was not a dyarchy for the simple reason that Vladimir Putin has kept the upper hand on all important matters in domestic as well as foreign affairs. The division of labour has functioned rather well, each doing his own chores, but the ultimate decision has never been made against Putin's will. It would be naïve to believe that Medvedev could have relied on formal institutions to enhance his personal clout. As was discussed in this book, year after year public institutions have lost function and authority. Many of them, like the Constitutional Court, have become hollow; others like the State Duma are fragile and unpopular. Political parties cannot prosper without the agreement of the administration and Putin's blessing. In such a context, how could a president, under the authority of the prime minister, win a power bid with weak public institutions when other structures and networks proved much stronger?

At regular intervals, Dmitry Medvedev had to admit that he shared the regalian attributes with his Prime Minister: defence and security, foreign affairs, all the '*siloviki*'. Invited to speak at the London School of Economics on 2 April 2009, Medvedev answered: 'Vladimir Putin and I work well together, he is a good head of government, not an easy task. I am the President of Russia and make decisions. As to the power structures (*silovoi blok*), we share the decision-making'.[28]

In actual fact, Putin has always been the most active in the management of Russia's economic resources and financial negotiations. With Deputy Prime Minister Igor Sechin, he masters important contracts with national and foreign bankers and businessmen, as well as foreign governments. His trips to the provinces of Russia and abroad aim at striking economic deals, and bear more significance than some of President Medvedev's formal visits. The latter rarely deals personally with business matters, his economic profile is enhanced mainly at G20 summit meetings. During bilateral talks with a foreign leader Medvedev defended Russia's economic positions, but he did not craft them in the Kremlin. The work is done in Putin's circles, by government and big companies officials, and intermediaries that lobby in Moscow and abroad.

In 2008–2011, Dmitry Medvedev occupied an important slot in the Putin constellation, but he was not an alternative power figure. A particular feature of the current power organization is that it revolves around Vladimir Putin, whatever the post he occupies. Putin cautiously prevents his loyal team of state *apparatchiki* and oligarchs from being institutionalized as a new Politburo. His conception of power is anti-constitutionalist and anti-functionalist. Allegiances are personal and corporatist and work in ways that are unwritten and shifting. The only iron rule is the lack of compromise with competitors and enemies, on the inside as well as the outside. Rare have been Putin's allies who have openly criticized the second war in Chechnya, or the murder of a journalist, the rigging of elections, the Yukos affair, the blackmail over natural gas and oil deliveries, or the tensions with Europe, Ukraine and Georgia. Dmitry Med-vedev has struggled to forge his own authority, in the shadow of Vladimir Putin, by promoting his own agenda and building on his international role. He has thus created a form of artificial plurality within the ruling group which has proven useful to compensate for the lack of real polit-ical alternative. But the tacit rules of the game, established in 2008, have prevented him from challenging his mentor. Similarly, efforts to promote fractions within the dominant party or create a new party which would deceive the eye and fake competition have failed. The blatantly fraudu-lent elections of December 2011 have caused outrage in Russia and abroad. They have undermined Vladimir Putin's authority and legitimacy. Blinded by overconfidence and deaf to critcism and opposition, the regime has gone too far and opened the door to political protest. Many Russian voters feel humiliated by the leadership's disregard of their preferences and violation of their rights as citizens.

CONCLUSION

Russia's marked deviation from the democratic trajectory which was followed by the Central European countries was not a foregone conclusion in 1991. All options were open to engage in a strategy of democratization along the definition given in the early pages of this book: respect for rights and freedoms, defence of public institutions, separation of powers, empowerment of citizens and those who govern them and an independent judiciary. The international situation was favourable; Russia and the former Soviet republics were open to engaging in the effort to improve security and cooperation and develop multilateralism and economic consultation. In the years of reform, Russia encountered great challenges, but also rich opportunities. Twenty years later, the country seems to be looking inward, protecting itself against innovation and influence from the outside. Until 2011, many Russians were willing to accept that there existed no other option but the present political and economic system. Their living standards had markedly improved since the beginning of the 2000s and they were grateful to Putin for it. They tended to embrace the leadership's rhetoric of 'specificity' or 'exceptionalism' of Russian development (*osobost'*), and the belief of 'no alternative' to the Putin system (*bezalternativnost'*). Their adaptation to the modes of thinking and methods of the ruling elites has been a strong factor in the consolidation of the regime. In the longer term, however, the lack of social dynamism, political participation and economic competitiveness may well work against the interests of the commanding groups.

The fluidity and adaptability in interpretation and implementation of the law give the Russian leaders precious advantages which they are not prepared to give up: the lack of fair accountability, the ability to control public and private ownership, impunity for their acts. The strengthening of the Putin system depends to a great extent on the control of information and the media so as to maintain a diffuse fear within society. This control, as we have seen, can remain effective even while tolerating a few independent newspapers, a radio station and websites that are fairly virulent in their criticism of the regime. Vladimir Putin has managed to adapt time-tested methods of repression to twenty-first-century conditions. Holding down a sealed lid is impossible; better to leave it slightly open to those who need fresh air and who submit to the tacit rule: 'Get rich, nourish yourself on free information but practise self-censorship on sensitive subjects and stay away from politics!'

This necessary tolerance towards economic elites has another advantage for the government. It divides Russian society between 'those who need to know', in order to establish their position and profit from it, and 'those who don't want to know', who protect themselves from the inherent risks of any criticism of the system. The achievement of Putin-style authoritarianism derives from the fact that it draws on the former, those who have the ability to doubt and criticize but who contribute dynamism, and not on the latter, who are perceived by the leaders as a social burden, but remain conveniently silent. Vladimir Putin has not conducted a unified policy for all, but a differentiated strategy that accommodates both and that fluctuates according to necessity. Throughout the 2000s, his strength resided in a form of flexibility and political ruse, served at once by brutal methods and an undeniable power of seduction. In 2011, that method reached its limits.

The strengths of the Russian system thus carry within them its weakness in the long term. Three paradigms appear decisive for the present and the future.

First, the relationship to the outside world remains a determining factor for developments inside Russia itself. This conclusion may seem at first paradoxical when one considers Russia's long history of isolation. Yet during the periods of opening and liberalization (the last one from 1986 to 1993), as well as during the periods of withdrawal and political tightening of the screws (the most recent being the current period starting in 1998–2000), the ambivalent push-and-pull with the West is at the heart of the Kremlin's strategy.

The most serious distortion in the Putin doctrine, because it is the most deeply engrained in people's minds, is the idea of belonging to a distinctive civilization, a 'specific' society, a Russian-style 'sovereign democracy'. It is an appeal to the vanity and intellectual laziness of the elites even while Russia is involved in the phenomenon of globalization, with an open economy (even if its competitiveness is imperfect) and ongoing foreign trade. The population is kept in a deceptive vision that is out of touch with reality. And some who are fervent about Russian culture in the West are mistaken when they think they are defending this culture by backing the regime's anti-Western propaganda.

However, and this is the second paradigm, the means of exercising authority and the relationship that individuals have with authority are the features that are the most resistant to change. The relationship between citizens and those who govern them is complex and not as distant as one might at first believe. Russians express their clear-sightedness and distrust, but remain dependent on the elites in their way of thinking and speaking. They know, for instance, that elections are rigged, but a good half of them still go out and vote. After 2011, however, they will be more inclined to vote against the regime.

Despite deep transformations in the economy and society, the elites have resisted remarkably and consolidated dominant positions in old and new ways. They have not yielded to liberal tendencies; they keep part of society dependent, and are scarcely accountable to anyone, from either an institutional or a personal standpoint. The Putin system has been shaped for the elites, not against them.

This phenomenon is disconcerting. It partly explains the reluctance that politicians, intellectuals, journalists and experts critical of the regime have in embarking on an open war against the authorities. In Russia, being alone against the authorities means being alone in the face of society. Conservatism is one kind of cement for the current political system.

The third paradigm is one that is the crux of the argument of this book: the state has been defeated in its post-Communist attempt at modernization. It will not easily rise up from the years of crisis and the illusion of normalization. Posited at first as a concept and key instrument of change, the state has retreated both as *res publica* and as an institutional ensemble in charge of governing and accommodating the community's development. Under Yeltsin and Putin, Russia has been a patent failure of constitutionalism and the rule of law.

The law and private ownership remain fragile institutions in Russia. These two foundations of democratic society have been abused in recent years, even before they managed to gain a firm foothold in the Russian landscape. The subordination of the judges and the rulers' irresponsibility are major obstacles to the respect for basic rights, which are nevertheless enshrined in the Constitution. When he became President, Medvedev acknowledged this fact and claimed to want to establish the rule of law, but many similar promises had been made by Yeltsin in 1991 and 1996, then by Putin in 2000.

The primitive aspects of the state and the predatory behaviour of its leaders will inevitably operate as an impediment to economic and social dynamism; for the two spheres are intrinsically linked together. The goals set by the power-wielders in terms of economic growth and modernization will be inexorably impeded by political control and interference in corporate affairs.

Social apathy makes the Putin system appear unchallenged and strong. Indeed, people do not mobilise *en masse* at the national level in defence of political liberalization or social reform. Levada Centre polls show that an increasing proportion of Russians do not feel concerned by policies decided at the top. 85 per cent declare they have no influence over the way their country is managed.[1]

Russians are nevertheless aware of the defects of the ruling system and uncertainty about the future. Substantial criticism is being expressed at the grassroots level, because of dissatisfaction with the way in which practical matters are managed, including employment, education, health, transport, bureaucratic inefficiency and corruption. Protest sentiments are growing in Russia and may lead to the rise of a civil society if opponents can have access to national channels of expression and political institutions. The elections of 2011 and 2012 put pressure on the leadership and the administration. Some limited pluralism is necessary for elections to look credible, and for citizens to have an incentive to vote. Protest vote now is the biggest challenge to the authoritarian regime. The hollowing out of public institutions and pressures against independent media, associations and political movements, as well as independent entrepreneurs, impede the process of social mobilization and political self-organization. By and large, people feel free as individuals, but they do not see how their society can be made free and responsible. The lack of legal protection for social activists and opposition politicians stands in the way of political competition.

A civil society does not make a political society, unless fundamental principles and institutions are restored: free and fair elections, competitive pluralism with full rights for opposition parties and movements, accountability of the executive organs and their administrations to Parliament, and an independent and potent judiciary. There are forces in Russia that work in favour of regime consolidation, and forces that work against it. The latter have been considerably weaker than the former until the electoral scandal of 2011, and are gaining strength as attitudes are changing and uncertainty is rising. More and more Russians express concern that an irremovable President is not a good prospect. They remember old jokes about Brezhnev and make fun of *zastoi* (stagnation) under an aging Putin.

The lack of institutional modes of protesting has served as the best protection of the regime against dissident views and alternative policies. Not any longer. The hollowing out of public institutions will produce a boomerang effect, as was exemplified in Tunisia, Egypt and in Libya in 2011. Massive repression is no longer an option in Russia. An open and dynamic political life and a society looking with some confidence at its own future are the necessary conditions for Russia's modernization and state consolidation.

CHRONOLOGY

1985   *15 March.* Mikhail Gorbachev becomes General Secretary of the Communist Party of the Soviet Union (CPSU).
July. The withdrawal of troops from Afghanistan and Mongolia begins—a slow process, completed in 1989.
October. Gorbachev visits France. It is his first official trip to a Western country since March 1985. (In December 1984, he had visited the United Kingdom and met Margaret Thatcher.)

1986   *Perestroika* is introduced.
26 April. Chernobyl nuclear power plant catastrophe.
11 October. Mikhail Gorbachev and American President Ronald Reagan meet in Reykjavik (Iceland) to discuss reducing intermediate-range nuclear weapons in Europe.
December. Andrey Sakharov is free after years of exile in Gorky (Nizhny Novgorod).

1987   *Glasnost* is introduced; the liberalization of the media begins. Mikhail Gorbachev publishes his book *Perestroika*, in Russia and abroad. The *New Thinking* and the *Common European Home* are key concepts in the Soviet Union's new foreign policy.
24 November. In Geneva, Ronald Reagan and Mikhail Gorbachev sign the intermediate-range nuclear forces treaty (INF), a major arms-control agreement.

1988   *February.* The USSR announces its withdrawal from Afghanistan.
Institutional reform begins.
November. The CPSU Central Committee passes a resolution announcing the revision of the Constitution, particularly revision of article 6 regarding one-party rule.

December. The Constitution is revised, providing for a new parliamentary structure and making it legal for parties other than the Communist Party to exist. Elections are announced.

1989   *26 March*. Elections of deputies to the new USSR Congress of People's Deputies.

April. Violent clashes in Tbilisi.

May-June. The Congress of People's Deputies is constantly in session. Debates are filmed by television crews and deputies freely debate the nature of the regime and the structure of the Soviet state.

25–28 May. Mikhail Gorbachev visits China. He is in Beijing during the Tiananmen Square peaceful demonstrations, a few days before the brutal armed repression of early June.

9 November. Fall of the Berlin Wall.

December. Another constitutional revision.

1990   Yavlinsky's 500 Days Programme.

January. Violent clashes in Azerbaijan. Elections to the parliaments of the Soviet republics between February and October.

May. The new parliament of the Soviet Republic of Russia (Congress of People's Deputies of Russia) meets and elects Boris Yeltsin as its President.

12 June. The Russian parliament declares the sovereignty of the Socialist Federal Republic of Russia.

September. Reunification of Germany.

15 October. The Nobel Peace Prize is awarded to Mikhail Gorbachev .

December. Gorbachev suggests a referendum on a new union of sovereign states.

1991   *January*. Repression in Vilnius and Riga; Gorbachev promptly puts an end to armed intervention.

February. Referendum on the sovereignty of Lithuania. Boris Yeltsin asks Mikhail Gorbachev to resign.

March. Referendum on the sovereignty of Latvia, Estonia and Georgia.

April. Nine out of fifteen Soviet republics approve a new Union treaty.

12 June. Boris Yeltsin is elected President of the Republic of Russia by direct universal suffrage.

July. Dissolution of the Warsaw Pact.

19 August. Putsch against Gorbachev in Crimea.

21 August. End of the putsch and Boris Yeltsin's victory over the putschists.

24 August. Mikhail Gorbachev resigns from his post of General Secretary of the Communist Party.

28 August. Ukraine takes control of the armed forces stationed on its territory.

29 August. The Russian Parliament dissolves the Communist Party.

September. Mikhail Gorbachev recognizes the independence of the three Baltic countries (which recover their full sovereignty).

1 December. Referendum on the independence of Ukraine and election of President Kravchuk by direct universal suffrage.

8 December. Meeting of the Russian, Ukrainian and Belarusian Presidents at Belovezhskaya Pushcha to prepare the end of the USSR.

21 December. At Alma Ata, the leaders of the Soviet republics (except the Baltic countries and Georgia) establish the Commonwealth of Independent States (CIS) and dissolve the USSR.

24 December. Russia announces it will occupy the USSR's seat at the United Nations.

25 December. Mikhail Gorbachev abandons his functions as President of the USSR because the USSR no longer exists. The 15 republics that made up the USSR, and Chechnya, autonomous republic within the Federal Republic of Russia, declare their independence or recover their sovereignty (the Baltic countries) during the year 1991.

1992   *January*. 'Shock therapy' begins with privatizations conducted by Yegor Gaidar, Deputy Prime Minister and later Prime Minister. The Russian economy enters a serious crisis.

December. Viktor Chernomyrdin becomes Prime Minister (a post he will leave in March 1998).

March–October. President Yeltsin is in open confrontation with Parliament.

June. Russian-Ukrainian accord on dividing the Black Sea fleet. Armed conflict between Ingushes and Ossetians, between

Abkhaz and Georgians, between Armenians and Azerbaijanis on the status of the various territories.

1993   *25 April.* Referendum on confidence in the President's and Parliament's policies and the pursuit of reforms. First elections of provincial governors.

21 September. Boris Yeltsin signs decree 1400 by which he disbands Parliament and announces he will rule by decree. A majority of deputies disobey.

3–4 October. Boris Yeltsin orders an assault on the White House, seat of Parliament, and the national television station, claiming at least 150 lives.

12 December. Referendum to approve the Constitution and the election of deputies to the State Duma, lower house of Parliament, and members of the Federation Council, upper house.

1994   *October.* Monetary crisis, the rouble collapses, Russians lose their savings. Poland, Hungary, the Czech Republic and Slovakia apply for NATO membership.

11 December. The Russian army invades Chechnya. Regional elections (on various dates).

May. US President Bill Clinton negotiates the opening of talks between NATO and Russia in Moscow.

17 December. Legislative elections.

1996   The accession process to NATO for former USSR satellite countries progresses.

3 July. Boris Yeltsin is narrowly re-elected in the second round of the presidential election.

August. Ceasefire in Chechnya, signed by Alexander Lebed and Aslan Maskhadov; Russian troops commence their withdrawal from the separatist republic.

December. Strikes to protest about unpaid wages.

1997   The economic crisis worsens.

12 May. Presidents Boris Yeltsin and Aslan Maskhadov sign a peace accord between Russia and Chechnya.

27 May. In Paris Yeltsin signs the Founding Act of the partnership between Russia and NATO.

1998   *23 March.* Yeltsin replaces Prime Minister Viktor Chernomyrdin with Sergey Kiriyenko.

May. Russia becomes a member of the new G8, an expansion of the G7 group of major industrialized countries.

17 August. Russian financial crisis, devaluation of the rouble.

11 September. Yevgeny Primakov becomes Prime Minister.

1999   *March.* Enlargement of NATO to include Poland, Hungary, the Czech Republic and Slovakia.

March–April. NATO strikes against Serbia to protect Kosovo; hostile reactions from Russia.

19 May. Sergey Stepashin replaces Yevgeny Primakov as head of government.

9 August. Vladimir Putin, chief of the FSB since July 1998, is appointed Prime Minister. The same day, Boris Yeltsin announces on television that Putin is his successor. Putin agrees to run for President in 2000.

August. Chechen commander Basayev makes an incursion into Dagestan, provoking Russian retaliation.

4 September. Terrorist attack in Buynaksk (Dagestan) followed by another serious attack in Moscow on 9 September perpetrated against an apartment building; more attacks on 13 September in Moscow and in Volgodonsk on 16 September.

1 October. After air raids against the suburbs of Grozny late September, a column of Russian tanks enters Chechnya. The second war in Chechnya begins.

19 December. Election of the State Duma.

31 December. Boris Yeltsin leaves his post as President of Russia, six months before the end of his second term.

2000   *26 March.* Vladimir Putin is elected President in the first round. Two powerful businessmen forced into exile: Vladimir Gusinsky and Boris Berezovsky.

May. Mikhail Kasyanov is appointed Prime Minister. Seven federal districts are created, each grouping together ten to fifteen regions and republics of the Federation.

12 August. Sinking of the *Kursk* submarine, 118 dead.

30 October. European Union-Russia summit in Paris.

2001   *April.* NTV television, the country's largest network, is placed under state control; creation of the new 'governing party', United Russia.

May. Putin appoints a close associate, Alexei Miller, head of Gazprom, the natural gas industry giant.

11 September. Al-Qaeda attacks in New York and Washington. Putin offers the United States his support in the fight against international terrorism.

2002   All television networks are brought under state control at the beginning of the year.

May. The NATO-Russia Council is formed.

23 October. Separatist Chechens take hostages at the Dubrovka Theatre in Moscow. Russian forces storm the building using a deadly gas. At least 120 people die.

2003   *March.* Start of the war in Iraq, conducted by the United States and a coalition of countries without a UN resolution.

31 May. EU-Russia summit, four 'common spaces' of cooperation defined.

5 October. Akhmad Kadyrov becomes President of Chechnya; the 'Chechenization' of the conflict progresses, but Russian troops remain.

25 October. Mikhail Khodorkovsky is arrested for tax evasion.

November. Dmitry Medvedev replaces Aleksandr Voloshin as Head of the Presidential Administration.

22–23 November. Rose Revolution in Georgia. Mikheil Saakashvili emerges as leader; President Shevardnadze is forced to step down.

7 December. Election of the State Duma.

2004   *February.* Mikhail Kasyanov's cabinet is forced to resign; the new Prime Minister is Mikhail Fradkov.

14 March. Vladimir Putin is re-elected President of Russia in the first round.

29 March. Lithuania, Estonia and Latvia (three former Soviet republics), along with four other countries, join NATO.

1 May. Enlargement of the European Union to ten new members, including Poland, Hungary, the Czech Republic, Slovakia, Lithuania, Latvia and Estonia.

9 May. Akhmad Kadyrov is assassinated in Grozny in an attack perpetrated during the ceremony commemorating the USSR's victory over Nazi Germany on 9 May 1945. Soon thereafter, his son Ramzan is appointed Prime Minister of the Chechen Republic.

27 June. Igor Sechin becomes President of Rosneft's Board of Directors.

1–3 September. Hostage taking at the Beslan school in North Ossetia, with over 330 victims, mostly children.

13 September. Vladimir Putin puts an end by decree to the election of provincial governors and presidents of republics in the Federation of Russia and undertakes an authoritarian reform of electoral laws and procedures.

November–December. Orange Revolution in Ukraine; tens of thousands of Ukrainians camp out on the main square in Kiev demanding a fair presidential election.

26 December. Another second round of the Ukraine presidential election is held under international observation; Viktor Yushchenko is elected President of Ukraine.

2005   Plans to build a gas pipeline under the Baltic Sea are reactivated to avoid Ukraine, Poland and Belarus; Germany backs the project, which will be named Nord Stream in 2006.

8 March. Separatist Chechen leader Aslan Maskhadov is killed.

31 May. Mikhail Khodokorvsky and Platon Lebedev are sentenced to nine years of imprisonment (reduced to eight years by the Appeal Court).

13 October. Terrorist assaults in the city of Nalchisk, Republic of Kabardino-Balkaria. More than a hundred killed.

2006   *January.* Energy crisis between Russia and Ukraine. Because of a dispute over prices and transit, Russia cuts off all gas supplies passing through Ukrainian territory, thereby reducing supply to most European countries; the price of Russian gas is raised.

11–12 July. Conference held in Moscow by The Other Russia, an organization that unites a number of opposition parties and movements.

15–17 July. G8 summit in Saint Petersburg.

October. Russia imposes a total embargo on Georgia covering mineral waters and wines, air and postal communications.

7 October. Anna Politkovskaya, investigative journalist and opponent of the regime, is murdered in Moscow.

1 November. Alexander Litvinenko is poisoned with polonium in London, and dies on 23 November.

Several repressive laws are passed during the year, particularly those on NGOs and on extremism.

2007   *1 January.* Enlargement of the European Union to 27. Bulgaria and Romania join the EU.

January. Oil pipeline dispute between Russia and Belarus.

4 July. The International Olympic Committee votes for Sochi in Russia to host the Winter Olympic Games of 2014.

July. The price of oil hits 100 dollars a barrel.

12 November. Referendum on independence in the separatist region of South Ossetia, in Georgia.

27 November. NATO Summit in Riga, which opens up the possibility of another enlargement to the East.

2 December. Election of the State Duma; the party led by Vladimir Putin wins a large majority of seats.

2008   *February.* Kosovo declares its independence.

2 March. Dmitry Medvedev is elected President of the Russian Federation in the first round; no independent mission of international observers is authorized.

8 May. Dmitry Medvedev is sworn in and appoints Vladimir Putin Prime Minister.

9 May. The State Duma votes to confirm the new government.

July. World oil price rises to $147 a barrel.

7–12 August. War between Georgia and Russia, triggered in South Ossetia, a separatist region of Georgia. Russian continues to bombard Georgia until 22 August.

26 August. After a unanimous vote in the State Duma on 25 August, the Russian President signs a decree recognizing the independence of Abkhazia and South Ossetia. No other CIS country recognizes them. Georgia cuts off diplomatic ties with Russia and leaves the CIS.

8 September. French President Nicolas Sarkozy, acting for the European Union, brokers an agreement with the Russian President for a military withdrawal from Georgian areas occupied by the Russian army after 7 August, the deployment of a small mission of European observers and a commitment to participate in an international conference on security in the region. Russia reinforces its military and economic presence in Abkhazia and South Ossetia. The so-called 'six-point plan' will not be fully implemented.

September–October. Russia is severely hit by the world economic crisis and credit crunch.

October. The Geneva multilateral talks about the situation in Georgia start. They will yield very limited results in the following years.

5 November. Dmitry Medvedev's first state-of-the-nation address to Parliament.

November. In a series of votes, the two houses of Parliament approve several amendments to the constitution by an overwhelming majority. Presidential terms are extended from four to six years. The State Duma term is extended from four to five years. The reform comes into force on 31 December.

2009   *January.* Once more, Russia cuts natural gas supplies to Ukraine, and subsequently to Europe, in a dispute over prices and unpaid bills.

March 6. Hillary Clinton presents Sergei Lavrov with a red 'reset button' to symbolize improved ties.

April. Russia officially declares the end of 'the counterterrorism operation' in Chechnya, and the 'normalization' of the situation in the republic.

July. US President Obama's first official visit to Moscow.

1 September. Putin commemorates the beginning of World War II in Gdansk, Poland.

27 November. Bomb in a Moscow-St Petersburg train: twenty-seven dead, a hundred injured.

2010   *January.* Another oil pipeline dispute between Russia and Belarus.

7 February. Viktor Yanukovich is elected President of Ukraine. Defeated rival Yulia Timoshenko contests the results.

14 March. Elections of a number of local and regional assemblies in Russian provinces.

29 March. Two suicide bombings in the Moscow Metro, killing 40 and injuring hundreds. Islamist terrorist Doku Umarov, self-proclaimed emir of the North-Caucasus, claims responsibility.

April-June. Series of riots and demonstrations across Kyrgyzstan lead to the ousting of President Bakiyev.

8 April. The New Start Treaty is signed in Prague by the USA and Russia. It calls for both sides to reduce their deployed warheads modestly to 1,550 from 2,200. The treaty also will ensure that each country has continued insight into the other's arsenal, with inspections and exchanges of information.

April. Russian authorities acknowledge the USSR's responsibility in the massacre of thousands of Polish officers in the Katyn forest, Smolensk region, in April 1940. Polish President dies in plane crash on his way to the Katyn commemoration. Improvement of Russian-Polish relations continues.

1 June. EU-Russia summit meeting in Rostov-on-Don.

9 June. Russia joins the new round of sanctions against Iran imposed by United Nations Security Council resolution 1929.

24 June. Russian President Medvedev's first official visit to the United States.

5 July. Customs union between Russia, Belarus and Kazakhstan comes into force after Minsk ratifies a key customs code.

August. A five-week heat wave and wildfires hit many regions of Russia, and some big cities, claiming many victims. The mortality rate is twice the normal rate.

28 September. Yury Luzhkov, Mayor of Moscow, is dismissed, after 18 years in office.

14 October. Elections of a number of local and regional assemblies. Edinaya Rossiya wins the majority of seats in all contests. Direct elections of the Mayor of Samara and Makhachkala, which are the last cases of mayors elected by direct universal suffrage (and not by their peers in elected assemblies or councils).

21 October. Sergey Sobyanin, nominated by President Medvedev, is elected mayor of Moscow by the city Duma. Sobyanin is a close ally of Vladimir Putin, Deputy Prime Minister and head of the government apparatus since 2008, head of Putin's presidential administration from 2005 to 2008.

October-November. Journalists suffer brutal aggressions, most notably the *Kommersant* newspaper's Oleg Kashin and *Khimkinskaya Pravda* Editor Mikhail Beketov who were severely beaten, as well as Konstantin Fetisov, environmentalist and defender of Khimki Forest.

1 November. Medvedev pays the first visit by a Russian president to the disputed Kurile Islands, sparking a diplomatic row with Japan.

19–20 November. In the framework of the NATO-Russia Council, Medvedev meets NATO leaders in Lisbon. At a closed-door meeting, he suggests uniting a missile shield being built by the 28 allies with Russia's own missile defence system.

11 December. Violent racist fights in the very centre of Moscow, between young nationalist Russians and non-Russian youth.

19 December. Presidential election in Belarus. Lukashenko is re-elected a fourth time. International observers denounce fraud and the brutal repression of a peaceful demonstration and arrest of several opposition candidates the very night of the election.

20 December. A court in Kiev charges opposition leader Yulia Timoshenko with misusing public funds. The former Prime Minister is accused of making the decision to use funds from the sale of quotas of greenhouse gases to cover expenses incurred through the payment of pensions.

30 December. After a second, 22-month trial, Mikhail Khodorkovsky and Platon Lebedev are sentenced to 14 years of imprisonment (from which the 7 years already served are subtracted), on charges of embezzlement and money-laundering.

2011   *January.* World oil price rises to $100 a barrel.

24 January. Terrorist attack in Moscow Domodedovo airport. 36 are killed, many more injured.

10 February. Medvedev orders the deployment of additional weapons on the disputed Kurile islands, 'an inseparable part' of Russia.

13 March. Elections of a number of local and regional assemblies. Edinaya Rossiya wins a majority of seats in all assemblies and councils (an average of 68 per cent of all mandates, but with only 46 per cent of the votes).

17 March. The United Nations Security Council adopts resolution 1973 on Libya. Russia abstains, along with China, Brazil, India and Germany. The resolution calls for a no-fly zone and for the protection of civilians. On 19 March, Russia opposes military intervention in Libya, launched by a coalition of Western states.

22 June. The Ministry of Justice refuses to register the new opposition Party of People's Freedom (*Parnas*) on the grounds that it had submitted a membership list with dead and underage members. Boris Nemtsov, Vladimir Ryzhkov, Vladimir Milov, and Ilya Yashin are leaders of the party.

24 September. At the United Russia party Congress, Vladimir Putin and Dmitri Medvedev announce that Putin will run for presidency in March 2012 and that Medvedev will take over the chairmanship of the party and head the list for the 4 December Duma elections. Putin also promises to appoint Medvedev Prime Minister in 2012.

1 October. The Russian government recognizes the National Transition Council as the ruling authority in Libya.

9 November. Georgia and Russia sign a trade agreement that clears the path for Russia to join the World Trade Organisation (effective on 15 December).

4 December. State Duma elections. The ruling party, United Russia, wins a majority of seats but numerous violations and frauds are reported. Protest demonstrations are organized in Moscow and many other cities on 10 and 24 December.

NB. The above historical milestones do not offer a detailed chronology of Russian political life since 1985. They are a selection of key dates and episodes mentioned in this book, as a guide to the reader.

NOTES

INTRODUCTION

1. See for example Dmitry Medvedev's article, 'Rossiya—vpered!' [Forward, Russia!], website gazeta.ru, September 2009, and reports by think tanks INSOR (Institute for contemporary development) and TsSR (Centre for strategic studies), posted on the web in March 2011, and commented on in *Moscow Times*, 28 March 2011.

1. THE MYTH OF A STRONG STATE: LEGACY OF THE EMPIRE AND AUTOCRACY

1. Anatole Leroy-Beaulieu, *L'Empire des tsars et les Russes*, volume 2, Lausanne, L'Âge d'Homme, 1988 (original edition 1888), p. 570. Published in English: *The Empire of the Tsars and Russians*, translated by Z. A. Ragozin, New York, G. P. Putnam, 1893–1896, reprinted by Kessinger Publishing LLC, 2007.
2. Levada Centre for the analysis of public opinion, surveys presented in *EU-Russia Centre Review*, no. 4, 2007.
3. Marc Raeff, 'Un empire pas comme les autres?', *Cahiers du Monde Russe et Soviétique*, vol. XXX (3–4), July-December 1989, p. 322.
4. Michel Heller, *Histoire de la Russie et de son empire*, Paris, Calmann-Lévy, 1997; Nicolas Riazanovsky, *Histoire de la Russie*, Paris, Robert Laffont, 1996.
5. Richard Pipes, *Russia Under the Old Regime*, London, Weidenfeld & Nicolson, 1974.
6. Vasily Klyuchevsky, *Kurs russkoi istorii*, 5 volumes, reprinted in Moscow, 1956–1958. English translation at London, J. M. Dent & Sons; New York, E. P. Dutton & Co., 1911–1931.
7. Richard Pipes, *Karamzin's Memoir on Ancient and Modern Russia: A Translation and Analysis*, New York, Atheneum, 1981.
8. Marc Raeff, 'Un empire pas comme les autres?', art. cit., pp. 323–4.
9. This slogan is appearing with increasing frequency in the discourse of the Putin Youth, the *Nashi* (Ours), and among some leaders of the ruling political party, United Russia. Official rhetoric, orchestrated by a few advisors, such as Vladislav Surkov, will be discussed in Chapter 5.

10. For a more historical analysis of the issue, see the author's 'Le mythe du nationalisme russe', in Pierre Birnbaum, *Sociologie des nationalismes*, Paris, Presses Universitaires de France, 1999, pp. 85–102.

11. Meetings with President Putin, conferences at the Valdai International Club, September 2004, September 2005 and September 2006, in which the author took part.

12. On autocracy and the sovereign, see Aleksandr Akhiezer, Igor Klyamkin and Igor Yakovenko, *Istoriya Rossii: konets ili novoe nachalo?* (History of Russia: End or new beginning?), Moscow, Liberal'naya Foundation Missiya, 2006; Oleg Kharkhordin, *Main Concepts of Russian Politics*, Lanham, MA, University Press of America, 2005.

13. '*Samoderzhavie, pravoslavie, narodnost*' in Russian. On the meaning of the word *narodnost*', see Alexandre Koyré, *La Philosophie et le problème national en Russie au début du 19ᵉ siècle* (first published: Paris, Librairie Honoré Champion, 1929), Paris, Gallimard, 1976, p. 234.

14. Richard Pipes, *The Formation of the Soviet Union*, Cambridge, MA, Harvard University Press, 1954, reprinted in 1997, p. 2.

15. Thomas M. Barrett, 'Lines of Uncertainty: The Frontiers of the North Caucasus', *Slavic Review*, 54, no. 3, Autumn 1999, p. 581.

16. Ibid., p. 579.

17. Donald W. Treadgold, *The Great Siberian Migration*, Princeton University Press, 1957.

18. The most recent history textbooks published in Russia faithfully reproduce the official line. The history of peoples and of societies is scant and poorly covered. One exception is the two-volume *Istoriya Rossii* (History of Russia), edited by Andrei Zubov, Moscow, Astrel, 2009.

19. Richard Pipes, *Karamzin's Memoir*, op. cit., p. 6.

20. Anatole Leroy-Beaulieu, *L'Empire des Tsars et les Russes*, op. cit., p. 72.

21. Ibid., pp. 70–1.

22. Igor Klyamkin et al., *Rossiiskoe gosudarstvo: vchera, sevodnya, zavtra* [Russian state: yesterday, today and tomorrow], Moscow, *Liberal'naya missiya*, *Novoe Izdatel'stvo* Foundation, 2007. Boris Mironov, *Sotsial'nyia istoriya Rossii* [Social history of Russia], Saint Petersburg, Dmitri Bulanin, 1999.

23. Richard Pipes, *Property and Freedom*, chapter entitled 'Patrimonial Russia', New York, Alfred Knopf, 2000, p. 191.

24. Karamzin, translated by Richard Pipes, ibid., pp. 204–5.

25. Karamzin, cited in Alexander Koyré, op. cit., p. 29.

26. Jonathan W. Daly, 'On the Significance of Emergency Legislation in Late Imperial Russia', *Slavic Review*, 54, no. 3, Autumn 1995, pp. 602–29.

27. Richard Pipes, *The Formation of the Soviet Union*, Cambridge, MA, Harvard University Press, 1994; Michel Heller, *Histoire de la Russie*, op. cit.

28. Michel Heller and Aleksandr Nekritch, *L'Utopie au pouvoir. Histoire de l'URSS de 1917 à nos jours*, Paris, Calmann-Lévy, 1982.

29. Merle Fainsod, *Smolensk Under Soviet Rule*, Cambridge, MA, Harvard University Press, 1953.

30. Richard Pipes, *The Formation of the Soviet Union*, op. cit.

31. The Republic of Georgia also included autonomous territories, in particular Abkhazia and South Ossetia, which were recognized as independent states by Russia in August 2008, after the Georgian-Russian war, and benefit from the financial support of Moscow.

32. Basile Kerblay, *La Société soviétique contemporaine*, Paris, Armand Colin, 1977, pp. 295–7.

33. Alexander Solzhenitsyn, *The Gulag Archipelago*, London, Collins/Fontana, 1974.

34. Nicolas Werth, *La terreur et le désarroi. Staline et son système*, Paris, Perrin, 2007.

35. Cf. Adam Ulam, *The Bolsheviks: The Intellectual and Political History of the Triumph of Communism in Russia*, New York, Collier Books, 1965; Isaiah Berlin, *Russian Thinkers*, New York, Penguin Books, 1979.

36. Alain Besançon, *Présent soviétique et passé russe*, reprint Paris, Hachette, 1986; Nathan Leites, *A Study of Bolshevism*, Glencoe, ILL, The Free Press, 1953; Nathan Leites, *The Operation Code of the Politburo*, New York, McGraw-Hill, 1951.

37. Boris Souvarine, *Stalin: A Critical Survey of Bolshevism*, trans. C. L. R. James, Alliance Book Corporation, 1939, reprinted by Kessinger Publishing LLC, 2005, pp. 20–1.

38. 14 December 1825: in the turbulent period following the death of Alexander I, some regiments of the Imperial Russian Guard rebelled. The rebellion was led by educated young officers, attracted by Western ideas of freedom and progress, who belonged to the upper nobility. The uprising was harshly put down, and the Decembrists were sent to prison in Siberia, but not killed. The 'Decembrists' were acclaimed as forerunners of the revolutionary movement.

39. Cf. The writings of Kireevsky, Koyré, Besançon, op. cit., and see the recent discussion at the Liberal'naya Missiya Foundation on the nation and post-imperial syndrome, particularly the lectures by Aleksey Miller, websites polit.ru and liberal.ru.

40. James H. Billington, *The Icon and the Axe: An Interpretative History of Russian Culture*, chapter entitled 'The Turn to Social Thought', New York, Vintage Books, 1970, p. 371.

41. Ibid., p. 377.

42. Ibid., p. 447.

43. Letter from Karl Marx to Dr Kugermann, 1871, cited in Richard Pipes, *Russian Revolution 1899–1919*, London, Fontana Press, 1992, p. 396.

44. Yuri Pivovarov and Andrey Fursov, '*Russkaya systema i reformy*' [The Russian system and reform], *Pro and Contra*, vol. 4, no. 4, Autumn 1999, pp. 176–97.

45. See Aleksander Auzan's analysis, 'Natsional'nye tsennosti i constitutsionnyi stroi'[National values and the constitutional edifice], polit.ru public lecture, 29 November 2007, www.polit.ru/lectures/2007/12/06/auzan.html.

2. DOMESTIC REFORM AND OPENING TO THE WORLD

1. The joke by the famous Soviet dissident is cited by Galia Ackerman, 'Le soviétisme et la nouvelle identité russe', in Stéphane Courtois (ed.), *Le jour se lève. L'héritage du totalitarisme en Europe. 1953–2005*, Monaco, Éditions du Rocher, 2006. The name of the Soviet state contains no geographical reference: Union of Soviet Socialist Republics. Only the ideological identity appears in the country's name.

2. Vladimir Putin's televised speech broadcast on 4 September 2004, the day after the tragedy of the school in Beslan. The word 'disaster' would henceforth be used regularly by Putin and his entourage to stigmatize the end of the USSR in 1991 (Putin had already spoken of 1991 as a disaster in February 2000, but did not use the word again in the following years).

3. Henri Mendras and Michel Forsé, *Le Changement social*, Paris, Armand Colin, 1983, pp. 28–32.

4. Anatoly Vishnevsky, *La Faucille et le rouble: La modernisation conservatrice en URSS*, Paris, Gallimard, 2000.

5. Merle Fainsod, *How Russia is Ruled*, Cambridge, MA, Harvard University Press, 1953; Basile Kerblay, *La société soviétique contemporaine*, Paris, Armand Colin, 1977.

6. During the presidential election of June 1996, five years after the collapse of the USSR and his enforced withdrawal from politics, Mikhail Gorbachev decided, for the first and last time, to stand for election against Boris Yeltsin, his sworn enemy. He obtained 0.5 per cent of the votes. The Russians held him responsible for the 1989–1991 upheavals and the destruction of their state.

7. Alexander Zinoviev, *The Radiant Future*, New York, Random House, 1980, and *The Yawning Heights*, New York, Random House, 1979.

8. Jon Elster, 'Active Negation and Passive Negation: Essay on Ivanian Sociology', *European Journal of Sociology/Archives Européennes de Sociologie*, 21, 1980, p. 334.

9. Mikhail Gorbachev, *Perestroika: New Thinking for our Country and the World*, New York, Harper & Row, 1987, pp. 255 and 234.

10. This period of Soviet history is the subject of numerous studies. Cf. the bibliography.

11. The strategic defence initiative launched by Ronald Reagan in 1982 was a programme of new anti-nuclear defence technologies that went far beyond the USSR's innovation capabilities at the time.

12. Marie Mendras and Marie-Thérèse Vernet-Stragiotti, 'Prélude à la perestroïka: le rapport de Tatiana Zaslavskaïa (Novosibirsk, 1983)', *Vingtième Siècle*, no. 38, April-June 1993, pp. 90–104.

13. Leonid Abalkin, *Etot trudnyi put* [This difficult path], Moscow, 1989, cited in Yuri Baturin et al., *Epokha Eltsina, Ocherki politicheskoi istorii* [The Yeltsin era: A snapshot of political history], Moscow, Vagrius, 2001, p. 170.

14. Mikhail Gorbachev, *Perestroika*, op. cit., and *Memoirs*, op. cit.

15. Interview with Anne Sinclair on the French TV programme *7 sur 7*, recorded on 5 December 1991, TF1.

16. Alexander Lukin, *Political Culture of Russian 'Democrats'*, Oxford University Press, 2000.

17. At this time, most Kremlinologists were sceptical with regard to the optimistic scenario presented by Gorbachev who believed in strengthening socialism and not destroying it.

18. Vladimir Voinovich, *The Anti-Soviet Soviet Union*, New York, Harcourt Brace Jovanovich, 1986, pp. xvi-xvii.

19. Yuri Afanasyev (ed.), *Inogo ne dano* [There is no other choice], Moscow, Progress, 1988.

20. Ronald Inglehart, *Culture Shift in Advanced Industrial Society*, Princeton University Press, 1990.

21. In an opinion poll carried out in July 1992 to the question 'Do you agree with those who say that Russia must remain a superpower even if it is detrimental to its relations with the rest of the world?', 69 per cent replied yes, 20 per cent no, with 11 per cent don't knows. Survey carried out by VTsIOM, Moscow, published in *Moskovskie Novosti*, 26 July 1992.

22. Gregory Guroff and Alexander Guroff, 'The Paradox of Russian National Identity', in *Russian Littoral Project*, Karen Dawisha and Bruce Parrott (eds), University of Maryland, no. 16, May 1993, p. 33. This analysis proved very pertinent but was a minority view in 1993 when most Western experts thought that Russia would 'become standardized' in the mould of a large European country of medium power. On this subject see the excellent collective work edited by Vladimir Baranovsky, *Russia and Europe: The Emerging Security Agenda*, SIPRI and Oxford University Press, 1997.

23. Lev Gudkov and Boris Dubin, '*Posttotalitarnyi sindrom: "upravliaemaya demokratyia" i apatiya mass*' [Post-totalitarian syndrome: 'directed democracy' and social apathy] in Maria Lipman and Andrey Ryabov, *Puti rossiiskogo postkommunizma* [The paths of Russian post-Communism], Moscow Carnegie Center, 2007, p. 8.

24. Ibid., p. 10.

25. Ibid., p. 14.

26. Donna Bahry, 'Society Transformed? Rethinking the Social Roots of Perestroika', *Slavic Review*, vol. 52, no. 3, Autumn 1993, pp. 512–54. See also James Gibson, Raymond Duch and Kent Tedin, 'Democratic Values and the Transformation of the Soviet Union', *The Journal of Politics*, vol. 54, no. 2, May 1992, pp. 329–71.

27. Juan Linz and Alfred Stepan, *Problems of Democratic Consolidation: Southern Europe, South America, and Post-Communist Europe*, Baltimore, Johns Hopkins University Press, 1996.

28. T. Carothers, 'The End of the Transition Paradigm', *Journal of Democracy*, vol. 13, no. 1, January 2002, pp. 5–21. Cf. the many articles devoted to this question in the *Journal of Democracy* since the 1990s.

29. Juan J. Linz, *Totalitarian and Authoritarian Regimes*, London and Boulder, Lynne Rienner Publishers, 2000

30. Martin Malia, *La Tragédie soviétique: Histoire du socialisme en Russie 1917–1991*, Paris, Seuil, 1995.

31. Nathan Leites, *The Operational Code of the Politburo*, op. cit.

32. Martin Malia's position was that the ideology shaped people's mentalities. See the fine article by Alain Besançon paying tribute to Malia, 'Tombeau pour un grand historien', *Commentaire*, no. 109, 2005, p. 171; see also the discussion between the author and Malia: 'L'écroulement du totalitarianisme en Russie', interview with Martin Malia, *Esprit*, no. 218, Jan-Feb 1996, pp. 40–53.

33. François Furet, *The Passing of an Illusion*, trans. Deborah Furet, University of Chicago Press, 1999. Furet points out this paradox: Napoleon left a great deal behind after his defeat; Lenin left nothing. 'Lenin in contrast left no estate. The October Revolution ended not by being defeated in war, but by liquidating all that it had created. When the Soviet empire fell apart, it was in the strange position of having been a superpower without incarnating a civilization' (p. viii). They were 'incapable of giving a meaning to the twentieth century, and thus to their past', concludes Furet.

34. Steven Solnick, *Stealing the State*, Cambridge, MA, Harvard University Press, 1998.

35. Ivan Kireevsky, cited in Alexandre Koyré, *Le problème national*, op. cit.

36. Richard Pipes, *Property and Freedom*, New York, Knopf, 2000, pp. 190–1.

37. Ibid., p. 161.

38. John Locke, *Second Treatise of Civil Government*, 1690, ch. 15 section 173, cited in Michel Lallement, *Histoire des idées sociologiques*, vol. 1, Paris, Nathan, 1993, p. 33.

39. Hilton Root, *The Fountain of Privilege: Political Foundations of Markets in Old Regime France and England*, California Series on Social Choice and Political Economy, University of California Press, 1994, p. 218.

40. Jürgen Habermas, *The Structural Transformation of the Public Sphere*, Massachusetts Institute of Technology, 1989 and 1991, p. 74. In 1804, Napoleon produced the classic of bourgeois law, the *Code Civil*.

41. Max Weber, *The Protestant Ethic and the Spirit of Capitalism*, trans. Talcott Parsons, London, Unwin University Books, 1930, and trans. Peter Behr and Gordon C. Wells, London, Penguin Modern Classics, 2002.

42. David Woodruff, *Money Unmade: Barter and the Fate of Russian Capitalism*, Ithaca, Cornell University Press, 1999. See also by Woodruff, 'Rules for Followers: Institutional Theory and the New Politics of Economic Backwardness in Russia', *Politics and Society*, vol. 28, no. 4, pp. 437–82, and 'Property Rights in Context: Privatization's Legacy for Corporate Legality in Poland and Russia', *Studies in Comparative International Development*, vol. 38, no. 4, winter 2004, pp. 82–108.

43. David Woodruff, 'Property Rights in Context: Privatization's Legacy for Corporate Legality in Poland and Russia', art. cit., pp. 82–108.

44. Ronald Inglehart, op. cit., p. 24.

45. On these anecdotes, see Amandine Régamey, *Prolétaires de tous pays, excusez-moi! Dérision et politique dans le monde soviétique*, Paris, Buchet-Chastel, 2007.

46. Hannah Arendt, *The Origins of Totalitarianism*, New York, Harcourt Brace Jovanovich, 1951; *On Violence*, New York, Harcourt Brace Jovanovich, 1970.

47. Ronald Inglehart, op. cit., p. 13.

48. The deputies elected Boris Yeltsin President of the new Parliament of the Republic of Russia on 28 May 1990. On 12 June, Parliament declared Russia's sovereignty. Yeltsin was elected President of Russia by direct universal suffrage on 12 June 1991.

49. Alexis Berelowitch, 'Le nationalisme russe', *Politique étrangère*, 1/1992, pp. 35–41.

50. Cited in Jonathan Steele, *Eternal Russia: Yeltsin, Gorbachev and the Mirage of Democracy*, London, Faber & Faber, 1994, p. 328.

51. Alexander Solzhenitsyn, *Rebuilding Russia* (Translation of *Kak nam obustroit' Rossiyu?*), London, Harvill, 1991.

52. See Alexander Verkhovsky, 'Religion et "idée nationale" dans la Russie de Poutine', *Les Cahiers Russie/Russia Papers*, no. 3, 2006. In December 2011, Kirill expressed criticism over the rigged elections.

53. I. Klyamkin and V. Lapkin, '*Russkii vopros v Rossii. 2*' ['The Russian question in Russia. 2'], *Politicheskie issledovaniya*, 1/1996, p. 80.

54. The following analyses are based on the surveys and publications of the Russian Centre for Public Opinion studies, VTsIOM (now the Levada Centre): *Monitoring obshchestvennogo mneniya*, Moscow, six issues a year, and on the surveys carried out by the Public Opinion Foundation.

55. I. Klyamkin and V. Lapkin, art. cit., pp. 78–96.

56. See the survey results in Richard Rose and William Maley, 'Conflict or Compromise in the Baltic States?', *RFE/RL Research Report*, vol. 3, no. 28, 15 July 1994, pp. 26–35.

3. THE DEFEAT OF CONSTITUTIONALISM

1. Yves Mény, 'Constitutionnalisme' entry in the *Dictionnaire Constitutionnel*, edited by Olivier Duhamel and Yves Mény, Paris, Presses Universitaires de France, 1991, p. 212.

2. See Gorbachev's account, *Memoirs*, op. cit., and that of Boris Yeltsin, *Against the Grain*, trans. Michael Glenny, London, Jonathan Cape, 1990. See also Richard Sakwa's analysis, *Russian Politics and Russian Society*, London, Routledge, 1993.

3. Marie Mendras, 'Les trois Russies. Analyse du referendum du 25 April 1993', *Revue Française de Science Politique*, vol. 43, no. 6, December 1993, pp. 897–939.

4. On 12 June 1991, in accordance with the revised former Constitution, the President of Russia was elected through direct universal suffrage, alongside a Vice President. Yeltsin and Rutskoi were therefore elected together. After the revolt of October 1993, this American-style system was abandoned once and for all.

5. Blocked by the constitutional Commission, in June-July 1993, Yeltsin called a 'Constitutional Conference' of experts and representatives from the republics and regions, which produced a new draft Constitution on 12 July 1993. This document was less presidentialist than the previous one and gave more powers to the subjects of the Federation. Cf. Vera Tolz, 'Drafting the New Russian Constitution', *RFE/RL Research Report*, no. 29, 16 July 1993, pp. 1–15.

6. Abkhazia, Adjara and South Ossetia are provinces of Georgia. Since the armed conflicts of 1992–1993, the status of Abkhazia and South Ossetia has been 'frozen' and the Russian Army has had an official presence there as a 'peacekeeping force'. Adjara reached agreement with Georgia in 2004. The armed conflict between Georgia and Russia in August 2008, and subsequent recognition by Russia of Abkhazia's and South Ossetia's independence, are consequences of the failed state-building process in the early 1990s.

7. Faced with political protest and the difficulties of drafting a new Constitution, Boris Yeltsin decided to hold a referendum on four questions: 1) Do you have confidence in Boris Yeltsin, the President of Russia? 2) Do you approve the social and economic policy of the President of Russia and Russia's government since 1992? 3) Do you consider an early presidential election necessary? 4) Do you consider an early election of People's Deputies of the Russian Federation necessary? As a majority turnout was required and not attained, the planned elections did not take place. See Marie Mendras, 'Les trois Russies', art. cit., p. 898.

8. Mikhail Gorbachev, *Memoirs*, op. cit., p. 685. Gorbachev gives his version of events: 'On 21 September 1993, the President, exceeding his powers, issued a decree suspending the Constitution and dissolving the Supreme Soviet. The majority of the deputies refused to comply, regarding the decree as a *coup d'Etat*. Forces loyal to Yeltsin surrounded the Parliament building. In its turn, the Supreme Soviet deprived Yeltsin of power and proclaimed Vice-President Rutskoi as provisional President. [...] Even those who supported the President's decree of 21 September insisted on negotiations. The Patriarch joined the negotiating process. There appeared a hope that bloodshed would be avoided'. (pp. 684–5).

9. In 1993, the Federation comprised 21 republics (including separatist Chechnya), 49 regions (*oblast'*), 10 territories (*krai*), 6 districts (*okrug*), 1 autonomous region and 2 cities with federal status, Moscow and Saint Petersburg. In 2008–2009, following the merging of some territories, the number of subjects in the Russian Federation dropped from 89 to 83 (see map at the beginning of the book).

10. Some of Boris Yeltsin's advisers gave their views in the book by Yuri Baturin et al., *Epokha Eltsina*, op. cit. See the contributions by Georgy Satarov and Mikhail Krasnov in particular.

11. 'Vlast'i voina v Chechne v rossiiskom obshchestvennom mnenii' [Political power and the war in Chechnya in Russian public opinion], *Sevodnya*, 23 February 1995.

12. M. Mendras, 'Toward a Post-imperial Identity', in Vladimir Baranovsky (ed.), *Russia and Europe: The Emerging Security Agenda*, Oxford University Press, 1997, pp. 90–103.

13. Yuri Burtin, *'Voina. Predvaritel'nye itogi'* [The War. Preliminary toll], *Moskovskie Novosti*, no. 3, 15–22 January 1995, p. 6.

14. Arkady Vaksberg, *'Ubiystvennaya igra'* [A game of slaughter], *Literaturnaya gazeta*, 25 January 1995. At the time, all the media, even those close to the Kremlin, criticized different aspects of the war, and numerous conferences on the issue were held in Russia. Leading sociologists, ethnologists, journalists, deputies, even government officials took part and condemned the recourse to armed violence. Cf. *Epokha Eltsina*, op. cit., and Gail Lapidus, 'Contested Sovereignty: The Case of Chechnya', *International Security*, 23/1, 1998, pp. 5–49.

15. Isabelle Astigarraga, *Tchétchénie, un peuple sacrifié*, Paris, L'Harmattan, 2000.

16. Eugene Huskey, 'Democracy and Institutional Design in Russia', in Archie Brown (ed.), *Contemporary Russian Politics*, Oxford University Press, 2001, p. 41.

17. Lilia Shevtsova and Igor Klyamkin, 'The Tactical Origins of Russia's New Political Institutions', ibid., p. 14.

18. On the elections in USSR-Russia since 1989, see Richard Rose (ed.), *How Russia Votes*, London, Chatham House, 1997, and Marie Mendras's articles in the journal *Pouvoirs*. See map p. 141, *Pouvoirs*, no. 80, January 1997.

19. *OMRI Daily Digest*, Prague, 17 January 1996.

20. Boris Yeltsin never agreed to join the party that was created to support him and his government. Vladimir Putin chose a different strategy in October 2007: he took the chairmanship of Edinaya Rossiya, the dominant party, in order to lead the Duma elections of December 2007 and position his 'successor', Dmitry Medvedev, on the winning lane to the presidential election of March 2008. See chapter 7.

21. In some regions, the Communists had a landslide victory. The *oblasti* (regions) of Kemerovo, Orel, Tambov, Volgograd, Penza and Bryansk ranked top with respectively 48.6 per cent, 40.2 per cent, 36.9 per cent, 36.6 per cent and 35.3 per cent of votes through the list system. In the Republic of Chuvashia, the CP won 33.5 per cent and the Agrarian Party 40.6 per cent. In North Ossetia, the CP is reported to have accounted for 70 per cent of the votes. The results for the republics of the North Caucasus should be considered with caution. The situation there is very tense and the voting and counting conditions were not observed so scrupulously. Results published by the Central Electoral Commission, Moscow, 19 December 1995.

22. The option of voting against all the candidates existed from 1993 to 2006, and was then abolished. It is a kind of remnant of the Soviet vote: then there was only one candidate and it was impossible not to go and vote, so the only form of protest possible was to spoil the voting slip by crossing out the name of the single candidate.

23. The author was an OSCE observer.

24. Surveys carried out by the VTsIOM, published in the bi-monthly review of the All-Russian Public Opinion Research Centre, *Monitoring obshchestvennogo mneniya*, during the 1990s.

25. See the analysis by the sociologist Vladimir Shlapentokh, chiefly based on opinion polls, 'Russian Patience: A Reasonable Behavior and a Social Strategy', *Archives Européennes de Sociologie/Journal of European Sociology*, vol. 36, no. 2, 1995, pp. 247–80.

26. Yuri Levada, 'Vybory: peyzaj posle bitvy—i pered nei' [The elections: the landscape after the battle and before the next], *Izvestiya*, 11 January 1996.

27. Ibid.

28. Interview with the author, at Our Home Is Russia campaign headquarters, 14 December 1995.

29. Interview with the author, Moscow, 19 December 2007. Vladimir Ryzhkov is listed among the enemies of Putin and of Russia officially declared in 2007 in a book published by the Gleb Pavlosvky Centre, part of the Kremlin's propaganda machine: *Vragi Putina* [Putin's enemies], Moscow, Europa, 2007.

30. Alexander Sobyanin and Vladislav Sukhovol'skii, 'Demokratam dorogo oboshlis' ambitsii ikh liderov' [Their leaders' ambitions cost the democrats dearly], *Izvestiya*, 23 December 1995, p. 4.

31. ITAR-TASS, Moscow, 11 January 1996.

32. On Berezovsky, see the book by the American journalist Paul Khlebnikov, who was murdered in 2004: *Godfather of the Kremlin: Boris Berezovsky and the Looting of Russia*, New York, Harcourt Brace, 2000.

33. In 1996, the seven oligarch-Boyars were Boris Berezovsky (Logovaz group and Obiedinienye Bank), Vladimir Gusinsky (Most group), Alexander Smolensky (Stolichny Bank), Vladimir Potanin (Onexim Bank), Mikhail Khodorkovsky (Menatep group), Piotr Aven and Mikhail Fridman (Alfa group).

34. Boris Yeltsin, *Midnight Diaries*, trans. Catherine A. Fitzpatrick, London, Weidenfeld & Nicolson, 2000, pp. 91–4.

35. Peter Reddaway and Vladimir Glinsky, *The Tragedy of Russian Reforms*, Washington, DC, The United States Institute of Peace Press, 2002; Chrystia Freeland, *Sale of the Century: Russia's Wild Rise from Communism to Capitalism*, New York, Crown Publishing, 2000; David Hoffman, *The Oligarchs: Wealth and Power in the New Russia*, New York, Public Affairs, 2002; Paul Khlebnikov, *Godfather of the Kremlin*, op. cit.; Peter Baker and Susan Baker, *Kremlin Rising: Vladimir Putin's Russia and the End of Revolution*, Washington, DC, Potomac Books, 2nd edn, 2007. Others began their ascent, like Roman Abramovich. See Natalie Nougayrède, 'Les oligarques et le pouvoir: la redistribution des cartes', in 'La Russie de Poutine', *Pouvoirs*, no. 112, 2005, p. 35.

36. See Marie Mendras, 'L'élection présidentielle de 1996 en Russie', *Revue Française de Science Politique*, vol. 45, no. 2, 1997.

37. Research trip to the Nizhni-Novgorod region, June 1996.

38. Overall the OCSE report on the presidential election of 1996 was positive, reflecting the West's 'politically correct' approach: don't make waves and be glad that the 'reformer' Yeltsin won against the 'reactionary' Zyuganov.

39. Boris Yeltsin was elected President of the Federal Republic of Russia through universal suffrage for the first time in June 1991, when it was still under the Soviet regime. A new Constitution was adopted on 12 December 1993, providing for a maximum of two successive terms. Yeltsin completed his first five-year term (according to the old Constitution) in June 1996 and was re-elected for four years, according to the new Constitution. The constitutional court ruled on this matter: Boris Yeltsin began his second term in 1996 and therefore could not seek a third.

40. On the government and society, see the six-article special issue: 'Qui gouverne en Russie?', *La Revue Tocqueville/The Tocqueville Review*, vol. 19, no. 1, 1998, pp. 3–135. NB: in July 1998 Vladimir Putin took over the helm of the intelligence service (FSB).

41. See Stephen Holmes, 'Plaidoyer pour un État libéral et fort en Russie', *Esprit*, July 1998, pp. 97–111.

42. On the legal system in the 1990s, see Peter Solomon, 'The Limits of Legal Order in Russia', *Post-Soviet Affairs*, vol. 11, no. 2, April-June 1995.

43. Lilia Shevtsova, *Russia Lost in Transition: The Yeltsin and Putin Legacies*, Washington, Carnegie Endowment for International Peace, 2007, p. 7.

44. Alexander Litvinenko and Yuri Felshtinsky led the investigation, published in their book *Blowing up Russia*, New York, Encounter Books, 2007. They claim the FSB was directly involved in these attacks designed to create a climate of terror and anti-Chechen xenophobia. Alexander Litvinenko was poisoned with polonium in London in November 2006.

45. Online surveys conducted in 1999–2000, especially those carried out by the VTsIOM (Russian centre for public opinion studies) and the FOM (Public opinion foundation).

46. Interview with the author, Moscow, October 1999.

47. The State Duma was elected half through the list ballot and half through the single-mandate system. There were 450 seats in total.

48. The other lists obtained less than 3 per cent and did not reach the 5 per cent threshold required to win a seat; 3.3 per cent voted 'against all', an option on every voting slip in Russia. The Union of Right Forces, gathered behind certain 'pro-reform' figures (Sergey Kiriyenko, Boris Nemtsov), quickly rallied to Putin's support. In the single-mandate vote, through which the other half of the deputies were elected, the 'governmental party' and the other groupings close to the government obtained mediocre results. However, more than 100 candidates presented themselves under no political label and many of them adopted a pro-government position after their election. The Narodni Deputat ('People's Deputy') fraction was an annex of the Edinstvo parliamentary group. Other elected candidates, particularly those of Zhirinovsky's party, supported the new government.

49. Research trips and electoral observation missions by the author to the regions of Ulyanovsk, Nizhni-Novgorod, Sverdlovsk, Krasnodar and Novgorod in 1999–2000.
50. 'Special Report/Election', *Moscow Times*, 9 September 2000.
51. Very often they are based in the offices of this administration whose head personally supervises the transmission of the results to Moscow via computer. In Krasnodar, during the night that followed the presidential election, observers from the OSCE received a very unpleasant welcome from the administration of one of the town districts. They noted how the data from each polling station were keyed into a computer at top speed, with no verification. Many *protokoly* were handwritten. In one of the rooms in the administration building, in the middle of the night, people were calmly filling in vote count forms (the author's participation in an electoral observation mission, Krasnodar, 23–8 March 2000).

4. THE POWER OF BUREAUCRACIES

1. Mikhail Saltykov-Shchedrin, *Le Bon vieux temps*, Lausanne, L'Âge d'Homme, 1997. Written between 1886 and 1889, the novel describes provincial Russia after the abolition of serfdom in 1861.
2. All three were former members of the KGB, very close to Putin: Gennady Timchenko has lived in Switzerland for years and is Head of the Gunvor trading company, which works closely with Putin's networks; Igor Sechin was Deputy Prime Minister and Chairman of the Board of the Rosneft petroleum company; and Sergei Ivanov, former Defence Minister, was Deputy Prime Minister and in charge of most weapons sales.
3. Merle Fainsod, *How Russia is Ruled*, Cambridge, Mass.: Harvard University Press, 1963, p. 387.
4. In post-Soviet Russia, there was an outpouring of new laws and regulations, since every area of public and private life had to be thoroughly overhauled.
5. Igor Klyamkin, 'Bureaucrates et hommes d'affaires', in *Comment fonctionne la Russie? Le politique, le bureaucrate et l'oligarque*, M. Mendras (ed.), Paris, Autrement, 2003, p. 41.
6. Ibid., p. 42.
7. V. Gelman, S. Ryzhenkov and M. Brie, *Rossiya regionov: transformatsiya politicheskikh rezhimov* [Russia of the regions: transformation of the political regimes], Moscow, Ves' Mir, 2000.
8. From 1 January 2008, the territories of the Federation numbered only 84. Effectively, most of those that were enclosed within another territory of the Federation were merged with the territory enclosing them. It should be noted that the Russian Soviet Federative Socialist Republic (RSFSR) was one of the 15 republics that made up the USSR. It therefore formally had a federal form, within the USSR, which itself was a federal state on paper. Soviet practice was the opposite, i.e., monolithic and centralized. The Russian Constitution of 1993 echoed the political and administrative structure of the RSFSR, with only minimal modifications.

9. On the autonomy of the provinces in the 1990s, see Nikolay Petrov and Michael McFaul, *Politicheskii Almanakh Rossii* [Political almanach of Russia], Moscow, Carnegie Centre, 1997 and 1999; Kathryn Stoner-Weiss, *Local Heroes: The Political Economy of Russian Regional Governance*, Princeton University Press, 1997; Marie Mendras (ed.), *Russie: Le gouvernement des provinces*, Geneva, CRES, 2004.

10. Basile Kerblay, *La Société soviétique contemporaine*, op. cit.; Merle Fainsod, *How Russia is Ruled*, op. cit.

11. See Svetlana Alexievich, *Voices from Chernobyl*, trans. Keith Gessen, Champaign, ILL, Dalkey Archive Press, 2005, and Galia Ackerman, *Tchernobyl: Retour sur un désastre*, Paris, Buchet-Chastel, 2006.

12. In 2007 the infant mortality rate was 10 per thousand, which was still much higher than the French rate of 3 per thousand. See the demographics website www.demoscope.ru. See also, for the importance of demographic indices for predicting the future of a political regime, Emmanuel Todd, *The Final Fall: Essay on the Decomposition of the Soviet System*, trans. John Waggoner, preface Jean-François Revel, New York, Karz, 1976.

13. Mikhail Gorbachev, *Memoirs*, op. cit.

14. Trip to Ekaterinburg and the Sverdlovsk region in October 1994.

15. Interview with Eduard Rossel in his office in Ekaterinburg. Rossel signed this agreement in 1995.

16. Trip to Saratov, February 1996.

17. Trip to Kostroma in May 1994.

18. Jean-Charles Lallemand, 'Politics for the Few: Elites in Bryansk and Smolensk', *Post-Soviet Affairs* (Berkeley, California), vol. 15, no. 4, December 1999, pp. 312–35.

19. The work of the author's CERI research group 'Gouvernement des provinces en Russie' (Provincial government in Russia) between 1992 and 2000 made it possible to develop an empirical and micro-political analysis of case studies, and an interpretation of the political and social development of Russia as a whole. This political anthropology approach proved fruitful since it started from the hypothesis that local protagonists were as significant as those in the centre. Most Russian experts made the contrary assumption: Moscow could, at will, reverse the trend and regain the upper hand, therefore there was little point in studying the local action. Until 2004, the leaders of the big cities and the regions and republics remained the main protagonists in Russia's political and economic history. Cf. 'Regions of Russia: A Special Issue', *Post-Soviet Affairs*, 1999, op. cit.

20. V. Gelman, S. Ryzhenkov and M. Brie, op. cit.; *Post-Soviet Affairs*, op. cit.

21. Most regional governors and presidents of the republics were reaching the end of their second and final term, in accordance with the provisions of the republics' constitutions. Unless they revised their fundamental laws to grant themselves a third term, their time was up. Putin therefore offered the regional leaders the opportunity to remain in post indefinitely, which he also took himself, in 2008,

becoming prime minister with an unlimited term. Putin decided to run for President a third time in 2012.

22. Interviews in Moscow with Natalia Kotikova, legal expert to the Federation Council, and Vladimir Ryzhkov, State Duma deputy, 10–11 May 2001.

23. Alexey Novikov, 'Le recul du fédéralisme en Russie: l'exemple du budget', *Pouvoirs*, no. 112, 2005, pp. 111–25.

24. Igor Klyamkin, Lev Timofeev, *Tenevaya Rossia* [Russia of the shadows], Moscow, RGGU, 2000.

25. Steven Solnick, *Stealing the State*, op. cit.

26. Merle Fainsod, op. cit., p. 387.

27. Arkady Vaksberg, *The Soviet Mafia*, New York, St Martin's Press, 1992.

28. Vladimir Gimpelson, *Chislennost' i sostav rossiiskoi biurokratii* [Size and composition of Russia's bureaucracy], Moscow, GU-VCHE, 2002.

29. Official figures, *Chitelnnost' rabotnikov organov gosudarstvennoi vlasti i mestnogo samoupravleniia po vetviam vlasti i urovniam upravleniya*, www.gks.ru/bgd/regl.

30. Vladimir Gimpelson, op. cit.

31. Michel Crozier and Erhard Friedberg, *L'Acteur et le système*, Paris, Seuil, 1977; François Dupuy and Jean-Claude Thoenig, *Sociologie de l'administration française*, Paris, Armand Colin, 1983.

32. Viktor Makarenko, 'Pravitelstvo i biurokratiya' [Government and Bureaucracy], *Sotsiologicheskiie issledovaniya*, no. 2, 1999, p. 4.

33. Basile Kerblay, op. cit.

34. On Russian society through expressions of opinion, see the book by the sociologist Yuri Levada, *Ot mneniia k ponimaniu* [From opinion to understanding], Moscow, Moskovskaya shkola politicheskikh issledovanii, 2000. See also Chapter 6 of this book.

35. Author's visits to Tver in April 1994, March 2004 and December 2007.

36. Vladimir Shlapentokh, 'Russian Patience: A Social Strategy and a Reasonable Behaviour', art. cit., pp. 247–80. Marie Mendras, 'La préférence pour le flou. Pourquoi la construction d'un régime démocratique n'est pas la priorité des Russes', *Le Débat*, no. 107, Nov.-Dec. 1999, pp. 35–50.

37. Merle Fainsod, op. cit., p. 329 and chapter 12: 'The Control of the Bureaucracy—Public Administration in the Soviet Union', pp. 327–53.

38. In 1991, with the independence of the Soviet republics, Russia's population was only around 150 million and, by 2011, due to a declining population, around 141 million.

39. On corruption during the Soviet era, see Arkady Vaksberg, *The Russian Mafia*, op. cit.; Leslie Holmes, *The End of Communist Power: Anti-Corruption Campaigns and Legitimation Crisis*, Boston, Polity Press, 1993; J. Kramer, 'Political Corruption in the USSR', *Western Political Quarterly*, vol. 30, 1977, pp. 213–24; M. Mendras, 'La Russie: administrations sans foi ni loi', in Donatella Della Porta and Yves Mény (eds), *Démocratie et corruption en Europe*, Paris, La Découverte, 1996, pp. 117–30.

40. Steven L. Solnick, *Stealing the State*, op. cit., p. 29.
41. Ibid., p. 24.
42. Stephen Holmes, art. cit., p. 108.
43. See in particular the research of the Levada Centre which publishes the *Monitoring obshchestvennogo mneniya* and the surveys carried out by various Russian centres and published in the periodical *Opinion Analysis* (USIA Office of Research and Media Reaction, Washington).
44. On the legal system, see Chapter 5 and Peter H. Solomon Jr, 'La difficile réforme de la justice en Russie', *Esprit*, no. 244, July 1998, pp. 112–25.

5. THE HOLLOWING OUT OF PUBLIC INSTITUTIONS

1. Yuri Olesha, *Kniga proshchaniya* ['The book of the farewell', translated into English under the title *Goodbye to the World*], Moscow, 1999, cited by Nikolai Sheiko, 'Histoire du théâtre russe', in Georges Nivat, *Les Sites de la mémoire russe*, vol. 1, Paris, Fayard, 2007, p. 702.
2. Vladislav Surkov, conversation at the Valdai conference, September 2005. Several ideological works were published with contributions from V. Surkov, by Europa publishers, edited by Gleb Pavlovsky, in charge of spreading the Kremlin's doctrine: *Suverenitet* [Sovereignty], 2006; *Suverennaya demokratiya. Ot idei—k doktrine* [Sovereign democracy: From the idea to the doctrine], 2007; *Pro suverennuiu demokratiiu* [For sovereign democracy], 2007.
3. In summer 1999, an investigation into money laundering was conducted into accounts at the Bank of New York. Very large sums had been deposited by people close to Boris Yeltsin, in particular his son-in-law Leonid Dyachenko and his adviser Pavel Borodin.
4. Cf. Anna Politkovskaya's articles in the *Novaya Gazeta* newspaper and the collection of her writings, *Za Shto?* [Why?], Moscow, 2007, published posthumously. The English translation of extracts from her writings, *A Russian Diary*, is published by Random House (May 2008).
5. Yuri Levada, 'D'Eltsine à Poutine: Les élections présidentielles (1991–2004)', in 'La Russie de Poutine', *Pouvoirs*, 2005, op. cit., p. 145.
6. Informal interviews with close advisers to the Kremlin, Valdai conference, September 2004 and September 2005. Note the contrast with Boris Yeltsin's team. In 1999, President Yeltsin apologized to the nation for the war in Chechnya. His adviser Georgy Satarov confirmed that Yeltsin bitterly regretted this mistake and the resulting human disaster (conversation in Vienna, April 2007).
7. A Russian expert speaking off the record, Carnegie Moscow Center, March 1999.
8. Yuri Levada, 'Les Russes et le terrorisme', *Esprit*, Aug-Sept 2002.
9. The best reporting on the second war was by Anna Politkovskaya, the great reporter for the *Novaya Gazeta* newspaper, from 1999 until the day she was murdered, 7 October 2006. Her works are published in English, in particular *A Dirty War, a Russian Reporter in Chechnya*, Vintage, 2005.

10. Cf. the biography of Vladimir Putin written by independent experts, on the panorama.ru website. Cf. also the series of interviews given by Putin to three journalists at the beginning of his first term, *Ot pervogo litsa* [In the first person], Moscow, Vagrius, 2001, published also in English: Natalya Gevorkyan, Natalya Timakova and Andrei Kolesnikov, *First Person: An Astonishingly Frank Self-Portrait by Russia's President* (PublicAffairs, 2000).

11. The intelligence services, including military intelligence, along with all the other 'power ministries', were reformed during Boris Yeltsin's first term. Their fragmentation and the lack of financial resources undermined them to the extent that many employees of these organizations moved into the private sector or joined alternative, sometimes criminal networks. Cf. Amy Knight, *Spies Without Cloaks: The KGB's Successors*, Princeton University Press, 1996; J. Michael Waller, 'Russia: Death and Resurrection of the KGB', *Demokratizatsiya*, vol. 12, no. 3, 2004, pp. 333–55; Barbara Vernon, 'Les élites en uniforme', in 'La Russie de Poutine', *Pouvoirs*, no. 112, op. cit., pp. 63–77.

12. On these attacks and the resumption of the war in Chechnya, see Chapter 3.

13. Elena Tregubova, *Bayki Kremlevskogo diggera* [Tales of the Kremlin digger], Moscow, Ad Marginem, 2003; *Proshchanie Kremlevskogo diggera* [Farewell to the Kremlin digger], Moscow, Ad Marginem, 2004.

14. Vladislav Surkov, art. cit.

15. Nikolay Petrov, '*Prezidentskie vybory 2000 goda: konets publichnoi politiki?*' [The Presidential election of 2000: the end of public life?], Moscow, *Briefing*, Carnegie Center, vol. 2, no. 3, p. 1. 3. Yuri Levada, 'D'Eltsine à Poutine', art. cit., p. 145.

16. The presidential election of March 2000 is analyzed at the end of Chapter 3.

17. Yuri Levada, 'From Yeltsin to Putin', art.cit., p. 145.

18. 'Polpredy Prezidenta' [The President's representatives], Moscow University, *Nauchnye doklady*, no. 3, Jan. 2001.

19. Interviews with Aleksey Titkov and Leonid Smirnyagin in Moscow, interviews with regional politicians in Ryazan, during gubernatorial election, December 2000. Cf. Aleksei Titkov's study on the 2000–2001 gubernatorial elections, 'Vybory v regionakh Rossii v 2000–2001g' [Elections in the Russian regions in 2000 and 2001], a study conducted by the CERI research group in May 2001.

20. Robert W. Orttung, 'How Effective Are Putin's Federal Reforms?', *Russian Regional Report*, East West Institute, vol. 6, no. 11, 21 March 2001 (digital edition).

21. The first trial took place in 2004–2005, the second in 2009–2010. Cf. the reports and articles by Khodorkovsky's lawyers, the website Khodorkovsky.ru, and the book by Valery Panyushkin, *Berezovsky*, 2006; French translation *Le Prisonnier du silence*, Paris, Calmann-Lévy, 2007. For the second conviction in December 2010, see chapter 9.

22. William Tompson, 'Putting Yukos in Perspective', *Post-Soviet Affairs*, vol. 21, no. 2, 2005, pp. 159–81.

23. Survey conducted between 4 and 9 March 2004, www.levada-tsentr.ru.

24. See Vladimir Putin's declarations on 4 September 2004 on Russian television, and the interview with his number two, Vladislav Surkov, on 28 September 2004, in *Komsomolskaya Pravda*.

25. The Council of Europe and the Organization for Security and Cooperation in Europe (OSCE) sent teams of observers. Their findings were highly critical.

26. See the analyses of the Moscow Carnegie Centre experts, www.carnegie.ru, and the post-electoral analyses in Moscow newspapers such as the *Moscow Times*, *Kommersant* and *Novaya Gazeta*.

27. The political parties not controlled by the Kremlin had lost their capacity for action and influence since 2000. Their access to the television media was very limited; their finances were modest in comparison to the increasingly large sums given to the 'legitimist' parties, particularly the Unity Party which became United Russia. Yabloko was one of the very first democratic parties: founded in 1991, it occupied a central role in the new party system. The Union of Right Forces, SPS, was formed before the legislative elections of December 1999. Although it had a strong presence at first, thanks to its well-known leaders, it was never able to build a sufficient activist base, or win over the Russians outside of the urban elites.

28. According to the preliminary results announced by the central electoral commission on its website www.izbirkom.ru on 15 March 2004.

29. Caroline McGregor, 'Election numbers do not add up', *Moscow Times*, 19 March 2004.

30. The economist Sergey Glaziev only won 4.1 per cent of the votes, and Oleg Malyshkin, Zhirinovky's man (Vladimir Zhirinovky had agreed not to stand so as not to tarnish Putin's victory), only won 2 per cent. Sergey Mironov, President of Parliament's upper house, gained less than 1 per cent.

31. Irina Khakamada campaigned alone, without the support of her former SPS friends or of the leaders of the Yabloko movement.

32. Francesca Mereu, 'Governors lining up to join the Party', *Moscow Times*, 24 September 2004. In May 2000, the newly elected President changed the composition of the Federation Council. Its members were now appointed, whereas previously the regional Governor, elected through direct universal suffrage, and the President of the provincial assembly, also elected, were *ex officio* members of the upper house.

33. Mikhail Krasnov, 'Putin iskazil Konstitutsiu' [Putin has twisted the Constitution], *gazeta.ru*, 14 September 2004.

34. 'The case against a lapdog judiciary', Comment, *Moscow Times*, 4 October 2004.

35. See the interview with Boris Yeltsin in *Moskovskie Novosti*, no. 36, 24 September 2004. He deplored 'the abandonment of the spirit and the letter of the Constitution which the nation adopted through referendum in 1993'.

36. 'In society, nobody trusts words any more', interview with Vsevolod Bogdanov, Novayagazeta.ru/data/2007/32/24html

37. Oleg Panfilov, 'Putin and the Press: The Revival of Soviet-Style Propaganda', The Foreign Policy Centre, London, June 2005.

38. Floriana Fossato, 'Vladimir Putin and Russian Television "Family"', *Les Cahiers Russie/Russia Papers*, CERI-Sciences Po, no. 1, 2006.

39. *Kommersant*, 9 October 2007.

40. Anne Gazier, 'Vingt ans de réforme des systèmes juridiques and judiciaires en Russie: quelques éléments pour un premier bilan', *Revue d'Études Comparatives Est-Ouest*, vol. 38, no. 2, 2007, p. 20.

41. Ibid., p. 23. Anne Gazier explains that, during the Soviet period, this judicial surveillance (*sudebnyi sobor*) allowed the higher courts to overrule the judgments of lower courts with an irreversible judgment. This power was not subject to any time frame. At present, 'the main failing of this authority is to prolong trials' and 'it is highly criticized by the Council of Europe'.

42. The Colonel Budanov case in 2001–2003 was the focus of all eyes. In 2003, tank commander Budanov was sentenced to ten years in prison for kidnapping, torturing and strangling a young Chechen girl, Elza Kungayeva. He was released on parole in 2009 and shot in a contract-style shooting in Moscow in June 2011, http://www.guardian.co.uk/world/2011/jun/10.

43. Levada Centre survey involving 1,600 people in Russia, 13–16 June 2007, www.levada.ru

44. The Beslan mothers committee was humiliated several times by the authorities. Even when Vladimir Putin finally agreed to meet them, one year after the tragedy, he did so in an unpleasant manner (he offered to meet them on the date of the anniversary, which was unbearable for most mothers who wanted to be at the graves of their children in Beslan, and not at the Kremlin) and without offering any apologies or true remorse. The committee was not even able to secure an honest trial against the local officials (*Moscow Times*, 4 May 2007).

45. Zoltan Barany, 'Civil-Military Relations and Institutional Decay: Explaining Russian Military Politics', *Europe-Asia Studies*, vol. 60, no. 4, June 2008, pp. 581–604.

46. *Le Monde*, 1–2 June 2008. The full version of the interview was available on the paper's website for a few days, and was then removed.

6. A DISTRUSTFUL SOCIETY

1. Yuri Levada, 'D'Eltsine à Poutine. Les élections présidentielles en Russie, 1991–2004', *art. cit.*, pp. 141–2.

2. Basile Kerblay, *La société soviétique contemporaine*, op. cit.

3. Yuri Levada, *Entre le passé et l'avenir. L'Homme soviétique ordinaire*, Paris, Presses de Sciences Po, 1993.

4. Interview with Andrey Illarionov by Maxime Blant, Liberal'naya Missiya foundation, Moscow, November 2006, website www.liberal.ru.

5. Meeting with Vladimir Putin, Valdai Club, 8 September 2005. From the author's notes.

6. Levada Centre opinion poll, *EU-Russia Centre Newsletter*, Brussels, Summer 2007.

7. Boris Dubin, 'Osobyi put' i sotsialnyi poryadok v sovremennoy Rossii', *Vestnik obshchestvennogo mneniya*, 1 (103), January-March 2010, pp. 10–1.

8. Opinion poll 'The state and its citizens', carried out between 13 and 16 June 2007, on a representative sample of 1,600 people in Russia. www.levada.ru/press/20070727

9. Levada.ru, poll conducted on 23–27 January 2009.

10. Natalya Gevorkyan writes for the independent website gazeta.ru. Quote from a conference at the EU-Russia Centre, Brussels, 12 December 2006. From the author's notes.

11. Floriana Fossato, 'Vladimir Putin and the Russian Television "Family"', *Les Cahiers Russie/Russia Papers*, CERI-Sciences Po, 2006.

12. Presentation by Georgy Bovt at the same conference of 12 December 2006. A Levada Centre survey carried out in July 2008 showed that 82 per cent of Russians never holiday abroad and 12 per cent very rarely, www.levada.ru.

13. Levada Centre opinion polls in 2004 and 2005. In March 2006, 61 per cent of respondents felt that an ordinary citizen could not expect a fair trial. *Russian Public Opinion Annual*, Levada Centre, Moscow, 2007, p. 80.

14. See the works of the sociologists Yuri Levada, Vladimir Shlapentokh and Boris Grushin (see bibliography at the end of this book), the book edited by Alexis Berelowitch and Michel Wieviorka, *Les Russes d'en bas: Enquête sur la Russie post-communiste*, Paris, Seuil, 1998; Gilles Favarel-Garrigues and Kathy Rousselet, *La société russe en quête d'ordre: Avec Vladimir Poutine?*, Paris, CERI-Autrement, 2004.

15. Montesquieu, *The Spirit of the Laws*, ed. and transl. Anne M. Cohler, Basia Carolyn Miller and Harold Samuel Stone, Cambridge University Press, 2008, Book III, ch. 9, p. 28.

16. Vladimir Shlapentokh, *Fear in Contemporary Society: Its Negative and Positive Effects*, New York, Palgrave Macmillan, 2006, p. 1.

17. Ibid., p. 2.

18. Basile Kerblay, *La société soviétique contemporaine*, op. cit.; Vladimir Voinovich, *The Anti-Soviet Soviet Union*, op. cit.

19. Alexander Zinoviev, *The Yawning Heights*, trans. G. Clough, London, Random House, 1979; idem, *Homo Sovieticus*, trans. C. Janson, London, Gollancz, 1985; Vladimir Bukovsky, *To Build a Castle*, New York, Viking, 1979.

20. Anna Politkovskaya, *A Russian Diary*, trans. Arch Tait, London, Harvill Secker, 2007 p. 107.

21. Montesquieu, op. cit., p. 57.

22. Interview with Vladimir Putin, *Le Monde*, 1–2 June 2008.

23. Debra Javeline, 'Political Passivity and Russia's Health Crisis', Woodrow Wilson International Center, Kennan Institute, *Occasional Paper* 287, 2003.

24. Murray Feshbach, *Russia's Health and Demographic Crises: Policy Implications and Consequences*, The Chemical and Biological Arms Control Institute, Washington,

2003. See also the website of the Russian demographer Anatoly Vishnevsky, demoscope.ru.

25. Documentary by Manon Loiseau, 'La fureur russe', *Envoyé spécial*, France 2, 7 December 2006.

26. Whereas foreign experts tried to highlight the fairness of universal models, the Russians replied yes in principle, but that in the specific case of Russia, it went against people's thinking and the administrations were not geared for it.

27. Boris Dubin, 'The Symbolic Figure of the President', conference 'Elections in France and in Russia', November 2004, Moscow region, author's notes. See also Yuri Levada, 'D'Eltsine à Poutine', art. cit.

28. Levada Centre survey, June 2008, www.levada.ru/press

29. The habitual rhetoric of some of the Putin regime spin doctors such as Gleb Pavlovsky or Sergey Markov, whose words are widely reproduced in the media.

30. Lilia Shevtsova, 'Rossiya pered novym politicheskim tsiklom: paradoksy stabil'nosti i Petro-State' [Russia on the verge of a new cycle: the paradoxes of stability and the Petro-State], in Aleksandr Smolar (ed.), *Putin's Empire*, Warsaw, Stefan Batory Foundation, 2007; e-book, www.batory.org.pl/doc/putins-empire.pdf

31. See the discussion around a panel session held on 26 April 2006, *Prognosis* magazine, 'Strakh kak politicheskii instrument' [Fear as a political instrument], prognosis.ru/print.html; see also Lev Gudkov, *Negativnaya identichnost* [Negative identity], Moscow, Novoe Literaturnoe Obozrenie, 2004.

32. Andrew Wilson, *Ukraine's Orange Revolution*, New Haven, Yale University Press, 2005.

33. Vladimir Putin's attitude came out clearly in one of his long television Q&A sessions 'with the people', on the programme *Pryamaya liniya*, Channel 1, Russian television, 25 October 2006.

34. Opinion poll, 15–18 August 2008, www.levada.ru

35. Igor Klyamkin, 'Negrazhdanskoe obshchestvo' [Uncivil society], in Aleksandr Smolar (ed.), *Putin's Empire*, Warsaw, Stefan Batory Foundation, 2007; online at www.batory.org.pl/doc/putins-empire.pdf.

36. Cf. the regular opinion polls carried out by the Levada Centre, Sarah Mendelson and Theodore Gerber's analysis, 'Us and Them: Anti-American View of the Putin Generation', *The Washington Quarterly*, Spring 2008, and the Russian report of the magazine *Pro and Contra* (Moscow Carnegie Centre), March-June 2008, devoted to Russian society's adaptation.

7. THE PUTIN SYSTEM: UNANIMITY AND AUTOCRACY

1. Russian anecdote inspired by Jean de la Fontaine's famous fable, "The Crow and The Fox". Cf. Amandine Régamey, *Prolétaires de tous pays, excusez moi!, op. cit.*, p. 220.

2. Jean-Charles Lallemand and Virginie Symaniec, *Biélorussie: Mécanique d'une dictature*, Paris, Les Petits Matins, 2007.

3. Article 81, paragraph 3, stipulates, 'No one person shall hold the office of President of the Russian Federation for more than two terms in succession'. Unsurprisingly, the prevailing interpretation in Russia in 2008 held that it is possible for a president who has already served two consecutive terms to run for President after a period during which the position has been held by another person.

4. *Epokha Eltsina*, op. cit.; Lilia Shevtsova and Igor Klyamkin, 'The Tactical Origins of Russia's New Political Institutions', in Archie Brown (ed.), *Contemporary Russian Politics*, Oxford University Press, 2001, pp. 14–6.

5. Cf. Chapter 3.

6. Aleksey Venediktov, interview in Paris with French specialists in Russia, October 2007.

7. On the programme *Pryamaya liniya* (direct line), RTR, Russians ask questions of their President, simulcast in several Russian cities. It was during the 25 October 2006 broadcast that these remarks were made to Putin.

8. Dmitry Oreshkin, 'Vybory i geographiya administrativnogo resursa' [Elections and the geography of 'administrative resources'], Geography Institute of the Russian Academy of Sciences; an abridged version of this study was published in *Novaya Gazeta*, November 2007. See below Oreshkin's analysis of the 2 December vote.

9. 'Russia and Europe' conference organized by the Krynica Forum in Vilnius, March 2006.

10. Dmitry Rogozin was appointed Russia's ambassador to NATO in December 2007. He had become a nuisance in Russia, as his populism was gaining ground, but his anti-Westernism and his extremist positions well served Moscow's aggressive strategy towards the West. He proved particularly useful during the crisis between Russia and the West in the summer of 2008, with regard to Russian military operations in Georgia to break up the country by orchestrating the secession of Abkhazia and South Ossetia.

11. Meetings with Vladimir Putin, Valdai Club, 8 September 2005 at the Kremlin and 9 September 2006 in Novo-Ogarevo, the President's official residence outside Moscow. Author's notes.

12. Few foreign officials criticized the distortion of the text and spirit of the Russian Constitution, and some, such as the French President and the Prime Minister of Italy, even congratulated Putin on the legislative elections of 2 December 2007, which he transformed into a plebiscite in highly controversial conditions, as will be seen further on.

13. Olga Kryshtanovskaya, 'Putin's Militocracy', *Post-Soviet Affairs*, 19, 4, 2003, pp. 289–306; 'Opasnye liudi v shtatskom' [Dangerous people in civilian clothes], *Ezhenedel'nyi Zhournal*, 15 March 2004.

14. On 25 August 2008, the State Duma *unanimously* voted to recognize the independence of Abkhazia and South Ossetia, two separatist provinces in Georgia. On 26 August, President Medvedev recognized the independence of these two little territories by decree.

15. Interview with Russian political scientist Maria Lipman, Editor-in-Chief of the Russian journal *Pro et contra* (Carnegie Moscow Center), Moscow, December 2007.

16. The 'Special Operation' was broadly criticized on independent websites such as polit.ru, novayagazeta.ru and panorama.ru.

17. The OSCE issued a very terse declaration on 16 November 2007, www.osce.org/item/27967.

18. Speech given at the conference on security issues, Munich, 10 February 2007, www.kremlin.ru/archives.

19. Cf. Chapter 5, where this notion, suggested by Vladislav Surkov, is defined.

20. Predictions of a few specialists in Moscow on the day of the election. And we came within 1 per cent of the preliminary results announced by the Central Election Commission (TsIK) on 4 December 2007.

21. As a reminder, the four political parties represented in the State Duma elected on 2 December 2007 are the dominant party, United Russia, presided over by Vladimir Putin; the other 'governing party', Fair Russia, presided over by the President of the Federation Council (upper house of parliament); the Communist Party (KPRF); and the liberal-democratic party run by Vladimir Zhirinovsky (nationalist right), very loyal to the Kremlin. Only the Communist Party is not a vassal of Putin, and its 56 elected members moreover voted against his appointment to the position of Prime Minister on 8 May 2008.

22. Interviews with the author, Tver, 30 November 2007.

23. Dmitry Oreshkin, *Novaya Gazeta*, December 2007, and *Esprit*, art.cit., January 2008; the articles by Yulia Latynina, *Moscow Times*, December 2007, www.themoscowtimes.ru. This author followed the campaign and vote in Tver and Moscow.

24. Mikhail Sokolov, 'Le vote confisqué en Russie. Études des élections régionales de 2007', *Les Cahiers Russie/Russia Papers*, no. 5, 2007.

25. www.levada.ru.

26. Election experts Andrey Buzin (member of the Moscow electoral commission since 2001), for Golos, and Dmitry Oreshkin and Vladimir Kozlov (Mercator Centre), authors of the article 'Kak nas poschitali. I za kogo' [How our votes were counted. And for whom], *Novaya Gazeta*, 24 April 2008. Available at www.novayagazeta.ru.

27. Polling stations visited in Moscow on 2 December 2007.

28. Meetings at the Valdai Club in Moscow, 8 and 9 September 2006.

29. Natalya Narochnitskaya, *Que reste-t-il de notre victoire? Russie-Occident: le malentendu*, Paris, Éditions des Syrtes, 2008. The Russian title is different: *Za chto i s kem my voevali?* [For what and with whom did we fight?].

30. The Khodorkovsky affair is discussed in Chapter 5.

31. Étienne de La Boétie, *De la servitude volontaire ou le Contr'un....*, Paris Gallimard, 1993, p. 79 (translated as *Discourse on Voluntary Servitude*, New York, Columbia

University Press, 1942, trans. Harry Kurz, available online at http://www.Constitution.org/la_boetie/serv_vol.htm, 15 June 2010.

32. Ibid., p. 84.
33. Ibid., p. 87.
34. Lev Gudkov, 'L'opinion des élites sur l'État et la modernisation en Russie', *Les Cahiers Russie/Russia Papers*, CERI-Sciences Po, no. 6, 2008, p. 11. This remarkable study of the Russian elites will be analyzed in greater detail in the following chapter.
35. Ibid.
36. Igor Klyamkin et al., *Rossiiskoe gosudarstvo: vchera, sevodnya, zavtra* [The Russian state: yesterday, today and tomorrow], Moscow, Liberal'naya Missiya Foundation, Novoe Izdatel'stvo, 2007.
37. The other four ministers of the presidium are the Ministers of the Economy, Agriculture, Social Development and Health, and Regional Development.

8. THE PUTIN SYSTEM: PATRONAGE AND THE ENRICHMENT OF THE ELITES

1. Cf. Vladimir Milov and Boris Nemtsov, 'Putin. Itogi' [Putin. An assessment], March 2008, http://grani.ru/politics/Russia/3236.html.
2. For an appraisal of the years 2000–2007, see Pekka Sutela, 'The Legacy of the Putin Era', *BOFIT online* 6/2008, Bank of Finland Institute for Economies in Transition, Helsinki; Françoise Daucé and Gilles Walter, 'Russie 2006. Entre dérive politique et succès économiques', *Le Courrier des Pays de l'Est*, no. 1059, 2007, pp. 6–29; Iwona Wisniewska, 'The Invisible Hand… of the Kremlin. Capitalism "à la russe"', Centre for Eastern Studies, Warsaw, February 2007.
3. Pekka Sutela, 'Forecasting the Russian Economy for 2010–2012', *Russian Analytical Digest*, no. 88, 29 November 2010, pp. 2–7; Julian Cooper, 'The Innovative Potential of the Russian Economy', ibid., pp. 8–11, available online: www.res.ethz.ch.
4. Cf. Igor Fedyukin, 'Putin's Eight Years', *Kommersant*, 2008, www.kommersant.com/p804651.
5. Andrey Illarionov, cited in Catrina Stewart, 'From Battered to "Island of Stability"', *Moscow Times*, 28 February 2008, www.moscowtimes.ru/stories/2008/02/28.
6. Interviews with Vladimir Milov, former Deputy Minister of Energy, who has become highly critical of the regime and its energy policy, and was Director of the Institute for Energy Policy, in January 2007 in Moscow, and in May 2009 in Brussels. See the studies conducted by this institute at www.energypolicy.ru and the annual OECD reports, www.oecd.com.
7. Pekka Sutela, "How Strong is Russia's Economic Foundation?", *Centre for European Reform Policy Brief*, October 2009, www.cer.org.uk.
8. Julian Cooper, art. cit., p. 8.
9. William Tompson, 'Back to the Future: Thoughts on State Capitalism in Russia', *Les Cahiers Russie/Russia Papers*, CERI-Sciences Po, no. 6, 2008.

10. The Economist Evgeny Yasin, former Minister of the Economy, head of the Higher School of Economics in Moscow, uses the notion of a corporatist state to criticize the rentier and clientelistic turn taken by the regime: 'Noveishii rossiiskii goskapitalizm' [The new Russian state capitalism], *Liberal'naya Missiya*, Moscow, www.liberal.ru/article.

11. Nadia Popova, 'Putin accuses Mechel of tax evasion', *Moscow Times*, 29 July 2008.

12. Sergey Aleksashenko, 'Russia Two Years after the Crisis', round table at the Carnegie Centre, Moscow, 12 October 2010, see www.carnegie.ru.

13. Cf. Max Delany, 'Record 87 Russians on *Forbes* Rich List', *Moscow Times*, 7 March 2008, www.moscowtimes.ru/stories//2008/03/07/002.

14. Alexander Voloshin, Chief of the Presidential Administration since the last years of Yeltsin's presidency, had to leave his post a few days after the Head of the oil giant Yukos was arrested. This moment symbolically marks the shift to a new stage in Putin's oligarchy, liberated from the Yeltsin legacy.

15. 'It's our country's justice system, we must trust it'. Conversation with Khodorkovsky's parents outside the court in May 2005.

16. Meeting with Robert Amsterdam at CERI-Sciences Po, November 2003, a few weeks after the arrest.

17. Interview with the author in Moscow, January 2005.

18. Interview with the author in Paris, October 2004.

19. Meeting of Valdai Club with Vladimir Putin, 6 September 2004, Author's notes.

20. N. Varlamova, *Sovremennyi rossiiskii federalizm: konstitutsionnaya model' I politico-pravovaya dinamika* [Contemporary Russian, federalism: Constitutional model and political-legal dynamic], Moscow, Institute of Law and Public Policy, p. 73. See Bill Bowring's analysis of Varlamova's work, 'The Russian Constitutional System', in Marc Weller and Katherine Nobbs (eds), *Asymmetric Autonomy and the Settlement of Ethnic Conflicts*, Philadelphia, University of Pennsylvania Press, 2010, pp. 60–1.

21. Montequieu, *The Spirit of the Laws*, op. cit., p. 28.

22. Ibid., p. 57.

23. Press conference given by President Putin at the Kremlin, Moscow, 14 February 2008.

24. Linda Aström, 'Gatekeepers of Democracy? A Comparative Study of Elite Support in Russia and the Baltic States', *Örebro Studies in Political Science* 18, Örebro, Sweden.

25. Since the early 2000s, the opacity of leadership circles has led some researchers to undertake to decipher the make-up of the most important institutions and point out the growing role of 'men in uniform'. Olga Kryshtanovskaya and Stephen White, *Europe-Asia Studies*, art. cit.; Barbara Vernon, 'Les élites en uniforme', *Pouvoirs*, 2005, art. cit.

26. Cf. the INDEM Foundation reports, Moscow, www.indem.ru.

27. Alena Ledeneva, *Russia's Economy of Favours: Blat, Networking and Informal Exchange*, Cambridge University Press, 1998.

28. Lev Gudkov, Boris Dubin, Yuri Levada, *Problema 'elity' v sevodnyashnei Rossii* (The Problem of elites in Russia today'), Moscow, Liberal'naya Missiya, 2007.

29. Gleb Pavlovsky, *Vragi Putina*, Moscow, Europa, 2007.

30. Lev Gudkov, *Analyse des élites russes*, seminar given at CERI-Sciences Po, Paris, 17 September 2007.

31. Lev Gudkov, 'Les élites dirigeantes ne croient pas à la modernisation de la Russie', *Les Cahiers Russie/Russia Papers*, CERI, Paris, no. 6, 2008.

32. Author's trips to Russian provinces, election monitoring, in the 1990s and 2000s.

33. Lev Gudkov, 'Les élites russes ne croient pas à la modernisation de la Russie', art. cit.

34. *Problema 'elity' v sevodnyashnei Rossii*, op. cit.

35. Ibid., p. 7 and p. 9.

36. Ibid., p. 14.

37. Respondents lived in the fourteen largest Russian cities. In Moscow, they earned over 1,500 euros per month, in Saint Petersburg over 1,000 euros and in the other cities over 800 euros per month. Average income in Russia was about 400 euros per month in 2008. Levada Centre, 'The Russian Middle Class. Its Views of its own Country and of Europe', Moscow, June 2008, survey taken for the EU-Russia Centre in Brussels.

38. Richard Rose and Neil Munro, 'Do Russians see their Future in Europe or the CIS?' *Europe-Asia Studies*, vol. 60, no. 1, January 2008, pp. 49–66.

39. In an opinion poll taken between 15 and 18 August 2008 on the conflict in Georgia, 74 per cent of the respondents answered that the fault lay with the United States, which took Georgia hostage, and 70 per cent believed that Russia did everything it could to curb escalation; www.levada.ru. Official propaganda carried more weight than alternative information sources on the Internet. Russia's leaders did not hesitate to accuse the Georgians of 'genocide' against the Ossetians, whereas the fighting between 8 and 11 August claimed a few hundred lives. It should be pointed out that 59 per cent of Russians were in favour of international mediation, which reflects the fear of a facedown between Moscow and Tbilisi.

40. The request to release Khodorkovsky on parole was rejected by the Ingodinski court in Chita, Siberia, 22 August 2008.

41. Khodorkovsky and Lebedev were found guilty on 27 December; it took judge Danilkin three days to read the judgment; the sentence was pronounced on 30 December 2010. See chapter 9.

42. 11 per cent gave no answer. 2005 poll, www.levada.ru website.

43. Conference, Stefan-Batory Foundation, Warsaw, 5–6 December 2006. Papers published as an edited book online, *Putin's Empire*, op. cit.

44. Nikolai Petrov, 'Regional Governors under Putin and Medvedev', paper presented at CERI-Sciences Po, Paris, June 2010, and Carnegie Briefing, 2011.

45. Olga Kryshtanovskaya, *Les Élites d'en haut*, working paper, presented at the Observatoire de la Russie seminar series, at CERI-Sciences Po, Paris, 17 January

2008. See also her analysis 'Has-Beens: Trends of Downward Mobility of the Russian Elite', *Sociological Research*, vol. 44, no. 2, March-April 2005, pp. 7–54.

46. Andrei Soldatov and Irina Borogan, *The New Nobility: The Restoration of Russia's Security State and the Enduring Legacy of the KGB*, New York, Public Affairs, 2010.

47. Author's interview with geographer and political scientist Dmitry Oreshkin, Moscow, September 2009.

48. See in particular Robert Coalson's article, 'The gun is hanging on the wall', *Moscow Times*, 10 January 2008, and the kreml.org website. Gleb Pavlovsky lost his job in the spring of 2011.

49. See the excellent demographic and sociological website, www.demoscope.ru, and Anatoli Vishnevsky, *Rossyia pered demograficheskim vyborom* [Russia faced with population choices], Moscow, Higher School of Economics, 2007.

50. Lev Gudkov, 'Pochemu my ne liubim priezhnikh?' [Why we don't like immigrants], www.demoscope.ru/weekly/2006/0231.

9. NATIONAL EXCEPTIONALISM

1. This final chapter provides an update and expansion of the book written in French in 2008. Owing to its limited scope, it is an epilogue rather than an exhaustive presentation of Russian political and social developments from 2009 to October 2011.

2. International Security Conference, Munich, 7 February 2007, available on www.youtube.com.

3. For an in-depth assessment of the spiral of violence between Moscow and Tbilisi in the 2000s see Roy Allison, 'Russia Resurgent? Moscow's Campaign to 'Coerce Georgia to Peace" *International Affairs*, 84: 6, 2008, pp. 1145–71; Ronald Asmus, *A Little War That Shook the World*, Basingstoke, Palgrave Macmillan, 2010; 'Russia-Georgia Relations', *Russian Analytical Digest*, no. 68, 23 November 2009.

4. President Sarkozy invited a few scholars and journalists to exchange views on the war and its aftermath, Elysée Palace, 2 September 2008. Author's notes.

5. www.ceiig.ch/Report.html

6. Levada Centre opinion poll, conducted in May 2009, posted on www.polit.ru, 16 June 2009.

7. Vladimir Mukhin, *Nezavisimaya Gazeta*, 22 February, quoted by Paul Goble, 'Window on Eurasia: Post-Soviet States Boost Arms Spending', 23 February 2011, www.windowoneurasia.blogspot.com.

8. Zbigniew Brzezinski argued this point early on, at a conference in Vilnius, under the aegis of President Adamkus, January 2005, author's notes; Bill Bowring, 'Russia and Human Rights: Incompatible Opposites', *Göttingen Journal of International Law*, 1 (2009) 2, pp. 257–78.

9. Aleksandr Smolar (ed.), *Putin's Empire*, Stefan Batory Foundation, Warsaw, 2007, online at www.batory.org.

10. See the poll results and Lev Gudkov's analysis posted on www.levada.ru, 2 February 2011.

11. Gennady Gudkov, lenta.ru, February 2011.

12. On religion and extremism, see the work of the SOVA Centre, led by Aleksandr Verkhovsky, www.sova.ru.

13. See Human Rights Watch reports, works by Tatyana Lokshina, Grigory Shvedov, and the CSIS study 'Violence in the North Caucasus. Summer 2010: Not Just a Chechen Conflict', www.csis.org.

14. Kremlin.ru and press coverage of the Davos conference of 2011.

15. A. Soldatov and I. Borogan, op. cit., p. 4.

16. Ibid., p. 173.

17. Ibid., p. 3.

18. Ibid., p. 64.

19. Bill Bowring, 'Russia and Human Rights: Incompatible Opposites?', *Göttingen Journal of International Law*, 1 (2009) 2, pp. 257–78.

20. Author's notes, Moscow, 28 October–2 November 2010, author's exchanges with Russian and foreign journalists who attended the closing days of the trial on 27–30 December.

21. Conversation with Karinna Moskalenko in Moscow, 31 October 2010.

22. *Wall Street Journal*, February 2011.

23. Discussion with economists from the Higher School of Economics, Moscow, November 2010.

24. Alena Ledeneva, *How Russia Really Works: The Informal Practices That Shaped Post-Soviet Politics and Business*, Ithaca, NY, Cornell University Press, 2006.

25. Masha Lipman, 'Putin's no-participation pact', *Moscow Times*, 1 April 2011, themoscowtimes.com

26. The forty-page booklet entitled 'Luzhkov. Itogi' [Luzhkov. An Assessment] appeared on 8 September.

27. Cohabitation occurred for the first time in the history of France's Fifth Republic in 1986 when the Socialist President François Mitterrand had to appoint the right-wing Jacques Chirac head of government after the Left's failure in the legislative elections.

28. Dmitry Medvedev's lecture at the London School of Economics, on the eve of the G20 summit meeting in London, 2 April 2009, author's notes.

CONCLUSION

1. A week after the Domodedovo terrorist attack in Domodedovo airport. See opinion polls and Lev Gudkov's analysis posted on 2 February 2011, www.levada.ru.

BIBLIOGRAPHY

State, Change, Democracy, Authoritarianism

Books

Arendt, Hannah, *The Origins of Totalitarianism*, New York: Harcourt, Brace and Company, 1951.

Aron, Raymond, *Les Étapes de la pensée sociologique*, Paris: Gallimard, 1965.

———— *Penser la liberté, penser la démocratie*, Paris: Gallimard, 'Quarto', 2005.

Badie, Bertrand and Pierre Birnbaum, *Sociologie de l'État*, Paris: Grasset, 1979.

Bell, Daniel, *The End of Ideology*, New York: The Free Press, 1962 (in particular chapter 14, 'Ten Theories in Search of Reality: The Prediction of Soviet Behavior').

Birnbaum, Pierre and Jean Leca (eds), *Sur l'individualisme*, Paris: Presses de la FNSP, 1965.

Courtois, Stéphane (ed.), *Le jour se lève. L'héritage du totalitarisme en Europe. 1953–2005*, Paris: Éditions du Rocher, 'Démocratie ou totalitarisme', 2006.

Elias, Norbert, *The Society of Individuals*, Oxford: Blackwell, 1991.

Foucault, Michel, *Sécurité, territoire, population. Cours au Collège de France, 1977–1978*, Paris: Seuil/Gallimard, 1994.

Gauchet, Marcel, *La Démocratie contre elle-même*, Paris: Gallimard, 2002.

Glucksmann, André, *La Cuisinière et le mangeur d'hommes*, Paris: Seuil, 1975.

Habermas, Jürgen, *The Structural Transformation of the Public Sphere*, Cambridge, MA: MIT Press, 1989 and 1991.

———— *The Postnational Constellation*, Cambridge, MA: MIT Press, 2001.

Hassner, Pierre, *La Violence et la paix. De la bombe atomique au nettoyage ethnique*, Paris: Seuil, 2000.

Hegel, Friedrich, *Elements of the Philosophy of Right*, Cambridge University Press, 1991.

Hirschman, Albert O., *Shifting Involvements. Private Interest and Public Action*, Princeton University Press, 1982 and 2002.

Hobbes, Thomas, *Leviathan or The Matter, Form and Power of a Common Wealth Ecclesiastical and Civil*, London: Barnes & Noble, 2004 [original publication 1651].

Holmes, Stephen, *Benjamin Constant and the Making of Modern Liberalism*, New Haven (Conn.): Yale University Press, 1984.

Linz, Juan J., *Totalitarian and Autoritarian Regimes*, Boulder: Lynne Rienner, 2000.

Locke, John, *Two Treatises of Government*, Cambridge University Press, 1988.

La Boétie, Étienne de, *De la servitude volontaire ou le Contr'un*, Paris: Gallimard, 1993.

Lallement, Michel, *Histoire des idées sociologiques*, tome 1: *Des origines à Weber*, Paris: Nathan, 1993.

Lefort, Claude, *L'Invention démocratique*, Paris: Fayard, 1994.

Machiavelli, Nicolas, *The Prince*, Oxford University Press, 1998 [original publication 1532].

Mendras, Henri and Michel Forsé, *Le Changement social*, Paris: Armand Colin, 1983.

Merton, Robert K., *Social Theory and Social Structure*, New York: Macmillan, 1968.

Mill, John Stuart, *On Liberty*, Minneapolis (Minn.): Filiquarian Publishing LLC, 2006.

Ozer, Atila, *L'État*, textes choisis et présentés, Paris: Flammarion, 1998.

Polanyi, Karl, *The Great Transformation*, Boston: Beacon Press, 2001.

Ricoeur, Paul, *L'Idéologie et l'utopie*, Paris: Seuil, 'Points', 1997.

Root, Hilton, *The Fountain of Privilege: Political Foundations of Markets in Old Regime France and England*, University of California Press, 1994.

Rosanvallon, Pierre, *Le Peuple introuvable*, Paris: Gallimard, 2006.

Weber, Max, *The Protestant Ethic and the Spirit of Capitalism*, London: Routledge, 2001.

——— *Economy and Society: An Outline of Interpretive Sociology*, University of California Press, 1978.

Journals

'La démocratie majoritaire', *Pouvoirs*, no. 85, pp. 5–19, Paris: Seuil, 1998.

'L'opposition', *Pouvoirs*, no. 108, Paris: Seuil, 2004.

The History of the State in Russia

Books

Berlin, Isaiah, *The Soviet Mind: Russian Culture under Communism*, Washington, DC: Brookings, 2004 (first publication in 1949).

Berdyaev, Nicolas, *The Origin of Russian Communism*, Ann Arbor: University of Michigan Press, 1960.

Besançon, Alain, *Le Tsarévitch immolé*, Paris: Plon, 1967.

——— *Présent soviétique et passé russe*, Hachette, 'Pluriel', 1980.

Billington, James H., *The Icon and the Axe: An Interpretative History of Russian Culture*, New York: Vintage, 1970.

Fainsod, Merle, *How Russia is Ruled*, Cambridge (Mass.): Harvard University Press, 1953.

Grossman, Vasily, *Life and Fate*, New York: Harper & Row, 1986.

Grushin, Boris, *Chetyre zhizni Rossii* ['Russia's four lives'], Moscow: Progress, 2001.

Heller, Michel, *Histoire de la Russie et de son empire*, Paris: Calmann-Lévy, 1997.

———— *La Machine et les rouages: La formation de l'homme soviétique*, Paris: Calmann-Lévy, 1985.

Heller, Michel and Aleksandr Nekritch, *L'Utopie au pouvoir. Histoire de l'URSS de 1917 à nos jours*, Paris: Calmann-Lévy, 1982.

Hosking, Geoffrey, *Rulers and Victims: The Russians in the Soviet Union*, Cambridge, Mass.: Harvard University Press, 2006.

Inkeles, Alex, *Social Change in Soviet Russia*, Cambridge (Mass.): Harvard University Press, 1968.

Kerblay, Basile, *La Société soviétique contemporaine*, Paris: Armand Colin, 1977.

Kliamkin, Igor *et al.*, *Natsional'nyi vopros* ['The national question'], Moscow: Liberal'naya Missiya, 2004.

Klyuchevsky, Vasily, *Kurs russkoi istorii* ['A lesson in Russian history'], Moscow, published in London: Dent, 1911.

Koyré, Alexandre, *La Philosophie et le problème national en Russie au début du XIXe siècle*, Paris: Librairie Honoré Champion, 1929.

Leites, Nathan, *The Operational Code of the Politburo*, Rand Corporation, New York: McGraw-Hill, 1951.

———— *A Study of Bolshevism*, Glencoe: The Free Press, 1953.

Leroy-Beaulieu, Anatole, *L'Empire des tsars et les Russes*, 3 volumes (first edition between 1881 and 1888), Lausanne: L'Âge d'Homme, 1988.

Martin, Malia, *The Soviet Tragedy: a History of Socialism in Russia*, New York: Free Press, 1992.

Pipes, Richard, *Russia Under the Old Regime*, London: Weidenfeld and Nicolson, 1974.

———— *The Formation of the Soviet Union: Communism and Nationalism 1917–1923*, Cambridge, MA : Harvard University Press, 1954 and 1997.

———— *Property and Freedom*, New York: Alfred A. Knopf, 2000.

Saltykov-Shchedrin, Mikhail, *Le Bon vieux temps*, Lausanne: L'Âge d'Homme, 1997 (this novel, written between 1886 and 1889, describes provincial life in Russia).

Shelley, Louise I., *Crime and Modernization: The Impact of Industrialization and Urbanization on Crime*, Carbondale: Southern Illinois University Press, 1981.

Sinyavsky, Andrei, *Soviet Civilization: a Cultural History*, New York: Arcade Pub., 1990.

Solnick, Steven, *Stealing the State*, Cambridge, MA: Harvard University Press, 1998.

Solzhenitsyn, Aleksandr, *The Gulag Archipelago*, New York: Harper & Row, 1978.

Ulam, Adam, *The Bolsheviks: The Intellectual, Personal and Political History of the Triumph of Communism in Russia*, New York: Collier Books, 1965.

Vishnevsky, Anatoly, *Serp i Rubl* ['Sickle and Rouble'], Moscow: OGI, 1998.

Voinovich, Vladimir, *The Anti-Soviet Soviet Union*, New York: Harcourt Brace Jovanovich, 1986.

Voslenski, Michael, *Nomenklatura: Anatomy of the Soviet Ruling Class*, London: The Bodley Head, 1984.

Zinovyev, Aleksandr, *Yawning Heights*, New York: Random House, 1979.

Articles

Raeff, Marc, 'Un empire comme les autres?', *Cahiers du Monde Russe et Soviétique*, vol. 30 (3–4), July-December 1989, p. 322.

The Transformation, 1985–1999

Books

Ackerman, Galia, *Tchernobyl, retour sur un désastre*, Paris: Buchet-Chastel, 2006.

Afanassiev, Yuri (ed.), *Inogo ne dano. Glasnost', demokratia, sotsializm* ['There is no other choice. Glasnost, democracy, socialism'], Moscow: Progress, 1988.

Baturin, Yuri et al., *Epokha Eltsina. Ocherki politicheskoi istorii* ['The Yeltsin era. Insight into a political history'], Moscow: Vagrius, 2001.

Berelowitch, Alexis and Michel Wievorka, *Les Russes d'en bas. Enquête sur la Russie post-communiste*, Paris: Seuil, 1996.

Gorbachev, Mikhail, *Perestroika. New Thinking For Our Country and the World*, New York: Harper & Row, 1987.

——— *Memoirs*, New York: Doubleday, 1996.

Levada, Yuri, *Entre le passé et l'avenir. L'homme soviétique ordinaire*, Paris: Presses de la FNSP, 1993.

Lukin, Alexander, *Political Culture of Russian "Democrats"*, Oxford University Press, 2000.

Mendras, Marie (ed.), *Un État pour la Russie*, Brussels: Complexe, 1992.

Reddaway, Peter, and Dmitri Glinski, *The Tragedy of Russia's Reforms: Market Bolshevism against Democracy*, Washington, DC: The United States Institute of Peace Press, 2001.

Ruble, Blair A., Hodi Koehn and Nancy Popson, (eds), *Fragmented Space in the Russian Federation*, Baltimore: Johns Hopkins University Press, 2001.

Sakwa, Richard, *Russian Politics and Society*, London: Routledge, 1993.

Shlapentokh, Vladimir, *Soviet Public Opinion and Ideology: The Interaction between Mythology and Pragmatism*, New York: Praeger, 1986.

——— *The Public and Private Life of the Soviet People*, New York and Oxford University Press, 1989.

Solomon, Peter H. (ed.), *Reforming Justice in Russia. 1864–1994: Power, Culture and the Limits of Legal Order*, New York: Armonk, 1997.

Todd, Emmanuel, *The Final Fall: an Essay on the Decomposition of the Soviet Sphere*, New York: Karz Publishers, 1979.

Wilson, Andrew, *Ukraine's Orange Revolution*, New Haven: Yale University Press, 2005.

Woodruff, David, *Money Unmade: Barter and the Fate of Russian Capitalism*, Ithaca: Cornell University Press, 1999.

Zaslavskaya, Tatyana (ed.), *Kuda idet Rossia? 1999* ['Where is Russia heading? 1999'], Moscow: Logos, 1999.

Zielonka, Jan and Alex Pravda, *Democratic Consolidation in Eastern Europe. International and Transnational Factors*, vol. 2, Oxford University Press, 2001.

Articles and journals

'Can Democracy Take Root in Post-Soviet Russia? Explorations in State Society Relations', collection of articles, *American Political Science Review*, 95 (1), 2001.

'L'URSS de Gorbatchev', *Pouvoirs*, no. 45, 1988.

'Qui gouverne en Russie?', collection of articles, *La Revue Tocqueville/The Tocqueville Review*, vol. XIX, no. 1, 1998, pp. 3–135.

Mendras, Marie (ed.), 'Russie. Le gouvernement des provinces', *Nouveaux Mondes*, no. 7, winter 1997.

The War in Chechnya

Chechnya Committee, *Tchétchénie. Dix clés pour comprendre*, Paris: La Découverte, 2003.

Dunlop, John, *Russia Confronts Chechnya: Roots of a Separatist Conflict*, Cambridge University Press, 1998.

Hughes, James, *Chechnya: From Nationalism to Jihad*, Philadelphia: University of Pennsylvania Press, 2007.

Politovskaya, Anna, *A Dirty War: A Russian Reporter in Chechnya*, London: Harvill, 2001.

———— *A Small Corner of Hell: Dispatches from Chechnya*, University of Chicago Press, 2003.

Riabukhina, Nadezhda (ed.), *Beslan. Kto vinovat?* ['Beslan. Who's to blame?'], Moscow: Sovershenno Sekretno, 2005.

Contemporary Russia

Books

Baker, Peter and Susan Glasser, *Kremlin Rising: Vladimir Putin's Russia and the End of Revolution*, Washington, DC: Potomac Books, 2007.

Barany, Zoltan, *Democratic Breakdown and the Decline of the Russian Military*, Princeton and Oxford: Princeton University Press, 2007.

Brown, Archie (ed.), *Contemporary Russian Politics: A Reader*, Oxford University Press, 2001.

Dubin, Boris, *Intellektualnye gruppy i simvolicheskie formy. Ocherki sotsiologii sovremennoi kultury* ['Intellectual groups and symbolic forms. Sociological studies of contemporary culture'], Moscow: Novoe Izdatel'stvo, 2004.

———— (ed.), *Rossiya nulevykh: politicheskaya kul'tura, istoricheskaya pamyat', povsednevnaya zhizn'* (Russia of the 2000s: political culture, historical memory, everyday life), Moscow: Rosspen, 2011.

———— Lev Gudkov and Yuri Levada, *Problema «elity» v sevodniashnei Rossii* '['The question of the 'elite' in today's Russia']', Moscow: Liberal'naya missia, 2007.

Dunlop, John, *The 2002 Dubrovka and 2004 Beslan Hostage Crises: A Critique of Russian Counter-Terrorism*, Stuttgart: Ibidem-Verlag, 2006.

Evans, Alfred, and Vladimir Gelman, *The Politics of Local Government in Russia*, Lanham: Rowman & Littlefield, 2004.

Favarel-Garrigues, Gilles, *Policing Economic Crime in Russia*, London: Hurst Publishers, 2011.

Favarel-Garrigues, Gilles and Kathy Rousselet, *La Société russe en quête d'ordre: avec Vladimir Poutine?*, Paris: CERI/Autrement, 2004.

———— (eds), *La Russie contemporaine*, Paris: Fayard, 2010.

Galeotti, Mark (ed.), *The Politics of Security in Modern Russia*, Aldershot: Ashgate (coll. 'Post-Soviet Politics'), 2009.

Gessat-Anstett, Élisabeth, *Une Atlantide russe: Anthropologie de la mémoire en Russie postsoviétique*, Paris: La Découverte, 2007.

Gudkov, Lev, *Negativnaya identichnost'* '['Negative identity"], Moscow: Novoe Literaturnoe Obozrenie, 2004.

———— *Abortivnaya Modernizatsiya* [aborted modernization], Moscow: Rosspen, 2011.

Guillemoles, Alain and Alla Lazareva, *Gazprom, le nouvel empire*, Paris: Les Petits Matins, 2008.

Hommage à Anna Politkovskaïa, collective of authors, Paris: Buchet-Chastel, 2008.

Kagarlitsky, Boris, *Russia under Yeltsin and Putin: Neo-liberal Autocracy*, London: Pluto Press, 2002.

Kharkhordin, Oleg, *Main Concepts of Russian Politics*, Lanham: University Press of America, 2005.

Khodorkovski, Mikhail, *Paroles libres*, Paris: Fayard, 2011.

Kliamkin, Igor (ed.), *Posle imperii* ('After the empire'), Moscow: Liberal'naya missiya, 2007.

Kliamkin, Igor et al., *Rossiiskoe gosudarstvo: vchera, sevodnia, zavtra* '['The Russian state: past, present and future"], Moscow: Liberal'naya missiya Novoe Izdatel'stvo, 2007.

Korkhonen, Ikka and Laura Solanko (eds), *From Soviet Plans to Russian Reality*, Helsinki: WSOYpro Oy, 2011.

Lane, David and Ross Cameron, *The Transition from Communism to Capitalism. Ruling Elites From Gorbachev to Yeltsin*, New York: St Martins Press, 1999.

Laruelle, Marlène (ed.), *Le Rouge et le Noir: Extrême droite et nationalisme en Russie*, Paris: Éditions du CNRS, 2007.

Laruelle, Marlène, *In the Name of the Nation: Nationalism and Politics in Contemporary Russia*, New York: Palgrave Macmillan, 2009.

Ledeneva, Alena, *Russia's Economy of Favours: Blat, Networking and Informal Exchange*, Cambridge University Press, 1998.

Le Huérou, Anne, and Élisabeth Sieca-Kozlowski, (eds), *Culture militaire et patriotisme dans la Russie d'aujourd'hui*, Paris: Karthala, 2007.

Levada, Yuri, *Ishchem cheloveka. Sotsiologicheskie ocherki 2000–2005* ['In search of the individual. Sociological studies"], Moscow: Novoe Izdatel'stvo, 2006.

Lipman, Maria and Andrey Ryabov (eds), *Puti rossiskogo postkommunizma* ['The paths of postcommunism in Russia"], Moscow: Carnegie Centre, Elinina, 2007.

Lokshina, Tanya, Ray Thomas and Mary Mayer, *The Imposition of a Fake Political Settlement in the Northern Caucasus*, Stuttgart: Ibidem-Verlag, 2005.

McFaul, Michael, *Russia's Unfinished Revolution: Political Change from Gorbachev to Putin*, Ithaca: Cornell University Press, 2001.

———— Nikolay Petrov and Andrey Ryabov, *Between Dictatorship and Democracy: Russian Post-Communist Political Reform*, Washington, DC: Carnegie Endowment for International Peace, 2004.

Mendras, Marie (ed.), *Comment fonctionne la Russie? Le politique, le bureaucrate et l'oligarque*, Paris: CERI/Autrement, 2003.

Ot pervogo litsa. Razgavory s Vladimirom Putinom ['In the first person. Conversations with Vladimir Putin"], Moscow: Vagrius, 2000.

Piontovsky, Andrei, *Tretii put'… k Rabstvu* (A third way… to Slavery), Moscow: M-Graphics, 2010.

Politkovskaya, Anna, *Putin's Russia: Life in a Failing Democracy*, New York: Metropolitan Books, 2005.

———— *A Russian Diary: a Journalist's Final Account of Life, Corruption, and Death in Putin's Russia*, New York: Random House, 2007.

Popescu, Nicu and Andrew Wilson, *The Limits of Enlargement-lite: European and Russian Power in the Troubled Neighbourhood*, European Council on Foreign Relations, London, June 2009.

Reddaway, Peter and Robert Orttung (eds), *The Dynamics of Russian Politics: Putin's Reform of Federal-Regional Relations*, Vol. 1, Lanham, Md, Rowman and Littlefield, 2004.

Régamey, Amandine, *Prolétaires de tous pays, excusez-moi! Dérision et politique dans le monde soviétique*, Paris: Buchet-Chastel, 2007.

Rose, Richard and Neil Munro, *Elections without Order. Russia's Challenge to Vladimir Putin*, Cambridge University Press, 2002.

Rossiia Putina. Istoria bolezni ['Putin's Russia. History of a disease"], Moscow: Centre Panorama, 2004.

Shevtsova, Lilia, *Putin's Russia*, Washington, DC: Carnegie Endowment for International Peace, 2003.

————*Russia Lost in Transition: The Yeltsin and Putin Legacies*, Washington, DC: Carnegie Endowment for International Peace, 2007.

Shevtsova, Lilia, and Andrew Wood, *Change or Decay?*, Washington, D.C.: Carnegie Endowment for Peace, 2011.

Soldatov, Andrei, and Irina Borogan, *The New Nobility: The Restoration of Russia's Security State and the Enduring Legacy of the KGB*, New York: PublicAffairs, 2010.

Trenin, Dmitri V., *Getting Russia Right*, Washington, DC.: Carnegie Endowment for Peace, 2007.

Vishnevsky, Anatoly, *Rossiia pered demograficheskim byborom* '[Russia faced with a demographic choice'], Moscow: Vyshchaya Shkola Ekonomiki, 2007.

White, Stephen, *Understanding Russian Politics*, Cambridge University Press, 2011.

Wilson, Andrew, *Ukraine's Orange Revolution*, New Haven, London: Yale University Press, 2005.

Zapadniki i natsionalisty: vozmozhen li dialog? '[Pro-Westerners and nationalists: is dialogue possible?'], Moscow: Liberal'naya missia, OGI, 2003.

Articles and journals

'Putin and Putinism', Special issue, ed. by Ronald J. Hill and Ottorino Capelli, *The Journal of Communist Studies and Transition Politics*, vol. 24, no. 4, December 2008, pp. 473–656.

'Russia and the other CIS countries in 2006', *Le Courrier des pays de l'Est*, Paris: La Documentation Française, no. 1059, January-February 2007.

'Russia's Authoritarian Elections', A Special Issue, *Europe-Asia Studies*, June 2011.

Obshchestvo na fone '['Society as background"], published on polit.ru, Moscou, OGI, 2001.

Russian Public Opinion. Annual, Centre Levada, summary of opinion polls, in English, published each year.

'*Sotsum i vlast' v Rossii*' ['Social conscience and power in Russia'], series of articles in *Polis*, no. 5, 2007, pp. 35–80.

'*Vremya Preemnika*' ['The time of the successor"], report in the journal *Pro et contra*, Moscow, nos 4–5 (38), July-October 2007, pp. 6–159.

'Symposium on the Post-Soviet Media', *Europe-Asia Studies*, vol. 59, no. 8, December 2007, pp. 1243–403.

'*Régime nouveau. Rossiia v 1998–2006 gody*' ['New regime. Russia in the years 1998–2006"], collection of articles, *Neprikosnovennyi Zapas*, 6 (050), Moscow, 2006.

Mendras, Marie (ed.), 'Regions of Russia: A Special Issue', *Post-Soviet Affairs*, vol. 15, no. 4, October-November 1999.

Shlapentokh, Vladimir, 'Hobbes and Locke at Odds in Putin's Russia', *Europe-Asia Studies*, vol. 55, no. 7, 2003, pp. 981–1007.

Young, John F. and Gary N. Wilson, 'The View From Below: Local Government and Putin's Reforms', *Europe-Asia Studies*, vol. 59, no. 7, November 2007, pp. 1071–88.

Propaganda documents since 2000

Danilin, Pavel, Natalia Kryshtal and Dmitri Poliakov, *Vragi Putina* ['Putin's enemies"], Moscow: Europa, 2007.

Filippov, A. V., *Noveïshaia istoriia Rossii, 1945–2006. Kniga dlya uchitelya* ('Recent history of Russia 1945–2006. Teaching manual'), Moscow: Prosveshchenie, 2007.

Narotchnitskaya, Natalia, *Que reste-t-il de notre victoire?*, Paris: Éditions des Syrtes, 2008.

Suverenitet ['Sovereignty' collection of articles], Moscow: Europa, 2006.

Surkov, Vladislav, *Suverenaya demokratiya*, Moscow: 2007.

Poliakov, Leonid (ed.), *PRO suverennuyu demokratiyu* ['For sovereign democracy'] Moscow: Europa, 2007.

Russian Websites

Ej.ru
Demoscope.ru (demography)
Grani.ru
Gazeta.ru
Kremlin.ru
Levada.ru
Libelal.ru
Novayagazeta.ru
Nz.ru (*neprikosnovennyi zapas*)
Panorama.ru
Polit.ru

INDEX

INDEX